Ideology and Utopia

Ideology and Utopia

An Introduction to the
Sociology of Knowledge

By

KARL MANNHEIM

The London School of Economics and Political Science
(University of London)
Formerly Professor of Sociology in the University of Frankfurt/Main

With a Preface by LOUIS WIRTH

Associate Professor in the University of Chicago

LONDON AND HENLEY
ROUTLEDGE & KEGAN PAUL

First published in England 1936
by Routledge & Kegan Paul Ltd
39 Store Street, London WC1E 2DD and
Newtown Road, Henley-on-Thames, Oxon. RG9 1EN
Reprinted 1940, 1946, 1948, 1949, 1952, 1954
Reprinted and first published
as a Routledge Paperback 1960
Reprinted 1966, 1968, 1972 and 1976

Printed in Great Britain by
Lowe & Brydone (Printers) Ltd, Thetford, Norfolk

ISBN 0 7100 3123 8 *(c)*
ISBN 0 7100 4609 x *(p)*

Translated from the German
By
Louis Wirth and Edward Shils
(University of Chicago)

To
JULIA MANNHEIM-LÁNG

TABLE OF CONTENTS

vii

CONTENTS

FOREWORD

THE present volume combines a number of different writings of the author. Parts II–IV represent Professor Mannheim's *Ideologie und Utopie* (F. Cohen, Bonn, 1929—now, Schulte-Bulmke, Frankfurt-am-Main) ; Part V consists of his article " Wissenssoziologie ", originally published in Alfred Vierkandt's *Handwörterbuch der Soziologie* (F. Enke, Stuttgart, 1931). Part I was especially written to introduce the present volume to the Anglo-Saxon reader.

Whereas Parts II–IV deal with the central problems of the sociology of knowledge and exemplify the method of this emerging discipline as applied to some of the most significant phases of recent and contemporary social life, the last part seeks to formulate a concise prospectus of this new scientific interest.

Stylistically the first four parts of this book will be found to differ markedly from the last. Whereas the former develop their respective themes rather fully, the latter, being originally an article for an Encyclopædia, is scarcely more than a schematic outline.

A classified bibliography is appended containing all of the works cited by Professor Mannheim in the above-mentioned article. To these items have been added some of the more significant representative contributions of American, English, French, and German thought on this subject which appeared to the translators to be relevant and suggestive.

Despite the involved language of the original, the translators have thought it worth while to adhere as closely as possible to the German text. While certain modifications have at times seemed necessary for the sake of intelligibility, strenuous efforts have been made to convey the author's meaning accurately.

Thanks are due to Professor Robert Cooley Angell, of the University of Michigan, for reading sections of Parts II and V, and to Mr. Arthur Bergholz, of the University of Chicago, who read sections 1–9 of " Ideology and Utopia ". Thanks are also tendered to Mrs. E. Ginsberg (M.A., Oxon), and Miss Jean McDonald (B.Sc. (Econ.), Lond.), for their help and valuable suggestions concerning the editing of the translation. The Social Science Research Committee of the University of Chicago generously provided assistance in typing the manuscript.

Louis Wirth.
Edward A. Shils.

PREFACE

By LOUIS WIRTH

THE original German edition of *Ideology and Utopia* appeared in an atmosphere of acute intellectual tension marked by widespread discussion which subsided only with the exile or enforced silence of those thinkers who sought an honest and tenable solution to the problems raised. Since then the conflicts which in Germany led to the destruction of the liberal Weimar Republic have been felt in various countries all over the world, especially in Western Europe and the United States. The intellectual problems which at one time were considered the peculiar preoccupation of German writers have enveloped virtually the whole world. What was once regarded as the esoteric concern of a few intellectuals in a single country has become the common plight of the modern man.

In response to this situation there has arisen an extensive literature which speaks of the " end ", the " decline ", the " crisis ", the " decay ", or the " death " of Western civilization. But despite the alarm which is heralded in such titles, one looks in vain in most of this literature for an analysis of the basic factors and processes underlying our social and intellectual chaos. In contrast with these Professor Mannheim's work stands out as a sober, critical, and scholarly analysis of the social currents and situations of our time as they bear upon thought, belief, and action.

It seems to be characteristic of our period that norms and truths which were once believed to be absolute, universal, and eternal, or which were accepted with blissful unawareness of their implications, are being questioned. In the light of modern thought and investigation much of what was once taken for granted is declared to be in need of demonstration and proof. The criteria of proof themselves have become subjects of dispute. We are witnessing not only a general distrust of the validity of ideas but of the motives of those who assert them. This situation is aggravated by a war of each against all in the intellectual arena where personal self-aggrandizement rather than truth has come to be the coveted prize. Increased secularization of life, sharpened social antagonisms and the accentuation of the spirit of personal competition have permeated regions which were once thought to be wholly under the reign of the disinterested and objective search for truth.

However disquieting this change may appear to be, it has had its wholesome influences as well. Among these might be mentioned the tendency toward a more thoroughgoing self-scrutiny and toward a more comprehensive awareness of the interconnections between ideas and situations than had hitherto been suspected. Although it may seem like grim humour to speak of the beneficent influences arising out of an upheaval that has shaken the foundations of our social and intellectual order, it must be asserted that the spectacle of change and confusion, which confronts social science, presents it at the same time with unprecedented opportunities for fruitful new development. This new development, however, depends on taking full cognizance of the obstacles which beset social thought. This does not imply that self-clarification is the only condition for the further advancement of social science, as will be indicated in what follows, but merely that it is a necessary pre-condition for further development.

I

The progress of social knowledge is impeded if not paralysed at present by two fundamental factors, one impinging upon knowledge from without, the other operating within the world of science itself. On the one hand the powers that have blocked and retarded the advance of knowledge in the past still are not convinced that the advance of social knowledge is compatible with what they regard as their interests, and, on the other hand, the attempt to carry over the tradition and the whole apparatus of scientific work from the physical to the social realm has often resulted in confusion, misunderstanding, and sterility. Scientific thought about social affairs up to now has had to wage war primarily against established intolerance and institutionalized suppression. It has been struggling to establish itself against its external enemies, the authoritarian interest of church, state, and tribe. In the course of the last few centuries, however, what amounts at least to a partial victory against these outside forces has been won, resulting in a measure of toleration of untrammelled inquiry, and even encouragement of free thought. For a brief interlude between the eras of medieval, spiritualized darkness and the rise of modern, secular dictatorships, the Western world gave promise of fulfilling the hope of the enlightened minds of all ages that by the full exercise of intelligence men might triumph over the adversities of nature and the perversities of culture. As so often in the past, however, this hope seems now to be chastened. Whole nations have officially and proudly given themselves up to the cult of irrationality, and even the Anglo-Saxon world which was for so long the haven of freedom and reason has recently provided revivals of intellectual witch hunts.

In the course of the development of the Western mind the pursuit of knowledge about the physical world resulted, after the travail of theological persecution, in the concession to natural science of an autonomous empire of its own. Since the sixteenth century, despite some spectacular exceptions, theological dogmatism has receded from one domain of inquiry after another until the authority of the natural sciences was generally recognized. In the face of the forward movement of scientific investigation, the church has yielded and time after time readjusted its doctrinal interpretations so that their divergence from scientific discoveries would not be too glaring.

At length the voice of science was heard with a respect approximating the sanctity which formerly was accorded only to authoritarian, religious pronouncements. The revolutions which the theoretical structure of science has undergone in recent decades have left the prestige of the scientific pursuit of truth unshaken. Even though in the last five years the cry has occasionally been raised that science was exerting a disruptive effect upon economic organization and that its output should therefore be restricted, whatever slowing down of the pace of natural science research has taken place during this period is probably more the result of the decreasing economic demand for the products of science than the deliberate attempt to hamper scientific progress in order to stabilize the existing order.

The triumph of natural science over theological and metaphysical dogma is sharply contrasted with the development in the studies of social life. Whereas the empirical procedure had made deep inroads on the dogmas of the ancients concerning nature, the classical social doctrines proved themselves more impervious to the onslaught of the secular and empirical spirit. This may in part have been due to the fact that the knowledge and theorizing about social affairs on the part of the ancients was far in advance of their notions about physics and biology. The opportunity for demonstrating the practical utility of the new natural science had not yet come, and the disutility of existing social doctrines could not be convincingly established. Whereas Aristotle's logic, ethics, æsthetics, politics, and psychology were accepted as authoritative by subsequent periods, his notions of astronomy, physics, and biology were progressively being relegated to the scrap-heap of ancient superstitions.

Until early in the eighteenth century political and social theory was still under the dominance of the categories of thought elaborated by the ancient and medieval philosophers and operated largely within a theological framework. That part of social science that had any practical utility was concerned, primarily, with administrative matters. Cameralism and political arithmetic, which represented this current, confined themselves to the homely facts of every-day life and rarely took flights into theory. Consequently that part of social knowledge which was concerned with questions most subject to controversy could scarcely lay claim to the practical value which the natural sciences, after a certain point in their development, had achieved. Nor could those social thinkers from whom alone an advance could come expect the support of the church or the state from whom the more orthodox wing derived its financial and moral sustenance. The more secularized social and political theory became and the more thoroughly it dispelled the sanctified myths which legitimized the existing political order, the more precarious became the position of the emerging social science.

A dramatic instance of the difference between the effects of and the attitude toward technological as contrasted with social knowledge is furnished by contemporary Japan. Once that country was opened to the streams of Western influence the technical products and methods of the latter were eagerly accepted. But social, economic, and political influences from the outside are even to-day regarded with suspicion and tenaciously resisted.

The enthusiasm with which the results of physical and biological science are embraced in Japan contrasts strikingly with the cautious and guarded cultivation of economic, political, and social investigation. These latter subjects are still, for the most part, subsumed under what the Japanese call *kikenshiso* or " dangerous thoughts ". The authorities regard discussion of democracy, constitutionalism, the emperor, socialism, and a host of other subjects as dangerous because knowledge on these topics might subvert the sanctioned beliefs and undermine the existing order.]

But lest we think that this condition is peculiar to Japan, however, it should be emphasized that many of the topics that come under the rubric of " dangerous thought " in Japan were until recently taboo in Western society as well. Even to-day open, frank, and " objective " inquiry into the most sacred and cherished institutions and beliefs is more or less seriously restricted in every country of the world. It is virtually impossible, for instance, even in England and America, to inquire into the actual facts regarding communism, no matter how disinterest-edly, without running the risk of being labelled a communist.

That there is an area of " dangerous thought " in every society is, therefore, scarcely debatable. While we recognize that what it is dangerous to think about may differ from country to country and from epoch to epoch, on the whole the subjects marked with the danger signal are those which the society or the controlling elements in it believe to be so vital and hence so sacred that they will not tolerate their profanation by discussion. But what is not so easily recognized is the fact that thought, even in the absence of official censorship, is disturbing, and, under certain con-ditions, dangerous and subversive. [For thought is a catalytic agent that is capable of unsettling routines, disorganizing habits, breaking up customs, undermining faiths, and generating scepticism.]

The distinctive character of social science discourse is to be sought in the fact that every assertion, no matter how objective it may be, has ramifications extending beyond the limits of science itself. Since every assertion of a " fact " about the social world touches the interests of some individual or group, one cannot even call attention to the existence of certain " facts " without courting the objections of those whose very *raison d'être* in society rests upon a divergent interpretation of the " factual " situation.

II

The discussion centring around this issue has traditionally been known as the problem of objectivity in science. In the language of the Anglo-Saxon world to be objective has meant to be impartial, to have no preferences, predilections or prejudices,

B

no biases, no preconceived values or judgments in the presence of the facts. This view was an expression of the older conception of natural law in accord with which the contemplation of the facts of nature, instead of being coloured by the norms of conduct of the contemplator, automatically supplied these norms.[1] After the natural law approach to the problem of objectivity subsided, this non-personal way of looking at the facts themselves again found support for a time through the vogue of positivism. Nineteenth century social science abounds in warnings against the distorting influences of passion, political interest, nationalism, and class feeling and in appeals for self-purification.

Indeed a good share of the history of modern philosophy and science may be viewed as a trend, if not a concerted drive, toward this type of objectivity. This, it has been assumed, involves the search for valid knowledge through the elimination of biased perception and faulty reasoning on the negative side and the formulation of a critically self-conscious point of view and the development of sound methods of observation and analysis on the positive side. If it may appear, at first glance, that in the logical and methodological writings on science the thinkers of other nations have been more active than the English and Americans, this notion might well be corrected by calling attention to the long line of thinkers in the English-speaking world who have been preoccupied with these very same problems without specifically labelling them methodology. Certainly the concern with the problems and pitfalls involved in the search for valid knowledge has constituted more than a negligible portion of the works of a long line of brilliant thinkers from Locke through Hume, Bentham, Mill, and Spencer to writers of our own time. We do not always recognize these treatments of the processes of knowing as serious attempts to formulate the epistemological, logical, and psychological premises of a sociology of knowledge, because they do not bear the explicit label and were not deliberately intended as such. Nonetheless wherever scientific activity has been carried on in an organized and self-conscious fashion, these problems have always received a considerable

---

[1] It is precisely to that current of thought which subsequently developed into the sociology of knowledge and which constitutes the main theme of this book that we owe the insight that political-ethical norms not only cannot be derived from the direct contemplation of the facts, but themselves exert a moulding influence upon the very modes of perceiving the facts. Cf. among others the works of Thorstein Veblen, John Dewey, Otto Bauer and Maurice Halbwachs.

amount of attention. In fact, in such works as J. S. Mill's *System of Logic* and Herbert Spencer's brilliant and much neglected *Study of Sociology*, the problem of objective social knowledge has received forthright and comprehensive treatment. In the period that followed Spencer this interest in the objectivity of social knowledge was somewhat deflected by the ascendancy of statistical techniques as represented by Francis Galton and Karl Pearson. But in our own day the works of Graham Wallas and John A. Hobson, among others, signalize a return to this interest.

America, despite the barren picture of its intellectual landscape that we so generally find in the writings of Europeans, has produced a number of thinkers who have concerned themselves with this issue. Outstanding in this respect is the work of William Graham Sumner, who, although he approached the problem somewhat obliquely through the analysis of the influence of the folkways and mores upon social norms rather than directly through epistemological criticism, by the vigorous way in which he directed attention to the distorting influence of ethnocentrism upon knowledge, placed the problem of objectivity into a distinctively concrete sociological setting. Unfortunately his disciples have failed to explore further the rich potentialities of his approach and have largely interested themselves in elaborating other phases of his thought. Somewhat similar in his treatment of this problem is Thorstein Veblen who, in a series of brilliant and penetrating essays, has explored the intricate relationships between cultural values and intellectual activities. Further discussion of the same question along realistic lines is found in James Harvey Robinson's *The Mind in the Making*, in which this distinguished historian touches on many of the points which the present volume analyses in detail. More recently Professor Charles A. Beard's *The Nature of the Social Sciences* has dealt with the possibilities of objective social knowledge from a pedagogical point of view in a manner revealing traces of the influence of Professor Mannheim's work.

Necessary and wholesome as the emphasis on the distorting influence of cultural values and interests upon knowledge was, this negative aspect of the cultural critique of knowledge has arrived at a juncture where the positive and constructive significance of the evaluative elements in thought had to be recognized. If the earlier discussion of objectivity laid stress upon the elimination of personal and collective bias, the more modern approach calls attention to the positive cognitive importance of this bias. Whereas the former quest for objectivity tended to posit an " object " which was distinct from the " subject ", the latter sees an intimate relationship between the object and the perceiving subject. In fact, the most recent view maintains that the object emerges for the subject when, in the course of experience, the interest of the subject is focused upon that particular aspect of the world. Objectivity thus appears in a two-fold aspect : one, in which object and subject are discrete and separate entities, the other in which the interplay between them is emphasized. Whereas objectivity in the first sense refers to the reliability of our data and the validity of our conclusions, objectivity in the second sense is concerned with relevance to our interests. In the realm of the social, particularly, truth is not merely a matter of a simple correspondence between thought and existence, but is tinged with the investigator's interest in his subject matter, his standpoint, his evaluations, in short the definition of his object of attention. This conception of objectivity, however, does not imply that henceforth no distinction between truth and error is ascertainable. It does not mean that whatever people imagine to be their perceptions, attitudes, and ideas or what they want others to believe them to be corresponds to the facts. Even in this conception of objectivity we must reckon with the distortion produced not merely by inadequate perception or incorrect knowledge of oneself, but also by the inability or unwillingness under certain circumstances to report perceptions and ideas honestly.

This conception of the problem of objectivity which underlies Professor Mannheim's work will not be found totally strange by those who are familiar with that current of American philosophy represented by James, Peirce, Mead, and Dewey. Though Professor Mannheim's approach is the product of a different intellectual heritage, in which Kant, Marx, and Max Weber have played the leading roles, his conclusions on many pivotal issues are identical with those of the American pragmatists. This convergence runs, however, only as far as the limits of the field of social psychology. Among American sociologists this point of view has been explicitly expressed by the late Charles H. Cooley, and R. M. MacIver, and implicitly by W. I. Thomas and Robert E. Park. One reason why we do not immediately connect the works of these writers with the problem complex of the present volume is that in America what the sociology of knowledge deals with

systematically and explicitly has been touched on only incidentally within the framework of the special discipline of social
psychology or has been an unexploited by-product of empirical
research.

The quest for objectivity gives rise to peculiarly difficult
problems in the attempt to establish a rigorous scientific method
in the study of social life. Whereas in dealing with the objects
in the physical world the scientist may very well confine himself
to the external uniformities and regularities that are there
presented without seeking to penetrate into the inner meaning
of the phenomena, in the social world the search is primarily
for an understanding of these inner meanings and connections.
It may be true that there are some social phenomena and,
perhaps, some aspects of all social events that can be viewed
externally as if they were things. But this should not lead to
the inference that only those manifestations of social life which
find expression in material things are real. It would be a very
narrow conception of social science to limit it to those concrete
things which are externally perceivable and measurable.

The literature of social science amply demonstrates that
there are large and very definite spheres of social existence in
which it is possible to obtain scientific knowledge which is not
only reliable but which has significant bearings on social policy
and action. It does not follow from the fact that human beings
are different from other objects in nature that there is nothing
determinate about them. Despite the fact that human beings
in their actions show a kind of causation which does not apply
to any other objects in nature, namely motivation, it must
still be recognized that determinate causal sequences must be
assumed to apply to the realm of the social as they do to the
physical. It might of course be argued that the precise knowledge
we have of causal sequences in other realms has not as yet been
established in the social realm. But if there is to be any knowledge at all beyond the sensing of the unique and transitory
events of the moment, the possibility of discovering general
trends and predictable series of events analogous to those to
be found in the physical world must be posited for the social
world as well. The determinism which social science presupposes,
however, and of which Professor Mannheim treats so under-
standingly in this volume, is of a different sort from that involved
in the Newtonian celestial mechanics.

There are, to be sure, some social scientists who claim that science must restrict itself to the causation of actual phenomena, that science is not concerned with what should be done, not with what ought to be done, but rather with what can be done and the manner of doing it. According to this view social science should be exclusively instrumental rather than a goal-setting discipline. But in studying what is, we cannot totally rule out what ought to be. In human life, the motives and ends of action are part of the process by which action is achieved and are essential in seeing the relation of the parts to the whole. Without the end most acts would have no meaning and no interest to us. But there is, nevertheless, a difference between taking account of ends and setting ends. Whatever may be the possibility of complete detachment in dealing with physical things, in social life we cannot afford to disregard the values and goal of acts without missing the significance of many of the facts involved. In our choice of areas for research, in our selection of data, in our method of investigation, in our organization of materials, not to speak of the formulation of our hypotheses and conclusions, there is always manifest some more or less clear, explicit or implicit assumption or scheme of evaluation.

There is, accordingly, a well-founded distinction between objective and subjective facts, which results from the difference between outer and inner observation or between " knowledge about " and " acquaintance with ", to use William James's terms. If there is a difference between physical and mental processes—and there seems to be little occasion to talk this important distinction out of existence—it suggests a corresponding differentiation in the modes of knowing these two kinds of phenomena. Physical objects can be known (and natural science deals with them exclusively as if they could be known) purely from the outside, while mental and social processes can be known only from the inside, except in so far as they also exhibit themselves externally through physical indexes, into which in turn we read meanings. Hence insight may be regarded as the core of social knowledge. It is arrived at by being on the inside of the phenomenon to be observed, or, as Charles H. Cooley put it, by sympathetic introspection. It is the participation in an activity that generates interest, purpose, point of view, value, meaning, and intelligibility, as well as bias.

If then the social sciences are concerned with objects that have meaning and value the observer who attempts to understand them must necessarily do so by means of categories which in turn depend on his own values and meanings. This point has been stated time and again in the dispute which has raged for many years between the behaviourists among the social scientists who would have dealt with social life exclusively as the natural scientist deals with the physical world, and those who took the position of sympathetic introspectionism and understanding along the lines indicated by such a writer as Max Weber.

But on the whole, while the evaluative element in social knowledge has received formal recognition, there has been relatively little attention given, especially among English and American sociologists, to the concrete analysis of the role of actual interests and values as they have been expressed in specific historical doctrines and movements. An exception must be made in the case of Marxism which, although it has raised this issue to a central position, has not formulated any satisfactory systematic statement of the problem.

It is at this point that Professor Mannheim's contribution marks a distinctive advance over the work that has hitherto been done in Europe and America. Instead of being content with calling attention to the fact that interest is inevitably reflected in all thought, including that part of it which is called science, Professor Mannheim has sought to trace out the specific connection between actual interest groups in society and the ideas and modes of thought which they espoused. He has succeeded in showing that ideologies, i.e. those complexes of ideas which direct activity toward the maintenance of the existing order, and utopias—or those complexes of ideas which tend to generate activities toward changes of the prevailing order—do not merely deflect thought from the object of observation, but also serve to fix attention upon aspects of the situation which otherwise would be obscured or pass unnoticed. In this manner he has forged out of a general theoretical formulation an effective instrument for fruitful empirical research.

The meaningful character of conduct does not warrant the inference, however, that this conduct is invariably the product of conscious reflection and reasoning. Our quest for understanding arises out of action and may even be consciously preparatory for further action, but we must recognize that conscious reflection or the imaginative rehearsal of the situation that we call " thinking " is not an indispensable part of every act. Indeed, it seems to be generally agreed among social psychologists that ideas are not spontaneously generated and that, despite the assertion of an antiquated psychology, the act comes before the thought. Reason, consciousness and conscience characteristically occur in situations marked by conflict. Professor Mannheim, therefore, is in accord with that growing number of modern thinkers who, instead of positing a pure intellect, are concerned with the actual social conditions in which intelligence and thought emerges. If, as seems to be true, we are not merely conditioned by the events that go on in our world but are at the same time an instrument for shaping them, it follows that the ends of action are never fully statable and determined until the act is finished or is so completely relegated to automatic routines that it no longer requires consciousness and attention.

The fact that in the realm of the social the observer is part of the observed and hence has a personal stake in the subject of observation is one of the chief factors in the acuteness of the problem of objectivity in the social sciences. In addition we must consider the fact that social life and hence social science is to an overwhelming extent concerned with beliefs about the ends of action. When we advocate something, we do not do so as complete outsiders to what is and what will happen. It would be naïve to suppose that our ideas are entirely shaped by the objects of our contemplation which lie outside of us or that our wishes and our fears have nothing whatever to do with what we perceive or with what will happen. It would be nearer the truth to admit that those basic impulses which have been generally designated as " interests " actually are the forces which at the same time generate the ends of our practical activity and focus our intellectual attention. While in certain spheres of life, especially in economics and to a lesser degree in politics, these " interests " have been made explicit and articulate, in most other spheres they slumber below the surface and disguise themselves in such conventional forms that we do not always recognize them even when they are pointed out to us. The most important thing, therefore, that we can know about a man is what he takes for granted, and the most elemental and important facts about a society are those that are seldom debated and generally regarded as settled.

But we look in vain in the modern world for the serenity and calm that seemed to characterize the atmosphere in which some thinkers of ages past lived. The world no longer has a common faith and our professed " community of interest " is scarcely more than a figure of speech. With the loss of a common purpose and common interests, we have also been deprived of common norms, modes of thought, and conceptions of the world. Even public opinion has turned out to be a set of " phantom " publics. Men of the past may have dwelled in smaller and more parochial worlds, but the worlds in which they lived were apparently more stable and integrated for all the members of the community than our enlarged universe of thought, action, and belief has come to be.

A society is possible in the last analysis because the individuals in it carry around in their heads some sort of picture of that society. Our society, however, in this period of minute division of labour, of extreme heterogeneity and profound conflict of interests, has come to a pass where these pictures are blurred and incongruous. Hence we no longer perceive the same things as real, and coincident with our vanishing sense of a common reality we are losing our common medium for expressing and communicating our experiences. The world has been splintered into countless fragments of atomized individuals and groups. The disruption in the wholeness of individual experience corresponds to the disintegration in culture and group solidarity. When the bases of unified collective action begin to weaken, the social structure tends to break and to produce a condition which Emile Durkheim has termed *anomie*, by which he means a situation which might be described as a sort of social emptiness or void. Under such conditions suicide, crime, and disorder are phenomena to be expected because individual existence no longer is rooted in a stable and integrated social milieu and much of life's activity loses its sense and meaning.

That intellectual activity is not exempt from such influences is effectively documented by this volume, which, if it may be said to have a practical objective, apart from the accumulation and ordering of fresh insights into the preconditions, the processes, and problems of intellectual life, aims at inquiring into the prospects of rationality and common understanding in an era like our own that seems so frequently to put a premium upon irrationality and from which the possibilities of mutual understanding seem to have vanished. Whereas the intellectual world in earlier periods had at least a common frame of reference which offered a measure of certainty to the participants in that world and gave them a sense of mutual respect and trust, the contemporary intellectual world is no longer a cosmos but presents the spectacle of a battlefield of warring parties and conflicting doctrines. Not only does each of the conflicting factions have its own set of interests and purposes, but each has its picture of the world in which the same objects are accorded quite different meanings and values. In such a world the possibilities of intelligible communication and *à fortiori* of agreement are reduced to a minimum. The absence of a common apperception mass vitiates the possibility of appealing to the same criteria of relevance and truth, and since the world is held together to a large extent by words, when these words have ceased to mean the same thing to those who use them, it follows that men will of necessity misunderstand and talk past one another.

Apart from this inherent inability to understand one another there exists a further obstacle to the achievement of consensus in the downright obstinacy of partisans to refuse to consider or take seriously the theories of their opponents simply because they belong to another intellectual or political camp. This depressing state of affairs is aggravated by the fact that the intellectual world is not free from the struggle for personal distinction and power. This has led to the introduction of the wiles of salesmanship into the realm of ideas, and has brought about a condition where even scientists would rather be in the right than right.

III

If we feel more thoroughly appalled at the threatening loss of our intellectual heritage than was the case in previous cultural crises it is because we have become the victims of more grandiose expectations. For at no time prior to our own were so many men led to indulge in such sublime dreams about the benefits which science could confer upon the human race. This dissolution of the supposedly firm foundations of knowledge and the disillusionment that has followed it have driven some of the " tender minded " to romantic yearning for the return of an age that is past and for a certainty that is irretrievably lost. Faced by perplexity and bewilderment others have sought to ignore or circumvent the ambiguities, conflicts, and uncertainties of the intellectual world by humour, cynicism, or sheer denial of the facts of life.

At a time in human history like our own, when all over the world people are not merely ill at ease, but are questioning the bases of social existence, the validity of their truths, and the tenability of their norms, it should become clear that there is no value apart from interest and no objectivity apart from agreement. Under such circumstances it is difficult to hold tenaciously to what one believes to be the truth in the face of dissent, and one is inclined to question the very possibility of an intellectual life. Despite the fact that the Western world has been nourished by a tradition of hard-won intellectual freedom and integrity for over two thousand years, men are beginning to ask whether the struggle to achieve these was worth the cost if so many to-day accept complacently the threat to exterminate what rationality and objectivity has been won in human affairs. The widespread depreciation of the value of thought on the one hand and its repression on the other hand are ominous signs of the deepening twilight of modern culture. Such a catastrophe can be averted only by the most intelligent and resolute measures.

Ideology and Utopia is itself the product of this period of chaos and unsettlement. One of the contributions it makes toward the solution of our predicament is an analysis of the forces that have brought it about. It is doubtful whether such a book as this could have been written in any other period, for the issues with which it deals, fundamental as they are, could only be raised in a society and in an epoch marked by profound social and intellectual upheaval. It proffers no simple solution to the difficulties we face, but it does formulate the leading problems in a fashion that makes them susceptible of attack and carries the analysis of our intellectual crisis farther than has ever been done before. In the face of the loss of a common conception of the problems and in the absence of unanimously accepted criteria of truth, Professor Mannheim has sought to point out the lines along which a new basis for objective investigation of the controversial issues in social life can be constructed.

Until relatively recently, knowledge and thinking, while regarded as the proper subject matter of logic and psychology, were viewed as lying outside the realm of social science because they were not considered social processes. Whereas some of the ideas that Professor Mannheim presents are the result of the gradual development in the critical analysis of thought processes and are an integral part of the scientific heritage of the Western world, the distinctive contribution of the present volume may turn out to be the explicit recognition that thought, besides being a proper subject matter for logic and psychology, becomes fully comprehensible only if it is viewed sociologically. This involves the tracing of the bases of social judgments to their specific interest-bound roots in society, through which the particularity, and hence the limitations, of each view will become apparent. It is not to be assumed that the mere revelation of these divergent angles of vision will automatically cause the antagonists to embrace one another's conceptions or that it will result immediately in universal harmony. But the clarification of the sources of these differences would seem to be a precondition for any sort of awareness on the part of each observer of the limitations of his own view and at least the partial validity of the views of the others. While this does not necessarily involve the holding of one's interests in abeyance, it does make possible at least a working agreement on what the facts in an issue are, and on a limited set of conclusions to be drawn from them. It is in some such tentative fashion as this that social scientists, even though they are in disagreement on ultimate values, can to-day erect a universe of discourse within which they can view objects from similar perspectives and can communicate their results to one another with a minimum of ambiguity.

IV

To have raised the problems involved in the relations between intellectual activity and social existence squarely and lucidly is in itself a major achievement. But Professor Mannheim has not rested at this point. He has recognized that the factors at work in the human mind impelling and disturbing reason are the same dynamic factors that are the springs of all human activity. Instead of positing a hypothetical pure intellect that produces and dispenses truth without contaminating it by the so-called non-logical factors, he has actually proceeded to an analysis of the concrete social situations in which thought takes place and intellectual life is carried on.

The first four parts of the present volume demonstrate the fruitfulness of this sociological approach concretely and offer an exemplification of the methods of the new discipline, the formal foundations of which are sketched in Part V under the title, " The Sociology of Knowledge." This new discipline historically and logically falls within the scope of general sociology conceived as the basic social science. If the themes that Professor Mannheim has treated are systematically developed, the sociology of knowledge should become a specialized effort to deal in an integrated fashion, from a unifying point of view and by means of appropriate techniques, with a series of subject matters which hitherto have been only cursorily and discretely touched upon. It would be premature to define the exact scope which this new discipline will eventually take. The works of the late Max Scheler and of Professor Mannheim himself have, however, gone sufficiently far to allow of a tentative statement of the leading issues with which it must concern itself.

Of these the first and basic one is the social-psychological elaboration of the theory of knowledge itself, which has hitherto found a place in philosophy in the form of epistemology. Throughout the recorded history of thought this subject has haunted the succession of great thinkers. Despite the age-old effort to resolve the relationship between experience and reflection, fact and idea, belief and truth, the problem of the interconnection between being and knowing still stands as a challenge to the modern thinker. But it no longer is a problem that is the exclusive concern of the professional philosopher. It has become a central issue not merely in science, but in education and politics as well. To the further understanding of this ancient enigma the sociology of knowledge aspires to make a contribution. Such a task requires more than the application of well-established logical rules to the materials at hand, for the accepted rules of logic themselves are here called into question and are seen, in common with the rest of our intellectual tools, as parts and products of the whole of our social life. This involves the searching out of the motives that lie back of intellectual activity and an analysis of the manner and the extent to which the thought processes themselves are influenced by the participation of the thinker in the life of society.

A closely allied field of interest for the sociology of knowledge lies in the reworking of the data of intellectual history with a view to the discovery of the styles and methods of thought that are dominant in certain types of historical-social situations. In this connection it is essential to inquire into the shifts in intellectual interest and attention that accompany changes in other phases of social structure. It is here that Professor Mannheim's distinction between ideologies and utopias offers promising directives for research.

In analysing the mentality of a period or of a given stratum in society, the sociology of knowledge concerns itself not merely with the ideas and modes of thinking that happen to flourish, but with the whole social setting in which this occurs. This must necessarily take account of the factors that are responsible for the acceptance or the rejection of certain ideas by certain groups in society, and of the motives and interests that prompt certain groups consciously to promote these ideas and to disseminate them among wider sections.

The sociology of knowledge furthermore seeks to throw light on the question of how the interests and purposes of certain social groups come to find expression in certain theories, doctrines, and intellectual movements. Of fundamental importance for the understanding of any society is the recognition accorded to the various types of knowledge and the corresponding share of the resources of society devoted to the cultivation of each of these. Equally significant is the analysis of the shifts in social relationships brought about by the advances in certain branches of knowledge such as technical knowledge and the increased mastery over nature and society that the application of this knowledge makes possible. Similarly the sociology of knowledge, by virtue of its concern with the role of knowledge and ideas in the maintenance or change of the social order, is bound to devote considerable attention to the agencies or devices through which ideas are diffused and the degree of freedom of inquiry and expression that prevails. In connection with this attention will be focussed upon the types of educational systems that exist and the manner in which each reflects and moulds the society in which it operates. At this point the problem of indoctrination, which has recently received so much discussion in educational literature, finds a prominent place. In the same manner the functions of the press, of the popularization of knowledge and of propaganda receive appropriate treatment. An adequate understanding of such phenomena as these will contribute to a more precise conception of the role of ideas in political and social movements and of the value of knowledge as an instrument in controlling social reality.

Despite the vast number of specialized accounts of social institutions, the primary function of which centres around the intellectual activities in society, no adequate theoretical treatment of the social organization of intellectual life exists. One of the primary obligations of the sociology of knowledge consists, therefore, in a systematic analysis of the institutional organization within the framework of which intellectual activity is carried on. This involves, among other items, the study of schools, universities, academies, learned societies, museums, libraries, research institutes and laboratories, foundations, and publishing facilities. It is important to know how and by whom these institutions are supported, the types of activity they carry on, their policies, their internal organization and interrelations, and their place in the social organization as a whole.

Finally, and in all of its aspects, the sociology of knowledge is concerned with the persons who are the bearers of intellectual activity, namely the intellectuals. In every society there are individuals whose special function it is to accumulate, preserve, reformulate, and disseminate the intellectual heritage of the group. The composition of this group, their social derivation and the method by which they are recruited, their organization, their class affiliation, the rewards and prestige they receive, their participation in other spheres of social life, constitute some of the more crucial questions to which the sociology of knowledge seeks answers. The manner in which these factors express themselves in the products of intellectual activity provides the central theme in all studies which are pursued in the name of the sociology of knowledge.

In *Ideology and Utopia*, Professor Mannheim presents not merely the outlines of a new discipline which promises to give a new and more profound understanding of social life, but also offers a much-needed clarification of some of the major moral issues of to-day. It is in the hope that it will make some contribution to the solution of the problems which intelligent people in the English-speaking world are facing that the present volume has been translated.

I. PRELIMINARY APPROACH TO THE PROBLEM

1. The Sociological Concept of Thought

This book is concerned with the problem of how men actually think. The aim of these studies is to investigate not how thinking appears in textbooks on logic, but how it really functions in public life and in politics as an instrument of collective action.

Philosophers have too long concerned themselves with their own thinking. When they wrote of thought, they had in mind primarily their own history, the history of philosophy, or quite special fields of knowledge such as mathematics or physics. This type of thinking is applicable only under quite special circumstances, and what can be learned by analysing it is not directly transferable to other spheres of life. Even when it is applicable, it refers only to a specific dimension of existence which does not suffice for living human beings who are seeking to comprehend and to mould their world.

Meanwhile, acting men have, for better or for worse, proceeded to develop a variety of methods for the experiential and intellectual penetration of the world in which they live, which have never been analysed with the same precision as the so-called exact modes of knowing. When, however, any human activity continues over a long period without being subjected to intellectual control or criticism, it tends to get out of hand.

Hence it is to be regarded as one of the anomalies of our time that those methods of thought by means of which we arrive at our most crucial decisions, and through which we seek to diagnose and guide our political and social destiny, have remained unrecognized and therefore inaccessible to intellectual control and self-criticism. This anomaly becomes all the more monstrous when we call to mind that in modern times much more depends on the correct thinking through of a situation than was the case in earlier societies. The significance of social knowledge grows proportionately with the increasing necessity of regulatory intervention in the social process. This so-called pre-scientific inexact mode of thought, however (which, paradoxically, the logicians and philosophers also use when they have to make

C

practical decisions), is not to be understood solely by the use of logical analysis. It constitutes a complex which cannot be readily detached either from the psychological roots of the emotional and vital impulses which underlie it or from the situation in which it arises and which it seeks to solve.

It is the most essential task of this book to work out a suitable method for the description and analysis of this type of thought and its changes, and to formulate those problems connected with it which will both do justice to its unique character and prepare the way for its critical understanding. The method which we will seek to present is that of the sociology of knowledge.

The principal thesis of the sociology of knowledge is that there are modes of thought which cannot be adequately understood as long as their social origins are obscured. It is indeed true that only the individual is capable of thinking. There is no such metaphysical entity as a group mind which thinks over and above the heads of individuals, or whose ideas the individual merely reproduces.˙ Nevertheless it would be false to deduce from this that all the ideas and sentiments which motivate an individual have their origin in him alone, and can be adequately explained solely on the basis of his own life-experience.

Just as it would be incorrect to attempt to derive a language merely from observing a single individual, who speaks not a language of his own but rather that of his contemporaries and predecessors who have prepared the path for him, so it is incorrect to explain the totality of an outlook only with reference to its genesis in the mind of the individual. Only in a quite limited sense does the single individual create out of himself the mode of speech and of thought we attribute to him. He speaks the language of his group ; he thinks in the manner in which his group thinks. He finds at his disposal only certain words and their meanings. These not only determine to a large extent the avenues of approach to the surrounding world, but they also show at the same time from which angle and in which context of activity objects have hitherto been perceptible and accessible to the group or the individual.

The first point which we now have to emphasize is that the approach of the sociology of knowledge intentionally does not start with the single individual and his thinking in order then to proceed directly in the manner of the philosopher to the abstract heights of " thought as such ". Rather, the sociology of knowledge seeks to comprehend thought in the concrete setting of an historical-social situation out of which individually differentiated thought only very gradually emerges. Thus, it is not men in general who think, or even isolated individuals who do the thinking, but men in certain groups who have developed a particular style of thought in an endless series of responses to certain typical situations characterizing their common position.

Strictly speaking it is incorrect to say that the single individual thinks. Rather it is more correct to insist that he participates in thinking further what other men have thought before him. He finds himself in an inherited situation with patterns of thought which are appropriate to this situation and attempts to elaborate further the inherited modes of response or to substitute others for them in order to deal more adequately with the new challenges which have arisen out of the shifts and changes in his situation. Every individual is therefore in a two-fold sense predetermined by the fact of growing up in a society : on the one hand he finds a ready-made situation and on the other he finds in that situation preformed patterns of thought and of conduct.

The second feature characterizing the method of the sociology of knowledge is that it does not sever the concretely existing modes of thought from the context of collective action through which we first discover the world in an intellectual sense. Men living in groups do not merely coexist physically as discrete individuals. They do not confront the objects of the world from the abstract levels of a contemplating mind as such, nor do they do so exclusively as solitary beings. On the contrary they act with and against one another in diversely organized groups, and while doing so they think with and against one another. These persons, bound together into groups, strive in accordance with the character and position of the groups to which they belong to change the surrounding world of nature and society or attempt to maintain it in a given condition. It is the direction of this will to change or to maintain, of this collective activity, which produces the guiding thread for the emergence of their problems, their concepts, and their forms of thought. In accord with the particular context of collective activity in which they participate, men always tend to see the world which surrounds them differently. Just as pure logical analysis has severed individual thought from its group situation, so it also separated thought from action. It did this on the tacit assumption that those inherent connections which always exist in reality between thought on the one hand, and group and activity on the other, are either insignificant for " correct " thinking or can be detached from these foundations without any resultant difficulties. But the fact that one ignores something by no means puts an end to its existence. Nor can anyone who has not first given himself whole-heartedly to the exact observation of the wealth of forms in which men really think decide *a priori* whether this severance from the social situation and context of activity is always realizable. Nor indeed can it be determined offhand that such a complete dichotomy is fully desirable precisely in the interest of objective factual knowledge.

It may be that, in certain spheres of knowledge, it is the impulse to act which first makes the objects of the world accessible to the acting subject, and it may be further that it is this factor which determines the selection of those elements of reality which enter into thought. And it is not inconceivable that if this volitional factor were entirely excluded (in so far as such a thing is possible), the concrete content would completely disappear from the concepts, and the organizing principle which first makes possible an intelligent statement of the problem would be lost.

But this is not to say that in those domains where attachment to the group and orientation towards action seem to be an essential element in the situation, every possibility of intellectual, critical self-control is futile. Perhaps it is precisely when the hitherto concealed dependence of thought on group existence and its rootedness in action becomes visible that it really becomes possible for the first time, through becoming aware of them, to attain a new mode of control over previously uncontrolled factors in thought.

This brings us to the central problem of the book. These remarks should make it clear that a preoccupation with these problems and their solution will furnish a foundation for the social sciences and answer the question as to the possibility of the scientific guidance of political life. It is, of course, true that in the social sciences, as elsewhere, the ultimate criterion of truth or falsity is to be found in the investigation of the object, and the sociology of knowledge is no substitute for this. But the examination of the object is not an isolated act ; it takes place in a context which is coloured by values and collective-unconscious, volitional impulses. In the social sciences it is this intellectual interest, oriented in a matrix of collective activity, which provides not only the general questions, but the concrete hypotheses for research and the thought-models for the ordering of experience.   Only as we succeed in bringing into the area of conscious and explicit observation the various points of departure and of approach to the facts which are current in scientific as well as popular discussion, can we hope, in the course of time, to control the unconscious motivations and presuppositions which, in the last analysis, have brought these modes of thought into existence. A new type of objectivity in the social sciences is attainable not through the exclusion of evaluations but through the critical awareness and control of them.

2. The Contemporary Predicament of Thought

It is by no means an accident that the problem of the social and activistic roots of thinking has emerged in our generation. Nor is it accidental that the unconscious, which has hitherto motivated our thought and activity, has been gradually raised to the level of awareness and thereby made accessible to control. It would be a failure to recognize its relevance to our own plight if we did not see that it is a specific social situation which has impelled us to reflect about the social roots of our knowledge. It is one of the fundamental insights of the sociology of knowledge that the process by which collective-unconscious motives become conscious cannot operate in every epoch, but only in a quite specific situation.   This situation is sociologically determinable. One can point out with relative precision the factors which are inevitably forcing more and more persons to reflect not merely about the things of the world, but about thinking itself and even here not so much about truth in itself, as about the alarming fact that the same world can appear differently to different observers.

It is clear that such problems can become general only in an age in which disagreement is more conspicuous than agreement. One turns from the direct observation of things to the considera-tion of ways of thinking only when the possibility of the direct and continuous elaboration of concepts concerning things and situations has collapsed in the face of a multiplicity of funda-mentally divergent definitions. Now we are enabled to designate more precisely than a general and formal analysis makes possible, exactly in which social and intellectual situation such a shift of attention from things to divergent opinions and from there to the unconscious motives of thought must necessarily occur. In what follows we wish to point out only a few of the most significant social factors which are operating in this direction.

Above all, the multiplicity of ways of thinking cannot become a problem in periods when social stability underlies and guarantees the internal unity of a world-view. As long as the same meanings of words, the same ways of deducing ideas, are inculcated from childhood on into every member of the group, divergent thought-processes cannot exist in that society. Even a gradual modification in ways of thinking (where it should happen to arise), does not become perceptible to the members of a group who live in a stable situation as long as the tempo in the adaptations of ways of thinking to new problems is so slow that it extends over several generations. In such a case, one and the same generation in the course of its own life span can scarcely become aware that a change is taking place.

But in addition to the general dynamics of the historical process, factors of quite another sort must enter before the multiplicity of the ways of thinking will become noticeable and emerge as a theme for reflection. Thus it is primarily the intensification of social mobility which destroys the earlier illusion, prevalent in a static society, that all things can change, but thought remains eternally the same. And what is more, the two forms of social mobility, horizontal and vertical, operate in different ways to reveal this multiplicity of styles of thought. Horizontal mobility (movement from one position to another or from one country to another without changing social status) shows us that different peoples think differently. As long, however, as the traditions of one's national and local group remain unbroken, one remains so attached to its customary ways of thinking that the ways of thinking which are perceived in other groups are regarded as curiosities, errors, ambiguities, or heresies. At this stage one does not doubt either the correctness of one's own traditions of thought or the unity and uniformity of thought in general.

Only when horizontal mobility is accompanied by intensive vertical mobility, i.e. rapid movement between strata in the sense of social ascent and descent, is the belief in the general and eternal validity of one's own thought-forms shaken. Vertical mobility is the decisive factor in making persons uncertain and sceptical of their traditional view of the world. It is, of course, true that even in static societies with very slight vertical mobility, different strata within the same society have had different ways of experiencing the world. It is the merit of Max Weber [1] to have clearly shown in his sociology of religion how often the same religion is variously experienced by peasants, artisans, merchants, nobles, and intellectuals. In a society organized along the lines of closed castes or ranks the comparative absence of vertical mobility served either to isolate from each other the divergent world-views or if, for example, they experienced a common religion, according to their different contexts of life, they interpreted it in a different way. This accounts for the fact that the diversity of modes of thought of different castes did not converge in one and the same mind and hence could not become a problem. From a sociological point of view, the decisive change takes place when that stage of historical development is reached in which the previously isolated strata begin to communicate with one another and a certain social circulation sets in. The most significant stage of this communication is reached when the forms of thought and experience, which had hitherto developed independently, enter into one and the same consciousness impelling the mind to discover the irreconcilability of the conflicting conceptions of the world.

In a well stabilized society the mere infiltration of the modes of thought of the lower strata into the higher would not mean very much since the bare perception by the dominant group of possible variations in thinking would not result in their being intellectually shaken. As long as a society is stabilized on the basis of authority, and social prestige is accorded only to the achievements of the upper stratum, this class has little cause to call into question its own social existence and the value of its achievements. Apart from a considerable social ascent, it is not until we have a general democratization that the rise of the lower strata allows their thinking to acquire public significance. [2] This process of democratization first makes it possible for the ways of thinking of the lower strata, which formerly had no public validity, to acquire validity and prestige. When the stage of democratization has been reached, the techniques of thinking and the ideas of the lower strata are for the first time in a position to confront

---

[1] Max Weber, *Wirtschaft und Gesellschaft*, vol. i, chap. iv, § 7, *Religionssoziologie*: *Stände, Klassen und Religion* (Tübingen, 1925), pp. 267–296.
[2] Thus, for example, in our own time, pragmatism, as will be seen later, when viewed sociologically, constitutes the legitimation of a technique of thinking and of an epistemology which has elevated the criteria of everyday experience to the level of " academic " discussion.

the ideas of the dominant strata on the same level of validity. And now, too, for the first time these ideas and modes of thought are capable of impelling the person who thinks within their framework to subject the objects of his world to a fundamental questioning. It is with this clashing of modes of thought, each of which has the same claims to representational validity, that for the first time there is rendered possible the emergence of the question which is so fateful, but also so fundamental in the history of thought, namely, how it is possible that identical human thought-processes concerned with the same world produce divergent conceptions of that world. And from this point it is only a step further to ask : Is it not possible that the thought-processes which are involved here are not at all identical ? May it not be found, when one has examined all the possibilities of human thought, that there are numerous alternative paths which can be followed ?

Was it not this process of social ascent which in the Athenian democracy called forth the first great surge of scepticism in the history of Occidental thought ? Were not the Sophists of the Greek Enlightenment the expression of an attitude of doubt which arose essentially out of the fact that in their thinking about every object, two modes of explanation collided ? On the one hand was the mythology which was the way of thinking of a dominant nobility already doomed to decline. On the other hand was the more analytical habit of thought of an urban artisan lower stratum, which was in the process of moving upwards. Inasmuch as these two forms of interpreting the world converged in the thought of the Sophists, and since' for every moral decision there were available at least two standards, and for every cosmic and social happening at least two explanations, it is no wonder that they had a sceptical notion of the value of human thought. It is therefore pointless to censure them in schoolmaster fashion for having been sceptics in their epistemological efforts. They simply had the courage to express what every person who was really characteristic of the epoch felt, namely, that the previous unambiguity of norms and interpretations had been shattered, and that a satisfactory solution was to be found only in a thoroughgoing questioning and thinking through of the contradictions. This general uncertainty was by no means a symptom of a world doomed to general decay, but it was rather the beginning of a wholesome process which marked a crisis leading to recovery.

Was it not, furthermore, the great virtue of Socrates that he had the courage to descend into the abyss of this scepticism ? Was he not originally also a Sophist who took up the technique of raising questions and then raising further questions, and made it his own ? And did he not overcome the crisis by questioning even more radically than the Sophists and thus arrive at an intellectual resting-point which, at least for the mentality of that epoch, showed itself to be a reliable foundation ? It is interesting to observe that thereby the world of norms and of being came to occupy the central place in his inquiry. Furthermore, he was at least as intensively concerned with the question as to how individuals are able to think of and judge the same facts in different ways as he was with the facts themselves. Even at this stage in the history of thought it becomes apparent that in various periods the problems of thinking can be solved not solely by preoccupation with the object but rather only through dis-covering why opinions concerning them really differ.

In addition to those social factors which account for the early unity and subsequent multiplicity in the dominant forms of thought, another important factor should be mentioned. In every society there are social groups whose special task it is to provide an interpretation of the world for that society. We call these the " intelligentsia ". The more static a society is, the more likely is it that this stratum will acquire a well-defined status or the position of a caste in that society. Thus the magicians, the Brahmins, the medieval clergy are to be regarded as intellectual strata, each of which in its society enjoyed a mono-polistic control over the moulding of that society's world-view, and over either the reconstruction or the reconciliation of the differences in the naïvely formed world-views of the other strata. The sermon, the confession, the lesson, are, in this sense, means by which reconciliation of the different conceptions of the world takes place at less sophisticated levels of social development.

This intellectual stratum, organized as a caste and monopolizing the right to preach, teach, and interpret the world is conditioned by the force of two social factors. The more it makes itself the exponent of a thoroughly organized collectivity (e.g. the Church), the more its thinking tends towards " scholasticism ". It must give a dogmatically binding force to modes of thought which formerly were valid only for a sect and thereby sanction the ontology and epistemology implicit in this mode of thought. The necessity of having to present a unified front to outsiders compels this transition. The same result may also be brought about by the possibility that the concentration of power within the social structure will be so pronounced that uniformity of thought and experience can be imposed upon the members of at least one's own caste with greater success than heretofore.

The second characteristic of this monopolistic type of thought is its relative remoteness from the open conflicts of everyday life ; hence it is also " scholastic " in this sense, i.e. academic and life-less. This type of thought does not arise primarily from the struggle with concrete problems of life nor from trial and error, nor from experiences in mastering nature and society, but rather much more from its own need for systematization, which always refers the facts which emerge in the religious as well as in other spheres of life back to given traditional and intellec-tually uncontrolled premises. The antagonisms which emerge in these discussions do not embody the conflict of various modes of experience so much as various positions of power within the same social structure, which have at the time identified them-selves with the different possible interpretations of the dogmatized traditional " truth ". The dogmatic content of the premises with which these divergent groups start and which this thought then seeks in different ways to justify turns out for the most part to be a matter of accident, if judged by the criteria of factual evidence. It is completely arbitrary in so far as it depends upon which sect happens to be successful, in accordance with historical-political destiny, in making its own intellectual and experiential traditions the traditions of the entire clerical caste of the church.

From a sociological point of view the decisive fact of modern times, in contrast with the situation during the Middle Ages, is that this monopoly of the ecclesiastical interpretation of the world which was held by the priestly caste is broken, and in the place of a closed and thoroughly organized stratum of intellectuals, a free intelligentsia has arisen. Its chief characteristic is that it is increasingly recruited from constantly varying social strata and life-situations, and that its mode of thought is no longer subject to regulation by a caste-like organization. Due to the absence of a social organization of their own, the intellectuals have allowed those ways of thinking and experiencing to get a hearing which openly competed with one another in the larger world of the other strata. When one considers further that with the renunciation of the monopolistic privileges of a caste type of existence, free competition began to dominate the modes of intellectual production, one understands why, to the extent that they were in competition, the intellectuals adopted in an ever more pronounced fashion the most various modes of thought and experience available in society and played them off against one another. They did this inasmuch as they had to compete for the favour of a public which, unlike the public of the clergy, was no longer accessible to them without their own efforts. This competition for the favour of various public groups was accentuated because the distinctive modes of experiencing and thinking of each attained increasing public expression and validity.

In this process the intellectual's illusion that there is only one way of thinking disappears. The intellectual is now no longer, as formerly, a member of a caste or rank whose scholastic manner of thought represents for him thought as such. In this relatively simple process is to be sought the explanation for the fact that the fundamental questioning of thought in modern times does not begin until the collapse of the intellectual monopoly of the clergy. The almost unanimously accepted world-view which had been artificially maintained fell apart the moment the socially monopolistic position of its producers was destroyed. With the liberation of the intellectuals from the rigorous organization of the church, other ways of interpreting the world were increasingly recognized.

The disruption of the intellectual monopoly of the church brought about a sudden flowering of an unexampled intellectual richness. But at the same time we must attribute to the organizational disintegration of the unitary church the fact that the belief in the unity and eternal nature of thought, which had persisted since classical antiquity, was again shaken. The origins of the profound disquietude of the present day reach back to this period, even though in most recent times additional causes of a quite different nature have entered into the process. Out of this first upsurge of the profound disquietude of modern man there emerged those fundamentally new modes of thought and investigation, the epistemological, the psychological, and the sociological, without which to-day we could not even formulate our problem. For this reason we will attempt in the next section to show, in its main lines at least, how the many forms of questioning and investigation available to us arose from this unitary social situation.[1]

[1] On the nature of monopolistic thought, cf. K. Mannheim, " Die Bedeutung der Konkurrenz im Gebiete des Geistigen." Report delivered at the Sixth Congress of the German Sociological Society in Zurich (*Schriften der deutschen Gesellschaft für Soziologie*, vol. vi (Tübingen, 1929)).

3. The Origin of the Modern Epistemological, Psychological, and Sociological Points of View

Epistemology was the first significant philosophical product of the breakdown of the unitary world-view with which the modern era was ushered in. In this instance, as in antiquity, it was the first reflection of the unrest which emerged from the fact that those thinkers who were penetrating to the very foundations of thought were discovering not only numerous world-views but also numerous ontological orders. Epistemology sought to eliminate this uncertainty by taking its point of departure not from a dogmatically taught theory of existence, nor from a world-order which was validated by a higher type of knowledge, but from an analysis of the knowing subject.

All epistemological speculation is oriented within the polarity of object and subject.[1] Either it starts with the world of objects, which in one way or another it dogmatically presupposes as familiar to all, and with this as a basis explains the position of the subject in this world-order, deriving therefrom his cognitive powers ; or else it starts with the subject as the immediate and unquestioned datum and seeks to derive from him the possibility of valid knowledge. In periods in which the objective world-view remains more or less unshaken, and in epochs which succeed in presenting one unambiguously perceivable world-order, there exists the tendency to base the existence of the knowing human subject and his intellectual capacities on objective factors. Thus in the Middle Ages, which not only believed in an unambiguous world-order but which also thought that it knew the " existential value " to be attributed to every object in the hierarchy of things, there prevailed an explanation of the value of human capacities and thought which was based on the world of objects. But after the breakdown which we described, the conception of order in the world of objects which had been guaranteed by the dominance of the church became problematical, and there remained no alternative but to turn about and to take the opposite road, and, with the subject as the point of departure, to determine the nature and the value of the human cognitive act, attempting thereby to find an anchorage for objective existence in the knowing subject.

Although precursors for this tendency are already to be found

---

[1] Cf. K. Mannheim, *Die Strukturanalyse der Erkenntnistheorie.* Ergänzungsband der Kant-Studien, No. 57 (Berlin, 1922).

in medieval thought, it fully emerged for the first time in the rationalistic current of French and German philosophy from Descartes through Leibnitz to Kant on the one hand, and in the more psychologically oriented epistemology of Hobbes, Locke, Berkeley, and Hume on the other. This was above all else the meaning of Descartes' intellectual experiment, of the exemplary struggle in which he attempted to question all traditional theories in order, finally, to arrive at the no longer questionable *cogito ergo sum*. This was the only point from which he could again undertake anew to lay the foundations for a world-view.

All these attempts presuppose the more or less explicit consideration that the subject is more immediately accessible to us than the object which has become too ambiguous as a result of the many divergent interpretations to which it has been subjected. For this reason we must, wherever possible, empirically reconstruct the genesis of thought in the subject which is more accessible to our control. In the mere preference for the empirical observations and genetic criteria which gradually became supreme, the will to the destruction of the authoritarian principle was revealed in operation. It represents a centrifugal tendency in opposition to the church as the official interpreter of the universe. Only that has validity which I can control in my own perception, which is corroborated in my own experimental activity, or which I myself can produce or at least conceptually construct as producible.

Consequently, in place of the traditional, ecclesiastically guaranteed story of creation, there emerged a conception of the formation of the world, the various parts of which are subject to intellectual control. This conceptual model of the producibility of the world-view from the cognitive act led to the solution of the epistemological problem. It was hoped that through insight into the origins of cognitive representation one could arrive at some notion of the role and significance of the subject for the act of knowing and of the truth-value of human knowledge in general.

It was indeed appreciated that this circuitous approach through the subject was a substitute and a makeshift in the absence of anything better. A complete solution of the problem would be possible only if an extra-human and infallible mind were to render a judgment about the value of our thinking. But precisely this method had failed in the past, because the farther one progressed in the criticism of earlier theories, the more clear did it become that those philosophies which made the most absolute claims were the most likely to fall into easily perceivable self-deceptions. Hence, the method which meanwhile had proved itself the most suitable one in the natural orientation to the world and in the natural sciences, namely the empirical method, came to be preferred.

When, in the course of development, the philological and historical sciences were elaborated, the possibility arose in the analysis of thought of also drawing upon the historically evolving conceptions of the world and of understanding this wealth of philosophical and religious world-views in terms of the genetic process through which they had come into existence. Thus thought came to be examined at very different levels of its development and in quite different historical situations. It became evident that much more could be said about the manner in which the structure of the subject influenced his world-view when one made use of animal psychology, child psychology, the psychology of language, the psychology of primitive peoples, and the psychology of intellectual history than when one set about it with a purely speculative analysis of the achievements of a transcendent subject.

The epistemological recourse to the subject rendered possible in this way the emergence of a psychology which became ever more precise, including a psychology of thought which, as we have indicated above, broke up into numerous fields of specialization. However, the more precise this empirical psychology became, the greater the appreciation of the scope of empirical observation, the more evident it became that the subject was by no means such a safe point of departure for the attainment of a new conception of the world as had previously been assumed. It is indeed true, in a certain sense, that inner experience is more immediately given than external experience, and that the inner connection between experiences can be more surely comprehended, if, among other things, one is able to have a sympathetic understanding of the motivations which produce certain actions. However, it was nonetheless clear that one could not entirely avoid the risks involved in an ontology. The psyche, too, with all its inwardly immediately perceivable " experiences " is a segment of reality. And the knowledge of these experiences which it acquires presupposes a theory of reality, an ontology. However, just as such an ontology has become more ambiguous, as regards the outer world, so it became no less ambiguous as regards psychic reality.

The type of psychology which connected the Middle Ages with modern times, and which drew its contents from the self-observation of the religious man, does indeed still operate with certain concepts rich with content which evidence the continuing influence of a religious ontology of the soul. We are thinking, in this connection, of psychology as it has grown out of the inner struggle over the choice between good and evil, which was now conceived of as occurring in the subject. Such a psychology was developed in the conflicts of conscience and in the scepticism of men like Pascal and Montaigne down to Kierkegaard. Here we still find, pregnant with meaning, certain orientational concepts of an ontological sort such as despair, sin, salvation, and loneliness, which derive a certain richness from experience because every experience, which from its very beginning, is directed towards a religious goal, has its concrete content. Nonetheless these experiences, too, with the passage of time became more bare of content, thinner, and more formal as in the outer world their original frame of reference, their religious ontology, became enfeebled. A society in which diverse groups can no longer agree on the meaning of God, Life, and Man, will be equally unable to decide unanimously what is to be understood by sin, despair, salvation, or loneliness. Recourse to the subject along these lines provided no real assistance. Only he who immerses himself in his own self in such a manner that he does not destroy all of the elements of personal meaning and of value is in a position to find answers to questions that involve meaning. In the meantime, however, as a result of this radical formalization, scientific psychic inward observation took on new forms. Fundamentally this psychic inward observation involved the same process which characterized the experiencing and thinking through of the objects of the external world. Such meaning-giving interpretations with qualitatively rich contents (as, for instance, sin, despair, loneliness, Christian love) were replaced by formalized entities such as the feeling of anxiety, the perception of inner conflict, the experiencing of isolation, and the " libido ". These latter sought to apply interpretive schemes derived from mechanics to the inner experience of man. The aim here was not so much to comprehend as precisely as possible the inner contentual richness of experiences as they coexist in the individual and together operate towards the achievement of a meaningful goal ; the attempt was rather to exclude all distinctive elements in experience from the content in order that, wherever possible, the conception of psychic events should approximate the simple scheme of mechanics (position, motion, cause, effect). The problem becomes not how a person understands himself in terms of his own ideals and norms and how, against the background of such norms, his deeds and renunciations are given their meaning, but rather how an external situation can, with an ascertainable degree of probability, mechanically call forth an inner reaction. The category of external causality was increasingly used, operating with the idea of a regular succession of two formally simplified events, as is illustrated in the schema : " Fear arises when something unusual occurs," in which it was purposely overlooked that every type of fear changes completely with its content (fear in face of uncertainty and fear in face of an animal), and that the unusual, too, varies entirely in accord with the context in which things are usual. But it was precisely the formal abstraction of the common characteristics of these qualitatively differentiated phenomena that was sought after.

Or else the category of function was employed in the sense that single phenomena were interpreted from the point of view of their role in the formal functioning of the whole psychic mechanism, as, for instance, that when mental conflicts are interpreted, as, basically, the result of two unintegrated contradictory tendencies in the psychic sphere, they are the expressions of the subject's maladjustment. Their function is to compel the subject to reorganize his process of adaptation and to arrive at a new equilibrium.

It would be reactionary, with reference to the fruitful development of science, to deny the cognitive value of simplifying procedures such as these which are easily controllable and which are applicable, with a high degree of probability, to a great mass of phenomena. The fruitfulness of these formalizing sciences, working in terms of causes and functions, is still far from exhausted; and it would be harmful to impede their development. It is one thing to test a fruitful line of investigation and another to regard it as the only path to the scientific treatment of an object. In so far as the latter is the point at issue, it is already clear to-day that the formal approach alone does not exhaust what can be known of the world and particularly of the psychic life of human beings.

The interconnections of meaning which were in this procedure heuristically excluded (in the interests of scientific simplification) so that formal and easily definable entities could be arrived at, are not recaptured by a mere further perfection of formalization through the discovery of correlations and functions. It may indeed be necessary, for the sake of the precise observability of the formal sequence of experiences, to discard the concrete contents of experiences and values. It would, however, constitute a type of scientific fetishism to believe that such a methodical purification actually replaces the original richness of experience. It is even more erroneous to think that a scientific extrapolation and abstract accentuation of one aspect of a phenomenon, for the sole reason that it has been thought through in this form, is able to enrich the original life-experience.

Although we may know a great deal about the conditions under which conflicts arise, we may still know nothing about the inner situation of living human beings, and how, when their values are shattered, they lose their bearings and strive again to find themselves. Just as the most exact theory of cause and function does not answer the question as to who I actually am, what I actually am, or what it means to be a human being, so there can never arise out of it that interpretation of one's self and the world demanded by even the simplest action based on some evaluative decision.

The mechanistic and functionalistic theory is highly valuable as a current in psychological research. It fails, however, when it is placed in the total context of life-experience because it says nothing concerning the meaningful goal of conduct, and is therefore unable to interpret the elements of conduct with reference to it. The mechanistic mode of thought is of assistance only as long as the goal or the value is given from another source and the " means " alone are to be treated. The most important role of thought in life consists, however, in providing guidance for conduct when decisions must be made. Every real decision (such as one's evaluation of other persons or how society should be organized) implies a judgment concerning good and evil, concerning the meaning of life and mind.

At this point we encounter the paradox that this extrapolation of the formalized elements by means of general mechanics and the theory of function originally arose to help men in their activities to attain their goals more easily. The world of things and of the mind was mechanistically and functionally examined in order, through comparative analysis, to arrive at its ultimate constituent elements, and then to regroup them in accord with the goal of activity. When the analytical procedure was first used,

D

the end or goal prescribed by the activity was still in existence (often composed of fragments of an earlier, religiously understood world). Men strove to know the world so that they could mould it to conform to this ultimate goal ; society was analysed so as to arrive at a form of social life more just or otherwise more pleasing to God ; men were concerned with the soul in order to control the path to salvation. But the farther men advanced in analysis, the more the goal disappeared from their field of vision, so that to-day a research worker might say with Nietzsche " I have forgotten why I ever began " (*Ich habe meine Gründe vergessen*). If to-day one inquires concerning the ends served by analysis, the question is not to be answered with reference to either nature or the soul or society, or else we formally posit a purely technical, psychical, or social optimum condition, as, for example, the most " frictionless functioning ".[1] This goal appears as the only one when, for instance, disregarding all his complicated observations and hypotheses, one asks a psychoanalyst to what end he cures his patients. In most cases he has no other answer than the notion of an optimum of adaptation. As to what this optimum is, however, he can say nothing on the basis of his science alone, since every ultimate meaningful end has been eliminated from it from the very first.

Thereby another aspect of the problem is revealed. Without evaluative conceptions, without the minimum of a meaningful goal, we can do nothing in either the sphere of the social or the sphere of the psychic. By this we mean that even when one takes a purely causal and functional point of view one discovers only afterwards what sense there was originally concealed in the ontology on which one proceeded. It guarded against the atomization of the experience into isolated observations, i.e. atomization from the standpoint of the activity. Expressed in terms of modern Gestalt theory, the meanings which our ontology gives us served to integrate the units of conduct and to enable

---

[1] This may account for the deeper truth of the regulation that heads of ministries in parliamentary states must not be chosen from the ranks of the administrative staff, but rather from among the political leaders. The administrative bureaucrat, like every specialist and expert, inclines to lose sight of the context of his action and the end goal. It is assumed here that he who embodies the freely formed integration of the collective will in public life, the political leader, can integrate the available means which are necessary for the actions in question in a more organic fashion than the administrative expert who in questions of policy has been deliberately neutralized. Cf. section on the sociology of bureaucratic thinking, pp. 105 ff.

us to see in a configurative context the individual observational elements which otherwise would tend to remain discreet.

Even if all the meaning conveyed by the magical-religious view of the world had been " false ", it still served—when viewed from a purely functional standpoint—to make coherent the fragments of the reality of inner psychic as well as objective external experience, and to place them with reference to a certain complex of conduct. We see ever more clearly that from whatever source we get our meanings, whether they be true or false, they have a certain psychological-sociological function, namely to fix the attention of those men who wish to do something in common upon a certain " definition of the situation ". A situation is constituted as such when it is defined in the same way for the members of the group. It may be true or false when one group calls another heretics, and as such struggles against them, but it is only through this definition that the struggle is a social situation. It may be true or false that a group struggles only to realize a fascist or a communist society, but it is only by means of this meaning-giving, evaluating definition that events produce a situation where activity and counteractivity are distinguishable, and the totality of events are articulated into a process. The juxtaposition *ex post facto* of elements voided of meaningful content does not bring home the unity of conduct. As a result of the extensive exclusion of meaningful elements from psychological theory, it becomes more and more evident that in psychology, too, psychic situations, to say nothing of inner life histories, cannot be perceived without meaningful context.

Furthermore, from a purely functionalist point of view, the derivation of our meanings, whether they be true or false, plays an indispensable role, namely, it socializes events for a group. We belong to a group not only because we are born into it, not merely because we profess to belong to it, nor finally because we give it our loyalty and allegiance, but primarily because we see the world and certain things in the world the way it does (i.e. in terms of the meanings of the group in question). In every concept, in every concrete meaning, there is contained a crystallization of the experiences of a certain group. When someone says " kingdom ", he is using the term in the sense in which it has meaning for a certain group. Another for whom the kingdom is only an organization, as for instance an administrative organization such as is involved in a postal system, is not participating in those collective actions of the group in which the former meaning is taken for granted. In every concept, however, there is not only a fixation of individuals with reference to a definite group of a certain kind and its action, but every source from which we derive meaning and interpretation acts also as a stabilizing factor on the possibilities of experiencing and knowing objects with reference to the central goal of action which directs us.

The world of external objects and of psychic experience appears to be in a continuous flux. Verbs are more adequate symbols for this situation than nouns. The fact that we give names to things which are in flux implies inevitably a certain stabilization oriented along the lines of collective activity. The derivation of our meanings emphasizes and stabilizes that aspect of things which is relevant to activity and covers up, in the interest of collective action, the perpetually fluid process underlying all things. It excludes other configurational organizations of the data which tend in different directions. Every concept represents a sort of taboo against other possible sources of meaning— simplifying and unifying the manifoldness of life for the sake of action.

It is not improbable that the formalizing and functionalizing view of things became possible in our time only because the previously dominant taboos, which made man impervious to meanings derived from other sources, were already losing their force after the breakdown of the intellectual monopoly of the church. The opportunity gradually arose under these circumstances for every oppositional group openly to reveal to the world those contradictory meanings which corresponded to their own peculiarly conceived understanding of the world. What was a king for one was a tyrant for another. It has already been pointed out, however, that too many conflicting sources from which meanings with regard to a given object are derived in the same society leads in the end to the dissolution of every system of meaning. In such a society, internally divided with regard to any concrete system of meaning, consensus can be established only with reference to the formalized elements of the objects (e.g. the definition of monarch which asserts : " The monarch is he who in the eyes of a majority of persons in a country legally possesses the right of exercising absolute power "). In this and similar definitions everything substantial, every evaluation for which a consensus can no longer be found, is reinterpreted in functional terms.

Returning then to our discussion of the origins of modern psychology with the subject as the point of departure, it is now clear that the original difficulty, which was to have been solved through recourse to and concentration on the subject, was not thereby obviated. It is true that much that is new was discovered by the new empirical methods. They enabled us to gain insight into the psychic genesis of many cultural phenomena, but the answers which were brought forward deflected our attention from the fundamental question concerning the existence of mind in the order of reality. Especially was the unity of the mind as well as that of the person lost through the functionalization and mechanization of psychic phenomena. A psychology without a psyche cannot take the place of an ontology. Such a psychology was itself the outcome of the fact that men were attempting to think in the framework of categories which strove to negate every evaluation, every trace of common meaning, or of total configuration. What may be valuable for a specialized discipline as a research hypothesis may, however, be fatal for the conduct of human beings. The uncertainty which arises from relying upon scientific psychology in practical life becomes recurrently obvious as soon as the pedagogue or the political leader turns to it for guidance. The impression which he gets upon such an occasion is that psychology exists in another world and records its observations for citizens living in some society other than our own. This form of modern man's experience, which because of a highly differentiated division of labour tends towards directionlessness, finds its counterpart in the rootlessness of a psychology with whose categories not even the simplest life-process can be thought through. That this psychology actually constitutes a trained incapacity to deal with problems of the mind accounts for the fact that it offers no foothold to living human beings in their daily life.

Thus two fundamentally different tendencies characterize modern psychology. Both became possible because the medieval world which gave a single set of meanings to men in the Western world was in the process of dissolution. The first of these is the tendency to look behind every meaning and to understand it in terms of its genesis in the subject (the genetic point of view). The second tendency consists in the attempt to construct a sort of mechanical science of the elements of psychic experience which have been formalized and emptied of meaning (psychic mechanics). It becomes evident here that the mechanistic

thought-model is not, as was originally supposed, confined to
the world of mechanical objects. The mechanistic thought-model
represents primarily a kind of first approximation to objects
in general. Here the aim is not the exact comprehension of
qualitive peculiarities and unique constellations, but rather the
determination of the most obvious regularities and principles
of order obtaining between formalized simplified elements. We
have traced out this last-mentioned method in detail and seen
how the mechanistic method, in spite of the concrete achievements for which we are indebted to it, has, from the point of
view of life-orientation and conduct, contributed very much
to the general insecurity of modern man. The acting man must
know who he is, and the ontology of psychic life fulfils a certain
function in action. To the extent that mechanistic psychology
and its parallel in actual life, the social impulsion towards
all-embracing mechanization, negated these ontological values,
they destroyed an important element in the self-orientation of
human beings in their everyday life.

We should like to turn now to the genetic approach. Here
we should first point out that the genetic point of view, which
is bound up with the psychological approach, has contributed
in many ways to a deeper understanding of life in the sense
above indicated. The dogmatic exponents of classical logic
and philosophy are accustomed to maintain that the genesis
of an idea has nothing to say concerning its validity or meaning.
They always evoke the hackneyed example to the effect that
our knowledge of the life of Pythagoras and of his inner conflicts,
etc., is of little value in understanding the Pythagorean proposition. I do not believe, however, that this point holds for all
intellectual accomplishments. I believe that from the standpoint of strict interpretation, we are infinitely enriched when we
attempt to understand the biblical sentence, " The last shall be
first," as the psychic expression of the revolt of oppressed strata.
I believe that we shall understand it better if, as Nietzsche
and others have indicated in various ways, we consider and
become aware of the significance of resentment in the formation
of moral judgments. In this case, for example, one could say
in the case of Christianity, it was resentment which gave the
lower . strata courage to emancipate themselves, at least
psychically, from the domination of an unjust system of values
and to set up their own in opposition to it. We do not intend
to raise the question here whether with the aid of this

psychological-genetic analysis which deals with the value-generating function of resentment we can decide whether the Christians or the Roman ruling classes were in the right. In any case, through this analysis we are led more deeply into the comprehension of the meaning of the sentence. It is not irrelevant for an understanding of it to know that the phrase was not uttered by anybody in general and was not addressed to men in general, but rather that it has a real appeal only for those who, like the Christians, are in some manner oppressed and who, at the same time, under the impulse of resentment, wish to free themselves from prevailing injustices. The interconnection between psychic genesis, the motivation which leads to meaning, and the meaning itself is, in the case just cited, different from that which exists in the Pythagorean propositions. The specially concocted examples which logicians adduce may under certain circumstances make one unreceptive to the deepest differences between one meaning and another and may lead to generalizations which obscure relevant relationships.

The psychogenetic approach may then contribute in a great many cases to a deeper understanding of meaning, where we are concerned not with the most abstract and formal interrelationships but rather with meanings, the motivation of which can be sympathetically experienced, or with a complex of meaningful conduct, which can be understood in terms of its motivational structure and experiential context. So, for example, when I know what a man was as a child, what severe conflicts he experienced and in which situations they occurred and how he solved them, I will know more about him than if I merely had a few bare details of his external life-history. I will know the context [1] from which novelty is produced in him and in the light of which every detail of his experience will have to be interpreted. It is the great achievement of the psychogenetic method that it destroyed the earlier mechanical conception which treated norms and cultural values as material things. When confronted with a sacred text, the genetic method has replaced the formally acquiescent obedience to a norm with the living appreciation of the process in which norms and cultural values first arise and with which they must be kept in continual contact in order that they may be ever newly interpreted and

[1] It should be noted how the genetic point of view emphasizes interdependence in contrast with the mechanistic approach which concerns itself with the atomization of the elements of experience.

mastered. It has shown thereby that the life of a psychic phenomenon is the phenomenon itself. The meaning of history and
life is contained in their becoming and in their flux. These
insights were first stumbled upon by the Romantics and by Hegel,
but since then have had to be rediscovered again and again.

There was, however, from the very beginning a two-fold
limit to this concept of psychic genesis as it gradually developed
and penetrated into the cultural sciences (such as the history
of religions, literary history, art history, etc.) ; and this limit
threatened in time to become a definite restriction on the value
of this approach.

The most essential limitation of the psychogenetic approach
is the important observation that every meaning is to be understood in the light of its genesis and in the original context of
life-experience which forms its background. But this observation contains within it the injurious constriction that this approach
will be found only in an individualistic application. In most
cases the genesis of a meaning has been sought in the individual
context of experience rather than in its collective context.
Thus, for example, if one had before one some idea (let us take
the above-mentioned case of the transformation of a hierarchy
of moral values as it is expressed in the sentence : " The last
shall be first ") and wished to explain it genetically, one
would fasten upon the individual biography of the author and
attempt to understand the idea exclusively on the basis of
the special events and motivations of the author's personal
history. Now it is clear that very much can be done with this
method, for just as the experiences that truly motivate me have
their original source and locus in my own life-history, just so
the author's life-history is the locus of his experiences. But
it is also clear that while it may be sufficient for the genetic
explanation of a quite special individual mode of behaviour to
go back to the early period of an individual's history (as would,
for instance, be done by psycho-analysis to explain the symptoms
of later developments in character from the experiences of early
childhood), for a mode of behaviour of social significance, such
as the transvaluation of values which transforms the whole
system of life of a society in all its ramifications, preoccupation
with the purely individual life-history and its analysis is not
sufficient. The transvaluation, as indicated in the sentence
above, has its roots basically in a group situation in which
hundreds and thousands of persons, each in his own way,

participate in the overthrow of the existing society. Each of these persons prepares and executes this transvaluation in the sense that he acts in a new way in a whole complex of life-situations which impinge upon him. The genetic method of explanation, if it goes deep enough, cannot in the long run limit itself to the individual life-history, but must piece together so much that finally it touches on the interdependence of the individual life-history and the more inclusive group situation. For the individual life-history is only a component in a series of mutually intertwined life-histories which have their common theme in this upheaval ; the particular new motivation of a single individual is a part of a motivational complex in which many persons participate in various ways. It was the merit of the sociological point of view that it set alongside the individual genesis of meaning the genesis from the context of group life.

The two methods of studying cultural phenomena dealt with above, the epistemological and the psychological, had in common an attempt to explain meaning from its genesis in the subject. What is important in this case is not so much whether they were thinking of the concrete individual or of a generalized mind as such, but that in both cases the individual mind was conceived as separate from the group. Thereby they unwittingly brought false assumptions into the fundamental problems of epistemology and psychology which the sociological approach has had to correct. What is most important about the latter is that it puts an end to the fiction of the detachment of the individual from the group, within the matrix of which the individual thinks and experiences.

The fiction of the isolated and self-sufficient individual under-lies in various forms the individualistic epistemology and genetic psychology. Epistemology operated with this isolated and self-sufficient individual as if from the very first he possessed in essence all the capacities characteristic of human beings, including that of pure knowledge, and as if he produced his knowledge of the world from within himself alone, through mere juxta-position with the external world. Similarly in the individualistic developmental psychology, the individual passes of necessity through certain stages of development in the course of which the external physical and social environment have no other function than to release these preformed capacities of the individual. Both of these theories grew out of the soil of an exaggerated theoretical individualism (such as was to be found in the period of the Renaissance and of individualistic liberalism) which could have been produced only in a social situation in which the original connection between individual and group had been lost sight of. Frequently in such social situations the observer loses sight of the role of society in the moulding of the individual to the extent that he derives most of the traits, which are evidently only possible as the result of a common life and the interaction between individuals, from the original nature of the individual or from the germ plasm. (We attack this fiction not from some ultimate philosophical point of view but because it simply draws incorrect data into the picture of the genesis of knowledge and experience.)

In actuality it is far from correct to assume that an individual of more or less fixed absolute capacities confronts the world and in striving for the truth constructs a world-view out of the data of his experience. Nor can we believe that he then compares his world-view with that of other individuals who have gained theirs in a similarly independent fashion, and in a sort of discussion the true world-view is brought to light and accepted by the others. In contrast to this, it is much more correct to say that knowledge is from the very beginning a co-operative process of group life, in which everyone unfolds his knowledge within the framework of a common fate, a common activity, and the overcoming of common difficulties (in which, however, each has a different share). Accordingly the products of the cognitive process are already, at least in part, differentiated because not every possible aspect of the world comes within the purview of the members of a group, but only those out of which difficulties and problems for the group arise. And even this common world (not shared by any outside groups in the same way) appears differently to the subordinate groups within the larger group. It appears differently because the subordinate groups and strata in a functionally differentiated society have a different experiential approach to the common contents of the objects of their world. In the intellectual mastery of life problems, each is allotted different segments with which each deals quite differently according to his different life-interests. The degree in which the individualistic conception of the problem of knowledge gives a false picture of collective knowing corresponds to what would occur if the technique, mode of work, and productivity of an internally highly specialized factory of 2,000 workers were thought of as if each of the 2,000 workers worked in a separate cubicle, performed the same operations for himself at the same time and turned out each individual product from beginning to end by himself. Actually, of course, the workers do not do the same thing in parallel fashion but rather, through a division of functions, they collectively bring the total product into existence.

Let us ask ourselves for a moment what is lacking in the older theory in the instance of this individualistic re-interpretation of a process of collective work and achievement. In the first place, the framework which, in a real division of labour, determines the character of the work of every individual from the chairman of the board of directors down to the very last apprentice and which integrates in an intelligent manner the nature of each partial product turned out by the individual worker, is simply overlooked. The failure to observe the social character of knowing and experiencing was not primarily due, as many believe, to disregard for the role of the " mass " and over-emphasis of that of the great man. Its explanation is rather to be sought in the fact that the original social nexus in which every particular individual experience and perception in the group is nourished and developed was never analysed and appreciated.[1] This original interdependence of the elements of the life-process, which is analogous to but not identical with the division of labour, is different in an agrarian society from what it is in the urban world. Furthermore, within the latter the different groups participating in city life at any one time have different cognitive problems and arrive at their experiences through different avenues even with reference to the very same objects. Only when the point of view is introduced into the genetic approach from the very beginning, according to which a group of 2,000 persons do not perceive the same thing 2,000 times, but in which, in accord with the inner articulation of group life and with various functions and interests, subgroups arise which act and think collectively with and against each

---

[1] There is nothing more futile than to suppose that the contrast between the individualistic and the sociological points of view is the same as that between the " great personality " and the " mass ". There is nothing in the sociological approach that would exclude its concern with the description of the significance of the great personality in the social process. The real distinction is that the individualistic point of view is in most cases unable to see the significance of various forms of social life for the development of individual capacities, while the sociological viewpoint seeks from the very beginning to interpret individual activity in all spheres within the context of group experience.

other—only when things are seen from this angle can we achieve an understanding of how, in the same inclusive society, diverse meanings can arise due to the divergent social origins of the different members of the whole society.

An additional unconscious distortion committed by classical epistemology in its characterization of the genesis of the cognitive process is that it proceeds as if knowledge arose out of an act of purely theoretical contemplation. Here it seems to be elevating a marginal case to the level of a central principle. As a rule, human thought is not motivated by a contemplative impulse since it requires a volitional and emotional-unconscious under-current to assure the continuous orientation for knowledge in group life. Precisely because knowing is fundamentally collective knowing (the thought of the lone individual is only a special instance and a recent development), it presupposes a community of knowing which grows primarily out of a community of experiencing prepared for in the subconscious. However, once the fact has been perceived that the largest part of thought is erected upon a basis of collective actions, one is impelled to recognize the force of the collective unconscious. The full emergence of the sociological point of view regarding knowledge inevitably carries with it the gradual uncovering of the irrational foundation of rational knowledge.

That the epistemological and psychological analysis of the genesis of ideas came only belatedly upon the social factor in knowledge has its explanation in the fact that both these disciplines had their rise in the period of the individualistic form of society. They acquired the framework of their problems in periods of quite radical individualism and subjectivism, in the epoch of the disintegrating medieval social order, and in the liberal beginnings of the bourgeois-capitalistic era. In these periods, those who concerned themselves with these problems, the intellectuals and the well-to-do educated persons in bourgeois society, found themselves in circumstances in which the original interconnectedness of the social order must of necessity have been largely invisible to them. They could, therefore, in all good faith, present knowledge and experience as typically individualistic phenomena. Especially since they had in mind only that segment of reality which concerned the dominant minorities and which was characterized by the competition of individuals, social happenings could appear as though autono-mous individuals supplied from within themselves the initiative for acting and knowing. Seen from this segment, society appeared as if it were only an incalculably complex multiplicity of spontaneous individual acts of doing and knowing. This extremely individualistic character does not even hold for the so-called liberal social structure as a whole, inasmuch as here too the relatively free initiative of leading individuals both in acting and knowing is directed and guided by the circumstances of social life and by the tasks which they present. (Thus here, too, we find a hidden social interconnection underlying individual initiative.) On the other hand, this much is undoubtedly true, that there are social structures in which there is the possibility for certain strata (because of the larger area over which free competition obtains) to have a greater degree of individualization in their thought and conduct. It is, however, incorrect to define the nature of thought in general on the basis of this special historical situation in which a relatively individualized way of thinking was allowed to develop under exceptional conditions. It would do violence to the historical facts to regard this exceptional condition as if it were the axiomatic characteristic of the psychology of thought and of epistemology. We will not succeed in attaining an adequate psychology and theory of knowledge as a whole as long as our epistemology fails, from the very beginning, to recognize the social character of knowing, and fails to regard individualized thinking only as an exceptional instance.

In this case, too, it is obviously no accident that the sociological standpoint was added to the others only at a relatively advanced date. Nor is it by chance that the outlook which brings together the social and the cognitive spheres emerges in a time in which the greatest exertion of mankind once more consists in the attempt to counteract the tendency of an individualistic undirected society, which is verging toward anarchy, with a more organic type of social order. In such a situation there must arise a general sense of interdependence—of the interdependence which binds the single experience to the stream of experience of single individuals and these in turn to the fabric of the wider community of experience and activity. Thus, the newly arising theory of knowledge too is an attempt to take account of the rootedness of knowledge in the social texture. In it a new sort of life-orientation is at work, seeking to stay the alienation and disorganization which arose out of the exaggeration of the individualistic and mechanistic attitude. The epistemological, the psychological, and the sociological ways of stating problems are the three most important forms of raising questions about and investigating the nature of the cognitive process. We have sought to present them so that they would appear as parts of a unitary situation, emerging one after the other in a necessary sequence and reciprocally penetrating one another. In this form they provide the basis of the reflections recorded in this volume.

4. CONTROL OF THE COLLECTIVE UNCONSCIOUS AS A PROBLEM
OF OUR AGE

The emergence of the problem of the multiplicity of thought-styles which have appeared in the course of scientific develop-ment and the perceptibility of collective-unconscious motives hitherto hidden, is only one aspect of the prevalence of the intellectual restiveness which characterizes our age. In spite of the democratic diffusion of knowledge, the philosophical, psychological, and sociological problems which we presented above have been confined to a relatively small intellectual minority. This intellectual unrest came gradually to be regarded by them as their own professional privilege, and might have been considered as the private preoccupation of these groups had not all strata, with the growth of democracy, been drawn into the political and philosophical discussion.

The preceding exposition has already shown, however, that the roots of the discussion carried on by the intellectuals reached deeply into the situation of society as a whole. In many respects their problems were nothing else than the sublimated intensifica-tion and rational refinement of a social and intellectual crisis which at bottom embraced the entire society. The breakdown of the objective view of the world, of which the guarantee in the Middle Ages was the Church, was reflected even in the simplest minds. What the philosophers fought out among themselves in a rational terminology was experienced by the masses in the form of religious conflict.

When many churches took the place of one doctrinal system guaranteed by revelation with the aid of which everything essential in an agrarian-static world could be explained—when many small sects arose where there had formerly been a world religion, the minds of simple men were seized by tensions similar to those which the intellectuals experienced on the philosophical level in terms of the co-existence of numerous theories of reality and of knowledge.

At the beginning of modern times, the Protestant movement set up in the place of revealed salvation, guaranteed by the objective institution of the Church, the notion of the subjective certainty of salvation. It was assumed in the light of this doctrine that each person should decide according to his own subjective conscience whether his conduct was pleasing to God and conducive to salvation. Thus Protestantism rendered subjective a criterion which had hitherto been objective, thereby paralleling what modern epistemology was doing when it retreated from an objectively guaranteed order of existence to the individual subject. It was not a long step from the doctrine of the subjective certainty of salvation to a psychological standpoint in which gradually the observation of the psychic process, which developed into a veritable curiosity, became more important than the harkening to the criteria of salvation which men had formerly tried to detect in their own souls.

Nor was it conducive to the public belief in an objective world-order when most political states in the period of enlightened absolutism attempted to weaken the Church by means which they had taken over from the Church itself, namely, through attempting to replace an objective interpretation of the world guaranteed by the Church, by one guaranteed by the State. In doing this, it advanced the cause of the Enlightenment which at the same time was one of the weapons of the rising bourgeoisie. Both the modern state and the bourgeoisie achieved success in the measure that the rationalistic naturalistic view of the world increasingly displaced the religious one. This took place, however, without the permeation into the broadest strata of that fullness of knowledge required for rational thinking. Furthermore, this diffusion of the rationalistic world-view was realized without the strata involved in it being brought into a social position which would have allowed an individualization of the forms of living and thinking.

Without, however, a social life-situation compelling and tending toward individualization, a mode of life which is devoid of collective myths is scarcely bearable. The merchant, the entrepreneur, the intellectual, each in his own way occupies a position which requires rational decisions concerning the tasks set by everyday life. In arriving at these decisions, it is always necessary for the individual to free his judgments from those of others and to think through certain issues in a rational way from the point of view of his own interests. This is not true for peasants of the older type nor for the recently emerged mass of subordinate white-collar workers who hold positions requiring little initiative, and no foresight of a speculative kind. Their modes of behaviour are regulated to a certain extent on the basis of myths, traditions or mass-faith in a leader. Men who in their everyday life are not trained by occupations which impel toward individualization always to make their own decisions, to know from their own personal point of view what is wrong and what is right, who from this point on never have occasion to analyse situations into their elements and who, further, fail to develop a self-consciousness in themselves which will stand firm even when the individual is cut off from the mode of judgment peculiar to his group and must think for himself—such individuals will not be in a position, even in the religious sphere, to bear up under such severe inner crises as scepticism. Life in terms of an inner balance which must be ever won anew is the essentially novel element which modern man, at the level of individualization, must elaborate for himself if he is to live on the basis of the rationality of the Enlightenment. A society which in its division of labour and functional differentiation cannot offer to each individual a set of problems and fields of operation in which full initiative and individual judgment can be exercised, also cannot realize a thorough-going individualistic and rationalistic *Weltanschauung* which can aspire to become an effective social reality.

Although it would be false to believe—as intellectuals easily tend to do—that the centuries of the Enlightenment actually changed the populace in a fundamental way, since religion even though weakened lived on as ritual, cult, devotion, and ecstatic modes of experience, nonetheless their impact was sufficiently strong to shatter to a large extent the religious world-view. The forms of thought characteristic of industrial society gradually penetrated into those areas which had any contact whatever with industry and sooner or later undermined one element after another of the religious explanation of the world.

The absolute state, by claiming as one of its prerogatives the setting forth of its own interpretation of the world, took a step which later on with the democratization of society tended more and more to set a precedent. It showed that politics was able to use its conception of the world as a weapon and that politics was not merely a struggle for power but really first became fundamentally significant only when it infused its aims with a kind of political philosophy, with a political conception of the world. We can well dispense with sketching in detail the picture of how, with increasing democratization, not only the state but also political parties strove to provide their conflicts with philosophical foundation and systematization. First liberalism, then haltingly following its example conservatism, and finally socialism made of its political aims a philosophical credo, a world-view with well established methods of thought and prescribed conclusions. Thus to the split in the religious world-view was added the fractionalization of political outlooks. But whereas the churches and sects conducted their battles with diverse irrational articles of faith and developed the rational element in the last analysis only for the members of the clergy and the narrow stratum of lay intellectuals, the emergent political parties incorporated rational and if possible scientific arguments into their systems of thought to a much greater degree and attributed much more importance to them. This was due in part to their later appearance in history in a period in which science as such was accorded a greater social esteem and in part to the method by which they recruited their functionaries, since in the beginning, at least, these were chosen largely from the ranks of the above-mentioned emancipated intellectuals. It was in accord with the needs of an industrial society and of these intellectual strata for them to base their collective actions not on a frank enunciation of their creed but rather on a rationally justifiable system of ideas.

The result of this amalgamation of politics and scientific thought was that gradually every type of politics, at least in the forms in which it offered itself for acceptance, was given a scientific tinge and every type of scientific attitude in its turn came to bear a political colouration.

This amalgamation had its negative as well as its positive effects. It so facilitated the diffusion of scientific ideas that ever broader strata in the whole of their political existence had to seek theoretical justifications for their positions. They learned thereby —even though frequently in a very propagandistic manner— to think about society and politics with the categories of scientific analysis. It was also helpful to political and social science in that it gained a concrete grip on reality and in so doing gave itself a theme for stating its problems, which furnished a continuous link between it and that field of reality within which it had to operate, namely, society. The crises and the exigencies of social life offered the empirical subject-matter, the political and social interpretations, and the hypotheses through which events became analysable. The theories of Adam Smith as well as those of Marx—to mention only these two—were elaborated and extended with their attempts to interpret and analyse collectively experienced events.

The principal liability, however, in this direct connection between theory and politics lies in the fact that while knowledge always has to retain its experimental character if it wishes to do justice to new sets of facts, thinking which is dominated by a political attitude can not allow itself to be continuously readapted to new experiences. Political parties, because of the very fact of their being organized, can neither maintain an elasticity in their methods of thought nor be ready to accept any answer that might come out of their inquiries. Structurally they are public corporations and fighting organizations. This in itself already forces them into a dogmatic direction. The more intellectuals became party functionaries, the more they lost the virtue of receptivity and elasticity which they had brought with them from their previous labile situation.

The other danger which arises from this alliance between science and politics is that the crises affecting political thinking also become the crises of scientific thought. Out of this complex we will concentrate on only one fact which, however, became significant for the contemporary situation. Politics is conflict and tends increasingly to become a life-and-death struggle. The more violent this struggle became, the more tightly did it grip the emotional undercurrents which formerly operated unconsciously but all the more intensively, and forced them into the open domain of the conscious.

Political discussion possesses a character fundamentally different from academic discussion. It seeks not only to be in the right but also to demolish the basis of its opponent's social and intellectual existence. Political discussion, therefore, penetrates more profoundly into the existential foundation of thinking than the kind of discussion which thinks only in terms of a few selected " points of view " and considers only the " theoretical relevance " of an argument. Political conflict, since it is from the very beginning a rationalized form of the struggle for social predominance, attacks the social status of the opponent, his public prestige, and his self-confidence. It is difficult to decide in this case whether the sublimation or substitution of discussion for the older weapons of conflict, the direct use of force and oppression, really constituted a fundamental improvement in human life. Physical repression is, it is true, harder to bear externally, but the will to psychic annihilation, which took its place in many instances, is perhaps even more unbearable. It is therefore no wonder that particularly in this sphere every theoretical refutation was gradually transformed into a much more fundamental attack on the whole life-situation of the opponent, and with the destruction of his theories one hoped also to undermine his social position. Further, it is not surprising that in this conflict, in which from the very start one paid attention not only to what a person said but also the group for which he was the spokesman and with what action in view he set forth his arguments, one viewed thought in connection with the mode of existence to which it was bound. It is true that thought has always been the expression of group life and group action (except for highly academic thinking which for a time was able to insulate itself from active life). But the difference was either that in religious conflicts, theoretical issues were not of primary significance or that in analysing their adversaries, men did not get to an analysis of their adversaries' groups because, as we have seen, the social elements in intellectual phenomena had not become visible to the thinkers of an individualistic epoch.

In political discussion in modern democracies where ideas were more clearly representative of certain groups, the social and existential determination of thought became more easily visible. In principle it was politics which first discovered the sociological method in the study of intellectual phenomena. Basically it was in political struggles that for the first time men became aware of the unconscious collective motivations which had always guided the direction of thought. Political discussion is, from the very first, more than theoretical argumentation ; it is the tearing off of disguises—the unmasking of those unconscious motives which bind the group existence to its cultural aspirations and its theoretical arguments. To the extent, however, that modern politics fought its battles with theoretical weapons, the process of unmasking penetrated to the social roots of theory.

The discovery of the social-situational roots of thought at first, therefore, took the form of unmasking. In addition to the gradual dissolution of the unitary objective world-view, which to the simple man in the street took the form of a plurality of divergent conceptions of the world, and to the intellectuals presented itself as the irreconcilable plurality of thought-styles, there entered into the public mind the tendency to unmask the unconscious situational motivations in group thinking. This final intensification of the intellectual crisis can be characterized by two slogan-like concepts " ideology and utopia " which because of their symbolic significance have been chosen as the title for this book.

The concept " ideology " reflects the one discovery which emerged from political conflict, namely, that ruling groups can in their thinking become so intensively interest-bound to a situation that they are simply no longer able to see certain facts which would undermine their sense of domination. There is implicit in the word " ideology " the insight that in certain situations the collective unconscious of certain groups obscures the real condition of society both to itself and to others and thereby stabilizes it.

The concept of *utopian* thinking reflects the opposite dis-covery of the political struggle, namely that certain oppressed groups are intellectually so strongly interested in the destruction and transformation of a given condition of society that they unwittingly see only those elements in the situation which tend to negate it. Their thinking is incapable of correctly diagnosing an existing condition of society. They are not at all concerned with what really exists ; rather in their thinking they already seek to change the situation that exists. Their thought is never a diagnosis of the situation ; it can be used only as a direction for action. In the utopian mentality, the collective unconscious, guided by wishful representation and the will to action, hides certain aspects of reality. It turns its back on everything which would shake its belief or paralyse its desire to change things.

The collective unconscious and the activity impelled by it serve to disguise certain aspects of social reality from two directions. It is possible, furthermore, as we have seen above, to designate specifically the source and direction of the distortion. It is the task of this volume to trace out, in the two directions indicated, the most significant phases in the emergence of this discovery of the role of the unconscious as it appears in the history of ideology and utopia. At this point we are concerned only with delineating that state of mind which followed upon these insights since it is characteristic of the situation from which this book came forth.

At first those parties which possessed the new " intellectual weapons ", the unmasking of the unconscious, had a terrific advantage over their adversaries. It was stupefying for the latter when it was demonstrated that their ideas were merely distorted reflections of their situation in life, anticipations of their unconscious interests. The mere fact that it could be convincingly demonstrated to the adversary that motives which had hitherto been hidden from him were at work must have filled him with terror and awakened in the person using the weapon a feeling of marvellous superiority. It was at the same time the dawning of a level of consciousness which mankind had hitherto always hidden from itself with the greatest tenacity. Nor was it by chance that this invasion of the unconscious was dared only by the attacker while the attacked was doubly overwhelmed—first, through the laying bare of the unconscious itself and then, in addition to this, through the fact that the unconscious was laid bare and pushed into prominence in a spirit of enmity. For it is clear that it makes a considerable difference whether the unconscious is dealt with for purposes of aiding and curing or for the purpose of unmasking.

To-day, however, we have reached a stage in which this weapon of the reciprocal unmasking and laying bare of the unconscious sources of intellectual existence has become the property not of one group among many but of all of them. But in the measure that the various groups sought to destroy their adversaries' confidence in their thinking by this most modern intellectual weapon of radical unmasking, they also destroyed, as all positions gradually came to be subjected to analysis, man's confidence in human thought in general. The process of exposing the problematic elements in thought which had been latent since the collapse of the Middle Ages culminated at last in the collapse of confidence in thought in general. There is nothing accidental but rather more of the inevitable in the fact that more and more people took flight into scepticism or irrationalism.

Two powerful currents flow together here and reinforce one another with an overwhelming pressure : one, the disappearance of a unitary intellectual world with fixed values and norms ; and, two, the sudden surge of the hitherto hidden unconscious into the bright daylight of consciousness. Man's thought had from time immemorial appeared to him as a segment of his spiritual existence and not simply as a discrete objective fact. Reorientation had in the past frequently meant a change in man himself. In these earlier periods it was mostly a case of slow shifts in values and norms, of a gradual transformation of the frame of reference from which men's actions derived their ultimate orientation. But in modern times it is a much more profoundly disorganizing affair. The resort to the unconscious tended to dig up the soil out of which the varying points of views emerged. The roots from which human thought had hitherto derived its nourishment were exposed. Gradually it becomes clear to all of us that we cannot go on living in the same way once we know about our unconscious motives as we did when we were ignorant of them. What we now experience is more than a new idea, and the questions we raise constitute more than a new problem. What we are concerned with here is the elemental perplexity of our time, which can be epitomized in the symptomatic question " How is it possible for man to continue to think and live in a time when the problems of ideology and utopia are being radically raised and thought through in all their implications ? "

It is possible, of course, to escape from this situation in which the plurality of thought-styles has become visible and the existence of collective-unconscious motivations recognized simply by hiding these processes from ourselves. One can take flight into a supra-temporal logic and assert that truth as such is unsullied and has neither a plurality of forms nor any connection with unconscious motivations. But in a world in which the problem is not just an interesting subject for discussion but rather an inner perplexity, someone will soon come forth who will insist against these views that " our problem is not truth as such ; it is our thinking as we find it in its rootedness in action in the social situation, in unconscious motivations. Show us how we can advance from our concrete perceptions to your absolute definitions. Do not speak of truth as such but show us the way in which our statements, stemming from our social existence, can be translated into a sphere in which the partisanship, the fragmentariness of human vision, can be transcended, in which the social origin and the dominance of the unconscious in thinking will lead to controlled observations rather than to chaos ". The absoluteness of thought is not attained by warranting, through a general principle, that one has it or by proceeding to label some particular limited viewpoint (usually one's own) as supra-partisan and authoritative.

Nor are we aided when we are directed to a few propositions in which the content is so formal and abstract (e.g. in mathematics, geometry, and pure economics) that in fact they seem to be completely detached from the thinking social individual. The battle is not about these propositions but about that greater wealth of factual determinations in which man concretely diagnoses his individual and social situation, in which concrete interdependences in life are perceived and in which happenings external to us are first correctly understood. The battle rages concerning those propositions in which every concept is meaningfully oriented from the first, in which we use words like conflict, breakdown, alienation, insurrection, resentment—words which do not reduce complex situations for the sake of an externalizing, formal description without ever being able to build them up again and which would lose their content if their orientation, their evaluative elements, were dropped out.

We have already shown elsewhere that the development of modern science led to the growth of a technique of thought by means of which all that was only meaningfully intelligible was excluded. Behaviourism has pushed to the foreground this tendency towards concentration on entirely externally perceivable reactions, and has sought to construct a world of facts in which there will exist only measurable data, only correlations between series of factors in which the degree of probability of modes of behaviour in certain situations will be predictable. It is possible, and even probable, that sociology must pass through this stage in which its contents will undergo a mechanistic dehumanization and formalization, just as psychology did, so that out of devotion to an ideal of narrow exactitude nothing will remain except statistical data, tests, surveys, etc., and in the end every significant formulation of a problem will be excluded. All that can be said here is that this reduction of everything to a measurable or inventory-like describability is significant as a serious attempt to determine what is unambiguously ascertainable and, further, to think through what becomes of our psychic and social world when it is restricted to purely externally measurable relationships. There can no longer be any doubt that no real penetration into social reality is possible through this approach. Let us take for example the relatively simple phenomenon denoted by the term " situation ". What is left of it, or is it even at all intelligible when it is reduced to an external constellation of various reciprocally related but only externally visible patterns of behaviour ? It is clear, on the other hand, that a human situation is characterizable only when one has also taken into account those conceptions which the participants have of it, how they experience their tensions in this situation and how they react to the tensions so conceived. Or, let us take some milieu ; for instance, the milieu in which a certain family exists. Are not the norms which prevail in this family, and which are intelligible only through meaningful interpretation, at least as much a part of the milieu as the landscape or the furniture of the household ? Still further, must not this same family, other things being equal, be considered as a completely different milieu (e.g. from the point of the training of the children) if its norms have changed ? If we wish to comprehend such a concrete phenomenon as a situation or the normative content of a milieu, the purely mechanistic scheme of approach will never suffice and there must be introduced in addition concepts adequate for the understanding of meaningful and non-mensurative elements.

But it would be false to assume that the relations between these elements are less clear and less precisely perceivable than those that obtain between purely measurable phenomena. Quite on the contrary, the reciprocal interdependence of the elements making up an event is much more intimately comprehensible than that of strictly external formalized elements. Here that approach which, following Dilthey, I should like to designate as the understanding of the primary interdependence of experience (*das verstehei.de Erfassen des ,, ursprünglichen Lebenszusammenhanges* '' [1]) comes into its own. In this approach, by use of the technique of understanding, the reciprocal functional interpenetration of psychic experiences and social situations becomes immediately intelligible. We are confronted here with a realm of existence in which the emergence of psychic reactions from within becomes evident of necessity and is not comprehensible merely as is an external causality, according to the degree of probability of its frequency.

Let us take certain of the observations which sociology has worked up by the use of the method of understanding and consider the nature of its scientific evidence. When one has stated concerning the ethics of the earliest Christian communities, that it was primarily intelligible in terms of the resentment of oppressed strata, and when others have added that this ethical

[1] Here I use Dilthey's expression, leaving unsettled the question as to how his use of the term is different from that above.

outlook was entirely unpolitical because it corresponded to the mentality of that stratum which had as yet no real aspirations to rule ("Render unto Caesar the things that are Caesar's"), and when it has been said further that this ethic is not a tribal ethic but a world ethic, since it arose from the soil of the already disintegrated tribal structure of the Roman Empire, it is clear that these interconnections between social situations on the one hand and psychic-ethical modes of behaviour on the other are not, it is true, measurable but can none the less be much more intensively penetrated in their essential character than if coefficients of correlation were established between the various factors. The interconnections are evident because we have used an understanding approach to those primary interdependences of experience from which these norms arose.

It has become clear that the principal propositions of the social sciences are neither mechanistically external nor formal, nor do they represent purely quantitative correlations but rather situational diagnoses in which we use, by and large, the same concrete concepts and thought-models which were created for activistic purposes in real life. It is clear, furthermore, that every social science diagnosis is closely connected with the evaluations and unconscious orientations of the observer and that the critical self-clarification of the social sciences is intimately bound up with the critical self-clarification of our orientation in the everyday world. An observer who is not fundamentally interested in the social roots of the changing ethics of the period in which he himself lives, who does not think through the problems of social life in terms of the tensions between social strata, and who has not also discovered the fruitful aspect of resentment in his own experience, will never be in a position to see that phase of Christian ethics described above, to say nothing of being able to understand it. It is precisely in the degree in which he participates evaluationally (sympathetically or antagonistically) in the struggle for ascendancy of the lower strata, in the degree that he evaluates resentment positively or negatively, that he becomes aware of the dynamic significance of social tension and resentment. " Lower class," " social ascendancy," " resentment " instead of being formal concepts are meaningfully oriented concepts. If they were to be formalized, and the evaluations they contain distilled out of them, the thought-model characteristic of the situation, in which it is precisely resentment which produced the good and novel fruitful norm, would be totally inconceivable. The more closely one examines the word " resentment " the more clear it becomes that this apparently non-evaluative descriptive term for an attitude is replete with evaluations. If these evaluations are left out, the idea loses its concreteness. Furthermore, if the thinker had no interest in reconstructing the feeling of resentment, the tension which permeated the above-described situation of early Christianity would be entirely inaccessible to him. Thus here, too, the purposefully oriented will is the source of the understanding of the situation.

In order to work in the social sciences one must participate in the social process, but this participation in collective-unconscious striving in no wise signifies that the persons participating in it falsify the facts or see them incorrectly. Indeed, on the contrary, participation in the living context of social life is a presupposition of the understanding of the inner nature of this living context. The type of participation which the thinker enjoys determines how he shall formulate his problems. The disregard of qualitative elements and the complete restraint of the will does not constitute objectivity but is instead the negation of the essential quality of the object.

But, at the same time, the reverse the greater the bias, the greater the objectivity, is not true. In this sphere there obtains a peculiar inner dynamic of modes of behaviour in which, through the retention of the *élan politique*, this *élan* subjects itself to an intellectual control. There is a point at which the *élan politique* collides with something, whereupon it is thrown back upon itself and begins to subject itself to critical control. There is a point where the movement of life itself, especially in its greatest crisis, elevates itself above itself and becomes aware of its own limits. This is the point where the political problem-complex of ideology and utopia becomes the concern of the sociology of knowledge, and where the scepticism and relativism arising out of the mutual destruction and devalution of divergent political aims becomes a means of salvation. For this relativism and scepticism compel self-criticism and self-control and lead to a new conception of objectivity.

What seems to be so unbearable in life itself, namely, to continue to live with the unconscious uncovered, is the historical prerequisite of scientific critical self-awareness. In personal life, too, self-control and self-correction develop only when in our originally blind vital forward drive we come upon an obstacle which throws us back upon ourselves. In the course of this collision with other possible forms of existence, the peculiarity of our own mode of life becomes apparent to us. Even in our personal life we become masters of ourselves only when the unconscious motivations which formerly existed behind our backs suddenly come into our field of vision and thereby become accessible to conscious control. Man attains objectivity and acquires a self with reference to his conception of his world not by giving up his will to action and holding his evaluations in abeyance but in confronting and examining himself. The criterion of such self-illumination is that not only the object but we ourselves fall squarely within our field of vision. We become visible to ourselves, not just vaguely as a knowing subject as such but in a certain role hitherto hidden from us, in a situation hitherto impenetrable to us, and with motivations of which we have not hitherto been aware. In such moments the inner connection between our role, our motivations, and our type and manner of experiencing the world suddenly dawns upon us. Hence the paradox underlying these experiences, namely the opportunity for relative emancipation from social determination, increases proportionately with insight into this determination. Those persons who talk most about human freedom are those who are actually most blindly subject to social determination, inasmuch as they do not in most cases suspect the profound degree to which their conduct is determined by their interests. In constrast with this, it should be noted that it is precisely those who insist on the unconscious influence of the social determinants in conduct, who strive to overcome these determinants as much as possible. They uncover unconscious motivations in order to make those forces which formerly ruled them more and more into objects of conscious rational decision.

This illustration of how the extension of our knowledge of the world is closely related to increasing personal self-knowledge and self-control of the knowing personality is neither accidental nor peripheral. The process of the self-extension of the individual represents a typical example of the unfolding of every kind of situationally determined knowledge, i.e. of every kind of knowledge which is not merely the simple objective accumulation of information about facts and their causal connections, but which is interested in the understanding of an inner interdependence in the life process. Inner interdependence can be grasped only by the understanding method of interpretation, and the stages of this understanding of the world are bound at every step to the process of individual self-clarification. This structure, in accordance with which self-clarification makes possible the extension of our knowledge of the world about us, obtains not only for individual self-knowledge but is also the criterion of group self-clarification. Although here, too, it should again be emphasized that only individuals are capable of self-clarification (there is no such thing as a " folk mind " and groups as wholes are as incapable of self-clarification as they are of thinking), it makes a powerful difference whether an individual becomes conscious of those quite special unconscious motivations which have characterized particularly his previous thinking and acting or whether he is made aware of those elements in his motivations and outlook which tie him to the members of a particular group.

It is a problem in itself as to whether the sequence which the stages of self-clarification follow is entirely a matter of chance. We are inclined to believe that individual self-clarification occupies a position in a stream of self-clarification, the social source of which is a situation common to the different individuals. But whether we are here concerned with the self-clarification of individuals or of groups, one thing is common to both, namely, their structure. The centrally important feature of this structure is that in so far as the world does become a problem it does not do so as an object detached from the subject but rather as it impinges upon the fabric of the subject's experiences. Reality is discovered in the way in which it appears to the subject in the course of his self-extension (in the course of extending his capacity for experience and his horizon).

What we have hitherto hidden from ourselves and not integrated into our epistemology is that knowledge in the political and social sciences is, from a certain point on, different from formal mechanistic knowledge ; it is different from that point where it transcends the mere enumeration of facts and correlations, and approximates the model of situationally determined knowledge to which we shall refer many times in the present work.

Once the interrelationship between social science and situationally-bound thinking, as it is for instance found in political orientation, becomes evident, we have reason to investigate the positive potentialities as well as the limits and dangers of this type of thinking. It is furthermore important that we take our point of departure in that state of crisis and uncertainty in which were disclosed the dangers of this sort of thinking as well as those new possibilities of self-criticism through which it was hoped that a solution could be found.

If the problem is attacked from this point of view, the uncertainty which had become an ever more unbearable grief in public life becomes the soil from which modern social science gains entirely new insights. These fall into three main tendencies : first, the tendency towards the self-criticism of collective-unconscious motivations, in so far as they determine modern social thinking ; second, the tendency towards the establishment of a new type of intellectual history which is able to interpret changes in ideas in relation to social-historical changes ; and, third, the tendency towards the revision of our epistemology which up to now has not taken the social nature of thought sufficiently into account. The sociology of knowledge is, in this sense, the *systematization* of the doubt which is to be found in social life as a vague insecurity and uncertainty. The aim of this book is on the one hand the clearer theoretical formulation of one and the same problem from different angles, and on the other the elaboration of a method which will enable us, on the basis of increasingly precise criteria, to distinguish and isolate diverse styles of thinking and to relate them to the groups from which they spring.

Nothing is simpler than to maintain that a certain type of thinking is feudal, bourgeois or proletarian, liberal, socialistic, or conservative, as long as there is no analytical method for demonstrating it and no criteria have been adduced which will provide a control over the demonstration. Hence the chief task in the present stage of research is to elaborate and concretize the hypotheses involved in such a way that they can be made the basis of inductive studies. At the same time, the segments of reality with which we deal must be analysed into factors in a much more exact manner than we have been accustomed to do in the past. Our aim then is, first, to refine the analysis of meaning in the sphere of thought so thoroughly that grossly undifferentiated terms and concepts will be supplanted by increasingly exact and detailed characterizations of the various thought-styles ; and, second, to perfect the technique of reconstructing social history to such an extent that, instead of scattered isolated facts, one will be able to perceive the social structure as a whole, i.e. the web of interacting social forces from which have arisen the various modes of observing and thinking through the existing realities that presented themselves at different times.

There are such vast possibilities of precision in the combination of meaning-analysis and sociological situational diagnosis that in time it may be possible to compare them with the methods of the natural sciences. This method will have, in addition, the advantage that it will not have to disregard the realm of meaning as uncontrollable but will on the contrary make the interpretation of meaning a vehicle of precision.[1] If the interpretive technique of the sociology of knowledge should succeed in attaining this degree of exactness, and if with its help the significance of social life for intellectual activity should become demonstrable through ever more precise correlation, then it would also bring with it the advantage that in the social sciences it would no longer be necessary, in order to be exact, to renounce the treatment of the most important problems. For it is not to be denied that the carrying over of the methods of natural science to the social sciences gradually leads to a situation where one no longer asks what one would like to know and what will be of decisive significance for the next step in social development, but attempts only to deal with those complexes of facts which are measurable according to a certain already existent method. Instead of attempting to discover what is most significant with the highest degree of precision possible under the existing circumstances, one tends to be content to attribute importance to what is measurable merely because it happens to be measurable.

[1] The author has attempted to work out this method of sociological analysis of meaning in his study, " Das konservative Denken : Soziologische Beiträge zum Werden des politisch-historischen Denkens in Deutschland," *Archiv für Sozialwissenschaft und Sozialpolitik* (1927), vol. 57. There he attempted to analyse as precisely as possible all the important thinkers of a single political current with reference to their style of thinking and to show how they used every concept differently from the way it was used by other groups, and how with the change in their social basis their thought-style also changed. Whereas in that study we proceeded " microscopically ", so to speak, in the sense that we made a precise investigation of a limited section of intellectual and social history, in the studies contained in the present volume we use an approach which might be termed " macroscopic ". We seek to diagnose the most important steps in the history of the ideology-utopia complex ; or, in other words, to illuminate those turning-points which appear to be crucial when looked at from a distance. The macroscopic approach is the more fruitful one when, as in the case of this book, one is attempting to lay the foundations of a comprehensive problem-complex ; the microscopic, when one is seeking to verify details of limited range. Basically they belong together and must always be applied alternatively and complementarily. The reader who wishes to obtain a complete picture of the applicability of the sociology of knowledge in historical research is referred to this study.

At the present stage of development we are still far from having unambiguously formulated the problems connected with the theory of the sociology of knowledge, nor have we yet worked out the sociological analysis of meaning to its ultimate refinement. This feeling of standing at the beginning of a movement instead of the end conditions the manner in which the book is presented. There are problems about which neither textbooks nor perfectly consistent systems can be written. They are those questions which an age has as yet neither fully perceived nor fully thought through. For such problems earlier centuries, which were shaken by the repercussions of the revolution in thought and experience from the sixteenth to the eighteenth centuries, invented the form of the scientific essay. The technique of the thinkers of that period consisted in leaping into any immediate problem which was conveniently at hand and observing it for so long and from so many angles that finally some marginal problem of thought and existence was disclosed and illuminated by means of the accidental individual case. This form of presentation, which since has so frequently proved its worth, served as a prototype to the author when in the present volume, with the exception of the last part, he chose to employ the essay form and not the systematic style of treatment.

These studies are attempts to apply a new way of looking at things and a new method of interpretation to various problems and bodies of facts. They were written at different times and independently of one another and, although they centre about a unitary problem, each of these essays has its own intellectual objective.

This essayistic-experimental attitude in thought also explains why here and there repetitions have not been eliminated and contradictions resolved. The reason for not eliminating repetitions was that the same idea presented itself in a new context and was therefore disclosed in a new light. Contradictions have not been corrected because it is the author's conviction that a given theoretical sketch may often have latent in it varied possibilities which must be permitted to come to expression in order that the scope of the exposition may be truly appreciated.[1] It is his

[1] In this connection it should be noted how in the second part of this book the so-called relativistic possibilities of the same ideas, how in the fourth the activistic-utopian elements, and in the last the tendency toward a harmonious-synthetic solution of the same fundamental issues comes to the fore. To the extent that the experimental method of thinking devotes itself to the exploration of the various possibilities contained in germinal ideas

further conviction that frequently in our time various notions derived from contradictory styles of thought are at work in the same thinker. We do not note them, however, only because the systematic thinker carefully hides his contradictions from himself and his readers. Whereas contradictions are a source of discomfiture to the systematizer, the experimental thinker often perceives in them points of departure from which the fundamentally discordant character of our present situation becomes for the first time really capable of diagnosis and investigation.

A brief summary of the contents of the parts that follow should provide a background for the analyses undertaken in them :—

Part II examines the most important changes in the conception of Ideology, pointing out on the one hand how these changes in meaning are bound up with social and historical changes, and attempting on the other hand to demonstrate with concrete examples how the same concept in different phases of its history can mean at one time an evaluative and at another time a non-evaluative attitude, and how the very ontology of the concept is involved in its historical changes, which pass almost unnoticed.

Part III deals with the problem of scientific politics : how is a science of politics possible in face of the inherently ideological character of all thought ? In this connection an attempt will be made to work out empirically an important example of an analysis of the meaning of a concept along the lines of the sociology of knowledge. It will be shown, for example, how the concepts of Theory and Practice differ in the vocabularies of different groups, and how these differences in the uses of words arise out of the positions of the different groups and can be understood by a consideration of their different situations.

Part IV deals with the " Utopian Mentality ", and turns to an analysis of the utopian element in our thought and experience. An attempt is made to indicate with reference to only a few crucial cases how extensively the changes in the utopian element in our thought influence the frame of reference we use for the ordering and evaluation of our experiences, and how such changes can be traced back to social movements.

Part V offers a systematic summary and prospectus of the new discipline of the Sociology of Knowledge.

the point illustrated above becomes apparent—that the same " facts ", under the influence of the will and the changing point of view, can often lead to divergent conceptions of the total situation. As long, however, as a connection between ideas is still in the process of growth and becoming, one should not hide the possibilities which are still latent in it but should submit it in all its variations to the judgment of the reader.

II. IDEOLOGY AND UTOPIA

1. DEFINITION OF CONCEPTS

In order to understand the present situation of thought, it is necessary to start with the problems of " ideology ". For most people, the term " ideology " is closely bound up with Marxism, and their reactions to the term are largely determined by the association. It is therefore first necessary to state that although Marxism contributed a great deal to the original statement of the problem, both the word and its meaning go farther back in history than Marxism, and ever since its time new meanings of the word have emerged, which have taken shape independently of it.

There is no better introduction to the problem than the analysis of the meaning of the term " ideology " : firstly we have to disentangle all the different shades of meaning which are blended here into a pseudo-unity, and a more precise statement of the variations in the meanings of the concept, as it is used to-day, will prepare the way for its sociological and historical analysis. Such an analysis will show that in general there are two distinct and separable meanings of the term " ideology "—the particular and the total.

The particular conception of ideology is implied when the term denotes that we are sceptical of the ideas and representations advanced by our opponent. They are regarded as more or less conscious disguises of the real nature of a situation, the true recognition of which would not be in accord with his interests. These distortions range all the way from conscious lies to half-conscious and unwitting disguises ; from calculated attempts to dupe others to self-deception. This conception of ideology, which has only gradually become differentiated from the common-sense notion of the lie is particular in several senses. Its particularity becomes evident when it is contrasted with the more inclusive total conception of ideology. Here we refer to the ideology of an age or of a concrete historico-social group, e.g. of a class, when we are concerned with the characteristics

49

F

and composition of the total structure of the mind of this epoch or of this group.

The common as well as the distinctive elements of the two concepts are readily evident. The common element in these two conceptions seems to consist in the fact that neither relies solely on what is actually said by the opponent in order to reach an understanding of his real meaning and intention.[1] Both fall back on the subject, whether individual or group, proceeding to an understanding of what is said by the indirect method of analysing the social conditions of the individual or his group. The ideas expressed by the subject are thus regarded as functions of his existence. This means that opinions, statements, propositions, and systems of ideas are not taken at their face value but are interpreted in the light of the life-situation of the one who expresses them. It signifies further that the specific character and life-situation of the subject influence his opinions, perceptions, and interpretations.

Both these conceptions of ideology, accordingly, make these so-called " ideas " a function of him who holds them, and of his position in his social milieu. Although they have something in common, there are also significant differences between them. Of the latter we mention merely the most important :—

(a) Whereas the particular conception of ideology designates only a part of the opponent's assertions as ideologies—and this only with reference to their content, the total conception calls into question the opponent's total *Weltanschauung* (including his conceptual apparatus), and attempts to understand these concepts as an outgrowth of the collective life of which he partakes.

(b) The particular conception of " ideology " makes its analysis of ideas on a purely psychological level. If it is claimed for instance that an adversary is lying, or that he is concealing or distorting a given factual situation, it is still nevertheless assumed that both parties share common criteria of validity—it is still assumed that it is possible to refute lies and eradicate sources of error by referring to accepted criteria of objective validity

---

[1] If the interpretation relies solely upon that which is actually said we shall speak of an " immanent interpretation " : if it transcends these data, implying thereby an analysis of the subject's life-situation, we shall speak of a " transcendental interpretation ". A typology of these various forms of interpretation is to be found in the author's " Ideologische und soziologische Interpretation der geistigen Gebilde ", *Jahrbuch für Soziologie*, vol. ii (Karlsruhe, 1926), p. 424 ff.

common to both parties. The suspicion that one's opponent is the victim of an ideology does not go so far as to exclude him from discussion on the basis of a common theoretical frame of reference. The case is different with the total conception of ideology. When we attribute to one historical epoch one intellectual world and to ourselves another one, or if a certain historically determined social stratum thinks in categories other than our own, we refer not to the isolated cases of thought-content, but to fundamentally divergent thought-systems and to widely differing modes of experience and interpretation. We touch upon the theoretical or noological level whenever we consider not merely the content but also the form, and even the conceptual framework of a mode of thought as a function of the life-situation of a thinker. " The economic categories are only the theoretical expressions, the abstractions, of the social relations of production. . . . The same men who establish social relations conformably with their material productivity, produce also the principles, the ideas, the categories, conformably with their social relations." (Karl Marx, *The Poverty of Philosophy*, being a translation of *Misère de la Philosophie*, with a preface by Frederick Engels, translated by H. Quelch, Chicago, 1910, p. 119.) These are the two ways of analysing statements as functions of their social background ; the first operates only on the psychological, the second on the noological level.

(c) Corresponding to this difference, the particular conception of ideology operates primarily with a psychology of interests, while the total conception uses a more formal functional analysis, without any reference to motivations, confining itself to an objective description of the structural differences in minds operating in different social settings. The former assumes that this or that interest is the cause of a given lie or deception. The latter presupposes simply that there is a correspondence between a given social situation and a given perspective, point of view, or apperception mass. In this case, while an analysis of constellations of interests may often be necessary it is not to establish causal connections but to characterize the total situation. Thus interest psychology tends to be displaced by an analysis of the correspondence between the situation to be known and the forms of knowledge.

Since the particular conception never actually departs from the psychological level, the point of reference in such analyses is always the individual. This is the case even when we are dealing with groups, since all psychic phenomena must finally be reduced to the minds of individuals. The term " group ideology " occurs frequently, to be sure, in popular speech. Group existence in this sense can only mean that a group of persons, either in their immediate reactions to the same situation or as a result of direct psychic interaction, react similarly. Accordingly, conditioned by the same social situation, they are subject to the same illusions. If we confine our observations to the mental processes which take place in the individual and regard him as the only possible bearer of ideologies, we shall never grasp in its totality the structure of the intellectual world belonging to a social group in a given historical situation. Although this mental world as a whole could never come into existence without the experiences and productive responses of the different individuals, its inner structure is not to be found in a mere integration of these individual experiences. The individual members of the working-class, for instance, do not experience *all* the elements of an outlook which could be called the proletarian *Weltanschauung*.   Every individual participates only in certain fragments of this thought-system, the totality of which is not in the least a mere sum of these fragmentary individual experiences. As a totality the thought-system is integrated systematically, and is no mere casual jumble of fragmentary experiences of discrete members of the group. Thus it follows that the individual can only be considered as the bearer of an ideology as long as we deal with that conception of ideology which, by definition, is directed more to detached contents than to the whole structure of thought, uncovering false ways of thought and exposing lies. As soon as the total conception of ideology is used, we attempt to reconstruct the whole outlook of a social group, and neither the concrete individuals nor the abstract sum of them can legitimately be considered as bearers of this ideological thought-system as a whole. The aim of the analysis on this level is the reconstruction of the systematic theoretical basis underlying the single judgments of the individual. Analyses of ideologies in the particular sense, making the content of individual thought largely dependent on the interests of the subject, can never achieve this basic reconstruction of the whole outlook of a social group. They can at best reveal the collective psychological aspects of ideology, or lead to some development of mass psychology, dealing either with the different behaviour of the individual in the crowd, or with the results of the mass integration of the psychic experiences of many individuals. And although the collective-psychological aspect may very often approach the problems of the total ideological analysis, it does not answer its questions exactly. It is one thing to know how far my attitudes and judgments are influenced and altered by the co-existence of other human beings, but it is another thing to know what are the theoretical implications of my mode of thought which are identical with those of my fellow members of the group or social stratum.

We content ourselves here merely with stating the issue without attempting a thorough-going analysis of the difficult methodological problems which it raises.

2. THE CONCEPT IDEOLOGY IN HISTORICAL PERSPECTIVE

Just as the particular and total conceptions of ideology can be distinguished from one another on the basis of their differences in meaning, so the historical origins of these two concepts may also be differentiated even though in reality they are always intertwined. We do not as yet possess an adequate historical treatment of the development of the concept of ideology, to say nothing of a sociological history of the many variations [1]

[1] As a partial bibliography of the problem, the author indicates the following of his own works :—

Mannheim, K., " Das Problem einer Soziologie des Wissens," *Archiv für Sozialwissenschaft und Sozialpolitik*, 1925, vol. 54.

Mannheim, K., " Ideologische und soziologische Interpretation der geistigen Gebilde," *Jahrbuch für Soziologie*, edited by Gottfried Salomon, ii (Karlsruhe, 1926), pp. 424 ff.

Other relevant materials are to be found in :—

Krug, W. T., *Allgemeines Handwörterbuch der philosophischen Wissenschaften nebst ihrer Literatur und Geschichte*, 2nd edit., Leipzig, 1833

Eisler's *Philosophisches Wörterbuch*.

Lalande, *Vocabulaire de la philosophie* (Paris, 1926).

Salomon, G., " Historischer Materialismus und Ideologienlehre ", *Jahrbuch für Soziologie*, ii, pp. 386 ff.

Ziegler, H. O., " Ideologienlehre," *Archiv für Sozialwissenschaft und Sozialpolitik*, vol. 57, pp. 657 ff.

The majority of the studies of ideology never reach the level of attempting a systematic analysis, confining themselves usually to historical references or to the most general considerations. As examples, we cite the well-known works of Max Weber, Georg Lukács, Carl Schmitt, and more recently—

Kelsen, Hans, " Die philosophischen Grundlagen der Naturrechtslehre und der Rechtspositivismus," No. 31 of the *Vorträge der Kant Gesellschaft*, 1928.

The standard works of W. Sombart, Max Scheler, and Franz Oppenheimer are too widely known to require detailed reference.

In a wider connection the following studies are of especial interest :—

Riezler, K., " Idee und Interesse in der politischen Geschichte," *Die Dioskuren*, vol. iii (Munich, 1924). (Continued on p. 54).

in its meaning. Even if we were in a position to do so, it would not be our task, for the purposes we have in mind, to write a history of the changing meanings in the concept of ideology. Our aim is simply to present such facts from the scattered evidence as will most clearly exhibit the distinction between the two terms made in the previous chapter, and to trace the process which gradually led to the refined and specialized meaning which the terms have come to possess. Corresponding to the dual meaning of the term ideology which we have designated here as the particular and total conceptions, respectively, are two distinct currents of historical development.

The distrust and suspicion which men everywhere evidence towards their adversaries, at all stages of historical development, may be regarded as the immediate precursor of the notion of ideology. But it is only when the distrust of man toward man, which is more or less evident at every stage of human history, becomes explicit and is methodically recognized, that we may properly speak of an ideological taint in the utterances of others. We arrive at this level when we no longer make individuals personally responsible for the deceptions which we detect in their utterances, and when we no longer attribute the evil that they do to their malicious cunning. It is only when we more or less consciously seek to discover the source of their untruthfulness in a social factor, that we are properly making an ideological interpretation. We begin to treat our adversary's views as ideologies only when we no longer consider them as calculated lies and when we sense in his total behaviour an unreliability which we regard as a function of the social situation in which he finds himself. The particular conception of ideology therefore signifies a phenomenon intermediate between a simple lie at one pole, and an error, which is the result of a distorted and faulty conceptual apparatus, at the other. It refers to a sphere of errors, psychological in nature, which, unlike deliberate deception, are not intentional, but follow inevitably and unwittingly from certain causal determinants.

(*Note continued from p. 53.*)

Szende, Paul, *Verhüllung und Enthüllung* (Leipzig, 1922).

Adler, Georg, *Die Bedeutung der Illusionen für Politik und soziales Leben* (Jena, 1904).

Jankelevitch, " Du rôle des idées dans l'évolution des sociétés," *Revue philosophique*, vol. 66, 1908, pp. 256 ff.

Millioud, M., " La formation de l'idéal," ibid., pp. 138 ff.

Dietrich, A., " Kritik der politischen Ideologien," *Archiv für Geschichte und Politik*, 1923.

According to this interpretation, Bacon's theory of the *idola* may be regarded to a certain extent as a forerunner of the modern conception of ideology. The " idols " were " phantoms " or " preconceptions ", and there were, as we know, the idols of the tribe, of the cave, of the market, and of the theatre. All of these are sources of error derived sometimes from human nature itself, sometimes from particular individuals. They may also be attributed to society or to tradition. In any case, they are obstacles in the path to true knowledge.[1] There is certainly some connection between the modern term " ideology " and the term as used by Bacon, signifying a source of error. Furthermore, the realization that society and tradition may become sources of error is a direct anticipation of the sociological point of view.[2] Nevertheless, it cannot be claimed that there is an actual relationship, directly traceable through the history of thought, between this and the modern conception of ideology.

It is extremely probable that everyday experience with political affairs first made man aware of and critical toward the ideological element in his thinking. During the Renaissance, among the fellow citizens of Machiavelli, there arose a new

---

[1] A characteristic passage from Bacon's *Novum Organum*, § 38. " The idols and false notions which have already preoccupied the human understanding and are deeply rooted in it, not only so beset men's minds that they become difficult of access, but even when access is obtained will again meet, and trouble us in the instauration of the sciences, unless mankind when forewarned guard themselves with all possible care against them," *The Physical and Metaphysical Works of Lord Bacon* (including the *Advancement of Learning* and *Novum Organum*). Edited by Joseph Devey, p. 389. G. Bell and Sons (London, 1891).

[2] " There are also idols formed by the reciprocal intercourse and society of man with man, which we call idols of the market from the commerce and association of men with each other ; for men converse by means of language, but words are formed at the will of the generality, and there arises from a bad and unapt formation of words a wonderful obstruction to the mind." Bacon, op. cit., p. 390, § 43. Cf. also § 59.

On " the idol of tradition " Bacon says :—

" The human understanding, when any proposition has once been laid down (either from general admission and belief, or from the pleasure it affords), forces everything else to add fresh support and confirmation : and although most cogent and abundant instances exist to the contrary, yet either does not observe or despises them or gets rid of and rejects them by some distinction, with violent and injurious prejudice, rather than sacrifice the authority of its first conclusion." Op. cit., § 46, p. 392.

That we are confronted here with a source of error is evinced by the following passage :—

" The human understanding resembles not a dry light, but admits a tincture of the will and passions, which generate their own system accordingly, for man always believes more readily that which he prefers." Op cit., § 49, pp. 393–4. Cf. also § 52.

adage calling attention to a common observation of the time—namely that the thought of the palace is one thing, and that of the public square is another.[1] This was an expression of the increasing degree to which the public was gaining access to the secrets of politics. Here we may observe the beginning of the process in the course of which what had formerly been merely an occasional outburst of suspicion and scepticism toward public utterances developed into a methodical search for the ideological element in all of them. The diversity of the ways of thought among men is even at this stage attributed to a factor which might, without unduly stretching the term, be denominated as sociological. Machiavelli, with his relentless rationality, made it his special task to relate the variations in the opinions of men to the corresponding variations in their interests. Accordingly when he prescribes a *medicina forte* for every bias of the interested parties in a controversy,[2] he seems to be making explicit and setting up as a general rule of thought what was implicit in the common-sense adage of his time.

There seems to be a straight line leading from this point in the intellectual orientation of the Western world to the rational and calculating mode of thought characteristic of the period of the Enlightenment. The psychology of interests seems to flow from the same source. One of the chief characteristics of the method of rational analysis of human behaviour, exemplified by Hume's *History of England*, was the presupposition that men were given to " feigning "[3] and to deceiving their fellows. The same characteristic is found in contemporary historians who operate with the particular conception of ideology. This mode of thought will always strive in accordance with the psychology of interests to cast doubt upon the integrity of the adversary and to deprecate his motives. This procedure, nevertheless, has positive value as long as in a given case we are interested in discovering the genuine meaning of a statement that lies concealed behind a camouflage of words. This " debunking " tendency in the thought of our time has become very marked.[4]

---

[1] Machiavelli, *Discorsi*, vol. ii, p. 47. Cited by Meinecke, *Die Idee der Staatsräson* (Munich and Berlin, 1925), p. 40.

[2] Cf. Meinecke, ibid.

[3] Meusel, Fr., *Edmund Burke und die französische Revolution* (Berlin 1913), p. 102, note 3.

[4] Carl Schmitt analysed this characteristic contemporary manner of thought very well when he said that we are in continual fear of being

And even though in wide circles this trait is considered undignified
and disrespectful (and indeed in so far as " debunking " is an
end in itself, the criticism is justified), this intellectual position
is forced upon us in an era of transition like our own, which
finds it necessary to break with many antiquated traditions and
forms.

3. FROM THE PARTICULAR TO THE TOTAL CONCEPTION OF IDEOLOGY

It must be remembered that the unmasking which takes
place on the psychological level is not to be confused with the
more radical scepticism and the more thoroughgoing and
devastating critical analysis which proceeds on the ontological
and noological levels. But the two cannot be completely separated.
The same historical forces that bring about continuous transformations in one are also operative in the other. In the former,
psychological illusions are constantly being undermined, in the
latter, ontological and logical formulations arising out of given
world-views and modes of thought are dissolved in a conflict
between the interested parties. Only in a world in upheaval,
in which fundamental new values are being created and old ones
destroyed, can intellectual conflict go so far that antagonists
will seek to annihilate not merely the specific beliefs and attitudes
of one another, but also the intellectual foundations upon which
these beliefs and attitudes rest.

As long as the conflicting parties lived in and tried to represent
the same world, even though they were at opposite poles in
that world, or as long as one feudal clique fought against its
equal, such a thoroughgoing mutual destruction was inconceivable. This profound disintegration of intellectual unity is
possible only when the basic values of the contending groups are
worlds apart. At first, in the course of this ever-deepening
disintegration, naïve distrust becomes transformed into a
systematic particular notion of ideology, which, however,
remains on the psychological plane. But, as the process continues,
it extends to the noological-epistemological sphere. The rising
bourgeoisie which brought with it a new set of values was not
content with merely being assigned a circumscribed place within

misled. Consequently we are perpetually on guard against disguises,
sublimations, and refractions. He points out that the word *simulacra*,
which appeared in the political literature of the seventeenth century,
may be regarded as a forerunner of the present attitude (*Politische
Romantik*, 2nd edit., (Munich and Leipzig, 1925), p. 19).

the old feudal order. It represented a new " economic system "
(in Sombart's sense), accompanied by a new style of thought
which ultimately displaced the existing modes of interpreting
and explaining the world. The same seems to be true of the
proletariat to-day as well. Here too we note a conflict between
two divergent economic views, between two social systems,
and, correspondingly, between two styles of thought.

What were the steps in the history of ideas that prepared
the way for the total conception of ideology ? Certainly it did
not merely arise out of the attitude of mistrust which gradually
gave rise to the particular conception of ideology. More fundamental steps had to be taken before the numerous tendencies
of thought moving in the same general direction could be
synthesized into the total conception of ideology. Philosophy
played a part in the process, but not philosophy in the narrow
sense (as it is usually conceived) as a discipline divorced from
the actual context of living. Its role was rather that of the ultimate
and fundamental interpreter of the flux in the contemporary
world. This cosmos in flux is in its turn to be viewed as a series
of conflicts arising out of the nature of the mind and its responses
to the continually changing structure of the world. We shall
indicate here only the principal stages in the emergence of the
total conception of ideology on the noological and ontological levels.

The first significant step in this direction consisted in the
development of a philosophy of consciousness. The thesis that
consciousness is a unity consisting of coherent elements sets
a problem of investigation which, especially in Germany, has
been the basis of monumental attempts at analysis. The
philosophy of consciousness has put in place of an infinitely
variegated and confused world an organization of experience
the unity of which is guaranteed by the unity of the perceiving
subject. This does not imply that the subject merely reflects
the structural pattern of the external world, but rather that,
in the course of his experience with the world, he spontaneously
evolves the principles of organization that enable him to understand it. After the objective ontological unity of the world had
been demolished, the attempt was made to substitute for it a unity
imposed by the perceiving subject. In the place of the medieval-
Christian objective and ontological unity of the world, there
emerged the subjective unity of the absolute subject of the
Enlightenment— " consciousness in itself."

Henceforth the world as " world " exists only with reference to the knowing mind, and the mental activity of the subject determines the form in which the world appears. This constitutes in fact the embryonic total conception of ideology, though it is, as yet, devoid of its historical and sociological implications.

At this stage, the world is conceived as a structural unity, and no longer as a plurality of disparate events as it seemed to be in the intermediate period when the breakdown of the objective order seemed to bring chaos. It is related in its entirety to a subject, but in this case the subject is not a concrete individual. It is rather a fictitious " consciousness in itself ". In this view, which is particularly pronounced in Kant, the noological level is sharply differentiated from the psychological one. This is the first stage in the dissolution of an ontological dogmatism which regarded the " world " as existing independently of us, in a fixed and definitive form.

The second stage in the development of the total conception of ideology is attained when the total but super-temporal notion of ideology is seen in historical perspective. This is mainly the accomplishment of Hegel and the Historical school. The latter, and Hegel to an even greater degree, start from the assumption that the world is a unity and is conceivable only with reference to a knowing subject. And now at this point, what is for us a decisive new element is added to the conception—namely, that this unity is in a process of continual historical transformation and tends to a constant restoration of its equilibrium on still higher levels. During the Enlightenment the subject, as carrier of the unity of consciousness, was viewed as a wholly abstract, super-temporal, and super-social entity : " consciousness in itself." During this period the *Volksgeist*, " folk spirit," comes to represent the historically differentiated elements of consciousness, which are integrated by Hegel into the " world spirit ". It is evident that the increasing concreteness of this type of Philosophy results from the more immediate concern with the ideas arising from social interaction and the incorporation of historical-political currents of thought into the domain of philosophy. Thenceforth, however, the experiences of everyday life are no longer accepted at face value, but are thought through in all their implications and are traced back to their presupposi-tions. It should be noted, however, that the historically changing nature of mind was discovered not so much by philosophy as by the penetration of political insight into the everyday life of the time.

The reaction following upon the unhistorical thought of the period of the French Revolution revitalized and gave new impetus to the historical perspective. In the last analysis, the transition from the general, abstract, world-unifying subject (" consciousness in itself ") to the more concrete subject (the nationally differentiated " folk spirit ") was not so much a philosophical achievement as it was the expression of a transformation in the manner of reacting to the world in all realms of experience. This change may be traced to the revolution in popular sentiment during and after the Napoleonic Wars when the feeling of nationality was actually born. The fact that more remote antecedents may be found for both the historical perspective and the *Volksgeist* does not detract from the validity of this observation.[1]

The final and most important step in the creation of the total conception of ideology likewise arose out of the historical-social process. When " class " took the place of " folk " or nation as the bearer of the historically evolving consciousness, the same theoretical tradition, to which we have already referred, absorbed the realization which meanwhile had grown up through the social process, namely—that the structure of society and its corresponding intellectual forms vary with the relations between social classes.

Just as at an earlier time, the historically differentiated " folk spirit " took the place of " consciousness as such ", so now the concept of *Volksgeist*, which is still too inclusive, is replaced by the concept of class consciousness, or more correctly class ideology. Thus the development of these ideas follows a two-fold trend—on the one hand, there is a synthesizing and integrating process through which the concept of consciousness comes to furnish a unitary centre in an infinitely variable world ; and on the other, there is a constant attempt to make more pliable and flexible the unitary conception which has been too rigidly and too schematically formulated in the course of the synthesizing process.

[1] For future reference, we state here that the sociology of knowledge, unlike the orthodox history of ideas, does not aim at tracing ideas back to all their remote historical prototypes. For if one is bent on tracing similar *motifs* in thought to their ultimate origins, it is always possible to find " precursors " for every idea. There is nothing which has been said, which has not been said before (*Nullum est iam dictum, quod non sit dictum prius*). The proper theme of our study is to observe how and in what form intellectual life at a given historical moment is related to the existing social and political forces. Cf. my study, " Das konservative Denken," loc. cit., p. 103, note 57.

The result of this dual tendency is that instead of a fictional unity of a timeless, unchanging " consciousness as such " (which was never actually demonstrable) we get a conception which varies in accordance with historic periods, nations, and social classes. In the course of this transition, we continue to cling to the unity of consciousness, but this unity is now dynamic and in constant process of becoming. This accounts for the fact that despite the surrender of the static conception of consciousness, the growing body of material discovered by historical research does not remain an incoherent and discontinuous mass of discrete events. This latest conception of consciousness provides a more adequate perspective for the comprehension of historical reality.

Two consequences flow from this conception of consciousness : first we clearly perceive that human affairs cannot be understood by an isolation of their elements. Every fact and event in an historical period is only explicable in terms of meaning, and meaning in its turn always refers to another meaning. Thus the conception of the unity and interdependence of meaning in a period always underlies the interpretation of that period. Secondly, this interdependent system of meanings varies both in all its parts and in its totality from one historical period to another. Thus the re-interpretation of that continuous and coherent change in meaning becomes the main concern of our modern historical sciences. Although Hegel has probably done more than anyone else in emphasizing the need for integrating the various elements of meaning in a given historical experience, he proceeded in a speculative manner, while we have arrived at a stage of development where we are able to translate this constructive notion, given us by the philosophers, into empirical research.

What is significant for us is that although we separated them in our analysis, the two currents which led to the particular and total conceptions of ideology, respectively, and which have approximately the same historical origin, now begin to approach one another more closely. The particular conception of ideology merges with the total. This becomes apparent to the observer in the following manner : previously, one's adversary, as the representative of a certain political-social position, was accused of conscious or unconscious falsification. Now, however, the critique is more thoroughgoing in that, having discredited the total structure of his consciousness, we consider him no longer capable of thinking correctly. This simple observation means, in the light of a structural analysis of thought, that in earlier attempts to discover the sources of error, distortion was uncovered only on the psychological plane by pointing out the personal roots of intellectual bias. The annihilation is now more thorough-going since the attack is made on the noological level and the validity of the adversary's theories is undermined by showing that they are merely a function of the generally prevailing social situation. Herewith a new and perhaps the most decisive stage in the history of modes of thought has been reached. It is difficult, however, to deal with this development without first analysing some of its fundamental implications. The total conception of ideology raises a problem which has frequently been adumbrated before, but which now for the first time acquires broader significance, namely the problem of how such a thing as the " false consciousness " (*falsches Bewusstsein*) —the problem of the totally distorted mind which falsifies everything which comes within its range—could ever have arisen. It is the awareness that our total outlook as distinguished from its details may be distorted, which lends to the total conception of ideology a special significance and relevance for the under-standing of our social life. Out of this recognition grows the profound disquietude which we feel in our present intellectual situation, but out of it grows also whatever in it is fruitful and stimulating.

4. OBJECTIVITY AND BIAS

The suspicion that there might be such a thing as " false consciousness ", every cognition of which is necessarily wrong, where the lie lay in the soul, dates back to antiquity. It is of religious origin, and has come down to us as part of our ancient intellectual heritage. It appears as a problem whenever the genuineness of a prophet's inspiration or vision is questioned either by his people or by himself.[1]

Here we seem to have an instance where an age-old conception underlies a modern epistemological idea, and one is tempted to assert that the essence of the observation was already present in the older treatment ; what is new is only its form. But

---

[1] " Beloved, believe not every spirit, but try the spirits whether they are of God, because many false prophets are gone out into the world," 1 John, iv, 1.

here, too, as elsewhere, we must maintain, in opposition to those who attempt to derive everything from the past, that the modern form taken by the idea is much more important than its origin. Whereas formerly, the suspicion that there might be such a thing as " false consciousness " was only a statement of observed fact, to-day, working with clearly defined analytical methods, we have been able to make a more fundamental attack on the problems of consciousness. What was formerly a mere traditional anathema, has in our time been transformed into a methodical procedure resting upon scientific demonstration.

Of even greater importance is the change which we are about to discuss. Since the problem has been torn out of its purely religious context, not only have the methods of proof, of demonstrating the falsity or truth of an insight changed, but even the scale of values by which we measure truth and falsity, reality and unreality have been profoundly transformed. When the prophet doubted the genuineness of his vision it was because he felt himself deserted by God, and his disquietude was based upon a transcendental source of reference. When, on the contrary, we, of to-day, become critical of our own ideas, it is because we fear that they do not measure up to some more secular criterion.

To determine the exact nature of the new criterion of reality which superseded the transcendental one, we must subject the meaning of the word " ideology " also in this respect to a more precise historical analysis. If, in the course of such an analysis, we are led to deal with the language of everyday life, this simply indicates that the history of thought is not confined to books alone, but gets its chief meaning from the experiences of everyday life, and even the main changes in the evaluations of different spheres of reality as they appear in philosophy eventually go back to the shifting values of the everyday world.

The word " ideology " itself had, to begin with, no inherent ontological significance; it did not include any decision as to the value of different spheres of reality, since it originally denoted merely the theory of ideas. The ideologists,[1] were, as we know,

---

[1] Cf. Picavet, *Les idéologues, essai sur l'histoire des idées et des théories scientifiques, philosophiques, réligieuses en France depuis 1789* (Paris, Alcan, 1891).

Destutt de Tracy, the founder of the above-mentioned school, defines the science of ideas as follows : " The science may be called ideology, if one considers only the subject-matter ; general grammar, if one considers only the methods ; and logic, if one considers only the purpose. Whatever the name, it necessarily contains these three subdivisions, since one cannot be treated adequately without also treating the two others. Ideology

the members of a philosophical group in France who, in the tradition of Condillac, rejected metaphysics and sought to base the cultural sciences on anthropological and psychological foundations.

The modern conception of ideology was born when Napoleon, finding that this group of philosophers was opposing his imperial ambitions, contemptuously labelled them " ideologists ". Thereby the word took on a derogatory meaning which, like the word " doctrinaire ", it has retained to the present day. However, if the theoretical implications of this contempt are examined, it will be found that the depreciative attitude involved is, at bottom, of an epistemological and ontological nature. What is depreciated is the validity of the adversary's thought because it is regarded as unrealistic. But if one asked further, unrealistic with reference to what ?—the answer would be, unrealistic with reference to practice, unrealistic when contrasted with the affairs that transpire in the political arena. Thenceforth, all thought labelled as " ideology " is regarded as futile when it comes to practice, and the only reliable access to reality is to be sought in practical activity. When measured by the standards of practical conduct, mere thinking or reflection on a given situation turns out to be trivial. It is thus clear how the new meaning of the term ideology bears the imprint of the position and the point of view of those who coined it, namely, the political men of action. The new word gives sanction to the specific experience of the politician with reality,[1] and it lends support to that practical irrationality which has so little appreciation for thought as an instrument for grasping reality.

During the nineteenth century, the term ideology, used in this sense, gained wide currency. This signifies that the politician's feeling for reality took precedence over and displaced the scholastic, contemplative modes of thought and of life. Henceforward the problem implicit in the term ideology—what is really real ?—never disappeared from the horizon.

But this transition needs to be correctly understood. The

seems to me to be the generic term because the science of ideas subsumes both that of their expression and that of their derivation." *Les éléments de l'idéologie*, 1st edit. (Paris, 1801), cited from the 3rd edit., the only one available to me (Paris, 1817), p. 4 n.

[1] From the conclusions of Part III it would be possible to define more exactly, according to the social position he occupies, the type of politician whose conception of the world and whose ontology we are here discussing, for not every politician is addicted to this irrational ontology. Cf. pp. 119 ff.).

question as to what constitutes reality is by no means a new one ; but that the question should arise in the arena of public discussion (and not just in isolated academic circles) seems to indicate an important change. The new connotation which the word ideology acquired, because it was redefined by the politician in terms of his experiences, seems to show a decisive turn in the formulation of the problem of the nature of reality. If, therefore, we are to rise to the demands put upon us by the need for analysing modern thought, we must see to it that a sociological history of ideas concerns itself with the actual thought of society, and not merely with self-perpetuating and supposedly self-contained systems of ideas elaborated within a rigid academic tradition. If erroneous knowledge was formerly checked by appeal to divine sanction, which unfailingly revealed the true and the real, or by pure contemplation, in which true ideas were supposedly discovered, at present the criterion of reality is found primarily in an ontology derived from political experience. The history of the concept of ideology from Napoleon to Marxism, despite changes in content, has retained the same political criterion of reality. This historical example shows, at the same time, that the pragmatic point of view was already implicit in the accusation which Napoleon hurled at his adversaries. Indeed we may say that for modern man pragmatism has, so to speak, become in some respects, the inevitable and appropriate outlook, and that philosophy in this case has simply appropriated this outlook and from it proceeded to its logical conclusion.

We have called attention to the nuance of meaning which Napoleon gave to the word ideology in order to show clearly that common speech often contains more philosophy and is of greater significance for the further statement of problems than academic disputes which tend to become sterile because they fail to take cognizance of the world outside the academic walls.[1]

We are carried a step farther in our analysis, and are able to bring out another aspect of this problem by referring to the example just cited in another connection. In the struggle which Napoleon carried on against his critics, he was able, as we have

---

[1] Concerning the structure and peculiarities of scholastic thought, and, for that matter, every type of thought enjoying a monopolistic position, cf. the author's paper delivered in Zürich at the Sixth Congress of the Deutsche Gesellschaft für Soziologie, " Die Bedeutung der Konkurrenz im Gebiete des Geistigen," *Verhandlungen des sechsten deutschen Soziolog-entages in Zürich* (J. C. B. Mohr, Tübingen, 1929).

G

seen, by reason of his dominant position to discredit them by pointing out the ideological nature of their thinking. In later stages of its development, the word ideology is used as a weapon by the proletariat against the dominant group. In short, such a revealing insight into the basis of thought as that offered by the notion of ideology cannot, in the long run, remain the exclusive privilege of one class. But it is precisely this expansion and diffusion of the ideological approach which leads finally to a juncture at which it is no longer possible for one point of view and interpretation to assail all others as ideological without itself being placed in the position of having to meet that challenge. In this manner we arrive inadvertently at a new methodological stage in the analysis of thought in general.

There were indeed times when it seemed as if it were the prerogative of the militant proletariat to use the ideological analysis to unmask the hidden motives of its adversaries. The public was quick to forget the historical origin of the term which we have just indicated, and not altogether unjustifiably, for although recognized before, this critical approach to thought was first emphasized and methodically developed by Marxism. It was Marxist theory which first achieved a fusion of the particular and total conceptions of ideology. It was this theory which first gave due emphasis to the role of class position and class interests in thought. Due largely to the fact that it originated in Hegelianism, Marxism was able to go beyond the mere psychological level of analysis and to posit the problem in a more comprehensive, philosophical setting. The notion of a " false consciousness " [1] hereby acquired a new meaning.

Marxist thought attached such decisive significance to political practice conjointly with the economic interpretation of events, that these two became the ultimate criteria for disentangling what is mere ideology from those elements in thought which are more immediately relevant to reality. Consequently it is no wonder that the conception of ideology is usually regarded as integral to, and even identified with, the Marxist proletarian movement.

But in the course of more recent intellectual and social developments, however, this stage has already been passed. It is no longer the exclusive privilege of socialist thinkers

---

[1] The expression " false consciousness " (falsches Bewusstsein) is itself Marxist in origin. Cf. Mehring, Franz, Geschichte der deutschen Sozial-demokratie, i, 386 ; cf. also Salomon, op. cit., p. 147.

to trace bourgeois thought to ideological foundations and thereby to discredit it. Nowadays groups of every standpoint use this weapon against all the rest. As a result we are entering upon a new epoch in social and intellectual development.

In Germany, the first beginnings in this direction were made by Max Weber, Sombart, and Troeltsch—to mention only the more outstanding representatives of this development. The truth of Max Weber's words becomes more clear as time goes on : "The materialistic conception of history is not to be compared to a cab that one can enter or alight from at will, for once they enter it, even the revolutionaries themselves are not free to leave it." [1] The analysis of thought and ideas in terms of ideologies is much too wide in its application and much too important a weapon to become the permanent monopoly of any one party. Nothing was to prevent the opponents of Marxism from availing themselves of the weapon and applying it to Marxism itself.

5. THE TRANSITION FROM THE THEORY OF IDEOLOGY TO THE SOCIOLOGY OF KNOWLEDGE

The previous chapter traced a process of which numerous examples can be found in social and intellectual history. In the development of a new point of view one party plays the pioneering role, while other parties, in order to cope with the advantage of their adversary in the competitive struggle, must of necessity themselves make use of this point of view. This is the case with the notion of ideology. Marxism merely discovered a clue to understanding and a mode of thought, in the gradual rounding out of which the whole nineteenth century participated. The complete formulation of this idea is not the sole achievement of any single group and is not linked exclusively with any single intellectual and social position. The role that Marxism played in this process was one that deserves a high rank in intellectual history and should not be minimized. The process, however, by which the ideological approach is coming into general use, is going on before our very eyes, and hence is subject to empirical observation.

It is interesting to observe that, as a result of the expansion of the ideological concept, a new mode of understanding has

[1] Cf. Weber, Max, " Politik als Beruf " in *Gesammelte Politische Schriften* (Munich, 1921), p. 446.

gradually come into existence. This new intellectual standpoint constitutes not merely a change of degree in a phenomenon already operating. We have here an example of the real dialectical process which is too often misinterpreted for scholastic purposes —for here we see indeed a matter of difference in degree becoming a matter of difference in kind. For as soon as all parties are able to analyse the ideas of their opponents in ideological terms, all elements of meaning are qualitatively changed and the word ideology acquires a totally new meaning. In the course of this all the factors with which we dealt in our historical analysis of the meaning of the term are also transformed accordingly. The problems of " false consciousness " and of the nature of reality henceforth take on a different significance. This point of view ultimately forces us to recognize that our axioms, our ontology, and our epistemology have been profoundly transformed. We will limit ourselves in what follows to pointing out through what variations in meaning the conception of ideology has passed in the course of this transformation.

We have already traced the development from the particular to the total conception. This tendency is constantly being intensified. Instead of being content with showing that the adversary suffers from illusions or distortions on a psychological or experiential plane, the tendency now is to subject his total structure of consciousness and thought to a thoroughgoing sociological analysis.[1]

As long as one does not call his own position into question but regards it as absolute, while interpreting his opponents' ideas as a mere function of the social positions they occupy, the decisive step forward has not yet been taken. It is true, of course, that in such a case the total conception of ideology is being used, since one is interested in analysing the structure of the mind of one's opponent in its totality, and is not merely singling out a few isolated propositions. But since, in such an instance, one is interested merely in a sociological analysis of the opponent's ideas, one never gets beyond a highly restricted, or what I should like to call a special, formulation of the theory. In contrast to this special formulation, the general [2] form of the

[1] This is not meant to imply that for certain aspects of the struggles of everyday life the particular conception of ideology is inapplicable.

[2] We add here another distinction to our earlier one of " particular and total ", namely that of " special and general ". While the first distinction concerns the question as to whether single isolated ideas or the entire mind is to be seen as ideological, and whether the social situation conditions

total conception of ideology is being used by the analyst when he has the courage to subject not just the adversary's point of view but all points of view, including his own, to the ideological analysis.

At the present stage of our understanding it is hardly possible to avoid this general formulation of the total conception of ideology, according to which the thought of all parties in all epochs is of an ideological character. There is scarcely a single intellectual position, and Marxism furnishes no exception to this rule, which has not changed through history and which even in the present does not appear in many forms. Marxism, too, has taken on many diverse appearances. It should not be too difficult for a Marxist to recognize their social basis.

With the emergence of the general formulation of the total conception of ideology, the simple theory of ideology develops into the sociology of knowledge. What was once the intellectual armament [1] of a party is transformed into a method of research in social and intellectual history generally. To begin with, a given social group discovers the " situational determination " (*Seinsgebundenheit*) of its opponents' ideas. Subsequently the recognition of this fact is elaborated into an all-inclusive principle according to which the thought of every group is seen as arising out of its life conditions.[2] Thus, it becomes the task of the sociological history of thought to analyse without regard for party biases all the factors in the actually existing social situation which may influence thought. This sociologically oriented history of ideas is destined to provide modern men with a revised view of the whole historical process.

It is clear, then, that in this connection the conception of ideology takes on a new meaning. Out of this meaning two alternative approaches to ideological investigation arise. The first is to confine oneself to showing everywhere the interrelationships between the intellectual point of view held and the social position occupied. This involves the renunciation of every

merely the psychological manifestations of concepts, or whether it even penetrates to the noological meanings, in the distinction of special *versus* general, the decisive question is whether the thought of all groups (including our own) or only that of our adversaries is recognized as socially determined.

[1] Cf. the Marxist expression " To forge the intellectual weapons of the proletariat ".

[2] By the term " situational determination of knowledge " I am seeking to differentiate the propagandistic from the scientific sociological content of the ideological concept.

intention to expose or unmask those views with which one is in disagreement.

In attempting to expose the views of another, one is forced to make one's own view appear infallible and absolute, which is a procedure altogether to be avoided if one is making a specifically non-evaluative investigation. The second possible approach is nevertheless to combine such a non-evaluative analysis with a definite epistemology. Viewed from the angle of this second approach there are two separate and distinct solutions to the problem of what constitutes reliable knowledge —the one solution may be termed *relationism*, and the other *relativism*.

Relativism is a product of the modern historical-sociological procedure which is based on the recognition that all historical thinking is bound up with the concrete position in life of the thinker (*Standortsgebundenheit des Denkers*). But relativism combines this historical-sociological insight with an older theory of knowledge which was as yet unaware of the interplay between conditions of existence and modes of thought, and which modelled its knowledge after static prototypes such as might be exemplified by the proposition $2 \times 2 = 4$. This older type of thought, which regarded such examples as the model of all thought, was necessarily led to the rejection of all those forms of knowledge which were dependent upon the subjective standpoint and the social situation of the knower, and which were, hence, merely " relative ". Relativism, then, owes its existence to the discrepancy between this newly-won insight into the actual processes of thought and a theory of knowledge which had not yet taken account of this new insight.

If we wish to emancipate ourselves from this relativism we must seek to understand with the aid of the sociology of knowledge that it is not epistemology in any absolute sense but rather a certain historically transitory type of epistemology which is in conflict with the type of thought oriented to the social situation. Actually, epistemology is as intimately enmeshed in the social process as is the totality of our thinking, and it will make progress to the extent that it can master the complications arising out of the changing structure of thought.

A modern theory of knowledge which takes account of the relational as distinct from the merely relative character of all historical knowledge must start with the assumption that there are spheres of thought in which it is impossible to conceive of absolute truth existing independently of the values and position of the subject and unrelated to the social context. Even a god could not formulate a proposition on historical subjects like $2 \times 2 = 4$, for what is intelligible in history can be formulated only with reference to problems and conceptual constructions which themselves arise in the flux of historical experience.

Once we recognize that all historical knowledge is relational knowledge, and can only be formulated with reference to the position of the observer, we are faced, once more, with the task of discriminating between what is true and what is false in such knowledge. The question then arises : which social standpoint *vis-à-vis* of history offers the best chance for reaching an optimum of truth ? In any case, at this stage the vain hope of discovering truth in a form which is independent of an historically and socially determined set of meanings will have to be given up. The problem is by no means solved when we have arrived at this conclusion, but we are, at least, in a better position to state the actual problems which arise in a more unrestricted manner. In the following we have to distinguish two types of approach to ideological inquiry arising upon the level of the general-total conception of ideology : first, the approach characterized by freedom from value-judgments and, second, the epistemological and metaphysically oriented normative approach. For the time being we shall not raise the question of whether in the latter approach we are dealing with relativism or relationism.

The non-evaluative general total conception of ideology is to be found primarily in those historical investigations, where, provisionally and for the sake of the simplification of the problem, no judgments are pronounced as to the correctness of the ideas to be treated. This approach confines itself to discovering the relations between certain mental structures and the life-situations in which they exist. We must constantly ask ourselves how it comes about that a given type of social situation gives rise to a given interpretation. Thus the ideological element in human thought, viewed at this level, is always bound up with the existing life-situation of the thinker. According to this view human thought arises, and operates, not in a social vacuum but in a definite social milieu.

We need not regard it as a source of error that all thought is so rooted. Just as the individual who participates in a complex of vital social relations with other men thereby enjoys a chance

of obtaining a more precise and penetrating insight into his
fellows, so a given point of view and a given set of concepts,
because they are bound up with and grow out of a certain social
reality, offer, through intimate contact with this reality, a
greater chance of revealing its meaning. (The example cited
earlier showed that the proletarian-socialistic point of view was
in a particularly favourable position to discover the ideological
elements in its adversaries' thought.)   The circumstance,
however, that thought is bound by the social- and life-situation
in which it arises creates handicaps as well as opportunities.
It is clearly impossible to obtain an inclusive insight into problems
if the observer or thinker is confined to a given place in society.
For instance, as has already been pointed out, it was not possible
for the socialist idea of ideology to have developed of itself into
the sociology of knowledge.   It seems inherent in the historical
process itself that the narrowness and the limitations which
restrict one point of view tend to be corrected by clashing with
the opposite points of view.   The task of a study of ideology,
which tries to be free from value-judgments, is to understand
the narrowness of each individual point of view and the interplay between these distinctive attitudes in the total social
process.   We are here confronted with an inexhaustible theme.
The problem is to show how, in the whole history of thought,
certain intellectual standpoints are connected with certain forms
of experience, and to trace the intimate interaction between
the two in the course of social and intellectual change.   In the
domain of morals, for instance, it is necessary to show not only
the continuous changes in human conduct but the constantly
altering norms by which this conduct is judged.   Deeper insight
into the problem is reached if we are able to show that morality
and ethics themselves are conditioned by certain definite
situations, and that such fundamental concepts as duty, transgression, and sin have not always existed but have made their
appearance as correlatives of distinct social situations.[1]   The
prevailing philosophic view which cautiously admits that the
content of conduct has been historically determined, but which
at the same time insists upon the retention of eternal forms of
value and of a formal set of categories, is no longer tenable.
The fact that the distinction between the content and the forms

---

[1] Cf. Weber, Max, *Wirtschaft und Gesellschaft*. Grundriss der Sozialökonomik, Part iii, p. 794, dealing with the social conditions which are
requisite to the genesis of the moral.

of conduct was made and recognized is an important concession to the historical-sociological approach which makes it increasingly difficult to set up contemporary values as absolutes.

Having arrived at this recognition it becomes necessary also to remember that the fact that we speak about social and cultural life in terms of values is itself an attitude peculiar to our time. The notion of " value " arose and was diffused from economics, where the conscious choice between values was the starting-point of theory. This idea of value was later transferred to the ethical, æsthetic, and religious spheres, which brought about a distortion in the description of the real behaviour of the human-being in these spheres. Nothing could be more wrong than to describe the real attitude of the individual when enjoying a work of art quite unreflectively, or when acting according to ethical patterns inculcated in him since childhood, in terms of conscious choice between values.

The view which holds that all cultural life is an orientation toward objective values is just one more illustration of a typically modern rationalistic disregard for the basic irrational mechanisms which govern man's relation to his world. Far from being permanently valid the interpretation of culture in terms of objective values is really a peculiar characteristic of the thought of our own time. But even granting for the moment that this conception had some merit, the existence of certain formal realms of values and their specific structure would be intelligible only with reference to the concrete situations to which they have relevance and in which they are valid.[1] There is, then, no norm which can lay claim to formal validity and which can be abstracted as a constant universal formal element from its historically changing content.

To-day we have arrived at the point where we can see clearly that there are differences in modes of thought, not only in different historical periods but also in different cultures. Slowly it dawns upon us that not only does the content of thought change but also its categorical structure. Only very recently has it become possible to investigate the hypothesis that, in the past as well as in the present, the dominant modes of thought are supplanted by new categories when the social basis of the group, of which

[1] Cf. Lask, E., *Die Logik der Philosophie und die Kategorienlehre* (Tübingen, 1911), uses the term *hingelten* in order to explain that cate-gorical forms are not valid in themselves but only with reference to their always changing content which inevitably reacts upon their nature.

these thought-forms are characteristic, disintegrates or is transformed under the impact of social change.

Research in the sociology of knowledge promises to reach a stage of exactness if only because nowhere else in the realm of culture is the interdependence in the shifts of meaning and emphasis so clearly evident and precisely determinable as in thought itself. For thought is a particularly sensitive index of social and cultural change. The variation in the meaning of words and the multiple connotations of every concept reflect polarities of mutually antagonistic schemes of life implicit in these nuances of meaning.[1]

Nowhere in the realm of social life, however, do we encounter such a clearly traceable interdependence and sensitivity to change and varying emphasis as in the meaning of words. The word and the meaning that attaches to it is truly a collective reality. The slightest nuance in the total system of thought reverberates in the individual word and the shades of meaning it carries. The word binds us to the whole of past history and, at the same time, mirrors the totality of the present. When, in communicating with others, we seek a common level of understanding the word can be used to iron out individual differences of meaning. But, when necessary, the word may become an instrument in emphasizing the differences in meaning and the unique experiences of each individual. It may then serve as a means for detecting the original and novel increments that arise in the course of the history of culture, thereby adding previously imperceptible values to the scale of human experience. In all of these investigations use will be made of the total and general conception of ideology in its non-evaluative sense.

6. THE NON-EVALUATIVE CONCEPTION OF IDEOLOGY

The investigator who undertakes the historical studies suggested above need not be concerned with the problem of what is ultimate truth. Interrelationships have now become evident, both in the present and in history, which formerly could never have been analysed so thoroughly. The recognition of this fact in all its

[1] For this reason the sociological analysis of meanings will play a significant role in the following studies. We may suggest here that such an analysis might be developed into a symptomatology based upon the principle that in the social realm, if we can learn to observe carefully, we can see that each element of the situation which we are analysing contains and throws light upon the whole.

ramifications gives to the modern investigator a tremendous advantage. He will no longer be inclined to raise the question as to which of the contending parties has the truth on its side, but rather he will direct his attention to discovering the approximate truth as it emerges in the course of historical development out of the complex social process. The modern investigator can answer, if he is accused of evading the problem of what is truth, that the indirect approach to truth through social history will in the end be more fruitful than a direct logical attack. Even though he does not discover " truth itself ", he will discover the cultural setting and many hitherto unknown " circumstances " which are relevant to the discovery of truth. As a matter of fact, if we believe that we already have the truth, we will lose interest in obtaining those very insights which might lead us to an approximate understanding of the situation. It is precisely our uncertainty which brings us a good deal closer to reality than was possible in former periods which had faith in the absolute.

It is now quite clear that only in a rapidly and profoundly changing intellectual world could ideas and values, formerly regarded as fixed, have been subjected to a thoroughgoing criticism.   In no other situation could men have been alert enough to discover the ideological element in all thinking. It is true, of course, that men have fought the ideas of their adversaries, but in the past, for the most part, they have done so only in order to cling to their own absolutes the more stubbornly. To-day, there are too many points of view of equal value and prestige, each showing the relativity of the other, to permit us to take any one position and to regard it as impregnable and absolute. Only this socially disorganized intellectual situation makes possible the insight, hidden until now by a generally stable social structure and the practicability of certain traditional norms, that every point of view is particular to a social situation.[1] It may indeed be true that in order to act we need a certain amount of self-confidence and intellectual self-assurance.   It may also be true that the very form of expression, in which we clothe our thoughts, tends to impose upon them an absolute tone.   In our epoch, however, it is precisely the function of historical investigation (and, as we shall see, of those social groups from which the scholars

---

[1] By social stability we do not mean uneventfulness or the personal security of individuals, but rather the relative fixity of the existing total social structure, which guarantees the stability of the dominant values and ideas.

are to be recruited), to analyse the elements that make up our self-assurance, so indispensable for action in immediate, concrete situations, and to counteract the bias which might arise from what we, as individuals, take for granted. This is possible only through incessant care and the determination to reduce to a minimum the tendency to self-apotheosis. Through this effort the one-sidedness of our own point of view is counteracted, and conflicting intellectual positions may actually come to supplement one another.

It is imperative in the present transitional period to make use of the intellectual twilight which dominates our epoch and in which all values and points of view appear in their genuine relativity. We must realize once and for all that the meanings which make up our world are simply an historically determined and continuously developing structure in which man develops, and are in no sense absolute.

At this point in history when all things which concern man and the structure and elements of history itself are suddenly revealed to us in a new light, it behooves us in our scientific thinking to become masters of the situation, for it is not inconceivable that sooner than we suspect, as has often been the case before in history, this vision may disappear, the opportunity may be lost, and the world will once again present a static, uniform, and inflexible countenance.

This first non-evaluative insight into history does not inevitably lead to relativism, but rather to relationism. Knowledge, as seen in the light of the total conception of ideology, is by no means an illusory experience, for ideology in its relational concept is not at all identical with illusion. Knowledge arising out of our experience in actual life situations, though not absolute, is knowledge none the less. The norms arising out of such actual life situations do not exist in a social vacuum, but are effective as real sanctions for conduct. Relationism signifies merely that all of the elements of meaning in a given situation have reference to one another and derive their significance from this reciprocal interrelationship in a given frame of thought. Such a system of meanings is possible and valid only in a given type of historical existence, to which, for a time, it furnishes appropriate expression. When the social situation changes, the system of norms to which it had previously given birth ceases to be in harmony with it. The same estrangement goes on with reference to knowledge and to the historical perspective. All knowledge is oriented toward some object and is influenced in its approach by the nature of the object with which it is pre-occupied. But the mode of approach to the object to be known is dependent upon the nature of the knower. This is true, first of all, with regard to the qualitative depth of our knowledge (particularly when we are attempting to arrive at an " understanding " of something where the degree of insight to be obtained presupposes the mental or intellectual kinship of the understander and of the understood). It is true, in the second place, with regard to the possibility of intellectually formulating our knowledge, especially since in order to be transmuted into knowledge, every perception is and must be ordered and organized into categories. The extent, however, to which we can organize and express our experience in such conceptual forms is, in turn, dependent upon the frames of reference which happen to be available at a given historical moment. The concepts which we have and the universe of discourse in which we move, together with the directions in which they tend to elaborate themselves, are dependent largely upon the historical-social situation of the intellectually active and responsible members of the group. We have, then, as the theme of this non-evaluative study of ideology, the relationship of all partial knowledge and its component elements to the larger body of meaning, and ultimately to the structure of historical reality. If, instead of fully reckoning with this insight and its implications, we were to disregard it, we would be surrendering an advanced position of intellectual achievement which has been painfully won.

Hence it has become extremely questionable whether, in the flux of life, it is a genuinely worthwhile intellectual problem to seek to discover fixed and immutable ideas or absolutes. It is a more worthy intellectual task perhaps to learn to think dynamically and relationally rather than statically. In our contemporary social and intellectual plight, it is nothing less than shocking to discover that those persons who claim to have discovered an absolute are usually the same people who also pretend to be superior to the rest. To find people in our day attempting to pass off to the world and recommending to others some nostrum of the absolute which they claim to have dis-covered is merely a sign of the loss of and the need for intellectual and moral certainty, felt by broad sections of the population who are unable to look life in the face. It may possibly be true that, to continue to live on and to act in a world like ours, it is vitally necessary to seek a way out of this uncertainty of multiple alternatives ; and accordingly people may be led to embrace some immediate goal as if it were absolute, by which they hope to make their problems appear concrete and real. But it is not primarily the man of action who seeks the absolute and immutable, but rather it is he who wishes to induce others to hold on to the *status quo* because he feels comfortable and smug under conditions as they are. Those who are satisfied with the existing order of things are only too likely to set up the chance situation of the moment as absolute and eternal in order to have something stable to hold on to and to minimize the hazardousness of life. This cannot be done, however, without resorting to all sorts of romantic notions and myths. Thus we are faced with the curiously appalling trend of modern thought, in which the absolute which was once a means of entering into communion with the divine, has now become an instrument used by those who profit from it, to distort, pervert, and conceal the meaning of the present.

7. The Transition from the Non-evaluative to the Evaluative Conception of Ideology

Thus it appears that beginning with the non-evaluative conception of ideology, which we used primarily to grasp the flux of continuously changing realities, we have been unwittingly led to an evaluative-epistemological, and finally an ontological-metaphysical approach. In our argument thus far the non-evaluative, dynamic point of view inadvertently became a weapon against a certain intellectual position. What was originally simply a methodological technique disclosed itself ultimately as a *Weltanschauung* and an instrument from the use of which the non-evaluative view of the world emerged. Here, as in so many other cases, only at the end of our activity do we at last become aware of those motives which at the beginning drove us to set every established value in motion, considering it as a part of a general historical movement.

We see then that we have employed metaphysical-ontological value-judgements of which we have not been aware.[1] But only

[1] Of course, the type of value-judgments and the ontology of which we made use, partly unconsciously and partly deliberately, represents a judgment upon an entirely different level, and is a quite different ontology from that of which we spoke when we were criticizing the trend towards absolutism which attempts to reconstruct (in the spirit of the German

those will be alarmed by this recognition who are prey to the positivistic prejudices of a past generation, and who still believe in the possibility of being completely emancipated in their thinking from ontological, metaphysical, and ethical presuppositions.[1] In fact, the more aware one becomes of the presuppositions underlying his thinking, in the interest of truly empirical research, the more it is apparent that this empirical procedure (in the social sciences, at least) can be carried on only on the basis of certain meta-empirical, ontological, and metaphysical judgments and the expectations and hypotheses that follow from them.   He who makes no decisions has no questions to raise and is not even able to formulate a tentative hypothesis which enables him to set a problem and to search history for its answer. Fortunately positivism did commit itself to certain metaphysical and onto-logical judgments, despite its anti-metaphysical prejudices and its pretensions to the contrary. Its faith in progress and its naïve realism in specific cases are examples of such ontological judg-ments. It was precisely those presuppositions which enabled positivism to make so many significant contributions, some of which will have to be reckoned with for some time to come. The danger in presuppositions does not lie merely in the fact that they exist or that they are prior to empirical knowledge.[2] It lies rather in the fact that an ontology handed down through tradition

romantic school) the debris of history. This unavoidable implicit ontology which is at the basis of our actions, even when we do not want to believe it, is not something which is arrived at by romantic yearning and which we impose upon reality at will. It marks the horizon within which lies our world of reality and which cannot be disposed of by simply labelling it ideology. At this point we see a glimmer of a " solution " to our problem even though nowhere else in this book do we attempt to offer one. The exposure of ideological and utopian elements in thought is effective in destroying only those ideas with which we ourselves are not too intimately identified. Thus it may be asked whether under certain circumstances, while we are destroying the validity of certain ideas by means of the ideological analysis, we are not, at the same time, erecting a new construction—whether in the very way we call old beliefs into question is not unconsciously implied the new decision—as a sage once said, " Frequently when someone comes to me to seek advice, I know as I listen to him how he advises himself."

[1] A somewhat more critical positivism was more modest and wished to admit only a " minimum of indispensable assumptions ". The question might be raised whether this " minimum of indispensable assumptions " will not turn out to be equivalent to the elemental irreducible ontology contained in our conditions of existence.

[2] If empirical knowledge were not preceded by an ontology it would be entirely inconceivable, for we can extract objectified meanings out of a given reality only to the extent that we are able to ask intelligent and revealing questions.

obstructs new developments, especially in the basic modes of thinking, and as long as the particularity of the conventional theoretical framework remains unquestioned we will remain in the toils of a static mode of thought which is inadequate to our present stage of historical and intellectual development. What is needed, therefore, is a continual readiness to recognize that every point of view is particular to a certain definite situation, and to find out through analysis of what this particularity consists. A clear and explicit avowal of the implicit metaphysical pre-suppositions which underlie and make possible empirical knowledge will do more for the clarification and advancement of research than a verbal denial of the existence of these presuppositions accompanied by their surreptitious admission through the back door.

8. ONTOLOGICAL JUDGMENTS IMPLICIT IN THE NON-EVALUATIVE CONCEPTION OF IDEOLOGY

We have taken this excursion into the fields of ontology [1] and positivism because it seemed essential to get a correct understanding of the movements of thought in this most recent phase of intellectual history. What we described as an invisible shift from the non-evaluative approach to the evaluative one not only characterizes our own thought : it is typical of the whole development of contemporary thought. Our conclusion as a result of this analysis is that historical and sociological investigation in this period was originally dominated by the non-evaluative point of view, out of which developed two significant, alternative, metaphysical orientations. The choice between these two alternatives resolves itself in the present situation into the following : on the one hand it is possible to accept as a fact the transitory character of the historical event, when one is of the belief that what really matters does not lie either in the change itself or in the facts which constitute that change. According to this view, all that is temporal, all that is social, all the collective myths, and all the content of meanings and interpretations usually attributed to historical events can be ignored, because it is felt that beyond the abundance and multiplicity of the details, out of which ordered historical

---

[1] Cf. the author's *Die Strukturanalyse der Erkenntnistheorie*, Ergänz-ungsband der Kant-Studien, No. 57 (Berlin, 1922), p. 37, n. 1 ; p. 52, n. 1.

sequence emerge, lie the ultimate and permanent truths which transcend history and to which historical detail is irrelevant. Accordingly there is thought to be an intuitive and inspired source of history which actual history itself only imperfectly reflects. Those who are versed in intellectual history will recognize that this standpoint is derived directly from mysticism. The mystics had already maintained that there are truths and values beyond time and space, and that time and space and all that occurs within them are merely illusory appearances, when compared with the reality of the mystic's ecstatic experience. But in their time the mystics were not able to demonstrate the truth of their statements. The daily order of events was accepted as a stable and concrete matter of fact and the unusual incident was thought of as the arbitrary will of God. Traditionalism was supreme in a world which although alive with events admitted only one way, and that a stable way, of interpreting them. Traditionalism moreover did not accept the revelations of mysticism in their pure form ; rather it interpreted them in the light of their relation with the supernatural, since this ecstatic experience was regarded as a communion with God. The general interdependence of all the elements of meaning and their historical relativity has in the meantime become so clearly recognized that it has almost become a common sense truth generally taken for granted. What was once the esoteric knowledge of a few initiates can to-day be methodically demonstrated to every-body. So popular has this approach become that the sociological interpretation, not unlike the historical interpretation, will under certain circumstances be used to deny the reality of everyday experience and of history by those who see reality as lying outside of history, in the realm of ecstatic and mystical experience.

On the other hand, there is an alternative mode of approach which may also lead to sociological and historical research. It arises out of the view that the changes in relationships between events and ideas are not the result of wilful and arbitrary design, but that these relationships, both in their simultaneousness and in their historical sequence, must be regarded as following a certain necessary regularity, which, although not superficially evident, does nevertheless exist and can be understood.

Once we understand the inner meaning of history and realize that no stage of history is permanent and absolute, but rather that the nature of the historical process presents an unsolved

H

and challenging problem, we will no longer be content with the mystic's self-satisfied disregard for history as " mere history ". One may admit that human life is always something more than it was discovered to be in any one historical period or under any given set of social conditions, and even that after these have been accounted for there still remains an eternal, spiritual realm beyond history, which is never quite subsumed under history itself and which puts meaning into history and into social experience. We should not conclude from this that the function of history is to furnish a record of what man is not, but rather we should regard it as the matrix within which man's essential nature is expressed. The ascent of human beings from mere pawns of history to the stature of men proceeds and becomes intelligible in the course of the variation in the norms, the forms and the works of mankind, in the course of the change in institutions and collective aims, in the course of its changing assumptions and points of view, in terms of which each social-historical subject becomes aware of himself and acquires an appreciation of his past. There is, of course, the disposition more and more to regard all of these phenomena as symptoms and to integrate them into a system whose unity and meaning it becomes our task to understand. And even if it be granted that mystical experience is the only adequate means for revealing man's ultimate nature to himself, still it must be admitted that the ineffable element at which the mystics aim must necessarily bear some relation to social and historical reality. In the final analysis the factors that mould historical and social reality somehow also determine man's own destiny. May it not be possible that the ecstatic element in human experience which in the nature of the case is never directly revealed or expressed, and the meaning of which can never be fully communicated, can be discovered through the traces which it leaves on the path of history, and thus be disclosed to us.

This point of view, which is based without doubt on a particular attitude towards historical and social reality, reveals both the possibilities and the limits inherent in it for the understanding of history and social life. Because of its contempt for history, a mystical view, which regards history from an other-worldly standpoint, runs the risk of overlooking whatever important lessons history has to offer. A true understanding of history is not to be expected from an outlook which depreciates the significance of historical reality. A more circumspect examination of the facts will show that even though no final crystallization emerges out of the historical process, something of profound significance does transpire in the realm of the historical. The very fact that every event and every element of meaning in history is bound to a temporal, spatial, and situational position, and that therefore what happens once cannot happen always, the fact that events and meanings in history are not reversible, in short the circumstance that we do not find absolute situations in history indicates that history is mute and meaningless only to him who expects to learn nothing from it, and that, in the case of history more than in that of any other discipline, the standpoint which regards history as " mere history ", as do the mystics, is doomed to sterility.

The study of intellectual history can and must be pursued in a manner which will see in the sequence and co-existence of phenomena more than mere accidental relationships, and will seek to discover in the totality of the historical complex the role, significance, and meaning of each component element. It is with this type of sociological approach to history that we identify ourselves. If this insight is progressively worked out in concrete detail, instead of being allowed to remain on a purely speculative basis, and if each advance is made on the basis of available concrete material we shall finally arrive at a discipline which will put at our disposal a sociological technique for diagnosing the culture of an epoch. We sought to approximate this aim in earlier chapters which attempted to show the value of the conception of ideology for the analysis of the contemporary intellectual situation. In analysing the different types of ideology we did not intend simply to list unrelated cases of meanings of the term, but aimed rather to present in the sequence of its changing meanings a cross-section of the total intellectual and social situation of our time. Such a method of diagnosing an epoch, though it may begin non-evaluatively, will not long remain so. We shall be forced eventually to assume an evaluative position. The transition to an evaluative point of view is necessitated from the very beginning by the fact that history as history is unintelligible unless certain of its aspects are emphasized in contrast to others. This selection and accentuation of certain aspects of historical totality may be regarded as the first step in the direction which ultimately leads to an evaluative procedure and to ontological judgments.

9. THE PROBLEM OF FALSE CONSCIOUSNESS

Through the dialectical process of history there inevitably proceeds the gradual transition from the non-evaluative, total, and general conception of ideology to the evaluative conception (cf. p. 78). The evaluation to which we now refer, however, is quite different from that previously known and described. We are no longer accepting the values of a given period as absolute, and the realization that norms and values are historically and socially determined can henceforth never escape us. The ontological emphasis is now transferred to another set of problems. Its purpose will be to distinguish the true from the untrue, the genuine from the spurious among the norms, modes of thought, and patterns of behaviour that exist alongside of one another in a given historical period. The danger of " false consciousness " nowadays is not that it cannot grasp an absolute unchanging reality, but rather that it obstructs comprehension of a reality which is the outcome of constant reorganization of the mental processes which make up our worlds. Hence it becomes intelligible why, compelled by the dialectical processes of thought, it is necessary to concentrate our attention with greater intensity upon the task of determining which of all the ideas current are really valid in a given situation. In the light of the problems we face in the present crisis of thought, the question of " false consciousness " is encountered in a new setting. The notion of " false consciousness " already appeared in one of its most modern forms when, having given up its concern with transcendental-religious factors, it transferred its search for the criterion of reality to the realm of practice and particularly political practice in a manner reminiscent of pragmatism. But contrasted with its modern formulation, it still lacked a sense of the historical. Thought and existence were still regarded as fixed and separate poles, bearing a static relationship to one another in an unchanging universe. It is only now that the new historical sense is beginning to penetrate and a dynamic concept of ideology and reality can be conceived of.

Accordingly, from our point of view, an ethical attitude is invalid if it is oriented with reference to norms, with which action in a given historical setting, even with the best of intentions, cannot comply. It is invalid then when the unethical action of the individual can no longer be conceived as due to his own personal transgression, but must be attributed rather to the compulsion of an erroneously founded set of moral axioms. The moral interpretation of one's own action is invalid, when, through the force of traditional modes of thought and conceptions of life, it does not allow for the accommodation of action and thought to a new and changed situation and in the end actually obscures and prevents this adjustment and transformation of man. A theory then is wrong if in a given practical situation it uses concepts and categories which, if taken seriously, would prevent man from adjusting himself at that historical stage. Antiquated and inapplicable norms, modes of thought, and theories are likely to degenerate into ideologies whose function it is to conceal the actual meaning of conduct rather than to reveal it. In the following paragraphs we cite a few characteristic examples of the most important types of the ideological thinking that has just been described.

The history of the taboo against taking interest on loans [1] may serve as an example of the development of an antiquated ethical norm into an ideology. The rule that lending be carried on without interest could be put into practice only in a society which economically and socially was based upon intimate and neighbourly relations. In such a social world " lending without interest " is a usage that commands observance without difficulty, because it is a form of behaviour corresponding fundamentally to the social structure. Arising in a world of intimate and neighbourly relations this precept was assimilated and formalized by the Church in its ethical system. The more the real structure of society changed, the more this ethical precept took on an ideological character, and became virtually incapable of practical acceptance. Its arbitrariness and its unworldliness became even more evident in the period of rising capitalism when, having changed its function, it could be used as a weapon in the hands of the Church against the emergent economic force of capitalism. In the course of the complete emergence of capitalism, the ideological nature of this norm, which expressed itself in the fact that it could be only circumvented but not obeyed, became so patent that even the Church discarded it.

As examples of " false consciousness " taking the form of an incorrect interpretation of one's own self and one's role, we may cite those cases in which persons try to cover up their " real " relations to themselves and to the world, and falsify to themselves

[1] Cf. Max Weber, *Wirtschaft und Gesellschaft* : Gurndriss der Sozialökonomik, Part iii, p. 801 ff., for historical documentation of this case.

the elementary facts of human existence by deifying, romanticizing, or idealizing them, in short, by resorting to the device of escape from themselves and the world, and thereby conjuring up false interpretations of experience. We have a case of ideological distortion, therefore, when we try to resolve conflicts and anxieties by having recourse to absolutes, according to which it is no longer possible to live. This is the case when we create "myths", worship "greatness in itself", avow allegiance to "ideals", while in our actual conduct we are following other interests which we try to mask by simulating an unconscious righteousness, which is only too easily transparent.

Finally an example of the third type of ideological distortion may be seen when this ideology as a form of knowledge is no longer adequate for comprehending the actual world. This may be exemplified by a landed proprietor, whose estate has already become a capitalistic undertaking, but who still attempts to explain his relations to his labourers and his own function in the undertaking by means of categories reminiscent of the patriarchal order. If we take a total view of all these individual cases, we see the idea of " false consciousness " taking on a new meaning. Viewed from this standpoint, knowledge is distorted and ideological when it fails to take account of the new realities applying to a situation, and when it attempts to conceal them by thinking of them in categories which are inappropriate.[1]

This conception of ideology (the concept utopia will be treated in Part IV),[2] may be characterized as evaluative and dynamic. It is evaluative because it presupposes certain judgments concerning the reality of ideas and structures of consciousness, and it is dynamic because these judgments are always measured by a reality which is in constant flux.[3]

Complicated as these distinctions may appear to be at first

[1] A perception may be erroneous or inadequate to the situation by being in advance of it, as well as by being antiquated. We will investigate this more precisely in Part IV, where we deal with the utopian mentality. It is sufficient for us at this time merely to note that these forms of perception can be in advance of the situation as well as lagging behind.

[2] We hope to demonstrate in our subsequent treatment of the utopian mentality that the utopian outlook, which transcends the present and is oriented to the future, is not a mere negative case of the ideological outlook which conceals the present by attempting to comprehend it in terms of the past.

[3] This conception of ideology is conceivable only on the level of the general and total type of ideology, and constitutes the second evaluative type of ideology which we have earlier distinguished from the first or non-evaluative concept. Cf. pp. 71 ff. and p. 68, note 2 ; p. 78, note 1 ; pp. 83 ff.

glance, we believe that they are not in the least artificial, because they are merely a precise formulation of and an explicit attempt to pursue logically implications already contained in the everyday language of our modern world.

This conception of ideology (and utopia) maintains that beyond the commonly recognized sources of error we must also reckon with the effects of a distorted mental structure. It takes cognizance of the fact that the "reality" which we fail to comprehend may be a dynamic one ; and that in the same historical epoch and in the same society there may be several distorted types of inner mental structure, some because they have not yet grown up to the present, and others because they are already beyond the present. In either case, however, the reality to be comprehended is distorted and concealed, for this conception of ideology and utopia deals with a reality that discloses itself only in actual practice. At any rate all the assumptions which are contained in the dynamic, evaluative conception of ideology rest upon experiences which at best might conceivably be understood in a manner different from the one here set forth, but which can under no conditions be left out of account.

10. THE QUEST FOR REALITY THROUGH IDEOLOGICAL AND
UTOPIAN ANALYSIS

The attempt to escape ideological and utopian distortions is, in the last analysis, a quest for reality. These two conceptions provide us with a basis for a sound scepticism, and they can be put to positive use in avoiding the pitfalls into which our thinking might lead us. Specifically they can be used to combat the tendency in our intellectual life to separate thought from the world of reality, to conceal reality, or to exceed its limits. Thought should contain neither less nor more than the reality in whose medium it operates. Just as the true beauty of a sound literary style consists in expressing precisely that which is intended— in communicating neither too little nor too much—so the valid element in our knowledge is determined by adhering to rather than departing from the actual situation to be comprehended.

In considering the notions of ideology and utopia, the question of the nature of reality thrusts itself once again upon the scene. Both concepts contain the imperative that every idea must be tested by its congruence with reality. Meanwhile, however, our conception of reality itself has been revised and called into question. All the conflicting groups and classes in society seek this reality in their thoughts and deeds, and it is therefore no wonder that it appears to be different to each of them.[1] If the problem of the nature of reality were a mere speculative product of the imagination, we could easily ignore it. But as we proceed, it becomes more and more evident that it is precisely the multiplicity of the conceptions of reality which produces the multiplicity of our modes of thought, and that every ontological judgment that we make leads inevitably to far-reaching consequences. If we examine the many types of ontological judgments with which different groups confront us, we begin to

[1] Regarding the differentiation of ontologies according to social positions cf. my " Das konservative Denken," loc. cit., part ii. Further, cf. Eppstein, P., " Die Fragestellung nach der Wirklichkeit im historischen Materialismus," *Archiv für Sozialwissenschaft und Sozialpolitik*, lx (1928), p. 449 ff.
The careful reader will perhaps note that from this point on the evaluative conception of ideology tends once more to take on the form of the non-evaluative, but this, of course, is due to our intention to discover an evaluative solution. This instability in the definition of the concept is part of the technique of research, which might be said to have arrived at maturity and which therefore refuses to enslave itself to any one particular standpoint which would restrict its view. This dynamic relationism offers the only possible way out of a world-situation in which we are presented with a multiplicity of conflicting viewpoints, each of which, though claiming absolute validity, has been shown to be related to a particular position and to be adequate only to that one. Not until he has assimilated all the crucial motivations and viewpoints, whose internal contradictions account for our present social-political tension, will the investigator be in a position to arrive at a solution adequate to our present life-situation. If the investigator, instead of at once taking a definite position, will incorporate into his vision each contradictory and conflicting current, his thought will be flexible and dialectical, rather than rigid and dogmatic. Such a conceptual elasticity and the frank recognition that there are many as yet unreconciled contradictions need not, as happens so often in practice, becloud the vision of the investigator. Indeed the discovery of hitherto unsolved contradictions should serve as an impetus to the type of thought required by the present situation. As we have indicated before, it is our aim to bring all that is ambiguous and questionable in our contemporary intellectual life within the scope of overt consciousness and control by constantly pointing out the often concealed and carefully disguised elements in our thinking. Such a procedure will result in a dynamic relationism which would rather do without a closed system if it is to be brought about by a systematization of particular and discrete elements, the limitations of which have already become apparent. Furthermore we might ask whether the possibility of and the need for a closed or open system does not vary from epoch to epoch and from one social position to another. Even these few remarks should make it clear to the reader that whatever the types of formulations we use in our thinking, they are not arbitrary creations, but are rather more or less adequate means of comprehending and mastering the constantly changing forms of existence and thought that are expressed in them. For some comments concerning the sociological implication of " systems " of thought cf. " Das konservative Denken ", loc. cit., p. 86 ff.

suspect that each group seems to move in a separate and distinct world of ideas and that these different systems of thought, which are often in conflict with one another, may in the last analysis be reduced to different modes of experiencing the " same " reality.

We could, of course, ignore this crisis in our intellectual life as is generally done in everyday practical life, in the course of which we are content to encounter things and relationships as discrete events in no more than their immediate particular setting.[1] As long as we see the objects in our experience from a particular standpoint only and as long as our conceptual devices suffice for dealing with a highly restricted sphere of life, we might never become aware of the need for inquiring into the total interrelationship of phenomena. At best, under such circumstances, we occasionally encounter some obscurity which, however, we are usually able to overcome in practice. Thus everyday experience has operated for a very long time with magical systems of explanation ; and up to a certain stage of historical development, these were adequate for dealing empirically with the primitive life-situations encountered. The problem for earlier epochs as well as for ours may be stated as follows : under what conditions may we say that the realm of experience of a group has changed so fundamentally that a discrepancy becomes apparent between the traditional mode of thought and the novel objects of experience (to be understood by that mode of thought ?). It would be too intellectualistic an explanation

---

[1] Nothing could be more pointless, and incorrect than to argue as follows : Since every form of historical and political thought is based to a certain degree upon metatheoretical assumptions, it follows that we cannot put our trust in any idea or any form of thought, and hence it is a matter of indifference what theoretical arguments are employed in a given case. Hence each one of us ought to rely upon his instinct, upon his personal and private intuitions, or upon his own private interests, whichever of these will suit him best. If we did this each one of us, no matter how partisan his view, could hold it in good conscience and even feel quite smug about it. To defend our analysis against the attempt to use it for such propagandistic purposes, let it be said that there exists a fundamental difference between, on the one hand, a blind partisanship and the irrationalism which arises out of mere mental indolence, which sees in intellectual activity no more than arbitrary personal judgments and propaganda, and on the other the type of inquiry which is seriously concerned with an objective analysis, and which, after eliminating all conscious evaluation, becomes aware of an irreducible residue of evaluation inherent in the structure of all thought. (For a more detailed statement cf. my concluding statements in the discussion of my paper, " Die Bedeutung der Konkurrenz im Gebiete des Geistigen," and my remarks on W. Sombart's paper on methodology at the same meeting. *Verhandlungen des sechsten deutschen Soziologentages*, loc. cit.)

to assume that the older explanations were abandoned for any theoretical reasons. But in these earlier periods it was the actual change in social experiences which brought about the elimination of certain attitudes and schemes of interpretation which were not congruous with certain fundamental new experiences.

The special cultural sciences from the point of view of their particularity are no better than everyday empirical knowledge. These disciplines, too, view the objects of knowledge and formulate their problems abstracted and torn from their concrete settings. Sometimes it happens that the coherent formulation of the problems proceeds according to the actual organic connection in which they are encountered and not merely in the sense that they fall within the scope of one discipline. But often when a certain stage is reached, this organic and coherent order is suddenly lost. Historical questions are always monographic, either because of the limited manner in which the subject is conceived or because of the specialization of treatment. For history this is indeed necessary, since the academic division of labour imposes certain limitations. But when the empirical investigator glories in his refusal to go beyond the specialized observation dictated by the traditions of his discipline, be they ever so inclusive, he is making a virtue out of a defence mechanism which insures him against questioning his presuppositions.

Even the sort of investigation which never transcends the limits of its specialization can add to our data and enrich our experience. It is perhaps even true that at one time this point of view was the appropriate one. But just as the natural sciences too must question their hypotheses and their assumptions as soon as a discrepancy appears among their facts, and just as further empirical research becomes possible only when the general canons of explanation have been revised, so to-day in the cultural sciences we have arrived at a point at which our empirical data compel us to raise certain questions about our presuppositions.

Empirical research which limits itself to a particular sphere is for a long time in the same position as common sense : i.e. the problematic nature and incoherence of its theoretical basis remain concealed because the total situation never comes into view. It has been justly maintained that the human mind can make the most lucid observations with the fuzziest of concepts. But a crisis is reached when an attempt is made to reflect upon these observations and to define the fundamental concepts of the disciplines concerned. The correctness of this view is borne out by the fact that in certain disciplines empirical investigation goes on as smoothly as ever while a veritable war is waged about the fundamental concepts and problems of the science.

But even this view is a limited one because it formulates in the guise of a scientific proposition, intended to have general significance, a situation in science which is characteristic only of a given period. When these ideas began to be formulated about the beginning of the present century, the symptoms of the crisis were visible only on the periphery of research, in discussions concerning principles and definitions. To-day the situation has changed—the crisis has penetrated even into the heart of empirical research. The multiplicity of possible points of departure and of definitions and the competition between the various points of view colour even the perception of what formerly appeared to be a single and uncomplicated relationship.

No one denies the possibility of empirical research nor does any one maintain that facts do not exist. (Nothing seems more incorrect to us than an illusionist theory of knowledge.) We, too, appeal to " facts " for our proof, but the question of the nature of facts is in itself a considerable problem. They exist for the mind always in an intellectual and social context. That they can be understood and formulated implies already the existence of a conceptual apparatus. And if this conceptual apparatus is the same for all the members of a group, the presuppositions (i.e. the possible social and intellectual values), which underlie the individual concepts, never become perceptible. The somnambu- listic certainty that has existed with reference to the problem of truth during stable periods of history thus becomes intelligible. However, once the unanimity is broken,[1] the fixed categories which used to give experience its reliable and coherent character undergo an inevitable disintegration. There arise divergent and conflicting modes of thought which (unknown to the thinking subject) order the same facts of experience into different systems of thought, and cause them to be perceived through different logical categories.

This results in the peculiar perspective which our concepts impose upon us, and which causes the same object to appear differently, according to the set of concepts with which we view

[1] For further details as to the sociological cause of this disintegration cf. the author's paper, "Die Bedeutung der Konkurrenz im Gebiete des Geistigen " loc. cit.

it. Consequently, our knowledge of " reality ", as it assimilates more and more of these divergent perspectives, will become more comprehensive. What formerly appeared merely to be an unintelligible margin, which could not be subsumed under a given concept, has to-day given rise to a supplementary and sometimes opposite concept, through which a more inclusive knowledge of the object can be gained.

Even in empirical research we recognize ever more clearly how important a problem is the identity or lack of identity in our fundamental points of view. For those who have thought seriously about it, the problem presented by the multiplicity of points of view is clearly indicated by the particular limitation of every definition. This limitation was recognized by Max Weber, for instance, but he justified a particularistic point of view on the grounds that the particular interest motivating the investigation determines the specific definition to be used.

Our definition of concepts depends upon our position and point of view which, in turn, is influenced by a good many unconscious steps in our thinking. The first reaction of the thinker on being confronted with the limited nature and ambiguity of his notions is to block the way for as long as possible to a systematic and total formulation of the problem. Positivism, for example, took great pains to conceal from itself the abyss which lies behind all particularist thought. This was necessary on the one hand to promote the safe continuation of its search for facts, but on the other hand this refusal to deal with the problem often led to obscurity and ambiguity with reference to questions about the " whole ".

Two typical dogmas were particularly prone to prevent the raising of fundamental issues. The first of these was the theory which simply regarded metaphysical, philosophical, and other borderline questions as irrelevant. According to this theory, only the specialized forms of empirical knowledge had any claim to validity. Even philosophy was regarded as a special discipline whose primary legitimate preoccupation was logic. The second of these dogmas, which blocked the way to a perspective of the whole, attempted to compromise by dividing the field into two mutually exclusive areas to be occupied by empirical science and philosophy respectively,—to particular and immediate questions the former provided unchallengeable and certain answers, while in general questions and problems of the " whole ", " loftier " philosophical speculations were resorted to. This involved for philosophy the surrender of the claim that its conclusions were based upon generally valid evidence.

Such a solution is strangely like the dictum of the theorists of constitutional monarchy, which states : " The king reigns but does not govern." Philosophy is thus granted all the honours. Speculation and intuition are, under certain circumstances, regarded as higher instruments of knowledge, but only on the condition that they do not meddle with positive, democratically, and universally valid empirical investigation. Thereby the problem of the " whole " is once more avoided. Empirical science has brushed this problem aside, and philosophy cannot be held to account since it is responsible only to God. Its evidence is valid only in the realm of speculation and is confirmed only by pure intuition. The consequence of such a dichotomy is that philosophy, which should have the vital task of providing clarification of the observer's own mind in the total situation, is not in a position to do this, since it has lost contact with the whole, confining itself only to a " higher " realm. At the same time, the specialist, with his traditional (particularistic) point of view, finds it impossible to arrive at this more comprehensive vision which is made so necessary by the present condition of empirical investigation. For mastery of each historical situation, a certain structure of thought is required which will rise to the demands of the actual, real problems encountered, and is capable of integrating what is relevant in the various conflicting points of view. In this case, too, it is necessary to find a more fundamental axiomatic point of departure, a position from which it will be possible to synthesize the total situation. A fearful and uncertain concealment of contradictions and gaps will no more lead us out of the crisis than the methods of the extreme right and left, who exploit it in propaganda for the glorification of the past or future, forgetting for the moment that their own position is subject to the same criticism. Nor will it be of much help to interpret the onesidedness and limited character of the adversary's perspective as merely another proof of the crisis in his camp. This is practicable only if one's method is not challenged by any one else, and as long, consequently, as one is not conscious of the limitations of one's own point of view.

Only when we are thoroughly aware of the limited scope of every point of view are we on the road to the sought-for comprehension of the whole. The crisis in thought is not a crisis affecting merely a single intellectual position, but a crisis of a whole world which has reached a certain stage in its intellectual develcp-ment. To see more clearly the confusion into which our social and intellectual life has fallen represents an enrichment rather than a loss. That reason can penetrate more profoundly into its own structure is not a sign of intellectual bankruptcy. Nor is it to be regarded as intellectual incompetence on our part when an extraordinary broadening of perspective necessitates a thorough-going revision of our fundamental conceptions. Thought is a process determined by actual social forces, continually questioning its findings and correcting its procedure. (It would be fatal on that account to refuse to recognize, because of sheer timidity, what has already become clear.) The most promising aspect of the present situation, however, is that we can never be satisfied with narrow perspectives, but will constantly seek to understand and interpret particular insights from an ever more inclusive context.

Even Ranke in his *Politische Gespräch* put the following words into the mouth of Frederick : " You will never be able to arrive at truth by merely listening to extreme statements. Truth always lies outside the realm where error is to be found. Even from all the forms of error taken together it would be impossible to extract truth. Truth will have to be sought and found for its own sake, in its own realm. All the heresies in the world will not teach you what Christianity is—it can be learned only from the Gospel." [1] Such simple and unsophisticated ideas as these, in their purity and *naïveté*, are reminiscent of some intellectual Eden that knows nothing of the upheaval of knowledge after the Fall. Only too often is it found that the synthesis, which is presented with the assurance that it embraces the whole, turns out in the end to be the expression of the narrowest provincialism, and that an unquestioning espousal of any point of view that is at hand is one of the most certain ways of preventing the attain-ment of the ever broadening and more comprehensive under-standing which is possible to-day.

Totality in the sense in which we conceive it is not an immediate and eternally valid vision of reality attributable only to a divine eye. It is not a self-contained and stable view. On the contrary, a total view implies both the assimilation and trans-cendance of the limitations of particular points of view. It represents the continuous process of the expansion of knowledge, and has as its goal not achievement of a super-temporally valid

[1] Ranke, *Das politische Gespräch*, ed. by Rothacker (Halle, 1925), p. 13.

conclusion but the broadest possible extension of our horizon of vision.

To draw a simple illustration from everyday experience of the striving towards a total view, we may take the case of an individual in a given position of life who occupies himself with the concrete individual problems that he faces and then suddenly awakens to discover the fundamental conditions which determine his social and intellectual existence. In such a case, a person, who continually and exclusively occupies himself with his daily tasks, would not take a questioning attitude towards himself and his position, and yet such a person would, despite his self-assurance, be enslaved by a particularistic and partial point of view until he reached the crisis which brought disillusionment. Not until the moment, when he for the first time conceived of himself as being a part of a larger concrete situation, would the impulse awaken in him to see his own activities in the context of the whole. It is true that his perspective may still be as limited as his narrow range of experience allows ; perhaps the extent to which he analysed his situation would not transcend the scope of the small town or the limited social circle in which he moves. Nevertheless to treat events and human beings as parts of situations similar to those situations in which he finds himself, is something quite different from merely reacting immediately to a stimulus or to a direct impression. Once the individual has grasped the method of orienting himself in the world, he is inevitably driven beyond the narrow horizon of his own town and learns to understand himself as part of a national, and later of a world, situation. In the same manner he will be able to understand the position of his own generation, his own immediate situation within the epoch in which he lives, and in turn this period as part of the total historical process.

In its structural outlines this sort of orientation to one's situation represents in miniature the phenomenon that we speak of as the ever-widening drive towards a total conception. Although the same material is involved in this reorientation as in the individual observations which constitute empirical investigation, the end here is quite different. The situational analysis is the natural mode of thinking in every form of experience which rises above the commonplace level. The possibilities of this approach are not fully utilized by the special disciplines because ordinarily their objects of study are delimited by highly specialized points of view. The sociology of knowledge, however, aims to see even the crisis in our thought as a situation which we then strive to view as part of a larger whole.

If in as complicated a situation as our own, preceded by as differentiated an intellectual development as ours has been, new problems of thought arise, men must learn to think anew, because man is a kind of creature who must continually readapt himself to his changing history. Until the present, our attitudes towards our intellectual processes (despite all logical pretensions) were not much different from those of any naïve person. That is, men were accustomed to act in situations without clearly understanding them. But just as there was a moment in political history at which the difficulties of action became so great that they could not be directly overcome without reflecting on the situation itself, and just as man was forced to learn more and more to act, first on the basis of external impressions of the situation and afterwards by structurally analysing it, just so we may regard it as the natural development of a tendency, that man is actually grappling with the critical situation that has arisen in his thinking and is striving to envisage more clearly the nature of this crisis.

Crises are not overcome by a few hasty and nervous attempts at suppressing the newly arising and troublesome problems, nor by flight into the security of a dead past. The way out is to be found only through the gradual extension and deepening of newly-won insights and through careful advances in the direction of control.

III. THE PROSPECTS OF SCIENTIFIC POLITICS: THE RELATIONSHIP BETWEEN SOCIAL THEORY AND POLITICAL PRACTICE

1. WHY IS THERE NO SCIENCE OF POLITICS?

The emergence and disappearance of problems on our intellectual horizon are governed by a principle of which we are not yet fully aware. Even the rise and disappearance of whole systems of knowledge may ultimately be reduced to certain factors and thus become explicable. There have already been attempts in the history of art to discover why and in what periods such plastic arts as sculpture, relief-modelling or other arts arise and become the dominant art-form of a period. In the same manner the sociology of knowledge should seek to investigate the conditions under which problems and disciplines come into being and pass away. The sociologist in the long run must be able to do better than to attribute the emergence and solution of problems to the mere existence of certain talented individuals. The existence of and the complex interrelationship between the problems of a given time and place must be viewed and understood against the background of the structure of the society in which they occur, although this may not always give us an understanding of every detail. The isolated thinker may have the impression that his crucial ideas occurred to him personally, independent of his social setting. It is easy for one living in a provincial and circumscribed social world to think that the events which touch him are isolated facts for which fate alone is responsible. Sociology, however, cannot be content with understanding immediate problems and events emerging from this myopic perspective which obscures every significant relationship. These seemingly isolated and discrete facts must be comprehended in the ever-present but constantly changing configurations of experience in which they actually are lived. Only in such a context do they acquire meaning. If the sociology of knowledge should have any measure of success in this type of analysis, many problems which hitherto, as regards their origins at least, have been unsolved, would be cleared up. Such

I

a development would also enable us to see why sociology and economics are of such recent birth and why they advanced in one country and were retarded and beset by so many obstacles in others. Likewise it will be possible to solve a problem which has always gone unanswered : namely why we have not yet witnessed the development of a science of politics. In a world which is as permeated by a rationalistic ethos, as is our own, this fact represents a striking anomaly.

There is scarcely a sphere of life about which we do not have some scientific knowledge as well as recognized methods of communicating this knowledge. Is it conceivable then, that the sphere of human activity on the mastery of which our fate rests, is so unyielding that scientific research cannot force it to give up its secrets ? The disquieting and puzzling features of this problem cannot be disregarded. The question must have already occurred to many whether this is merely a temporary condition, to be overcome at a later date, or whether we have reached, in this sphere, the outermost limit of knowledge which can never be transcended ?

It may be said in favour of the former possibility that the social sciences are still in their infancy. It would be possible to conclude that the immaturity of the more fundamental social sciences explains the retardation of this " applied " science. If this were so, it would be only a question of time until this backwardness were overcome, and further research might be expected to yield a control over society comparable to that which we now have over the physical world.

The opposite point of view finds support in the vague feeling that political behaviour is qualitatively different from any other type of human experience, and that the obstacles in the way of its rational understanding are much more insurmountable than is the case in other realms of knowledge. Hence, it is assumed that all attempts to subject these phenomena to scientific analysis are foredoomed to failure because of the peculiar nature of the phenomena to be analysed.

Even a correct statement of the problem would be an achievement of value. To become aware of our ignorance would bring considerable relief since we would then know why actual knowledge and communication are not possible in this case. Hence the first task is a precise definition of the problem which is—What do we mean when we ask : Is a science of politics possible ?

There are certain aspects of politics which are immediately intelligible and communicable.   An experienced and trained political leader should know the history of his own country, as well as the history of the countries immediately connected with his own and constituting the surrounding political world. Consequently, at the least, a knowledge of history and the relevant statistical data are useful for his own political conduct. Furthermore, the political leader should know something about the political institutions of the countries with which he is concerned.   It is essential that his training be not only juristic but also include a knowledge of the social relations which underlie the institutional structure and through which it functions. He must likewise be abreast of the political ideas which mould the tradition in which he lives.   Similarly he cannot afford to be ignorant of the political ideas of his opponents.   There are still further though less immediate questions, which in our own times have undergone continual elaboration, namely the technique for manipulating crowds without which it is impossible to get on in mass-democracies.   History, statistics, political theory, sociology, history of ideas, and social psychology, among many other disciplines, represent fields of knowledge important to the political leader.   Were we interested in setting up a curriculum for the education of the political leader, the above studies would no doubt have to be included.   The disciplines mentioned above, however, offer no more than practical knowledge which, if one happens to be a political leader, might be of use. But even all of these disciplines added together do not produce a science of politics.   At best they may serve as auxiliary disciplines to such a science.   If we understood by politics merely the sum of all those bits of practical knowledge which are useful for political conduct, then there would be no question about the fact that a science of politics in this sense existed, and that this science could be taught.   The only pedagogical problem would consist, then, in selecting from the infinite store of existing facts those most relevant for the purposes of political conduct.

However, it is probably evident from this somewhat exaggerated statement that the questions " Under what conditions is a science of politics possible and how may it be taught ? " do not refer to the above-mentioned body of practical information. In what then does the problem consist ?

The disciplines which were listed above are structurally related only in so far as they deal with society and the state as if they were the final products of past history. Political conduct, however, is concerned with the state and society in so far as they are still in the process of becoming. Political conduct is confronted with a process in which every moment creates a unique situation and seeks to disentangle out of this ever-flowing stream of forces something of enduring character. The question then is : " Is there a science of this becoming, a science of creative activity ? "

The first stage in the delineation of the problem is thus attained. What (in the realm of the social) is the significance of this contrast between what has already become and what is in the process of becoming ?

The Austrian sociologist and statesman, Albert Schäffle,[1] pointed out that at any moment of socio-political life two aspects are discernible—first, a series of social events which have acquired a set pattern and recur regularly ; and, second, those events which are still in the process of becoming, in which, in individual cases, decisions have to to be made that give rise to new and unique situations. The first he called the "routine affairs of state", laufendes Staatsleben ; the second " politics ". The meaning of this distinction will be clarified by a few illustrations. When, in the accustomed life of an official, current business is disposed of in accordance with existing rules and regulations, we are, according to Schäffle, in the realm of " administration " rather than of " politics ". Administration is the domain where we can see exemplified what Schäffle means by " routine affairs of state ". Wherever each new case may be taken care of in a prescribed manner, we are faced not with politics but with the settled and recurrent side of social life. Schäffle uses an illuminating expression from the field of adminis-tration itself to give point to his distinction. For such cases as can be settled by merely consulting an established rule, i.e. according to precedent, the German word Schimmel,[2] which is derived from the Latin simile is used, signifying that the case in hand is to be disposed of in a manner similar to precedents that already exist. We are in the realm of politics when envoys to foreign countries conclude treaties which were never made before ; when parliamentary representatives carry through new measures of taxation ; when an election campaign is waged ;

---

[1] Cf. Schäffle, A., " Über den wissenschaftlichen Begriff der Politik," Zeitschrift für die gesamte Staatswissenschaften, vol. 53 (1897).
[2] The German word Schimmel means " mould ". [Translator's note.]

when certain opposition groups prepare a revolt or organize strikes—or when these are suppressed.

It must be admitted that the boundary between these two classes is in reality rather flexible. For instance, the cumulative effect of a gradual shift of administrative procedure in a long series of concrete cases may actually give rise to a new principle. Or, to take a reverse instance, something as unique as a new social movement may be deeply permeated with " stereotyped " and routinizing elements. Nevertheless the contrast between the " routine affairs of state " and " politics " offers a certain polarity which may serve as a fruitful point of departure. If the dichotomy is conceived more theoretically, we may say : Every social process may be divided into a rationalized sphere consisting of settled and routinized procedures in dealing with situations that recur in an orderly fashion, and the " irrational " by which it is surrounded.[1] We are, therefore, distinguishing between the " rationalized " structure of society and the " irrational " matrix. A further observation presents itself at this point. The chief characteristic of modern culture is the tendency to include as much as possible in the realm of the rational and to bring it under administrative control—and, on the other hand, to reduce the " irrational " element to the vanishing point.

A simple illustration will clarify the meaning of this assertion. The traveller of 150 years ago was exposed to a thousand

[1] For the sake of precision, the following remark should be added : The expression " settled routinized elements " is to be regarded figuratively. Even the most formalized and ossified features of society are not to be regarded as things held in store in an attic, to be taken out when needed for use. Laws, regulations, and established customs only have an existence in that living experiences constantly call them into being. This settledness signifies merely that social life, while constantly renewing itself, conforms to rules and formal processes already inherent in it and this constantly generates itself anew in a recurrent manner. Similarly, the use of the expression " rationalized sphere " must be taken in the broader sense. It may mean either a theoretical, rational approach, as in the case of a technique which is rationally calculated and determined ; or it may be used in the sense of " rationalization " in which a sequence of events follows a regular, expected (probable) course, as is the case with convention, usage, or custom, where the sequence of events is not fully understood, but in its structure seems to have a certain settled character. Max Weber's use of the term "stereotype" as the broader class might be used here, and two sub-classes of the stereotyping tendency then distinguished, (a) traditionalism, (b) rationalism. Inasmuch as this distinction is not relevant for our present purpose, we will use the concept " rationalized structure " in the more comprehensive sense in which Max Weber uses the general notion of stereotyping.

accidents. To-day everything proceeds according to schedule. Fare is exactly calculated and a whole series of administrative measures have made travel into a rationally controlled enterprise. The perception of the distinction between the rationalized scheme and the irrational setting in which it operates provides the possibility for a definition of the concept " conduct ".

The action of a petty official who disposes of a file of documents in the prescribed manner, or of a judge who finds that a case falls under the provisions of a certain paragraph in the law and disposes of it accordingly, or finally of a factory worker who produces a screw by following the prescribed technique, would not fall under our definition of " conduct ". Nor for that matter would the action of a technician who, in achieving a given end, combined certain general laws of nature. All these modes of behaviour would be considered as merely " reproductive " because they are executed in a rational framework, according to a definite prescription entailing no personal decision whatsoever. Conduct, in the sense in which we use it, does not begin until we reach the area where rationalization has not yet penetrated, and where we are forced to make decisions in situations which have as yet not been subjected to regulation. It is in such situations that the whole problem of the relations between theory and practice arises. Concerning this problem, on the basis of the analyses thus far made, we may even at this stage venture a few further remarks.

There is no question that we do have some knowledge concerning that part of social life in which everything and life itself has already been rationalized and ordered. Here the conflict between theory and practice does not become an issue because, as a matter of fact, the mere treatment of an individual case by subjecting it to a generally existing law can hardly be designated as political practice. Rationalized as our life may seem to have become, all the rationalizations that have taken place so far are merely partial since the most important realms of our social life are even now anchored in the irrational. Our economic life, although extensively rationalized on the technical side, and in some limited connections calculable, does not, as a whole, constitute a planned economy. In spite of all tendencies towards trustification and organization, free competition still plays a decisive role. Our social structure is built along class lines, which means that not objective tests but irrational forces of social competition and struggle decide the place and function of the individual in society.   Dominance in national and international life is achieved through struggle, in itself irrational, in which chance plays an important part.   These irrational forces in society form that sphere of social life which is unorganized and unrationalized, and in which conduct and politics become necessary.   The two main sources of irrationalism in the social structure (uncontrolled competition and domination by force) constitute the realm of social life which is still unorganized and where politics becomes necessary.   Around these two centres there accumulate those other more profound irrational elements, which we usually call emotions.   Viewed from the sociological standpoint there is a connection between the extent of the unorganized realm of society where uncontrolled competition and domination by force prevail, and the social integration of emotional reactions.

The problem then must be stated :   What knowledge do we have or is possible concerning this realm of social life and of the type of conduct which occurs in it ? [1]   But now our original problem has been stated in the most highly developed form in which it seems to lend itself to clarification.   Having determined where the realm of the political truly begins, and where conduct in a true sense is possible, we can indicate the difficulties existing in the relationship between theory and practice.

The great difficulties which confront scientific knowledge in this realm arise from the fact that we are not dealing here with rigid, objective entities but with tendencies and strivings in a constant state of flux.   A further difficulty is that the constellation of the interacting forces changes continuously.   Wherever the same forces, each unchanging in character, interact, and their interaction, too, follows a regular course, it is possible to formulate general laws.   This is not quite so easy where new forces are incessantly entering the system and forming unforeseen combinations.   Still another difficulty is that the observer himself does not stand outside the realm of the irrational, but is a participant in the conflict of forces.   This participation inevitably binds him to a partisan view through his evaluations and interests. Furthermore, and most important, is the fact that not only is the

---

[1] It is necessary here to repeat that the concept of the " political " as used in conjunction with the correlative concepts, rationalized structure, and irrational field, represents only one of many possible concepts of the " political ".   While particularly suited for the comprehension of certain relationships, it must not be regarded as absolutely the only one.   For an opposite notion of the " political " cf. C. Schmitt, " Der Begriff des Politischen," *Archiv für Sozialwissenschaft und Sozialpolitik*, vol. 58 (1928).

political theorist a participant in the conflict because of his values, and interests, but the particular manner in which the problem presents itself to him, his most general mode of thought including even his categories, are bound up with general political and social undercurrents. So true is this that, in the realm of political and social thinking, we must, in my judgment, recognize actual differences in styles of thought—differences that extend even into the realm of logic itself.

In this, doubtless, lies the greatest obstacle to a science of politics. For according to ordinary expectations a science of conduct would be possible only when the fundamental structure of thought is independent of the different forms of conduct being studied. Even though the observer be a participant in the struggle, the basis of his thinking, i.e. his observational apparatus and his method of settling intellectual differences, must be above the conflict. A problem cannot be solved by obscuring its difficulties, but only by stating them as sharply and as pronouncedly as possible. Hence it is our task definitely to establish the thesis that in politics the statement of a problem and the logical techniques involved vary with the political position of the observer.

2. THE POLITICAL AND SOCIAL DETERMINANTS OF KNOWLEDGE

We shall now make an effort to show by means of a concrete example that political-historical thinking assumes various forms, in accordance with different political currents. In order not to go too far afield, we shall concentrate primarily on the relationship between theory and practice. We shall see that even this most general and fundamental problem of a science of political conduct is differently conceived by the different historical-political parties.

This may be easily seen by a survey of the various political and social currents of the nineteenth and twentieth centuries. As the most important representative ideal-types, we cite the following :—

1. Bureaucratic conservatism.
2. Conservative historicism.
3. Liberal-democratic bourgeois thought.
4. The socialist-communist conception.
5. Fascism.

The mode of thought of bureaucratic conservatism will be considered first. The fundamental tendency of all bureaucratic thought is to turn all problems of politics into problems of administration. As a result, the majority of books on politics in the history of German political science are *de facto* treatises on administration. If we consider the role that bureaucracy has always played, especially in the Prussian state, and to what extent the intelligentsia was largely an intelligentsia drawn from the bureaucracy, this onesidedness of the history of political science in Germany becomes easily intelligible.

The attempt to hide all problems of politics under the cover of administration may be explained by the fact that the sphere of activity of the official exists only within the limits of laws already formulated. Hence the genesis or the development of law falls outside the scope of his activity. As a result of his socially limited horizon, the functionary fails to see that behind every law that has been made there lie the socially fashioned interests and the *Weltanschauungen* of a specific social group. He takes it for granted that the specific order prescribed by the concrete law is equivalent to order in general. He does not understand that every rationalized order is only one of many forms in which socially conflicting irrational forces are reconciled.

The administrative, legalistic mind has its own peculiar type of rationality. When faced with the play of hitherto unharnessed forces, as, for example, the eruption of collective energies in a revolution, it can conceive of them only as momentary disturbances. It is, therefore, no wonder that in every revolution the bureaucracy tries to find a remedy by means of arbitrary decrees rather than to meet the political situation on its own grounds. It regards revolution as an untoward event within an otherwise ordered system and not as the living expression of fundamental social forces on which the existence, the preservation, and the development of society depends. The juristic administrative mentality constructs only closed static systems of thought, and is always faced with the paradoxical task of having to incorporate into its system new laws, which arise out of the unsystematized interaction of living forces as if they were only a further elaboration of the original system.

A typical example of the military-bureaucratic mentality is every type of the " stab in the back " legend, *Dolchstoss-legende* which interprets a revolutionary outbreak as nothing but a serious interference with its own neatly planned strategy.

The exclusive concern of the military bureaucrat is military action and, if that proceeds according to plan, then all the rest of life is in order too. This mentality is reminiscent of the joke about the specialist in the medical world, who is reputed to have said : "The operation was a splendid success. Unfortunately, the patient died."

Every bureaucracy, therefore, in accord with the peculiar emphasis on its own position, tends to generalize its own experience and to overlook the fact that the realm of administration and of smoothly functioning order represents only a part of the total political reality. Bureaucratic thought does not deny the possibility of a science of politics, but regards it as identical with the science of administration. Thus irrational factors are overlooked, and when these nevertheless force themselves to the fore, they are treated as " routine matters of state ". A classic expression of this standpoint is contained in a saying which originated in these circles : " A good administration is better than the best constitution." [1]

In addition to bureaucratic conservatism, which ruled Germany and especially Prussia to a very great extent, there was a second type of conservatism which developed parallel to it and which may be called historical conservatism. It was peculiar to the social group of the nobility and the bourgeois strata among the intellectuals who were the intellectual and actual rulers of the country, but between whom and the bureaucratic conservatives there always existed a certain amount of tension. This mode of thought bore the stamp of the German universities, and especially of the dominant group of historians. Even to-day, this mentality still finds its support largely in these circles.

Historical conservatism is characterized by the fact that it is aware of that irrational realm in the life of the state which cannot be managed by administration. It recognizes that there is an unorganized and incalculable realm which is the proper sphere of politics. Indeed it focuses its attention almost exclusively on the impulsive, irrational factors which furnish the real basis for the further development of state and society. It regards these forces as entirely beyond comprehension and infers that, as such, human reason is impotent to understand or to control them. Here only a traditionally inherited instinct, " silently working " spiritual forces, the " folk spirit ", *Volksgeist*, drawing

[1] Obituary of Böhlau by the jurist Bekker. *Zeitschrift der Savigny-Stiftung*. Germanist. Abtlg., vol. viii, p. vi ff.

their strength out of the depths of the unconscious, can be of aid in moulding the future.

This attitude was already stated at the end of the eighteenth century by Burke, who served as the model for most of the German conservatives, in the following impressive words : " The science of constructing a commonwealth or renovating it or reforming it, is like every other experimental science, not to be taught *a priori*. Nor is it a short experience that can instruct us in that practical science." [1]   The sociological roots of this thesis are immediately evident. It expressed the ideology of the dominant nobility in England and in Germany, and it served to legitimatize their claims to leadership in the state. The *je ne sais quoi* element in politics, which can be acquired only through long experience, and which reveals itself as a rule only to those who for many generations have shared in political leadership, is intended to justify government by an aristocratic class. This makes clear the manner in which the social interests of a given group make the members of that group sensitive to certain aspects of social life to which those in another position do not respond. Whereas the bureaucracy is blinded to the political aspect of a situation by reason of its administrative preconceptions, from the very beginning the nobility is perfectly at home in this sphere. Right from the start, the latter have their eyes on the arena where intra- and inter-state spheres of power collide with one another. In this sphere, petty textbook wisdom deserts us and solutions to problems cannot be mechanically deduced from premises. Hence it is not individual intelligence which decides issues. Rather is every event the resultant of actual political forces.

The historical conservative theory, which is essentially the expression of a feudal tradition [2] become self-conscious, is primarily concerned with problems which transcend the sphere of administration. The sphere is regarded as a completely irrational one which cannot be fabricated by mechanical methods but which grows of its own accord. This outlook relates everything to the decisive dichotomy between " construction according to calculated plan " and " allowing things to grow ".[3] For the political leader it is not sufficient to possess merely the correct knowledge and the mastery of certain laws and norms. In

---

[1] Burke's *Reflections on the Revolution in France*, edited by F. G. Selby (London : Macmillan and Co., 1890), p. 67.
[2] Cf. " Das konservative Denken," loc. cit., pp. 89, 105, 133 ff.
[3] Ibid., p. 472, n. 129.

addition to these he must possess that inborn instinct, sharpened through long experience, which leads him to the right answer.

Two types of irrationalism have joined to produce this irrational way of thinking : on the one hand, precapitalistic, traditionalistic irrationalism (which regards legal thinking, for instance, as a way of sensing something and not as mechanical calculation), and, on the other hand, romantic irrationalism. A mode of thought is thus created which conceives of history as the reign of pre- and super-rational forces. Even Ranke, the most eminent representative of the historical school, spoke from this intellectual outlook when he defined the relations of theory and practice.[1] Politics is not, according to him, an independent science that can be taught. The statesman may indeed study history profitably, but not in order to derive from it rules of conduct, but rather because it serves to sharpen his political instinct. This mode of thought may be designated as the ideology of political groups which have traditionally occupied a dominant position but which have rarely participated in the administrative bureaucracy.

If the two solutions thus far presented are contrasted, it will become clear that the bureaucrat tends to conceal the political sphere while the historicist sees it all the more sharply and exclusively as irrational even though he singles out for emphasis the traditional factors in historical events and in the acting subjects. At this stage we come to the chief adversary of this theory which, as has been pointed out, arose originally out of aristocratic feudal mentality, namely, the liberal-democratic bourgeoisie and its theories.[2] The rise of the bourgeoisie was attended by an extreme intellectualism. Intellectualism, as it is used in this connection, refers to a mode of thought which either does not see the elements in life and in thought which are based on will, interest, emotion, and *Weltanschauung*—or, if it does recognize their existence, treats them as though they were equivalent to the intellect and believes that they may be mastered by and subordinated to reason. This bourgeois intellectualism expressly demanded a scientific politics, and actually proceeded to found such a discipline. Just as the bourgeoisie found the first institutions into which the political struggle could be

[1] Cf. Ranke, *Das politische Gespräch* (1836), ed. by Rothacker (Halle a.d., Saale, 1925), p. 21 ff. Also other essays on the same theme : " Reflexionen " (1832), " Vom Einfluss der Theorie," " Über die Verwandtschaft und den Unterschied der Historie und der Politik."

[2] For the sake of simplicity we do not distinguish liberalism from democracy, although historically and socially they are quite different.

canalized (first parliament and the electoral system, and later
the League of Nations), so it also created a systematic place
for the new discipline of politics. The organizational anomaly
of bourgeois society appears also in its social theory.   The
bourgeois attempt at a thorough-going rationalization of the
world is forced nevertheless to halt when it reaches certain
phenomena. By sanctioning free competition and the class
struggle, it even creates a new irrational sphere. Likewise in
this type of thought, the irrational residue in reality remains
undissolved.   Furthermore, just 'as parliament is a formal
organization, a formal rationalization of the political conflict
but not a solution of it, so bourgeois theory attains merely an
apparent, formal intellectualization of the inherently irrational
elements.

The bourgeois mind is, of course, aware of this new irrational
realm, but it is intellectualistic in so far as it attempts solely
through thought, discussion, and organization to master, as if
they were already rationalized, the power and other irrational
relationships that dominate here. Thus, *inter alia*, it was believed
that political action could without difficulty be scientifically
defined. The science in question was assumed to fall into three
parts :—

> First—the theory of ends, i.e. the theory of the ideal State.
> Second—the theory of the positive State.
> Third—" politics," i.e. the description of the manner in
> which the existing State is transformed into a perfect State.

As an illustration of this type of thought we may refer to the
structure of Fichte's " Closed Commercial State " which in this
sense has recently been very acutely analysed by Heinrich
Rickert [1] who himself, however, completely accepts this position.
There is then a science of ends and a science of means. The
most striking fact about 'it is the complete separation between
theory and practice, of the intellectual sphere from the emotional
sphere. Modern intellectualism is characterized by its tendency
not to tolerate emotionally determined and evaluative thinking.
When, nevertheless, this type of thought is encountered (and
all political thought is set essentially in an irrational context)
the attempt is made so to construe the phenomena that the

---

[1] Cf. Rickert, Heinrich, " Über idealistische Politik als Wissenschaft.
Ein Beitrag zur Problemgeschichte der Staatsphilosophie," *Die Akademie*,
Heft 4, Erlangen.

evaluative elements will appear separable, and that there will remain at least a residue of pure theory. In this the question is not even raised whether the emotional element may not under certain circumstances be so intertwined with the rational as to involve even the categorical structure itself and to make the required isolation of the evaluative elements *de facto* unrealizable. Bourgeois intellectualism, however, does not worry over these difficulties. With undaunted optimism, it strives to conquer a sphere completely purged of irrationalism.

As regards ends, this theory teaches that there is one right set of ends of political conduct which, in so far as it has not already been found, may be arrived at by discussion. Thus the original conception of parliamentarism was, as Carl Schmitt has so clearly shown, that of a debating society in which truth is sought by theoretical methods.[1] We know all too well and can understand sociologically wherein the self-deception in this mode of thought lay. To-day we recognize that behind every theory there are collective forces expressive of group-purposes, -power, and -interests. Parliamentary discussions are thus far from being theoretical in the sense that they may ultimately arrive at the objective truth : they are concerned with very real issues to be decided in the clash of interests. It was left for the socialist movement which arose subsequently as the opponent of the bourgeoisie to elaborate specifically this aspect of the debate about real issues.

In our treatment of socialist theory we are not for the time being differentiating between socialism and communism, for we are here concerned not so much with the plethora of historical phenomena as with the tendencies which cluster around the opposite poles that essentially determine modern thought. In the struggle with its bourgeois opponent, Marxism discovered anew that in historical and political matters there can be no " pure theory ". It sees that behind every theory there lie collective points of view. The phenomenon of collective thinking, which proceeds according to interests and social and existential situations, Marx spoke of as ideology.

In this case, as so often in political struggles, an important discovery was made, which, once it became known, had to be followed up to its final conclusion. This was the more so since this discovery contained the heart of the problem of political

---

[1] Cf. Carl Schmitt, *Die geistesgeschichtliche Lage des heutigen Parlamentarismus*, 2nd edit. (Leipzig, 1926).

thought in general. The concept ideology serves to point out the problem, but the problem is thereby by no means solved or cleared up.[1] A thoroughgoing clarification is attainable only by getting rid of the one-sidedness inherent in the original conception. First of all, therefore, it will be necessary for our purpose to make two corrections. To begin with, it could easily be shown that those who think in socialist and communist terms discern the ideological element only in the thinking of their opponents while regarding their own thought as entirely free from any taint of ideology. As sociologists there is no reason why we should not apply to Marxism the perceptions which it itself has produced, and point out from case to case its ideological character. Moreover, it should be explained that the concept " ideology " is being used here not as a negative value-judgment, in the sense of insinuating a conscious political lie, but is intended to designate the outlook inevitably associated with a given historical and social situation, and the *Weltanschauung* and style of thought bound up with it. This meaning of the term, which bears more closely on the history of thought, must be sharply differentiated from the other meaning. Of course, we do not deny that in other connections it may also serve to reveal conscious political lies.

Through this procedure nothing that has a positive value for scientific research in the notion of ideology has been discarded. The great revelation it affords is that every form of historical and political thought is essentially conditioned by the life situation of the thinker and his groups. It is our task to disentangle this insight from its one-sided political encrustation, and to elaborate in a systematic manner the thesis that how one looks at history and how one construes a total situation from given facts, depends on the position one occupies within society. In every historical and political contribution it is possible to determine from what vantage point the objects were observed. However, the fact that our thinking is determined by our social position is not necessarily a source of error. On the contrary, it is often the path to political insight. The

[1] For what follows Part II should be referred to for further discussion of the problem, of which only the essentials will be repeated here. The concept of total, general, and non-evaluative ideology, as described earlier, is the one used in the present context (cf. p. 71 ff.). Part IV will deal with the evaluative conceptions of ideology and utopia. Henceforth the concept to be used will be determined by the immediate purposes of the investigation.

significant element in the conception of ideology, in our opinion, is the discovery that political thought is integrally bound up with social life. This is the essential meaning of the oft-quoted sentence, " It is not the consciousness of men that determines their existence but, on the contrary, their social existence which determines their consciousness." [1]

But closely related to this is another important feature of Marxist thought, namely a new conception of the relationship between theory and practice. Whereas the bourgeois theorist devoted a special chapter to setting forth his ends, and whereas this always proceeded from a normative conception of society, one of the most significant steps Marx took was to attack the utopian element in socialism. From the beginning he refused to lay down an exhaustive set of objectives. There is no norm to be achieved that is detachable from the process itself : " Communism for us is not a condition that is to be established nor an ideal to which reality must adjust itself. We call communism the actual movement which abolishes present conditions. The conditions under which this movement proceeds result from those now existing." [2]

If to-day we ask a communist, with a Leninist training, what the future society will actually be like, he will answer that the question is an undialectical one, since the future itself will be decided in the practical dialectical process of becoming. But what is this practical dialectical process ?

It signifies that we cannot calculate *a priori* what a thing should be like and what it will be like. We can influence only the general trend of the process of becoming. The ever-present concrete problem for us can only be the next step ahead. It is not the task of political thought to set up an absolute scheme of what should be. Theory, even including communist theory, is a function of the process of becoming. The dialectical relationship between theory and practice consists in the fact that, first of all, theory arising out of a definitely social impulse clarifies the situation. And in the process of clarification reality undergoes a change. We thereby enter a new situation out of which a new theory emerges. The process is, then, as follows : (1) Theory is a function of reality ; (2) This theory leads to a certain kind

---

[1] Marx, Karl, *A Contribution to the Critique of Political Economy*, tr. by N. I. Stone (Chicago, 1913), pp. 11–12.

[2] Cf. *Marx-Engels Archiv*, ed. by D. Ryazanov (Frankfurt a.M.), vol. i, p. 252.

of action ; (3) Action changes the reality, or in case of failure, forces us to a revision of the previous theory. The change in the actual situation brought about by the act gives rise to a new theory.[1]

This view of the relationship between theory and practice bears the imprint of an advanced stage in the discussion of the problem. One notes that it was preceded by the one-sidedness of an extreme intellectualism and a complete irrationalism, and that it had to circumvent all the dangers which were already revealed in bourgeois and conservative thought and experience. The advantages of this solution lie in the fact that it has assimilated the previous formulation of the problem, and in its awareness of the fact that in the realm of politics the usual run of thought is unable to accomplish anything. On the other hand, this outlook is too thoroughly motivated by the desire for knowledge to fall into a complete irrationalism like conservatism. The result of the conflict between the two currents of thought is a very flexible conception of theory. A basic lesson derived from political experience which was most impressively formulated by Napoleon in the maxim, " *On s'engage, puis on voit*," [2] here finds its methodological sanction.[3] Indeed, political thought cannot be carried on by speculating about it from the outside. Rather thought becomes illuminated when a concrete

---

[1] " When the proletariat by means of the class struggle changes its position in society and thereby the whole social structure, in taking cognizance of the changed social situation, i.e. of itself, it finds itself face to face not merely with a new object of understanding, but also changes its position as a knowing subject. The theory serves to bring the proletariat to a consciousness of its social position, i.e. it enables it to envisage itself—simultaneously both as an object and a subject in the social process." (Lukács, Georg, *Geschichte und Klassenbewusstsein*, Berlin, 1923.)

" This consciousness in turn becomes the motive force of new activity, since theory becomes a material force once it seizes the masses." (Marx-Engels, *Nachlass*, i, p. 392.)

[2] Indeed both Lenin and Lukács, as representatives of the dialectical approach, find justification in this Napoleonic maxim.

[3] " Revolutionary theory is the generalization of the experiences of the labour movement in all countries. It naturally loses its very essence if it is not connected with revolutionary practice, just as practice gropes in the dark if its path is not illumined by revolutionary theory. But theory can become the greatest force in the labour movement if it is indissolubly bound up with revolutionary practice, for it alone can give to the movement confidence, guidance, strength, and understanding of the inner relations between events and it alone can help practice to clarify, the process and direction of class movements in the present and near future." (Joseph Stalin, *Foundations of Leninism*, rev. ed. New York and London, 1932, pp. 26–7.)

K

situation is penetrated, not merely through acting and doing, but also through the thinking which must go with them.

Socialist-communist theory is then a synthesis of intuitionism and a determined desire to comprehend phenomena in an extremely rational way. Intuitionism is present in this theory because it denies the possibility of exact calculations of events in advance of their happening. The rationalist tendency enters because it aims to fit into a rational scheme whatever novelty comes to view at any moment. At no time is it permissible to act without theory, but the theory that arises in the course of action will be on a different level from the theory that went before.[1] It is especially revolutions that create a more valuable type of knowledge. This constitutes the synthesis which men are likely to make when they live in the midst of irrationality and recognize it as such, but do not despair of the attempt to interpret it rationally. Marxist thought is akin to conservative thought in that it does not deny the existence of an irrational sphere and does not try to conceal it as the bureacratic mentality does, or treat it in a purely intellectual fashion as if it were rational, as liberal-democratic thinkers do. It is distinguished from conservative thought, however, in that it conceives of this relative irrationality as potentially comprehensible through new methods of rationalization.[2] For even in this type of thought,

---

[1] Revolution, particularly, creates the situation propitious to significant knowledge : " History in general, the history of revolutions in particular, has always been richer, more varied, and variform, more vital and ' cunning ' than is conceived of by the best parties, by the most conscious vanguards of the most advanced classes. This is natural, for the best vanguards express the consciousness, will, passions, and fancies of but tens of thousands, whereas the revolution is effected at the moment of the exceptional exaltation and exertion of all the human faculties— consciousness, will, passion, phantasy, of tens of millions, spurred on by the bitterest class war." (N. Lenin, " *Left" Communism : an Infantile Disorder*, published by the Toiler, n.d. pp. 76–7, also New York and London, 1934.)

It is interesting to observe that from this point of view revolution appears not as an intensification of the passions resident in men nor as mere irrationality. This passion is valuable only because it makes possible the fusion of the accumulated rationality tested out experimentally in the individual experiences of millions.

[2] Thus, fate, chance, everything sudden and unexpected, and the religious view which arises therefrom, are conceived of as functions of the degree in which our understanding of history has not yet reached the stage of rationality.

" Fear of the blind forces of capitalism, blind because they cannot be foreseen by the masses of the people, forces which at every step in the lives of the proletariat and the small traders threaten to bring and do bring ' sudden ', ' unexpected ', ' accidental ' disaster and ruin, converting

the sphere of the irrational is not entirely irrational, arbitrary, or incomprehensible. It is true that there are no statically fixed and definite laws to which this creative process conforms, nor are there any exactly recurring sequences of events, but at the same time only a limited number of situations can occur even here. And this after all is the decisive consideration. Even when new elements in historical development emerge they do not constitute merely a chain of unexpected events ; the political sphere itself is permeated by tendencies which, even though they are subject to change, through their very presence do nevertheless determine to a large extent the various possibilities.

Therefore, the first task of Marxism is the analysis and rationalization of all those tendencies which influence the character of the situation. Marxist theory has elaborated these structural tendencies in a threefold direction. First, it points out that the political sphere in a given society is based on and is always characterized by the state of productive relations prevailing at the time.[1] The productive relations are not regarded statically as a continually recurring economic cycle, but, dynamically, as a structural interrelationship which is itself constantly changing through time.

Secondly, it sees that changes in this economic factor are most closely connected with transformations in class relations, which involves at the same time a shift in the kinds of power and an ever-varying distribution of power.

But, thirdly, it recognizes that it is possible to understand the inner structure of the system of ideas dominating men at any period and to determine theoretically the direction of any change or modification in this structure.

Still more important is the fact that these three structural patterns are not considered independently of one another.

them into beggars, paupers, or prostitutes, and condemn them to starvation ; these are the roots of modern religion, which the materialist, if he desires to remain a materialist, must recognize. No educational books will obliterate religion from the minds of those condemned to the hard labour of capitalism, until they themselves learn to fight in a united, organized, systematic, conscious manner the roots of religion, the domination of capital in all its forms." (*Selections from Lenin—The Bolshevik Party in Action, 1904-1914*, ii. From the essay, " The Workers' Party and Religion," New York, pp. 274-5.)

[1] " The mode of production in material life determines the general character of the social, political, and spiritual processes of life." Marx, *Contribution to the Critique of Political Economy*, tr. by N. I. Stone (Chicago, 1913), p. 11.

It is precisely their reciprocal relations which are made to constitute a single group of problems. The ideological structure does not change independently of the class structure, and the class structure does not change independently of the economic structure. And it is precisely the interconnection and intertwining of this threefold formulation of the problem, the economic, the social, and the ideological, that gives to Marxist ideas their singularly penetrating quality. Only this synthetic power enables it to formulate ever anew the problem of the structural totality of society, not only for the past but also for the future. The paradox lies in the fact that Marxism recognizes relative irrationality and never loses sight of it. But unlike the historical school it does not content itself with a mere acceptance of the irrational. Instead it tries to eliminate as much of it as possible by a new effort at rationalization.

Here again the sociologist is confronted with the question of the general historical-social form of existence and the particular situation from which the mode of thought peculiar to Marxism arose. How can we explain its singular character which consists in combining an extreme irrationalism with an extreme rationalism in such a manner that out of this fusion there arises a new kind of " dialectical " rationality ?

Considered sociologically, this is the theory of an ascendent class which is not concerned with momentary successes, and which therefore will not resort to a " putsch " as a means for seizing power, but which, because of its inherent revolutionary tendencies, must always be sensitive and alert to unpredictable constellations in the situation. Every theory which arises out of a class position and is based not on unstable masses but on organized historical groups must of necessity have a long range view. Consequently, it requires a thoroughly rationalized view of history on the basis of which it will be possible at any moment to ask ourselves where we are now and at what stage of development does our movement find itself.[1]

Groups of pre-capitalistic origin, in which the communal element prevails, may be held together by traditions or by common sentiments alone. In such a group, theoretical reflection is of entirely secondary importance. On the other hand, in groups which are not welded together primarily by such organic bonds of community life, but which merely occupy similar

[1] " Without a revolutionary theory there can be no revolutionary movement." Lenin, What Is To Be Done? New York and London, 1931.

positions in the social-economic system, rigorous theorizing is a prerequisite of cohesion. Viewed sociologically this extreme need for theory is the expression of a class society in which persons must be held together not by local proximity but by similar circumstances of life in an extensive social sphere. Sentimental ties are effective only within a limited spatial area, while a theoretical *Weltanschauung* has a unifying power over great distances.   Hence a rationalized conception of history serves as a socially unifying factor for groups dispersed in space, and at the same time furnishes continuity to generations which continuously grow up into similar social conditions.   In the formation of classes, a similar position in the social order and a unifying theory are of primary importance.   Emotional ties which subsequently spring up are only a reflection of the already existing situation and are always more or less regulated by theory.   Despite this extreme rationalizing tendency, which is implicit in the proletarian class position, the limits of the rationality of this class are defined by its oppositional, and particularly, by its allotted revolutionary position.

Revolutionary purpose prevents rationality from becoming absolute.   Even though in modern times the tendency toward rationalization proceeds on such an extensive scale that revolts,[1] which originally were only irrational outbursts, are organized on this plane after a bureaucratic fashion, still there must remain somewhere in our conception of history and our scheme of life a place for the essential irrationality which goes with revolution.

Revolution means that somewhere there is an anticipation of and an intent to provoke a breach in the rationalized structure of society.   It necessitates, therefore, a watchfulness for the favourable moment in which the attack must be risked.   If the whole social and political sphere were conceived of as thoroughly rationalized, it would imply that we would no longer have to be on the lookout for such a breach.   The moment, however, is nothing more than that irrational element in the " here and now ", which every theory, by virtue of its generalizing tendency, obscures.   But since, so long as one needs and wants revolution, one cannot allow this favourable moment, during which the

[1] " The armed uprising is a special form of the political struggle. It has developmental laws of its own and these must be learned.   Karl Marx expressed this with extraordinary vividness when he wrote that ' the revolt is just as much an art as war '." (Lenin, *Ausgewählte Werke*, Wien, 1925, p. 448.)

breach occurs, to pass, there develops a gap in the theoretical picture which indicates that the irrational element is valued for what it really is—is valued essentially in its irrationality.

All this dialectical thinking begins by rationalizing what seemed to the historical-conservative groups totally irrational; it does not, however, go so far in its rationalizing tendency as to yield a totally static picture of what is in process of becoming.

This element of the irrational is embodied in the concept of dialectical transformation. The dominant tendencies in the political sphere are not here construed as mathematically calculable combinations of forces, but rather as capable, at a certain point, of sudden transformation when thrown out of the orbit of their original tendencies. Naturally, this transformation is never subject to prediction; on the contrary, it always depends on the revolutionary act of the proletariat. Thus intellectualism is by no means deemed legitimate in all situations. Quite on the contrary, there appear to be two occasions in which the intuition necessary to comprehend the situation is aroused. First, it always remains incalculable and is left for political intuition to ascertain when the situation is ripe for revolutionary transformation and, second, historical events are never so exactly determinable in advance that it is superfluous to invoke action to change them.

Marxist thought appears as the attempt to rationalize the irrational. The correctness of this analysis is vouched for by the fact that to the extent that Marxian proletarian groups rise to power, they shake off the dialectical elements of their theory and begin to think in the generalizing methods of liberalism and democracy, which seek to arrive at universal laws, whilst those who, because of their position, still have to resort to revolution, cling to the dialectical element (Leninism).

Dialectical thinking is in fact rationalistic but it culminates in irrationalism. It is constantly striving to answer two questions:—first, what is our position in the social process at the moment? second, what is the demand of the moment? Action is never guided simply by impulse but by a sociological understanding of history. Nevertheless it is not to be assumed that irrational impulses can be entirely eliminated by a logical analysis of the situation and of momentary occurrences. Only through acting in the situation do we address questions to it, and the answer we derive is always in the form of the success or failure of the action. Theory is not torn from its essential connection with action, and action is the clarifying medium in which all theory is tested and develops.

The positive contribution of this theory is that out of its own concrete social experience it shows more and more convincingly that political thought is essentially different from other forms of theorizing. This dialectical mode of thought is further significant in that it has incorporated within itself the problems of both bourgeois rationalism and the irrationalism of historicism.

From irrationalism it has derived the insight that the historical-political sphere is not composed of a number of lifeless objects and that therefore a method which merely seeks laws must fail. Furthermore this method is fully cognizant of the completely dynamic character of the tendencies that dominate the political realm and since it is conscious of the connection between political thinking and living experience, it will not tolerate an artificial separation of theory and practice. From rationalism, on the other hand, it has taken over the inclination to view rationally even situations which have previously defied rational interpretation.

As a fifth claimant to a place among modern currents of thought we should mention fascism, which first emerged in our own epoch. Fascism has its own conception of the relations of theory and practice. It is, on the whole, activistic and irrational. It couples itself, by preference, with the irrationalist philosophies and political theories of the most modern period. It is especially Bergson, Sorel, and Pareto who, after suitable modification of course, have been incorporated into its *Weltanschauung*. At the very heart of its theory and its practice lies the apotheosis of direct action, the belief in the decisive *deed*, and in the significance attributed to the initiative of a leading *élite*. The essence of politics is to recognize and to grapple with the demands of the hour. Not programmes are important, but unconditional subordination to a leader.[1] History is made neither by the masses, nor by ideas, nor by " silently working " forces, but by the *élites* who from time to time assert themselves.[2] This is a complete

[1] Mussolini : " Our programme is quite simple ; we wish to rule over Italy. People are always asking us about our programme. There are too many already. Italy's salvation does not depend on programmes but on men and strong wills. (Mussolini, *Reden*. ed. by H. Meyer (Leipzig, 1928), p. 105. Cf. also pp. 134 ff.)

[2] Mussolini (loc. cit., p. 13) : " You know that I am no worshipper of the new god, the masses. At any rate, history proves that social changes have always been first brought about by minorities, by a mere handful of men."

irrationalism but characteristically enough not the kind of irrationalism known to the conservatives, not the irrational which is at the same time the super-rational, not the folk spirit (*Volksgeist*), not silently working forces, not the mystical belief in the creativeness of long stretches of time, but the irrationalism of the deed which negates even interpretation of history. " To be youthful means being able to forget. We Italians are, of course, proud of our history, but we do not need to make it the conscious guide of our actions—it lives in us as part of our biological make-up." [1]

A special study would be necessary to ascertain the different meanings of the various conceptions of history. It would be easy to show that the diverse intellectual and social currents have different conceptions of history. The conception of history contained in Brodrero's statement is not comparable either to the conservative, the liberal-democratic, or the socialistic conceptions. All these theories, otherwise so antagonistic, share the assumption that there is a definite and ascertainable structure in history within which, so to speak, each event has its proper position.

---

[1] From a statement by Brodrero at the Fourth International Congress for Intellectual Co-operation, Heidelburg, October, 1927.

It is rather difficult to organize fascist ideas into a coherent doctrine. Apart from the fact that it is still undeveloped, fascism itself lays no particular weight upon an integrally knit theory. Its programme changes constantly, depending on the class to which it addresses itself. In this case, more than in most others, it is essential to separate mere propaganda from the real attitude, in order to gain an understanding of its essential character. This seems to lie in its absolute irrationalism and its activism, which explain also the vacillating and volatile theoretical character of fascist theory. Such institutional ideas as the corporative state, professional organizations, etc., are deliberately omitted from our presentation. Our task is to analyse the attitude towards the problem of theory and practice and the view of history which results therefrom. For this reason, we will find it necessary from time to time to give some attention to the theoretical forerunners of this conception, namely Bergson, Sorel, and Pareto. In the history of fascism, two periods may be distinguished, each of which has had distinct ideological repercussions. The first phase, about two years in length, during which fascism was a mere movement, was marked by the infiltration of activistic-intuitive elements into its intellectual-spiritual outlook. This was the period during which syndicalist theories found entrance to fascism. The first " fasci " were syndicalist and Mussolini at that time was said to be a disciple of Sorel. In the second phase, beginning in November, 1921, fascism becomes stabilized and takes a decisive turn towards the right. In this period nationalistic ideas come to the fore. For a discussion of the manner in which its theory became transformed, in accordance with the changing class basis, and especially the transformations since high finance and large-scale industry allied themselves to it, cf. Beckerath, E. v., *Wesen und Werden des fascistischen Staates* (Berlin, 1927).

Not everything is possible in every situation.[1] This framework which is constantly changing and revolving must be capable of comprehension. Certain experiences, actions, modes of thought, etc., are possible only in certain places and in certain epochs. Reference to history and the study of history or of society are valuable because orientation to them can and must become a determining factor in conduct and in political activity.

However different the picture which conservatives, liberals, and socialists have derived from history, they all agree that history is made up of a set of intelligible interrelations. At first it was believed that it revealed the plan of divine providence, later that it showed the higher purpose of a dynamically and pantheistically conceived spirit. These were only metaphysical gropings towards an extremely fruitful hypothesis for which history was not merely a heterogeneous succession of events in time, but a coherent interaction of the most significant factors. The understanding of the inner structure of history was sought in order to derive therefrom a measuring-rod for one's own conduct.

While the liberals and socialists continued to believe that the historical structure was completely capable of rationalization the former insisting that its development was progressively unilinear, and the latter viewing it as a dialectical movement, the conservatives sought to understand the structure of the totality of historical development intuitively by a morphological approach. Different as these points of view were in method and content, they all understood political activity as proceeding on an historical background, and they all agreed that in our own epoch, it becomes necessary to orient oneself to the total situation in which one happens to be placed, if political aims are to be realized. This idea of history as an intelligible scheme disappears in the face of the irrationality of the fascist apotheosis of the deed. To a certain degree this was already the case with its syndicalist forerunner, Sorel,[2] who had already denied the idea of evolution

---

[1] In contrast to this, Mussolini said : " For my own part I have no great confidence in these ideals [i.e. pacifism]. Nonetheless, I do not exclude them. I never exclude anything. Anything is possible, even the most impossible and most senseless " (loc. cit., p. 74).

[2] As regards Mussolini's relations with Sorel : Sorel knew him before 1914 and, indeed in 1912, is reported to have said the following concerning him : " Mussolini is no ordinary Socialist. Take my word, some day you will see him at the head of a sacred battalion, saluting the Italian flag. He is an Italian in the style of the fifteenth century—a veritable condottiere. One does not know him yet, but he is the only man active enough to be capable of curing the weakness of the government." Quoted

in a similar sense. The conservatives, the liberals, the socialists were one in assuming that in history it can be shown that there is an interrelationship between events and configurations through which everything, by virtue of its position, acquires significance. Not every event could possibly happen in every situation. Fascism regards every interpretation of history as a mere fictive construction destined to disappear before the deed of the moment as it breaks through the temporal pattern of history.[1]

That we are dealing here with a theory which holds that history is meaningless is not changed by the fact that in fascist ideology, especially since its turn to the right, there are found the ideas of the " national war " and the ideology of the " Roman Empire ". Apart from the fact that these ideas were, from the very first, consciously experienced as myths, i.e. as fictions, it should be understood that historically oriented thought and activity do not mean the romantic idealization of some past epoch or event, but consist rather in the awareness of one's place in the historical process which has a clearly articulated structure. It is this clear articulation of the structure which makes one's own participation in the process intelligible.

The intellectual value of all political and historical knowledge *qua* knowledge, disappears in the face of this purely intuitional approach, which appreciates only its ideological and mythological aspect. Thought is significant here only in so far as it exposes the illusory character of these fruitless theories of history and unmasks them as self-deceptions. For this activistic intuitionism, thought only clears the way for the pure deed free from illusions. The superior person, the leader, knows that all political and historical ideas are myths. He himself is entirely emancipated from them, but he values them—and this is the obverse side of his attitude—because they are " derivations " (in Pareto's

from Pirou, Gaëtan, *Georges Sorel* (1847–1922), Paris (Marcel Rivière), 1927, p. 53.   Cf. also the review by Ernst Posse in *Archiv für die Geschichte des Sozialismus und der Arbeiterbewegung*, vol. 13, pp. 431 ff.

[1] Cf. the essay by Ziegler, H. O., " Ideologienlehre " in *Archiv für Sozialwissenschaft und Sozialpolitik*, 1927, vol. 57, pp. 657 ff. This author undertakes from the point of view of Pareto, Sorel, etc., to demolish the " myth of history ".   He denies that history contains any ascertainable coherence and points out various contemporary currents of thought which also affirm this unhistorical approach.   Mussolini expressed the same thought in political-rhetorical form : " We are not hysterical women fearfully awaiting what the future will bring.   We are not waiting for the destiny and revelation of history " (loc. cit., p. 129) and further— " We do not believe that history repeats itself, that it follows a prescribed route."

sense) which stimulate enthusiastic feelings and set in motion
irrational " residues " in men, and are the only forces that lead
to political activity.[1] This is a translation into practice of what
Sorel and Pareto [2] formulated in their theories of the myth and
which resulted in their theory of the role of the *élites* and advance
guards.

The profound scepticism towards science and especially cultural
sciences which arises from the intuitional approach is not difficult
to understand. Whereas Marxism placed an almost religious
faith in science, Pareto saw in it only a formal social mechanics.
In fascism we see the sober scepticism of this representative
of the late bourgeois epoch combined with the self-confidence
of a movement still in its youth. Pareto's scepticism towards
the knowable is maintained intact, but is supplemented by a faith
in the deed as such and in its own vitality.[3]

When everything which is peculiarly historical is treated as
inaccessible to science, all that remains for scientific research
is the exploration of that most general stratum of regularities
which are the same for all men and for all times. Apart from
social mechanics, social psychology alone is recognized. The
knowledge of social psychology is of value to the leaders purely
as a technique for manipulating the masses. This primitive
deep-lying stratum of man's psyche is alike in all men whether
we deal with the men of to-day, or of ancient Rome, or of the
Renaissance.

We find here that this intuitionism has suddenly fused with
the quest of the contemporary bourgeoisie for general laws. The
result was the gradual elimination from positivism, as represented
by Comte for instance, of all traces of a philosophy of history
in order to build a generalizing sociology. On the other hand, the
beginnings of the conception of ideology which marks the theory
of useful myths may be traced largely to Marxism. There are,
nevertheless, upon closer examination essential differences.

Marxism, too, raises the issue of ideology in the sense of the
" tissue of lies ", the " mystifications ", the " fictions " which

[1] Cf. Sorel, G., *Réflexions sur la violence* (Paris, 1921), chap. 4, pp. 167 ff.
[2] A concise statement of Pareto's sociological views may be found in
Bousquet's *Précis de sociologie d'après Vilfredo Pareto* (Paris, 1925).
[3] Mussolini, in one of his speeches, said : " We have created a myth.
This myth is a faith, a noble enthusiasm. It does not have to be a reality [!],
it is an impulse and a hope, belief, and courage. Our myth is the nation,
the great nation which we wish to make into a concrete reality." (Quoted
from Carl Schmitt, *Die geistesgeschichtliche Lage des heutigen Parlamentarismus*, p. 89.)

it seeks to expose. It does not, however, bring every attempt at an interpretation of history into this category but only those to which it is in opposition. Not every type of thought is labelled " ideology ". Only social strata who have need for disguises and who, from their historical and social situation will not and cannot perceive the true interrelations as they actually exist, necessarily fall victims to these deceptive experiences. But every idea, even a correct one, through the very fact that it can be conceived, appears to be related to a certain historical-social situation. The fact that all thought is related to a certain historical-social situation does not, however, rob it of all possibility of attaining the truth. The intuitional approach on the other hand, which so repeatedly asserts itself in fascist theory, conceives of knowledge and rationalizability as somewhat uncertain and of ideas as of altogether secondary significance.[1] Only a limited knowledge about history or politics is possible—namely that which is contained in the social mechanics and social psychology referred to above.

For fascism, the Marxian idea of history as a structural integration of economic and social forces in the final analysis is also merely a myth. Just as the character of the historical process is, in the course of time, disintegrated, so the class conception of society is rejected too. There is no proletariat—there are only proletariats.[2] It is characteristic of this type of thought and this mode of life that history dissolves itself into a number of transitory situations in which two factors are decisive ; on the one hand, the *élan* of the great leader and of the vanguard or *élites* and on the other the mastery of the only type of knowledge which it is believed possible to obtain concerning the psychology of the masses and the technique of their manipulation. Politics is then possible as a science only in a limited sense—in so far, namely, as it clears the way for action.

It does this in a twofold manner : first, by destroying all the illusions which make us see history as a process ; and, secondly, by reckoning with and observing the mass-mind, especially its power-impulses and their functioning. Now to a great extent this mass psyche does, in fact, follow timeless laws because it itself stands outside the course of historical development. By

[1] " Temperaments divide men more than ideas." Mussolini, op. cit., p. 55.
[2] Cf. Beckerath, E. v., op. cit., p. 142. Also Mussolini, op. cit., p. 96.

way of contrast, the historical character of the social psyche is perceptible only to groups and persons occupying a definite position in the historical social structure.

In the final analysis, this theory of politics has its roots in Machiavelli, who already laid down its fundamental tenets. The idea of *virtù* anticipates the *élan* of the great leader. A disillusioning realism which destroys all idols, and constant recourse to a technique for the psychic manipulation of the deeply despised masses, are also to be found in his writings, even though they may differ in detail from the fascist conceptions. Finally, the tendency to deny that there is a plan in history and the espousal of the theory of direct intervention of the deed are likewise anticipated. Even the bourgeoisie has often made room in its theory for this doctrine concerning political technique and placed it, as Stahl quite rightly saw, alongside the idea of natural law, which served a normative function,[1] without, however, connecting the two. The more bourgeois ideals and the corresponding view of history were in part realized and in part disintegrated by disillusionment through the accession to power of the bourgeoisie, the more this rational calculation, without any consideration for the historical setting of facts, was recognized as the only form of political knowledge. In the most recent period, this totally detached political technique became associated with activism and intuitionism which denied the intelligibility of history. It became the ideology of those groups who prefer a direct, explosive collision with history to a gradual evolutionary change. This attitude takes many forms—appearing first in the anarchism of Bakunin and Proudhon, then in the Sorelien syndicalism, and finally in the fascism of Mussolini.[2]

From a sociological point of view this is the ideology of " putschist " groups led by intellectuals who are outsiders to the liberal-bourgeois and socialist stratum of leaders, and who hope to seize power by exploiting the crises which constantly beset modern society in its period of transformation. This period of transformation, whether it leads to socialism or to a capitalistically planned economy, is characterized by the fact that it offers intermittent opportunities for the use of putschist tactics. In the degree that it contains within itself the irrational factors

[1] Cf. Stahl, F. J., *Die Philosophie des Rechts*, vol. i, 4th ed., book 4, chap. 1, " Die neuere Politik."
[2] Cf. Schmitt, *Parlamentarismus*, ch. 4.

of modern social and economic life, it attracts the explosive irrational elements in the modern mind.

The correctness of the interpretation of this ideology as the expression of a certain social stratum is proved by the fact that historical interpretations made from this point of view are oriented towards the irrational sphere referred to above. Being psychologically and socially situated at a point from which they can discern only the unordered and unrationalized in the development of society, the structural development and the integrated framework of society remain completely hidden from their view.

It is almost possible to establish a sociological correlation between the type of thinking that appeals to organic or organized groups and a consistently systematic interpretation of history. On the other hand, a deep affinity exists between socially uprooted and loosely integrated groups and an a-historical intuitionism. The more organized and organic groups are exposed to disintegration, the more they tend to lose the sense for the consistently ordered conception of history, and the more sensitive they become to the imponderable and the fortuitous. As spontaneously organized putschist groups become more stable they also become more hospitable to long range views of history and to an ordered view of society. Although historical complications often enter into the process, this scheme should be kept in mind because it delineates tendencies and offers fruitful hypotheses. A class or similar organic group never sees history as made up of transitory disconnected incidents ; this is possible only for spontaneous groups which arise within them. Even the unhistorical moment of which activism conceives and which it hopes to seize upon is actually torn out of its wider historical context. The concept of practice in this mode of thought is likewise an integral part of the putschist technique, while socially more integrated groups, even when in opposition to the existing order, conceive of action as a continuous movement toward the realization of their ends.[1]

The contrast between the *élan* of great leaders and *élites* on the one hand and the blind herd on the other reveals the marks of an

---

[1] Mussolini himself speaks convincingly concerning the change which the putschist undergoes after attaining power. " It is incredible how a roving, free-lance soldier can change when he becomes a deputy or a town official. He acquires another face. He begins to appreciate that municipal budgets must be studied, and cannot be stormed." (Op. cit., p. 166.)

ideology characteristic of intellectuals who are more intent on providing justifications for themselves than on winning support from the outside.   It is a counter-ideology to the pretensions of a leadership which conceives itself to be an organ expressing the interests of broad social strata.   This is exemplified by the stratum of conservative leaders who regarded themselves as the organ of the " people ",[1] by the liberals who conceived of themselves as the embodiment of the spirit of the age (*Zeitgeist*), and by the socialists and communists who think of themselves as the agents of a class-conscious proletariat.

From this difference in methods of self-justification, it is possible to see that groups operating with the leader-mass dichotomy are ascendant *élites* which are still socially unattached, so to speak, and have yet to create a social position for themselves. They are not primarily interested in overthrowing, reforming, or preserving the social structure—their chief concern is to supplant the existing dominant *élites* by others.   It is no accident that the one group regards history as a circulation of *élites*, while for the others, it is a transformation of the historical-social structure. Each gets to see primarily only that aspect of the social and historical totality towards which it is oriented by its purpose.

In the process of transformation of modern society, there are, as has already been mentioned, periods during which the mechanisms which have been devised by the bourgeoisie for carrying on the class struggle (e.g. parliamentarianism) prove insufficient.   There are periods when the evolutionary course fails for the time being and crises become acute. Class relations and class stratification become strained and distorted.   The class-consciousness of the conflicting groups becomes confused. In such periods it is easy for transitory formations to emerge, and the mass comes into existence, individuals having lost or forgotten their class orientations.   At such moments a dictatorship becomes possible.   The fascist view of history and its intuitional approach which serves as a preparation for immediate action have changed what is no more than a partial situation into a total view of society.

With the restoration of equilibrium following the crisis, the organized, historical-social forces again become effective. Even if the *élite* which has come to the top in the crisis is able

---

[1] Savigny in this sense created the fiction for evolutionary conservatism that the jurists occupied a special status as the representatives of the folk spirit.   (*Vom Beruf unserer Zeit zur Gesetzgebung und Rechtswissenschaft*, Freiburg, 1892, p. 7.)

to adjust itself well to the new situation, the dynamic forces of social life nevertheless reassert themselves in the old way. It is not that the social structure has changed, but rather that there has been a reshuffling—a shift in personnel among the various social classes within the frame of the social process which continues to evolve. An example of such a dictatorship has, with certain modifications, already been witnessed in modern history in the case of Napoleon. Historically this signified nothing more than the rise of certain *élites*.   Sociologically it was an indication of the triumph of the ascendant bourgeoisie which knew how to exploit Napoleonic imperialism for its own purposes.

It may be that those elements of the mind which have not as yet been rationalized become crystallized ever anew in a more stable social structure. It may be, too, that the position which underlies this irrationalistic philosophy is inadequate to comprehend the broad trends of historical and social development. None the less the existence of these short-lived explosions directs attention to the irrational depths which have not as yet been comprehended and which are incomprehensible by ordinary historical methods.   That which has not yet been rationalized here joins with the non-historical and with those elements in life which cannot be reduced to historical categories.   We are given a glimpse of a realm which up to the present appears to have remained unchanging.   It includes the blind biological instincts which in their eternal sameness underlie every historical event.   These forces can be mastered externally by a technique, but can never reach the level of meaning and can never be internally understood.   Besides this sub-historical biological element a spiritual, transcendental element is also to be found in this sphere.   It is of this element which is not fully embodied in history, and which, as something unhistorical and alien to our thought, eludes understanding, that the mystics spoke. Although the fascists do not mention it, it must nevertheless rank as the other great challenge to the historical rationalism.

All that has become intelligible, understandable, rationalized, organized, structuralized, artistically, and otherwise formed, and consequently everything historical seems in fact to lie between these two extreme poles. If we attempt to view the interrelations of phenomena from this middle ground, we never get to see what lies above and below history. If, on the other hand, we stand at either of these irrational, extreme poles, we completely lose sight of historical reality in its concreteness.

The attractions of the fascist treatment of the problem of the relations between theory and practice lie in its designation of all thought as illusion. Political thought may be of value in arousing enthusiasm for action, but as a means for scientific comprehension of the field of " politics " which involves the prognostication of the future it is useless. It seems nothing less than remarkable that man, living in the blinding glare of the irrational, is still able to command from instance to instance the empirical knowledge necessary to carry on his everyday life. Sorel once remarked apropos of this : " We know that the social myths do not prevent men from being able to take advantage of all the observations made in the course of everyday life, nor do they interfere with their execution of their regular tasks." In a footnote he added : " It has often been noted that American and English sectarians, whose religious exaltation is sustained by apocalyptic myths, are none the less in many cases very practical people." [1] Thus man can act despite the fact that he thinks.

It has often been insisted that even Leninism contains a tinge of fascism. But it would be misleading to overlook the differences in emphasizing the similarities. The common element in the two views is confined merely to the activity of aggressive minorities. Only because Leninism was originally the theory of a minority uncompromisingly determined to seize power by revolutionary means did the theory of the significance of leading groups and of their decisive energy come to the fore. But this theory never took flight into a complete irrationalism. The Bolshevist group was only an active minority within a class movement of an increasingly self-conscious proletariat so that the irrational activistic aspects of its doctrines were constantly supported by the assumption of the rational intelligibility of the historical process.

The a-historical spirit of fascism can be derived in part from the spirit of a bourgeoisie already in power. A class which has already risen in the social scale tends to conceive of history in terms of unrelated, isolated events. Historical events appear as a process only as long as the class which views these events still expects something from it.   Only such expectations can give rise to utopias on the one hand, and concepts of process on the other. Success in the class struggle, however, does away with the utopian element, and forces long range views into the background the better to devote its powers to its immediate tasks. The

[1] Sorel, op. cit., p. 177.

L

consequence is that in place of a view of the whole which formerly took account of tendencies and total structures, there appears a picture of the world composed of mere immediate events and discrete facts. The idea of a " process " and of the structural intelligibility of history becomes a mere myth.

Fascism finds itself serenely able to take over this bourgeois repudiation of history as a structure and process without any inconvenience, since fascism itself is the exponent of bourgeois groups. It accordingly has no intention of replacing the present social order by another, but only of substituting one ruling group for another within the existing class arrangements.[1] The chances for a fascist victory as well as for the justification of its historical theory depend upon the arrival of junctures in which a crisis so profoundly disorganizes the capitalist-bourgeois order, that the more evolutionary means of carrying on the conflict of interests no longer suffice. At moments like these, the chances for power are with him who knows how to utilize the moment with the necessary energy by stimulating active minorities to attack, thus seizing power.

3. Synthesis of the Various Perspectives as a Problem of Political Sociology

In the preceding pages we attempted to show concretely how one and the same problem, namely the relation between theory and practice, took a different form in accordance with the differing political positions from which it was approached. What holds true for this basic question of any scientific politics is valid also for all other specific problems. It could be shown in all cases that not only do fundamental orientations, evaluations, and the content of ideas differ but that the manner of stating a problem, the sort of approach made, and even the categories in which experiences are subsumed, collected, and ordered vary according to the social position of the observer.

If the course of political struggles thus far has decisively shown that there is an intimate relationship between the nature of political decisions and intellectual perspective, then it would seem to follow that a science of politics is impossible. But it is

[1] As regards Mussolini's attitude towards capitalism : " . . . the real history of capitalism will now begin. Capitalism is not just a system of oppression—on the contrary it represents the choice of the fittest, equal opportunities for the most gifted, a more developed sense of individual responsibility," op. cit., p. 96.

precisely at this point, where the difficulties become most pronounced, that we reach a turning point.

It is at this juncture that two new possibilities emerge and at this stage in the formulation of the problem we see two paths which may be followed. On the one hand it is possible to say : Since in the realm of politics the only knowledge that we have is a knowledge which is limited by the position which we occupy, and since the formation of parties is structurally an ineradicable element in politics, it follows that politics can be studied only from a party viewpoint and taught only in a party school. I believe, in fact, that this will prove one road from which immediate developments will follow.

But it has become evident and promises to become more so that, owing to the complicated character of contemporary society, the traditional methods of training the next generation of political leaders, which have had hitherto a largely accidental character, are not adequate to supply the present-day politician with the requisite knowledge. The political parties will therefore find it necessary to develop their party schools with increasing care and elaborateness. Not only will they provide the factual knowledge which will enable prospective political leaders to formulate factual judgments concerning concrete problems, but they will also inculcate the respective points of view from which experience may be organized and mastered.

Every political point of view implies at the same time more than the mere affirmation or rejection of an indisputable set of facts. It implies as well a rather comprehensive *Weltanschauung*. The significance that political leaders attach to the latter is shown by the efforts of all parties to mould the thinking of the masses, not only from a party standpoint, but also from the point of view of a *Weltanschauung*. Political pedagogy signifies the trans-mission of a particular attitude towards the world which will permeate all aspects of life. Political education to-day signifies further a definite conception of history, a certain mode of inter-preting events, and a tendency to seek a philosophical orientation in a definite manner.

This cleavage in modes of thought and *Weltanschauungen* and this increasing differentiation according to political positions has been going on with an increasing intensity since the beginning of the nineteenth century. The formation of party schools will accentuate this tendency, and carry it to its logical conclusion.

But the formation of party schools and the development

of party theories is only one of the inevitable consequences of the present situation. It is one which will appeal to those who, because they occupy an extreme position in the social order, must cling to their partisanship, must conceive of antagonisms as absolutes, and suppress any conception of the whole.

The present situation provides still another possibility. It rests, so to speak, on the reverse side of the fundamentally partisan character of political orientation. This alternative, which is at least as important as the other, consists in the following : not only the necessary partisan character of every form of political knowledge is recognized, but also the peculiar character of each variety. It has become incontrovertibly clear to-day that all knowledge which is either political or which involves a world-view, is inevitably partisan. The fragmentary character of all knowledge is clearly recognizable. But this implies the possibility of an integration of many mutually complementary points of view into a comprehensive whole.

Just because to-day we are in a position to see with increasing clarity that mutually opposing views and theories are not infinite in number and are not products of arbitrary will but are mutually complementary and derive from specific social situations, politics as a science is for the first time possible. The present structure of society makes possible a political science which will not be merely a party science, but a science of the whole. Political sociology, as the science which comprehends the whole political sphere, thus attains the stage of realization.

With this there comes the demand for an institution with a broader base than a party school where this science of the political totality may be pursued. Before going into the possibility and structure of this type of investigation, it is necessary to establish more firmly the thesis that each particular point of view needs to be complemented by all the others. Let us recall the instance which we used to illustrate the partisan setting of every problem.

We found that only certain limited aspects and areas of historical and political reality reveal themselves to each of the various parties. The bureaucrat restricted his range of vision to the stabilized part of the life of the state, historical conservatism could see only the regions in which the silently working *Volksgeist* was still operating, in which as in the realm of custom and usage, in religious and cultural association organic and not organized forces were at work. Historical conservatism also was aware that there was a place for a peculiar type of rationality in this sphere of organic forces: it had to decipher the inherent tendencies of growth.   Even though the one-sidedness of historical conservatism consisted in the exaggeration of the significance of the irrational elements in the mind and of the irrational social forces corresponding to it in social-historical reality it did nevertheless bring out an important point which could not have been perceived from another standpoint.   The same is true of the remaining points of view.   Bourgeois-democratic thought both discovered and developed the possibility of a rational means of carrying on the conflict of interests in society which will retain its reality and function in modern life as long as peaceful methods of class conflict are possible.

The development of this approach to political problems was an historical and lasting achievement of the bourgeoisie, and its value may be appreciated even though the one-sidedness of its intellectualism has been completely laid bare.   The bourgeois mind had a vital social interest in concealing from itself, by means of this intellectualism, the limits of its own rationalization.   Hence it acted as if real conflicts could be fully settled by discussion.   It did not realize, however, that closely connected with the realm of politics there arose a new kind of thinking in which theory could not be separated from practice nor thought from intent.

Nowhere is the mutually complementary character of socially-politically determined partial views more clearly visible than here.   For here it becomes once more apparent that socialist thought begins at that point where bourgeois-democratic thought reaches its limits, and that it threw new light on just those phenomena which its predecessors, because of the intimate connection with their own interests, had left in the dark.   To Marxism belongs the credit for discovering that politics does not consist merely in parliamentary parties and the discussions they carry on, and that these, in whatever concrete form they appear, are only surface expression of deeper-lying economic and social situations which can be made intelligible to a large extent through a new mode of thought.   These discoveries signalize the raising of the discussion to a higher level from which a more extensive and more inclusive view of history and a clearer conception of what actually constitutes the domain of politics can be obtained.   The discovery of the phenomenon of ideology is structurally closely bound up with this discovery.

Although quite one-sided, it represents the first attempt to define the position of socially bound thought as over against " pure theory ".

Finally, to return to the last antithesis, whereas Marxism focussed its attention too sharply on and overemphasized the purely structural foundation of the political and historical realm, fascism turned its attention to the amorphous aspects of life, to those " moments " in critical situations which are still present and still have significance, in which class forces become disjointed and confused, when the actions of men, acting as members of transitory masses, assume significance, and when the outcome entirely depends on the vanguards and their leaders who are dominating the situation at the moment. But here, too, it would be overemphasis of a single phase of historical reality to regard these eventualities, even though they are of frequent occurrence, as the essence of historical reality. The divergence of political theories is accounted for mainly by the fact that the different positions and social vantage points as they emerge in the stream of social life enable each one from its particular point in the stream to recognize the stream itself. Thus, at different times, different elementary social interests emerge and accordingly different objects of attention in the total structure are illuminated and viewed as if they were the only ones that existed.

All points of view in politics are but partial points of view because historical totality is always too comprehensive to be grasped by any one of the individual points of view which emerge out of it. Since, however, all these points of view emerge out of the same social and historical current, and since their partiality exists in the matrix of an emerging whole, it is possible to see them in juxtaposition, and their synthesis becomes a problem which must continually be reformulated and resolved. The continuously revised and renewed synthesis of the existing particular viewpoints becomes all the more possible because the attempts at synthesis have no less a tradition than has the knowledge founded upon partisanship. Did not Hegel, coming at the end of a relatively closed epoch, attempt to synthesize in his own work the tendencies which hitherto had developed independently ? Even though these syntheses time and again turned out to be partial syntheses, and disintegrated in the course of subsequent development, producing, e.g., left and right Hegelianism, though they were, nevertheless, not absolute but relative syntheses, as such they pointed in a very promising direction.

A demand for an absolute, permanent synthesis would, as far as we are concerned, mean a relapse into the static world view of intellectualism. In a realm in which everything is in the process of becoming, the only adequate synthesis would be a dynamic one, which is reformulated from time to time. There is still the necessity, however, to solve one of the most important problems that can be posited, namely, that of furnishing the most comprehensive view of the whole which is attainable at a given time.

Attempts at synthesis do not come into being unrelated to one another, because each synthesis prepares the road for the next by summarizing the forces and views of its time. A certain progress towards an absolute synthesis in the utopian sense may be noted in that each synthesis attempts to arrive at a wider perspective than the previous one, and that the later ones incorporate the results of those that have gone before.

At this stage of the discussion two difficulties arise even in connection with the relative synthesis.

The first comes from the fact that we can no longer conceive of the partiality of a point of view as merely being a matter of degree. If the cleavage in political and philosophical perceptions consisted merely in the fact that each was concerned with another side or section of the whole, that each illuminated only a particular segment of historical events, an additive synthesis would be possible without further ado. All that would be necessary would be to add up these partial truths and to join them into a whole.

But this simplified conception is no longer tenable when we have seen that the determination of particular viewpoints by their situations is based not only on the selection of subject-matter, but also on the divergence in aspects and in ways of setting the problem, and finally in the divergence of categorical apparatus and principles of organization. The question then is this : is it possible for different styles of thought (by which we mean the differences in modes of thinking just described) to be fused with one another and to undergo synthesis ? The course of historical development shows that such a synthesis is possible. Every concrete analysis of thinking which proceeds sociologically and seeks to reveal the historical succession of thought-styles indicates that styles of thought undergo uninterrupted fusion and interpenetration.

Moreover, syntheses in thought-styles are not made only by those who are primarily synthesists, and who more or less consciously attempt to comprehend a whole epoch in their thinking (as e.g. Hegel). They are achieved also by contending groups in so far as they try to unify and reconcile at least all those conflicting currents which they encounter in their own limited sphere. Thus Stahl essayed to bring together in conservatism all the hitherto existing contributory tendencies of thought, as, for example, connecting historicism with theism. Marx devoted himself to the fusion of the liberal-bourgeois generalizing tendency in thinking with Hegelian historicism, which itself was of conservative origin. It is clear then that not merely the contents of thought but also the basis of thought itself is subject to synthesis. This synthesis of hitherto separately developing thought-styles seems to be all the more necessary, since thinking must constantly aim to broaden the capacity of its categorical formal scope if it is to master the problems which daily grow in number and difficulty. If even those whose standpoints are party-bound are finding it necessary to have a broader perspective, this tendency should be all the more pronounced among those, who from the beginning have sought the most inclusive possible understanding of the totality.

4. The Sociological Problem of the "Intelligentsia"

The second difficulty arising at the present stage of the problem is this : How are we to conceive of the social and political bearers of whatever synthesis there is ? What political interest will undertake the problem of synthesis as its task and who will strive to realize it in society ?

Just as at an earlier period we should have slipped back into a static intellectualism if instead of aiming at a dynamic relative synthesis we had leaped into a super-temporal absolute one, similarly here we are in danger of losing sight of the hitherto constantly emphasized interest-bound nature of political thought and of assuming that the synthesis will come from a source outside the political arena. If it be once granted that political thought is always bound up with a position in the social order, it is only consistent to suppose that the tendency towards a total synthesis must be embodied in the will of some social group.

And indeed a glance at the history of political thought shows that the exponents of synthesis have always represented definite social strata, mainly classes who feel threatened from above and below and who, out of social necessity, seek a middle way out. But this search for a compromise from the very beginning assumes both a static as well as dynamic form.   The social position of the group with which the carriers of the synthesis are affiliated determines largely which of these two alternatives is to be emphasized.

The static form of mediation of the extremes was attempted first by the victorious bourgeoisie, especially in the period of the bourgeois monarchy in France, where it was expressed in the principle of the *juste milieu*.   This catch-phrase, however, is rather a caricature of a true synthesis than a solution of it, which can only be a dynamic one.   For that reason it may serve to show what errors a solution must avoid.

A true synthesis is not an arithmetic average of all the diverse aspirations of the existing groups in society.   If it were such, it would tend merely to stabilize the *status quo* to the advantage of those who have just acceded to power and who wish to protect their gains from the attacks of the " right " as well as the " left ". On the contrary a valid synthesis must be based on a political position which will constitute a progressive development in the sense that it will retain and utilize much of the accumulated cultural acquisitions and social energies of the previous epoch. At the same time the new order must permeate the broadest ranges of social life, must take natural root in society in order to bring its transforming power into play.   This position calls for a peculiar alertness towards the historical reality of the present.   The spatial " here " and the temporal " now " in every situation must be considered in the historical and social sense and must always be kept in mind in order to determine from case to case what is no longer necessary and what is not yet possible.

Such an experimental outlook, unceasingly sensitive to the dynamic nature of society and to its wholeness, is not likely to be developed by a class occupying a middle position but only by a relatively classless stratum which is not too firmly situated in the social order.   The study of history with reference to this question will yield a rather pregnant suggestion.

This unanchored, *relatively* classless stratum is, to use Alfred Weber's terminology, the " socially unattached intelligentsia " (*freischwebende Intelligenz*). It is impossible in this connection to give even the sketchiest outline of the difficult sociological problem raised by the existence of the intellectual. But the problems we are considering could not be adequately formulated, much less solved, without touching upon certain phases of the position of the intellectuals. A sociology which is oriented only with reference to social-economic classes will never adequately understand this phenomenon. According to this theory, the intellectuals constitute either a class or at least an appendage to a class. Thus it might describe correctly certain determinants and components of this unattached social body, but never the essential quality of the whole. It is, of course, true that a large body of our intellectuals come from rentier strata, whose income is derived directly or indirectly from rents and interest on investments. But for that matter certain groups of the officials and the so-called liberal professions are also members of the intelligentsia. A closer examination, however, of the social basis of these strata will show them to be less clearly identified with one class than those who participate more directly in the economic process.

If this sociological cross-section is completed by an historical view, further heterogeneity among the intellectuals will be disclosed. Changes in class relationships at different times affect some of these groups favourably, others unfavourably. Consequently it cannot be maintained that they are homogeneously determined. Although they are too differentiated to be regarded as a single class, there is, however, one unifying sociological bond between all groups of intellectuals, namely, education, which binds them together in a striking way. Participation in a common educational heritage progressively tends to suppress differences of birth, status, profession, and wealth, and to unite the individual educated people on the basis of the education they have received.

In my opinion nothing could be more wrong than to misinterpret this view and maintain that the class and status ties of the individual disappear completely by virtue of this. It is, however, peculiarly characteristic of this new basis of association that it preserves the multiplicity of the component elements in all their variety by creating a homogeneous medium within which the conflicting parties can measure their strength. Modern education from its inception is a living struggle, a replica, on a small scale of the conflicting purposes and tendencies which rage in society at large. Accordingly the educated man, as concerns his intellectual horizon, is determined in a variety of ways. This acquired educational heritage subjects him to the influence of opposing tendencies in social reality, while the person who is not oriented toward the whole through his education, but rather participates directly in the social process of production, merely tends to absorb the *Weltanschauung* of that particular group and to act exclusively under the influence of the conditions imposed by his immediate social situation.

One of the most impressive facts about modern life is that in it, unlike preceding cultures, intellectual activity is not carried on exclusively by a socially rigidly defined class, such as a priesthood, but rather by a social stratum which is to a large degree unattached to any social class and which is recruited from an increasingly inclusive area of social life. This sociological fact determines essentially the uniqueness of the modern mind, which is characteristically not based upon the authority of a priesthood, which is not closed and finished, but which is rather dynamic, elastic, in a constant state of flux, and perpetually confronted by new problems. Even humanism was already largely the expression of such a more or less socially emancipated stratum, and where the nobility became the bearer of culture it broke through the fixedness of a class-bound mentality in many respects. But not until we come to the period of bourgeois ascendency does the level of cultural life become increasingly detached from a given class.

The modern bourgeoisie had from the beginning a twofold social root—on the one hand the owners of capital, on the other those individuals whose only capital consisted in their education. It was common therefore to speak of the propertied and educated class, the educated element being, however, by no means ideologically in agreement with the property-owning element.[1]

There arises, then, in the midst of this society, which is being deeply divided by class cleavages, a stratum, which a sociology oriented solely in terms of class either can only slightly comprehend. Nevertheless, the specific social position of this stratum can be quite adequately characterized. Although situated between classes it does not form a middle class. Not, of course, that it is suspended in a vacuum into which social

---

[1] Cf. Fr. Brüggemann, "Der Kampf um die bürgerliche Welt- und Lebensanschauung in der deutschen Literatur des 18. Jahrhunderts," *Deutsche Vierteljahrsschrift für Literaturwissenschaft und Geistesgeschichte,* iii (Halle, 1925), pp. 94 ff. This affords a good treatment of the periodic recrudescence of the supra-bourgeois element in the bourgeois literary circles of the eighteenth century.

interests do not penetrate; on the contrary, it subsumes in itself all those interests with which social life is permeated. With the increase in the number and variety of the classes and strata from which the individual groups of intellectuals are recruited, there comes greater multiformity and contrast in the tendencies operating on the intellectual level which ties them to one another. The individual, then, more or less takes a part in the mass of mutually conflicting tendencies.

While those who participate directly in the process of production—the worker and the entrepreneur—being bound to a particular class and mode of life, have their outlooks and activities directly and exclusively determined by their specific social situations, the intellectuals, besides undoubtedly bearing the imprint of their specific class affinity, are also determined in their outlook by this intellectual medium which contains all those contradictory points of view. This social situation always provided the potential energy which enabled the more outstanding intellectuals to develop the social sensibility that was essential for becoming attuned to the dynamically conflicting forces. Every point of view was examined constantly as to its relevance to the present situation. Furthermore, precisely through the cultural attachments of this group, there was achieved such an intimate grasp of the total situation, that the tendency towards a dynamic synthesis constantly reappeared, despite the temporary distortions with which we have yet to deal.

Hitherto, the negative side of the " unattachedness " of the intellectuals, their social instability, and the predominantly deliberate character of their mentality has been emphasized almost exclusively. It was especially the politically extreme groups who, demanding a definite declaration of sympathies, branded this as " characterlessness ". It remains to be asked, however, whether in the political sphere, a decision in favour of a dynamic mediation may not be just as much a decision as the ruthless espousal of yesterday's theories or the one-sided emphasis on to-morrow's.

There are two courses of action which the unattached intellectuals have actually taken as ways out of this middle-of-the-road position : first, what amounts to a largely voluntary affiliation with one or the other of the various antagonistic classes ; second, scrutiny of their own social moorings and the quest for the fulfilment of their mission as the predestined advocate of the intellectual interests of the whole.

As regards the first way out, unattached intellectuals are to be found in the course of history in all camps. Thus they always furnished the theorists for the conservatives who themselves because of their own social stability could only with difficulty be brought to theoretical self-consciousness. They likewise furnished the theorists for the proletariat which, because of its social conditions, lacked the prerequisites for the acquisition of the knowledge necessary for modern political conflict. Their affiliation with the liberal bourgeoisie has already been discussed.

This ability to attach themselves to classes to which they originally did not belong, was possible for intellectuals because they could adapt themselves to any viewpoint and because they and they alone were in a position to choose their affiliation, while those who were immediately bound by class affiliations were only in rare exceptions able to transcend the boundaries of their class outlook. This voluntary decision to join in the political struggles of a certain class did indeed unite them with the particular class during the struggle, but it did not free them from the distrust of the original members of that class. This distrust is only a symptom of the sociological fact that the assimilability of intellectuals into an outside class is limited by the psychic and social characteristics of their own. Sociologically this peculiarity of belonging to the intelligentsia accounts for the fact that a proletarian who becomes an intellectual is likely to change his social personality. A detailed case-study of the path taken by the intellectual confronted by this distrust would not be in place here. We wish merely to point out that the fanaticism of radicalized intellectuals should be understood in this light. It bespeaks a psychic compensation for the lack of a more fundamental integration into a class and the necessity of over-coming their own distrust as well as that of others.

One could of course condemn the path taken by individual intellectuals and their endless wavering, but our sole concern here is to explain this behaviour by means of the position of intellectuals in the whole social structure. Such social dereliction and transgression may be regarded as no more than a negative misuse of a peculiar social position. The individual, instead of focussing his energies on the positive potentialities of the situation, falls victim to the temptations potential in the situation. Nothing would be more incorrect than to base one's judgment of the function of a social stratum on the apostatic behaviour of some of its members and to fail to see that the frequent

" lack of conviction " of the intellectuals is merely the reverse side of the fact that they alone are in a position to have intellectual convictions. In the long run, history can be viewed as a series of trial and error experiments in which even the failings of men have a tentative value and in the course of which the intellectuals were those who through their homelessness in our society were the most exposed to failure. The repeated attempts to identify themselves with, as well as the continual rebuffs received from, other classes must lead eventually to a clearer conception on the part of the intellectuals of the meaning and the value of their own position in the social order.

The first way, then, out of the predicament of the intellectuals, namely, the direct affiliation with classes and parties, shows a tendency, even though it is unconscious, towards a dynamic synthesis. It was usually the class in need of intellectual development which received their support. It was primarily the conflict of intellectuals which transformed the conflict of interests into a conflict of ideas. This attempt to lift the conflict of interests to a spiritual plane has two aspects : on the one hand it meant the empty glorification of naked interests by means of the tissues of lies spun by apologists ; on the other hand, in a more positive sense, it meant the infusion of certain intellectual demands into practical politics. In return for their collaboration with parties and classes, the intellectuals were able to leave this imprint upon them. If they had no other achievement to their credit, this alone would have been a significant accomplishment. Their function is to penetrate into the ranks of the conflicting parties in order to compel them to accept their demands. This activity, viewed historically, has amply shown wherein the sociological peculiarity and the mission of this unattached social stratum lie.

The second way out of the dilemma of the intellectuals consists precisely in becoming aware of their own social position and the mission implicit in it. When this is achieved, political affiliation or opposition will be decided on the basis of a conscious orientation in society and in accordance with the demands of the intellectual life.

One of the basic tendencies in the contemporary world is the gradual awakening of class-consciousness in all classes. If this is so, it follows that even the intellectuals will arrive at a consciousness—though not a class-consciousness—of their own general social position and the problems and opportunities it

involves. This attempt to comprehend the sociological phenomenon of the intellectuals, and the attempt, on the basis of
this, to take an attitude towards politics have traditions of their
own quite as much as has the tendency to become assimilated
into other parties.

We are not concerned here with examining the possibilities
of a politics exclusively suited to intellectuals. Such an examination would probably show that the intellectuals in the present
period could not become independently politically active.   In
an epoch like our own, where class interests and positions are
becoming more sharply defined and derive their force and
direction from mass action, political conduct which seeks other
means of support would scarcely be possible. This does not
imply; however, that their particular position prevents them
from achieving things which are of indispensable significance
for the whole social process.   Most important among these
would be the discovery of the position from which a total perspective would be possible. Thus they might play the part of watch-
men in what otherwise would be a pitch-black night.   It is
questionable whether it is desirable to throw overboard all of
the opportunities which arise out of their peculiar situation.

A group whose class position is more or less definitely fixed
already has its political viewpoint decided for it.   Where this
is not so, as with the intellectuals, there is a wider area of choice
and a corresponding need for total orientation and synthesis.
This latter tendency which arises out of the position of the
intellectuals exists even though the relation between the various
groups does not lead to the formation of an integrated party.
Similarly, the intellectuals are still able to arrive at a total
orientation even when they have joined a party. Should the
capacity to acquire a broader point of view be considered merely
as a liability ? Does it not rather present a mission ? Only
he who really has the choice has an interest in seeing the whole
of the social and political structure. Only in that period of
time and that stage of investigation which is dedicated to
deliberation is the sociological and logical locus of the development of a synthetic perspective to be sought. The formation
of a decision is truly possible only under conditions of freedom
based on the possibility of choice which continues to exist even
after the decision has been made. We owe the possibility of
mutual interpenetration and understanding of existent currents
of thought to the presence of such a relatively unattached

middle stratum which is open to the constant influx of individuals from the most diverse social classes and groups with all possible points of view. Only under such conditions can the incessantly fresh and broadening synthesis, to which we have referred, arise.

Even Romanticism, because of its social position, had already included in its programme the demand for a broad, dynamic mediation (*dynamische Vermittlung*) of conflicting points of view. In the nature of the case, this demand led to a conservative perspective. The generation that followed Romanticism, however, supplanted this conservative view with a revolutionary one as being in accord with the needs of the time. The essential thing in this connection is that only in this line of development did there persist the attempt to make this mediation a living one, and to connect political decisions with a prior total orientation. To-day more than ever it is expected of such a dynamic middle group that it will strive to create a forum outside the party schools in which the perspective of and the interest in the whole is safeguarded.

It is precisely to these latent tendencies that we owe our present realization that all political interest and knowledge are necessarily partisan and particular. It is only to-day, when we have become aware of all the currents and are able to understand the whole process by which political interests and *Weltanschauungen* come into being in the light of a sociologically intelligible process, that we see the possibility of politics as science. Since it is likely, in accord with the spirit of the age, that more and more party schools will arise, it is all the more desirable that an actual forum be established whether it be in the universities or in specialized higher institutions of learning, which shall serve the pursuit of this advanced form of political science. If the party schools address themselves exclusively to those whose political decisions have been made in advance by parties, this mode of study will appeal to those whose decision remains yet to be made. Nothing is more desirable than that those intellectuals who have a background of pronounced class interests should, especially in their youth, assimilate this point of view and conception of the whole.

Even in such a school it is not to be assumed that the teachers should be partyless. It is not the object of such a school to avoid arriving at political decisions. But there is a profound difference between a teacher who, after careful deliberation, addresses his students, whose minds are not yet made up, from a point of view which has been attained by careful thinking leading to a comprehension of the total situation and a teacher who is exclusively concerned with inculcating a party outlook already firmly established.

A political sociology which aims not at inculcating a decision but prepares the way for arriving at decisions will be able to understand relationships in the political realm which have scarcely even been noticed before. Such a discipline will be especially valuable in illuminating the nature of socially bound interests. It will uncover the determining factors underlying these class judgments, disclosing thereby the manner in which collective forces are bound up with class interests, of which everyone who deals with politics must take account. Relationships like the following will be clarified : Given such and such interests, in a given juncture of events, there will follow such and such a type of thinking and such and such a view of the total social process. However, what these specific sets of interest will be depends on the specific set of traditions which, in turn, depends on the structural determinants of the social situation. Only he who is able to formulate the problem in such a manner is in a position to transmit to others a survey of the structure of the political scene, and to aid them in getting a relatively complete conception of the whole. This direction in research will give a better insight into the nature of historical and political thought and will demonstrate more clearly the relationships that always exist between conceptions of history and political points of view. Those with this approach, however, are too sophisticated politically to believe that political decisions themselves are teachable or that they can, while they are still prevailing, be arbitrarily suspended. To summarize : whatever your interests, they are your interests as a political person, but the fact that you have this or that set of interests implies also that you must do this or that to realize them, and that you must know the specific position you occupy in the whole social process.[1]

While we believe that interests and purposes cannot be taught, the investigation and communication, however, of the structural relationship between judgment and point of view, between the

---

[1] Max Weber formulated the problems of political sociology somewhat similarly, although he started from entirely different premises. His desire for impartiality in politics represents the old democratic tradition. Although his solution suffers from the assumption of the separability of theory and evaluation, his demand for the creation of a common point of departure for political analysis is a goal worthy of the greatest efforts.

M

social process and the development of interest, is possible. Those who demand of politics as a science that it teach norms and ends should consider that this demand implies actually the denial of the reality of politics. The only thing that we can demand of politics as a science is that it see reality with the eyes of acting human beings, and that it teach men, in action, to understand even their opponents in the light of their actual motives and their position in the historical-social situation. Political sociology in this sense must be conscious of its function as the fullest possible synthesis of the tendencies of an epoch. It must teach what alone is teachable, namely, structural relationships ; the judgments themselves cannot be taught but we can become more or less adequately aware of them and we can interpret them.

5. THE NATURE OF POLITICAL KNOWLEDGE

The question, whether a science of politics is possible and whether it can be taught, must, if we summarize all that we have said thus far, be answered in the affirmative. Of course our solution implies a quite different form of knowledge from one customarily conceived. Pure intellectualism would not tolerate a science which is so intimately tied up with practice.

The fact that political science in its spontaneous form does not fit into the existing framework of science, as we understand it, and that it is in contradiction with our present-day conception of science does not mean that politics is at fault. Rather it should be a stimulus to the revision of our conception of science as a whole. Even a passing glance at contemporary notions of science and its institutional organization will show that we have not been able to deal satisfactorily with theories where the science in question is closely concerned with practical problems. There is no more of a science of pedagogy than there is a scientific politics. Still, there would be nothing gained if, after having realized that we have not been able to resolve the most important problems in these branches of science, we were to dismiss what is peculiarly pedagogical and political as " arts " or " intuitive skills ". All that would be accomplished thereby would be an escape from problems which must be faced.

Actual experience shows that in teaching as well as in politics it is precisely in the course of actual conduct that specific and relevant knowledge is attainable in increasing measure, and under certain conditions communicable.   Consequently, it appears that our conception of science is much narrower than the scope of present-day knowledge ; and that attainable and communicable knowledge by no means ends at the boundaries of established present-day sciences.

If, however, it is true, that life affords possibilities of knowledge and understanding even where science plays no part, it is no solution to designate such knowledge as " prescientific " or to relegate it to the sphere of " intuition ", simply in order to preserve the purity of an arbitrary definition of " science ". On the contrary, it is above all our duty to inquire into the inner nature of these still unformulated types of knowledge and then to learn whether the horizons and conceptions of science cannot be so extended as to include these ostensibly pre-scientific areas of knowledge.

The difference between " scientific " and " pre-scientific " depends of course on what we presuppose the limits of science to be. It should be evident by now that hitherto the definition has been too narrow, and that only certain sciences, for historical reasons, have become models of what a science should be. It is, for instance, well known how modern intellectual development reflects the dominant role of mathematics. Strictly speaking, from this point of view, only what is measurable should be regarded as scientific. In this most recent epoch, the ideal of science has been mathematically and geometrically demonstrable knowledge, while everything qualitative has been admissible only as a derivative of the quantitative. Modern positivism (which has always retained its affinity with the bourgeois-liberal outlook and which has developed in its spirit) has always adhered to this ideal of science and of truth. At the most, what it added in the way of a worthy form of knowledge was the quest for general laws. In accord with this prevailing ideal the modern mind has been permeated by measurement, formalization, and systematization on the basis of fixed axioms. This was quite successful for certain strata of reality which were accessible to a formal quantitative approach, or at least subsumption under generalizations.

Pursuing this mode of investigation it became obvious that it was adapted to the scientific comprehension of a homogeneous level of subject-matter, but that this subject matter by no means exhausted the fullness of reality. This one-sidedness is particularly apparent in the cultural sciences in which, in the nature of the case, we are not so much concerned with the narrow sphere of subject-matter which can be reduced to laws as with the wealth of unique, concrete phenomena and structures which are familiar to practical men of affairs but which are not attainable through the axioms of positivistic science. The upshot of this was that the practical man dealing with concrete situations, and applying his knowledge informally, was more intelligent than the theorist who observed only a limited sphere because he was imprisoned by the presuppositions of his science. It became more and more obvious that the former had some knowledge in realms where the latter—i.e. the modern intellectual theorist—long ago ceased to have any knowledge. It follows from this that the model of modern mathematical-natural science cannot be regarded as appropriate to knowledge as a whole.

The first feature to be displaced by this modern rationalist style of thought, which was, sociologically, closely tied up with the capitalist bourgeoisie, was the interest in the qualitative. But since the fundamental tendency of modern science was analytical, and since nothing was regarded as scientific unless it had been reduced to its constituent elements, the interest in the immediate and direct perception of totalities disappeared. It is no accident that Romanticism was the first to take up those tendencies in thought which showed a renewed emphasis on the specific cognitive value of qualitative knowledge and knowledge of the whole. And Romanticism, it should be recalled, represented the modern counter-current which in Germany delivered, even in the realm of politics, the counter attack against the bourgeois-rationalistic world outlook. Similarly, it is no accident that to-day the *Gestalt* theory of perception, and the theories of morphology and characterology, etc., which constitute a scientific and methodological counter attack against positivistic methodology, are coming to the fore in an atmosphere which derives its *Weltanschauung* and political outlook from neo-romanticism.

It is not our task here to give a detailed account of the interplay between political movements and currents in scientific methodology. However, the argument up to this point shows that the intellectualistic conception of science, underlying positivism, is itself rooted in a definite *Weltanschauung* and has progressed in close connection with definite political interests.

From the standpoint of the sociology of knowledge we have not fully revealed the essential character of this style of thinking when we have indicated its analytical and quantitative tendencies. We must refer back to the political and social interests which are expressed by these methodological tenets. This will be possible only after an examination of the basic criterion of reality assumed by the exponents of this style of thought. This is contained in the thesis that nothing is regarded as " true " or " knowable " except what could be presented as universally valid and necessary—these two requirements being predicated without further ado as synonymous. It was simply assumed without further analysis that only that is necessary which is universally valid, i.e. communicable to everyone.

Making these two synonymous, however, is not necessarily correct, since it is easily possible that there are truths or correct intuitions which are accessible only to a certain personal disposition or to a definite orientation of interests of a certain group. The democratic cosmopolitanism of the ascendant bourgeoisie denied the value and the right to existence of these insights. With this, there was revealed a purely sociological component in the criterion of truth, namely, the democratic demand that these truths should be the same for everyone.

This demand for universal validity had marked consequences for the accompanying theory of knowledge. It followed therefrom that only those forms of knowledge were legitimate which touched and appealed to what is common in all human beings. The elaboration of the notion of a " consciousness in itself " is no more than a distillation of those traits in the individual human consciousness which we may assume to be the same in all men, be they Negroes or Europeans, medievals or moderns. The primary common foundation of this common consciousness was found first of all in the conceptions of time and space, and in close connection therewith, in the purely formal realm of mathematics. Here, it was felt, a platform had been erected which every man could share. And, similarly, it was felt that an economic man, a political man, etc., irrespective of time and race, could be constructed on the basis of a few axiomatic characteristics. Only what could be known by the application of these axioms was considered as knowable. Everything else was simply due to the perverse " manifoldness of the real ", concerning which " pure " theory need not worry itself. The foremost aim of this mode of thought was a purified body of generally valid knowledge which is knowable by all and communicable to all.

All knowledge which depended upon the total receptivity of men, or upon certain historical-social characteristics of men in the concrete, was suspect and was to be eliminated. Thus, in the first place, all experience was suspect which rested upon the purely personal perceptions of the individual. The repudiation of qualitative knowledge, which has already been mentioned, grew out of this. Since the sense-perception of the individual, in its concrete and unique form, is a function of the living subject as a whole, and since this sense-perception could be communicated only with difficulty, one was inclined to deny it any specific value whatsoever.

Similarly, every kind of knowledge which only certain specific historical-social groups could acquire was distrusted. Only that kind of knowledge was wanted which was free from all the influences of the subject's *Weltanschauung*. What was not noticed was that the world of the purely quantifiable and analysable was itself only discoverable on the basis of a definite *Weltanschauung*. Similarly, it was not noticed that a *Weltanschauung* is not of necessity a source of error, but often gives access to spheres of knowledge otherwise closed.

Most important, however, was the attempt to eliminate the interests and values which constitute the human element in man. In the characterization of bourgeois intellectualism, attention was directed to the endeavour to eliminate interests even from politics and to reduce political discussion to a kind of general and universal consciousness which is determined by "natural law".

Thereby the organic connection between man as an historical subject and as a member of society on the one hand and his thought on the other hand was arbitrarily severed. This constitutes the chief source of the error with which, in this context, we must first deal. It may be said for formal knowledge that it is essentially accessible to all and that its content is unaffected by the individual subject and his historical-social affiliations. But, on the other hand, it is certain that there is a wide range of subject-matter which is accessible only either to certain subjects, or in certain historical periods, and which becomes apparent through the social purposes of individuals.

An illustration of the first is that only one who loves or hates gets to see in the loved or hated object certain characteristics which are invisible to others who are merely spectators. Furthermore, there is a type of knowledge which can never be conceived within the categories of a purely contemplative consciousness-as-such, and whose first assumption is the fact that we come to know our associates only in living and acting with them, not only because it takes time to observe things, but because human beings do not have " traits " which can be viewed apart from them and which, as we are erroneously accustomed to say, " automatically come to light." We are dealing here with a dynamic process in man, in that his characteristics emerge in the course of his concrete conduct and in confrontation with actual problems. Self-consciousness itself does not arise from mere self-contemplation but only through our struggles with the world—i.e. in the course of the process in which we first become aware of ourselves.

Here self-awareness and awareness of others are inseparably intertwined with activity and interest and with the processes of social interaction. Whenever the product is isolated from the process and from the participation in the act, the most essential facts are distorted. This, however, is the fundamental feature of the kind of thinking which is oriented towards a dead nature, in that it wishes at all costs to cancel out the subjective, volitional and processual relations from active knowledge in order to arrive at pure, homogeneously co-ordinated results.

The example just cited shows a case of the situational determination of knowledge as it operates in the relationship between specific types of personalities and specific forms of knowledge. But there are also certain domains of knowledge whose accessibility is not a matter of specific personalities, but rather of certain definite historical and social pre-conditions. Certain events in history and in the psychic life of men become visible only in certain historical epochs, which through a series of collective experiences, and a concurrently developed *Weltanschauung*, open up the way to certain insights. Furthermore, to return to our original theme, there are certain phenomena the perception of which depends upon the presence of certain collective purposes which reflect the interests of specific social strata. It appears then that clear-cut and readily objectifiable knowledge is possible in so far as it is a question of grasping those elements in social reality which, to begin with, we described as settled and routinized components of social life. There does not seem to be any obstacle to the formulation of laws in this domain, since the objects of attention themselves obey a recurrent rhythm of regular sequence.

When, however, we enter the realm of politics, in which everything is in process of becoming and where the collective element in us, as knowing subjects, helps to shape the process of becoming, where thought is not contemplation from the point of view of a spectator, but rather the active participation and reshaping of the process itself, a new type of knowledge seems to emerge, namely, that in which decision and standpoint are inseparably bound up together. In these realms, there is no such thing as a purely theoretical outlook on the part of the observer. It is precisely the purposes that a man has that give him his vision, even though his interests throw only a partial and practical illumination on that segment of the total reality in which he himself is enmeshed, and towards which he is oriented by virtue of his essential social purposes.

In such cases we must never sever interest, evaluation, and *Weltanschauung* from the product of thought, and must even, in case it has already been severed, establish the relationship anew. This is the task of sociology in so far as it is the science of the political. It accepts no theoretical contention as absolutely valid in itself, but reconstructs the original standpoints, viewed from which the world appeared thus and such, and tries to understand the whole of the views derived from the various perspectives through the whole of the process.

Politics as a science in the form of a political sociology is never a closed and finished realm of knowledge which can be separated from the continuous process out of which it developed. It is always in the process of becoming and is always nevertheless bound to the stream from which it derives. It arises in the dynamic unfolding of conflicting forces. Consequently it may be built either upon quite one-sided perspectives reflecting the interrelations of events as a given political party sees them, or it may appear in its most advanced form—as a constantly renewed attempt at synthesis of all the existent perspectives aiming at a dynamic reconciliation.

It may well be that our intellectualism will repeatedly stimulate in us the longing for a point of view beyond time and history—for a " consciousness as such " out of which there arise insights independent of particular perspectives, and capable of formulation into general laws which are eternally valid. But this objective cannot be attained without doing violence to the subject-matter. If we seek a science of that which is in process of becoming, of practice and for practice, we can realize it only by discovering a new framework in which this kind of knowledge can find adequate expression.

6. THE COMMUNICABILITY OF POLITICAL KNOWLEDGE

The original impetus to research in the problem of ideology has sprung from political life itself in its most recent developments. It does not represent a science which has been conjured up out of hairsplitting, intellectualistic subtleties. We have already too many such formulations of problems and it would indeed be harmful to increase their number. On the contrary, the student of ideology is merely trying to think out a problem which people have stumbled upon in the course of their effort to orient themselves in the everyday life of society. This problem consists essentially of the inescapable necessity of understanding both oneself and one's adversary in the matrix of the social process.

It is imperative at this point to introduce some reflections concerning the external forms of such a science, its communicability, and the requirements for its transmission to coming generations. It is evident from what has already been said that, as concerns the external form of the science, that part of political science which is made up of concrete factual knowledge is not subject to the problematic considerations just mentioned. What is peculiarly problematical in politics as science and in politics proper does not begin until we reach that sphere of life in which our interests and our perceptions are closely bound up with one another, and which makes what has gone before appear in a new light.

It has been shown that here too there are relationships which can be investigated, but which, just because they are in constant flux, can be taught only if, in the case of every phase to be communicated, there is taken into account the observational position which makes these interrelations assume their definite certain character. Every view should be equated with the social position of the observer. If possible, it should be investigated in every case why the relations appear as they do from every given standpoint. We cannot emphasize too much that the social equation does not always constitute a source of error but more frequently than not brings into view certain interrelations which would otherwise not be apparent. The peculiar one-sidedness of a social position is always most apparent when this position is seen in juxtaposition to all the others. Political life, involving, as it always does, thinking which proceeds from opposite poles, is modified in the course of its own development by toning down the exaggeration due to one point of view by what is revealed through another. In every situation, it is, therefore, indispensable to have a total perspective which embraces all points of view.

The greatest danger to an adequate representation of the relationships which concern us in the political sphere proper lies, however, in the assumption on the part of the investigator of a passive, contemplative attitude which tends to destroy the actual interrelations which, as such, interest the man of politics. It should always be kept in mind that behind all scientific work (impersonal as it may seem) there are types of mentality which to a large extent influence the concrete form of the science. Let us consider for a moment a neighbouring discipline which deals theoretically with non-theoretical materials —namely the history of art. The fundamental attitude of this discipline represents a fusion of the individual attitudes of connoisseurs, collectors, philologists, and historians of ideas. The histories of art would be quite different if they were written by artists for artists or from the standpoint of the appreciative spectator. The latter situation obtains for the most part only in contemporary art criticism.

Similarly, the theorizing subject is liable to be misled in the study of politics because his own contemplative attitude tends to subordinate his politically active attitude, thus concealing fundamental relationships rather than emphasizing them and tracing out their ramifications. The fact that sciences are cultivated in academic surroundings constitutes a danger in that the attitudes adequate to the understanding of an actual sector of human experience are suppressed in the contemplative atmosphere which prevails in academic institutions. To-day we almost take it for granted that science begins when it destroys our original approach and replaces it by one which is foreign to living experience. This is the most important reason why practice cannot profit by this kind of theory. This creates a tension between theory and practice which is increasingly aggravated by modern intellectualism. Summing up the main difference between this contemplative, intellectualistic point of view and the living standpoint which is accepted in the realm of practice, we might say that the scientist always approaches his subject-matter with an ordering and schematizing tendency, whereas the practical man—in our case the political person— seeks orientation with reference to action. It is one thing to aim at a schematically ordered bird's eye view ; it is quite another thing to seek a concrete orientation for action. The desire for concrete orientation leads us to view things only in the context of the life-situations in which they occur. A schematically ordered summary tears apart the organic interconnection in order to arrive at an ordered system which, although artificially constructed, is nevertheless occasionally useful.

An illustration will further illuminate this central distinction between the schematically ordering and actively orienting attitudes. There are three possible approaches to modern political theories : first, they may be presented by means of a typology which is detached from the historical moments and the concrete social situations to which they refer. This typology ranges the theories in an indifferent sort of series, and at best attempts to discover some purely theoretical principle for differentiating between them. This sort of typology, which is to-day very much in fashion, may be called a " surface " typology, because it represents an attempt to present the manifoldness of life upon an artificially uniform level. The only sensible justification such a scheme could possibly have is that there are different ways of life, and following one or the other of these is simply a matter of choice. This offers a survey, of course, but it is a purely schematic survey. According to this scheme, one can give names to the theories and attach labels to them, but their real interconnections are thereby obscured, since the theories originally are not modes of life in general, but merely ramifications of concrete situations. A somewhat more complex form of this two-dimensional typology is that already referred to which seeks to discover a basis of differentiation upon some principle—preferably a philosophical one. Thus, for instance, Stahl,[1] the first theorist and systematizer of the German party system, classified the different political tendencies of his time into variants of two theoretical principles —the principle of legitimism and the principle of revolution. His classification offers not merely a survey of, but also an insight into, existing party-ideologies. In reducing them to a philosophical dychotomy, no doubt, he deepens our understanding. The temptation of such a philosophical deduction is that it lays an undue stress on a theoretical principle which, of course, is

[1] Stahl, *Die gegenwärtigen Parteien in Staat und Kirche* (Berlin, 1863).

present in the development of the nineteenth century, but which happens not to be decisive. Typologies of that kind create the impression that political thought represents the working out of purely theoretical possibilities.

The first mode of exposition represents that of the collector, the second that of the philosophical systematizer. What happens in both cases is that the forms of experience of contemplative types of men are arbitrarily imposed upon political reality.

A further mode of presentation of political theories is the purely historical one. This procedure does not, of course, tear theories out of the immediate historical context in which they developed in order to juxtapose them upon an abstract level, but it commits the opposite error of clinging too closely to the historical. The ideal type of historian is interested accordingly in the unique complex of causes that account for these political theories. To arrive at these, he brings into the picture all the antecedents in the history of ideas and links the theories with the unique personalities of creative individuals. As a result, he becomes so involved in the historical uniqueness of the events that any sort of general conclusions about the historical and social process are impossible. Indeed, historians have even taken pride in the thesis that nothing can be learned from history. If, on the other hand, the first two types of presentation mentioned above erred by being so far removed from concrete events that it was impossible to find one's way back from the generalizations, types, and systems into history, the last mentioned historical approach is so bound up with the immediacies of history that its results hold only for the specific concrete situations with which it has dealt.

As over against these two extremes, there is a third possibility which consists in selecting the middle road between abstract schematization on the one hand and historical immediacy on the other. It is precisely in this third path that every clear-sighted political person lives and thinks, even though he may not always be aware of it. This third course proceeds by attempting to comprehend the theories and their mutations in close relation to the collective groups and typical total situations out of which they arose and whose exponents they are. The inner connections between thought and social existence must in this case be reconstructed. It is not " consciousness in itself " which arbitrarily chooses from several possible alternatives, nor does the single individual construct an *ad hoc* theory to suit the needs

of a given single situation ; but it is rather that social groups
having a certain type of structure formulate theories corresponding to their interests as perceived by them in certain
situations. As a result, for each specific social situation there are
discovered certain modes of thinking and possibilities of orientation. It is only because these structurally conditioned, collective
forces continue to exist beyond the duration of a single historical
situation that the theories and possibilities of orientation also
carry over.   It is not until their structural situations change
and are gradually displaced by others that the need for new
theories and new orientations arises.

Only he is able to follow the course of events intelligently
who comprehends the structural alignment which underlies and
makes possible a given historical situation and event.   Those,
however, who never transcend the immediate course of historical
events, as well as those who so completely lose themselves in
abstract generalities that they never find the way back to
practical life, will never be able to follow the changing meaning
of the historical process.

Every political figure operating on this level of consciousness
which is appropriate to our present stage of intellectual development thinks—implicitly, if not explicitly—in terms of structural
situations. This type of thinking alone gives meaning and concreteness to action oriented towards some far-off goal, though
momentary decisions may well rest on momentary orientations.
Thus, he is protected against empty and schematic generalities
and is at the same time given sufficient flexibility so that he will
not be overimpressed by some single event of the past as an
inadequate model for future action.

The man who is purposefully active will never ask how some
revered leader acted in a past situation, but rather how he would
really orient himself to the present situation.   This ability to
reorient oneself anew to an ever newly forming constellation of
factors constitutes the essential practical capacity of the type
of mind which is constantly seeking orientation for action. To
awaken this capacity, to keep it alert, and to make it effective
with reference to the material at hand is the specific task of
political education.

In the exposition of political interrelationships, the purely
contemplative attitude must never be allowed to displace the
original need of the political person for active orientation.
Considering the fact that our educational procedure is oriented

primarily to the contemplative attitude, and that, in the transmission of our subject-matter, we aim more at a schematic
survey than at a concrete orientation to life, it is imperative
to determine at least a point of departure for those problems
which concern the education of future generations in the realm
of the active and of the political.

All the ramifications of the problem cannot be dealt with here.
Let it suffice to present the structural principle of the essential
interrelationships that obtain here. The forms and methods of
transmitting the social and psychological subject-matter vary
with the peculiarity of the structural foundations of the group
on which they rest.[1] A certain form of social group and a certain
pedagogical technique is suitable for artistic training, another
for scientific training. Among the various sciences, mathematical
knowledge calls for different pedagogical methods and for different
relations between teacher and pupil than does the transmission
of cultural subject-matter. The same is true for philosophical
as contrasted with political subjects, etc.

History and practical life show a constant, if unconscious,
search for more adequate educational methods in the different
fields. Life is an incessant process of training and education.
Usages, customs, and habits are formed by processes and in
situations of which we are utterly unaware. The forms of association are continuously changing; relationships between individuals,
between individuals and groups, vary from moment to moment.
In one situation we are confronted with suggestion ; then with
spontaneous participation ; then with sensitiveness to others ;
then with restraint by others, etc. It is not possible to set up here
a complete typology of the forms of communication. They
emerge and pass away in the historical process, and they can
only be understood through their living context and its structural changes, and not in a vacuum.

As a first orientation, we present two tendencies of modern
life which play a significant role in the external and internal
shaping of the coming generation. On the one hand there is the

[1] The phenomenological school in particular has sought to show, in
opposition to modern intellectualism, that there is more than one form
of knowledge. Cf. particularly Max Scheler's *Die Formen des Wissens
und die Bildung* (Bonn, 1925) ; *Die Wissensformen und die Gesellschaft*
(Leipzig, 1926); Heidegger's " Sein und Zeit ", *Jahrbuch für Philosophie
und phänomenologische Forschung*, Bd. 8. (Halle, 1927), offers, even though
indirectly, much that is valuable in this respect. However, the specific
character of political knowledge is not treated there.

tendency, in accord with modern intellectualism, to make homogeneous and to intellectualize the forms of education and of the propagation of knowledge. As a countercurrent to this, there is Romanticism, which desires the return to older and more " original " forms of education.

The meaning of this will be made clear by an illustration. For the transmission of purely classificatory knowledge, the lecture is the most suitable type of pedagogical technique. If knowledge has to be systematized, classified into types, or otherwise ordered the most adequate pedagogical form seems to consist in that peculiar sort of subordination which is evident when one listens to a lecture. The " listener ", as mere " listener ", takes " cognizance " of it. Underlying this is the assumption—implicit in the lecture itself—that purely subjective personal factors have been eliminated. Thus intellect acts upon intellect in a rarified atmosphere detached from the concrete situation. But since the subject-matter of the lecture is not concerned with sacred and authoritative texts, but with materials that are public, and subject to free and independent investigation which can be checked, discussion after the lecture is possible. This justifies the so-called seminar procedure. Here, too, the essential feature is that subjective and emotional impulses and personal relations are pushed into the background as far as possible so that abstract possibilities are considered, one over against the other, on a factual basis.

From the standpoint of subject matter, this type of pedagogical association of lecturer and audience, and the type of communication it implies, seem to be justified in the case of those sciences which Alfred Weber [1] has called " civilizational ", i.e. those forms of knowledge which are not subject to the influences of *Weltanschauung* or of personal-volitional impulses. It is problematical whether this type of communication applies to the cultural sciences and even more to those oriented towards immediate practice. It is in accord with the type of knowledge and the tendency inherent in modern intellectualism that it should set up as a model this one specific mode of association between teacher and student and this specific form of communication, and attempt to carry it over into other realms of knowledge.

The educational institutions of medieval scholasticism and perhaps even more the universities in the age of absolutism,

[1] Alfred Weber, " Prinzipielles zur Kultursoziologie," *Archiv für Sozialwissenschaft und Sozialpolitik* (1920).

whose main purpose was the training of state officials, were instrumental in the elaboration and stabilization of this type of instruction. Only the sects and conventicles which were not primarily interested in specialized technical training and for which spiritual awakening was the prerequisite for knowledge and insight, developed the tradition of other forms of human association in the pedagogical process and cultivated other modes of intellectual transmission.

In our own epoch the inadequacy of an educational system which confined itself to merely handing down and communicating knowledge to the student by the lecture system, which subordinated the " listener " to the " lecturer ", became acutely evident in those fields which we are accustomed to refer to as the " arts ". Here, too, training in organized academies has displaced the older form of student-teacher association the prototype of which was the workshop (*atelier*). None the less, the type of association characteristic of the workshop is better suited to the sort of substratum to be communicated than is training in academies. The workshop brings about a relationship of mutual participation between master and apprentice. Here nothing is systematically expounded to be " taken cognizance of " by the apprentice. All that is communicated is shown in concrete situations " as opportunities arise ", and not merely " said ". Apprentice and master work together, assist one another, and participate in common in the completion of those creative enterprises which may have originated with either one of them. The initiative is transmitted from the teacher to the pupil, and there finds a response. Along with the transmission of the technique, there goes also the transmission of the idea, the style, not by means of theoretical discussion, but in the course of creative collaborative clarification of the aim which unites them. Thus the whole person is affected, and there is a wide difference between this human relationship and the mere " taking cognizance " which is involved in the lecture system. It is not a schematic system which is taught, but always a concrete orientation (in the case of the artistic process, a feeling for form is communicated). Here, too, analogous situations repeat themselves, but they are comprehended in the light of the character and the unity of the work newly to be created.

The Romantic impulse led to an instinctive recognition of the superiority of the form of association characteristic of the workshop. It emphasized that great damage had been done to the plastic arts by the academies ; or, to say the least, that creative art existed really not because but in spite of academies. Every movement which, in a related manner, tended to shape political or journalistic pedagogy in the same pattern was viewed with alarm. In this field, too, intellectualism finds a compensatory force in Romanticism. The ascendancy of this Romantic current has, in fact, achieved practical results in a few fields such as, e.g., in the crafts—or, to take a very different sphere, in nursery schools and kindergartens. It found acceptance in all those spheres of life in which intellectualism, not as an inherent necessity arising out of the facts of the situation, but rather because of a mere formal expansionistic urge, displaced the collaborative form of relationship of the workshop which had originally grown up. But the Romantic trend reaches its limit wherever systematic knowledge is an indispensable pre-requisite of modern life. The more advanced the level of training and the more complex the form of artistic workmanship, the more questionable does the use of workshop methods become, even though upon these higher levels of activity a great many excesses may be ascribed to a needless over-rationalization. (We note here an apt structural analogy with the phenomenon of over-rationalization and over-bureaucratization of capitalistic enterprises.) Thus we are able precisely to define the limits beyond which the Romantic countercurrent is no longer justified. The academic institutionalization of instruction in the case of architects, for instance, is not to be attributed exclusively to the exaggerated intellectualism of our age, but to the factual conditions of the complexity of the technical knowledge that is essential and must be mastered. Furthermore, it is essential to recognize that the existence and the dominance of our intellectualism is not itself an intellectually premeditated and contrived phenomenon, but has arisen naturally from the organic condition of the total process of social development. Hence it is not our task to drive intellectualism from the places where it actually fulfills an organic need that has arisen in recent times, but rather merely from those spheres in which, due to its inner formal urge for expansion, it tended to apply intellectualistic methods even where more spontaneous and direct approaches are to-day still effective. The purely technical requirements of engineering can no longer be taught in workshops. It is quite possible, how-ever, where we deal with creative impulses whose form is still in process of growth, to apply those more living forms of collaborative

N

educational association which are designed to " awaken " interest and transmit insight.

A solution is no longer to be found in one or the other extreme, but only on the basis of a realistic mediation between the various conflicting currents of our time, which requires that we seek to discover exactly, in each concrete case, to what extent, in accord with the particular subject-matter, the systematizing and to what extent the personal educational procedure is to be used.

What has been said here about the teaching of the " arts " applies *mutatis mutandis*, in a very large degree, to politics. Hitherto politics as an " art " has been taught and transmitted only incidentally " as occasion arose ".

Political knowledge and skill have thus far always been passed on in an informal and spasmodic fashion. The handing down of the specifically political has been left to chance occasions. What the studio has meant to creative art and the workshop to the handicrafts, the social form of the club has meant to liberal-bourgeois politics. The club is a specific form of human association which developed quite unintentionally as a suitable medium for social selection along party lines, as a basis for achieving a political career as well as for the cultivation of collective interests. The peculiar sociological structure of the club is the key to the understanding of the most significant forms of direct and informal transmission of political knowledge, growing out of the interest of those concerned. But in this case, as in the " arts ", we note that the more original and spontaneous forms of learning and training, which rest upon chance occasions, do not suffice. Our present-day world is much too complicated, and every decision, even if it is to be based only in part upon the knowledge and training made possible by present opportunities, requires too much specialized knowledge and too broad a perspective to permit the kind of knowledge and skill which has been acquired by casual association to suffice in the long run. The need for systematic training already tends, and in the future will tend even more strongly, towards the necessity of giving to the aspiring politician or journalist a specialized training. On the other hand, there is the danger that this specialized training will overlook the essentially political element. Purely encyclopædic knowledge which does not emphasize actual conduct will not be of much use. At the same time, a problem will arise, indeed it has already arisen for those of broader vision, namely, shall the training of politicians be left without further ado to party schools ?

In this respect, party schools have a certain advantage : the inculcation of the values, corresponding to certain interests, takes place almost automatically and permeates the subject-matter on every level of presentation. The atmosphere of the club which colours the interest of the members is quite unwittingly carried over into research and teaching. The real question is whether this form of political education is the only desirable one, for, upon closer examination, it turns out to be no more than the cultivation of a given set of values and perspectives, which are dictated by the partial point of view of a given social and political stratum.

But should there not and could there not be a form of political education which presupposes a relatively free choice among alternatives, which is and should become to an even greater degree the foundation of the modern intellectual stratum ? Would we not, without further ado, be giving up a significant achievement of European history precisely in the critical moment when party machinery threatens to overwhelm us, if we did not make the attempt to strengthen those tendencies which enable us to make decisions on the basis of a prior total orientation ? Can interests be aroused only by means of indoctrination ? Are not interests which have been subjected to and have arisen out of criticism also interests, and perhaps a higher type or form of interest which should not be renounced without considerable reflection ?

One should not allow oneself to be captivated by the limited doctrinal world, the terminology and outlook of the extremist groups. One must not assume that only inculcated interests are interests, and that only revolutionary or counter-revolutionary action is truly action. Here both the extreme wings of the political movement insist on imposing their one-sided conception of practice upon us and thereby conceal what is problematical. Must it be assumed that only that is politics which is preparation for an insurrection ? Is not the continual transformation of conditions and men also action ? The significance of the revolutionary phases can be understood from the standpoint of the whole, but even when they are so understood they are only a partial function in the total social process. Is it to be assumed that there is no tradition and form of education corresponding to precisely those interests seeking to establish a dynamic equilibrium, and which are oriented to the whole ? Would it not be in the true interest of the whole to set up more centres from which radiate those political interests imbued with the vitality of a critical point of view ?

There exists the need for the kind of political education in which the historical, legal, and economic subject-matter requisite to such critical orientation, the objective technique of mass-domination, and the formation and control of public opinion can be taught. Such an education should also take account of the fact that there are spheres in which interests are unavoidably bound up with insight. What is more, the subject-matter relating to these spheres should be presented in a manner which presupposes that we are dealing with people who are still searching for solutions and who have not yet arrived at final decisions. And, as a result, it will be possible to determine where the older forms of formal-theoretical educational association, and where the more living types of political association which are oriented towards action are applicable.

Thus it seems certain that the interrelations in the specifically political sphere can be understood only in the course of discussion, the parties to which represent real forces in social life. There is no doubt, for example, that in order to develop the capacity for active orientation, the teaching procedure must concentrate on events that are immediate and actual, and in which the student has an opportunity to participate. There is no more favourable opportunity for gaining insight into the peculiar structure of the realm of politics than by grappling with one's opponents about the most vital and immediate issues because on such occasions contradictory forces and points of view existing in a given period find expression.

Those who enjoy such a capacity for observation based on active orientation will see history differently from the majority of their contemporaries. History will, accordingly, no longer be studied only from the point of view of the archivist or moralist. Historiography has already passed from modest chronicle and legend, developing further as rhetoric, work of art, and vivid pictorial representation, until it arrived at a romantic yearning for immersion in the past. It has already undergone so many transformations that to-day it can once again undergo transformation.

These modes of historical interpretation corresponded to the dominant orientations that the respective epochs had to their past. Once this new mode of active orientation to life, which seeks to discover the sociological structural relationships, passes from political life back into the realm of scholarship, the corresponding new form of historiography will develop. This new form of historiography does not imply that the importance accorded to the study of the sources and the digging in the archives will decline, nor that other forms of historiography will cease to exist. There are to-day needs which are still satisfied by pure " political history ", and others which call for " morphological " presentation. But just those impulses, which, arising out of our present mode of orientation to life, lead us to see past events as a succession of changes in the social structure are still in their beginnings. Our present-day orientation to life cannot be complete until it has appreciated its continuity with the past. When once this point of view has established itself in life, then the past, too, will become intelligible in the light of the present.

7. THREE VARIETIES OF THE SOCIOLOGY OF KNOWLEDGE

Thus far we have not been able to offer a definitive solution to our problem, but have had to content ourselves with uncovering hidden interrelations and again calling into question issues which were seemingly settled. What would it avail to receive reassuring answers concerning politics as a science as long as political thinking in no way corresponded to these answers ?

We must first of all understand that political-historical thinking produces a kind of knowledge of its own which is not pure theory, but which nevertheless embodies real insight. Likewise it must be recognized that political-historical knowledge is always partial and sees things only from certain perspectives, that it arises in connection with collective group interests, and develops in close contact with these, but that nevertheless it does offer a view of reality as seen from a specific angle. For this reason we have made a detailed historical-sociological analysis of the formulation of the problem which was intended to show that the fundamental question of the relation between theory and practice varied in accordance with whether it was seen from a bureaucratic, historistic, liberal, social-communist, or fascist angle. In order to appreciate the peculiar nature of political thought, it is necessary to have grasped the distinction between knowledge which is oriented towards action and knowledge which aims merely at classification. Finally, the peculiarity of the forms of communication of knowledge had to be shown to be relevant to the specific requirements of political education. Hence the detailed treatment of forms of exposition and pedagogy.

Only when these differences have been clearly perceived, and the consequent difficulties taken into account, can there be an adequate solution to the problem of the possibility of a science of politics. Such an analysis, however, which constantly keeps in mind that political knowledge is involved with the mode of existence and which constantly attempts to understand the forms of exposition from the social-activistic angle, is offered by the sociology of knowledge. Without the type of formulation of problems made possible by the sociology of knowledge, the innermost nature of political knowledge would not be accessible to us. The sociology of knowledge still, however, leaves open three paths of analysis. First, after having recognized that political-historical knowledge is always bound up with a mode of existence and a social position, some will be inclined, precisely because of this social determination, to deny the possibility of attaining truth and understanding. This is the answer of those who take their criteria and model of truth from other fields of knowledge, and who fail to realize that every level of reality may possibly have its own form of knowledge. Nothing could be more dangerous than such a one-sided and narrow orientation to the problem of knowledge.

If one has already examined the problem from this point of view and arrived at these conclusions, there arises the possibility of taking another approach. This consists in the attempt to assign to the sociology of knowledge the task of discovering and analysing the " social equation " present in every historical-political view. This means that the sociology of knowledge has the task of disentangling from every concretely existing bit of " knowledge " the evaluative and interest-bound element, and eliminating it as a source of error with a view to arriving at a " non-evaluative ", " supra-social ", " supra-historical " realm of " objectively " valid truth.

There is no question that this approach has its justification, for there are, doubtless, areas of political-historical knowledge in which there is an autonomous regularity which may be formulated, in large measure, independently of one's *Weltanschauung* and political position. We have seen that there is a sphere in the psychic life which can be dealt with, to a large extent, by means of mass psychology, without going into the question of subjective meaning. Similarly, there is an area of social life in which may be perceived certain general structural regularities, i.e. the most general forms of human association (" formal sociology "). Max Weber, in his *Wirtschaft und Gesellschaft*, made it his central task to work out this stratum of purely " objectively " perceivable relations, in order to arrive at such a non-evaluative objective field of sociology. Finally, even the attempts to distill a pure theory out of the sphere of political economy, free from the entanglements of one's social position and *Weltanschauung*, is another instance of the aim to distinguish sharply between " evaluation " and " factual content ".

It is not yet certain how far the separation of these two spheres can go. It is by no means impossible that there are domains in which· this can be done. The " non-evaluative ", " supra-historical ", " supra-social " character of these spheres will be fundamentally assured only after we have analysed the body of axioms or the categorical apparatus which we employ with reference to its " roots " in a *Weltanschauung*. Altogether too frequently we are inclined to accept as " objective " those categorical structures and ultimate postulates which we ourselves have unconsciously read into our experience, and which, for the sociologist of knowledge, are revealed only subsequently as the partial, historically-, and socially-conditioned axioms of a particular current of thought. Nothing is more self-evident than that precisely the forms in which we ourselves think are those whose limited nature is most difficult for us to perceive, and that only further historical and social development gives us the perspective from which we realize their particularity. On that account, even those who are striving to attain a non-evaluative sphere separable from the rest of knowledge must at least as a corrective continually search out the social equation in their thinking by some such means as the sociology of knowledge.

While the result of such a procedure cannot be predicted in advance, this much may be said : if, after the influence of political-social position upon knowledge has been accounted for there should still remain a realm of non-evaluative knowledge (not merely in the sense of freedom from partisan political judgment, but in the sense of the employment of an unambiguous and non-evaluative categorical and axiomatic apparatus)—if there should turn out to be such a sphere, it would be attainable only by taking account of all the " social equations " in thinking which are accessible to us.

We arrive then at the third alternative to which we ourselves are committed. It is the view that, at the point where what is properly political begins, the evaluative element cannot easily be separated out, at least not in the same degree as is possible in formal sociological thinking and other sorts of purely formalizing knowledge. This position will insist that the voluntaristic element has an essential significance for knowledge in the political and historical sphere proper, even though in the course of history we may observe a gradual selection of categories which more and more acquire validity for all parties. Nonetheless, though there is a *consensus ex post* [1] or an increasingly broader stratum of knowledge which is valid for all parties, we should not allow ourselves to be misled by this or to overlook the fact that at every given historical point in time there is a substantial amount of knowledge which is accessible to us only seen in social perspective. But since we do not as yet live in a period free from mundane troubles and beyond history, our problem is not how to deal with a kind of knowledge which shall be " truth in itself ", but rather how man deals with his problems of knowing, bound as he is in his knowledge by his position in time and society. If we advocate a comprehensive view of that which is not yet synthesizable into a system, we do this because we regard it as the relative optimum possibility in our present situation, and because in so doing we believe (as is always the case in history) we are taking the necessary steps preparatory to the next synthesis. But having stated this solution to the problem, we should be ready to add at once that the disposition to achieve a synthesis from the most comprehensive and most progressive point of view also has implicit in it a prior judgment, namely, our decision to arrive at a dynamic intellectual mediation. Certainly we would be the last to deny that we have made this value-judgment. Indeed, it is our main thesis that political knowledge, as long as politics conforms to the definition previously made, is impossible without some such decision, and that this decision in favour of dynamic intellectual mediation must be seen as an element in the total situation. But it makes a good

[1] Cf. for further details the paper presented by the author in 1928 at Zürich (" Die Konkurrenz im Gebiete des Geistigen "), in which there is a discussion of the nature and genesis of *ex post* consensual knowledge.

deal of difference whether this presupposition influences one's point of view unconsciously and naïvely (which will hinder a fundamental enlargement of our perspective), or whether it appears only after everything of which we can become aware and which we already know has entered into our deliberations.

The very quintessence of political knowledge seems to us to lie in the fact that increased knowledge does not eliminate decisions but only forces them farther and farther back.   But what we gain through this retreat from decisions is an expansion of our horizon and a greater intellectual mastery of our world. Consequently, we may expect, from the advances in sociological research into ideology, that interrelations of social position, motives, and points of view, which have hitherto been only partially known, will now become more and more transparent. This will enable us, as we have already indicated, to calculate more precisely collective interests and their corresponding modes of thought and to predict approximately the ideological reactions of the different social strata.

The fact that the sociology of knowledge gives us a certain foundation does not free us from the responsibility of arriving at decisions. It does, however, enlarge the field of vision within the limits of which decisions must be made. Those who fear that an increased knowledge of the determining factors which enter into the formation of their decisions will threaten their " freedom " may rest in peace. Actually it is the one who is ignorant of the significant determining factors and who acts under the immediate pressure of determinants unknown to him who is least free and most thoroughly predetermined in his conduct. Whenever we become aware of a determinant which has dominated us, we remove it from the realm of unconscious motivation into that of the controllable, calculable, and objectified. Choice and decision are thereby not eliminated ; on the contrary, motives which previously dominated us become subject to our domination ; we are more and more thrown back upon our true self and, whereas formerly we were the servants of necessity, we now find it possible to unite consciously with forces with which we are in thorough agreement.

Increasing awareness of previously uncontrolled factors and the tendency to suspend immediate judgments until they are seen in a broader context appears to be the principal trend in the development of political knowledge. This corresponds to the fact, mentioned earlier, that the sphere of the rationalizable and of the rationally controllable (even in our most personal life) is always growing, while the sphere of the irrational becomes correspondingly narrower. We shall not discuss here whether such a development will ultimately lead us to a fully rationalized world in which irrationality and evaluation can no longer exist, or whether it will lead to the cessation of social determination in the sense of freedom through a complete awareness of all the social factors involved. This is a utopian and remote possibility and is therefore not subject to scientific analysis.

However, this much may be safely asserted : politics as politics is possible only as long as the realm of the irrational still exists (where it disappears, " administration " takes its place). Furthermore, it may be stated that the peculiar nature of political knowledge, as contrasted with the " exact " sciences, arises out of the inseparability, in this realm, of knowledge from interest and motivation. In politics the rational element is inherently intertwined with the irrational ; and, finally, there is a tendency to eliminate the irrational from the realm of the social, and in close connection therewith, there results a heightened awareness of factors which have hitherto dominated us unconsciously.

In the history of mankind this is reflected in man's original acceptance of social conditions as unalterable destiny in the same way that we shall probably always have to accept such natural and inevitable limitations as birth and death. Together with this outlook there went an ethical principle—the ethics of fatalism, the main tenet of which was submission to higher and inscrutable powers. The first break in this fatalistic outlook occurred in the emergence of the ethics of conscience in which man set his self over against the destiny inherent in the course of social events. He reserved his personal freedom, on the one hand, in the sense of retaining the ability through his own actions to set new causal sequences going in the world (even though he renounced the ability of controlling the consequences of these acts) and, on the other hand, through the belief in the indeterminateness of his own decisions.

Our own time seems to represent a third stage in this development : the world of social relations is no longer inscrutable or in the lap of fate but, on the contrary, some social interrelations are potentially predictable. At this point the ethical principle of responsibility begins to dawn. Its chief imperatives are, first, that action should not only be in accord with the dictates of conscience, but should take into consideration the possible consequences of the action in so far as they are calculable, and, second, which can be added on the basis of our previous discussion, that conscience itself should be subjected to critical self-examination in order to eliminate all the blindly and compulsively operating factors.

Max Weber has furnished the first acceptable formulation of this conception of politics. His ideas and researches reflect the stage in ethics and politics in which blind fate seems to be at least partially in the course of disappearance in the social process, and the knowledge of everything knowable becomes the obligation of the acting person. It is at this point, if at any, that politics can become a science, since on the one hand the structure of the historical realm, which is to be controlled, has become transparent, and on the other hand out of the new ethics a point of view emerges which regards knowledge not as a passive contemplation but as critical self-examination, and in this sense prepares the road for political action.

IV. THE UTOPIAN MENTALITY

1. UTOPIA, IDEOLOGY, AND THE PROBLEM OF REALITY

A state of mind is utopian when it is incongruous with the state of reality within which it occurs. *incompatible*

This incongruence is always evident in the fact that such a state of mind in experience, in thought, and in practice, is oriented towards objects which do not exist in the actual situation. However, we should not regard as utopian every state of mind which is incongruous with and transcends the immediate situation (and in this sense, " departs from reality "). Only those orientations transcending reality will be referred to by us as utopian which, when they pass over into conduct, tend to shatter, either partially or wholly, the order of things prevailing at the time.

In limiting the meaning of the term " utopia " to that type of orientation which transcends reality and which at the same time breaks the bonds of the existing order, a distinction is set up between the utopian and the ideological states of mind. One can orient himself to objects that are alien to reality and which transcend actual existence—and nevertheless still be effective in the realization and the maintenance of the existing order of things. In the course of history, man has occupied himself more frequently with objects transcending his scope of existence than with those immanent in his existence and, despite this, actual and concrete forms of social life have been built upon the basis of such " ideological " states of mind which were incongruent with reality. Such an incongruent orientation became utopian only when in addition it tended to burst the bonds of the existing order. Consequently representatives of a given order have not in all cases taken a hostile attitude towards orientations transcending the existing order. Rather they have always aimed to control those situationally transcendent ideas and interests which are not realizable within the bounds of the present order, and thereby to render them socially impotent, so that such ideas would be confined to a world beyond history and society, where they could not affect the *status quo*.

Every period in history has contained ideas transcending

the existing order, but these did not function as utopias ; they were rather the appropriate ideologies of this stage of existence as long as they were " organically " and harmoniously integrated into the world-view characteristic of the period (i.e. did not offer revolutionary possibilities). As long as the clerically and feudally organized medieval order was able to locate its paradise outside of society, in some other-worldly sphere which transcended history and dulled its revolutionary edge, the idea of paradise was still an integral part of medieval society. Not until certain social groups embodied these wish-images into their actual conduct, and tried to realize them, did these ideologies become utopian. If for the moment we follow Landauer's terminology,[1] and, in conscious opposition to the usual definition, call every actually existing and ongoing social order, a " topia " (from the word τόπος) then these wish-images which take on a revolutionary function will become utopias.

It is clear that a definite conception of " existence " and a corresponding conception of the transcendence of existence underlies the above distinction. This assumption must be thoroughly investigated before proceeding farther. The nature of " reality " or " existence as such " is a problem which belongs to philosophy, and is of no concern here. However, what is to be regarded as " real " historically or sociologically at a given time is of importance to us and fortunately can be definitely ascertained. Inasmuch as man is a creature living primarily in history and society, the " existence " that surrounds him is never " existence as such ", but is always a concrete historical form of social existence. For the sociologist, " existence " is that which is " concretely effective ", i.e. a functioning social order, which does not exist only in the imagination of certain individuals but according to which people really act.

Every concretely " operating order of life " is to be conceived and characterized most clearly by means of the particular economical and political structure on which it is based. But it embraces also all those forms of human " living-together " (specific forms of love, sociability, conflict, etc.) which the structure makes possible or requires ; and also all those modes and forms of experience and thought which are characteristic of this social system and are consequently congruous with it. (For the present statement of the problem this will be sufficiently

[1] Landauer, G., *Die Revolution*, vol. 13 of the series, *Die Gesellschaft*, ed. by Martin Buber (Frankfurt-am-Main, 1923).

precise. It is not to be denied that if the point of view from which the analysis is made were pressed further there would be much more to be explained. The extent to which a concept explains something can never be absolute ; it always keeps step with the expansion and intensification of insight into the total structure.) But every " actually operating " order of life is at the same time enmeshed by conceptions which are to be designated as " transcendent " or " unreal " because their contents can never be realized in the societies in which they exist, and because one could not live and act according to them within the limits of the existing social order.

In a word, all those ideas which do not fit into the current order are " situationally transcendent " or unreal. Ideas which correspond to the concretely existing and *de facto* order are designated as " adequate " and situationally congruous. These are relatively rare and only a state of mind that has been sociologically fully clarified operates with situationally congruous ideas and motives. Contrasted with situationally congruous and adequate ideas are the two main categories of ideas which transcend the situation—ideologies and utopias.

Ideologies are the situationally transcendent ideas which never succeed *de facto* in the realization of their projected contents. Though they often become the good-intentioned motives for the subjective conduct of the individual, when they are actually embodied in practice their meanings are most frequently distorted. The idea of Christian brotherly love, for instance, in a society founded on serfdom remains an unrealizable and, in this sense, ideological idea, even when the intended meaning is, in good faith, a motive in the conduct of the individual. To live consistently, in the light of Christian brotherly love, in a society which is not organized on the same principle is impossible. The individual in his personal conduct is always compelled—in so far as he does not resort to breaking up the existing social structure—to fall short of his own nobler motives.

The fact that this ideologically determined conduct always falls short of its intended meaning may present itself in several forms—and corresponding to these forms there is a whole series of possible types of ideological mentality. As the first type in this series we may regard the case in which the conceiving and thinking subject is prevented from becoming aware of the incongruence of his ideas with reality by the whole body of axioms involved in his historically and socially determined thought. As a second type of ideological mentality we may present the "cant mentality", which is characterized by the fact that historically it has the possibility of uncovering the incongruence between its ideas and its conduct, but instead conceals these insights in response to certain vital-emotional interests. As a final type there is the ideological mentality based on conscious deception, where ideology is to be interpreted as a purposeful lie. In this case we are not dealing with self-delusion but rather with purposeful deception of another. There is an endless number of transitional stages ranging all the way from good-intentioned, situationally transcendent mentality through " cant mentality " to ideology in the sense of conscious lies.[1] With these phenomena we need not occupy ourselves further at this point. It is necessary here to call attention to each of these types, however, in order to conceive more clearly in this connection the peculiarity of the utopian element.

Utopias too transcend the social situation, for they too orient conduct towards elements which the situation, in so far as it is realized at the time, does not contain. But they are not ideologies, i.e. they are not ideologies in the measure and in so far as they succeed through counteractivity in transforming the existing historical reality into one more in accord with their own conceptions. To an observer who has a relatively external view of them, this theoretical and completely formal distinction between utopias and ideologies seems to offer little difficulty. To determine concretely, however, what in a given case is ideological and what utopian is extremely difficult. We are confronted here with the application of a concept involving values and standards. To carry it out, one must necessarily participate in the feelings and motives of the parties struggling for dominance over historical reality.

What in a given case appears as utopian, and what as ideological, is dependent, essentially, on the stage and degree of reality to which one applies this standard. It is clear that those social strata which represent the prevailing social and intellectual order will experience as reality that structure of relationships of which they are the bearers, while the groups driven into opposition to the present order will be oriented towards the first stirrings of the social order for which they are striving and which is being realized through them. The representatives of a given order will label as utopian all conceptions of existence which *from their*

[1] For further details cf. Part II, " Ideology and Utopia."

point of view can in principle never be realized. According to this usage, the contemporary connotation of the term " utopian " is predominantly that of an idea which is in principle unrealizable. (We have consciously set apart this meaning of the term from the narrower definition.) Among ideas which transcend the situation there are, certainly, some which in principle can never be realized. Nevertheless, men whose thoughts and feelings are bound up with an order of existence in which they have a definite position will always evidence the tendency to designate as absolutely utopian all ideas which have been shown to be unrealizable only within the framework of the order in which they themselves live. In the following pages, whenever we speak of utopia we use the term merely in the relative sense, meaning thereby a utopia which seems to be unrealizable only from the point of view of a given social order which is already in existence.

The very attempt to determine the meaning of the concept " utopia " shows to what extent every definition in historical thinking depends necessarily upon one's perspective, i.e. it contains within itself the whole system of thought representing the position of the thinker in question and especially the political evaluations which lie behind this system of thought. The very way in which a concept is defined and the nuance in which it is employed already embody to a certain degree a prejudgment concerning the outcome of the chain of ideas built upon it. It is no accident that an observer who consciously or unconsciously has taken a stand in favour of the existing and prevailing social order should have such a broad and undifferentiated conception of the utopian ; i.e. one which blurs the distinction between absolute and relative unrealizability. From this position, it is practically impossible to transcend the limits of the *status quo*. This reluctance to transcend the *status quo* tends towards the view of regarding something that is unrealizable merely in the given order as completely unrealizable in any order, so that by obscuring these distinctions one can suppress the validity of the claims of the relative utopia. By calling everything utopian that goes beyond the present existing order, one sets at rest the anxiety that might arise from the relative utopias that are realizable in another order.

At the other extreme is the anarchist, G. Landauer (*Die Revolution*, pp. 7 ff.), who regards the existing order as one undifferentiated whole, and who, by according esteem only to revolution and utopia, sees in every topia (the present existing

o

order) evil itself. Just as the representatives of an existing order did not differentiate between the varieties of utopia (enabling us to speak of a utopia-blindness) so the anarchist may be accused of blindness to the existing order. We perceive in Landauer what is characteristic of all anarchists, namely the antithesis between the " authoritarian " and the " libertarian "—a contrast which simplifies everything and blurs all partial differences, which lumps together as authoritarian everything ranging from the police-state through the democratic-republican to the socialistic state, while only anarchism is regarded as libertarian. The same tendency towards simplification is also operative in the way history is pictured. This crude dichotomy obscures the undoubted qualitative differences in the individual forms of the state. Similarly, by laying the evaluative emphasis on utopia and revolution, the possibility of noting any kind of evolutionary trend in the realm of the historical and institutional is obscured. From this point of view every historical event is an ever-renewed deliverance from a topia (existing order) by a utopia, which arises out of it. Only in utopia and revolution is there true life, the institutional order is always only the evil residue which remains from ebbing utopias and revolutions. Hence, the road of history leads from one topia over a utopia to the next topia, etc.

The one-sidedness of this view of the world and conceptual structure is too obvious to require further elaboration. Its merit, however, is that in opposition to the " conservative " outlook which speaks for the established order, it prevents the existing order from becoming absolute, in that it envisages it as only one of the possible " topias " from which will emanate those utopian elements which in their turn will undermine the existing order. It is thus clear that in order to find the correct conception of utopia, or more modestly, the one most adequate for our present stage of thinking, the analysis based on the sociology of knowledge must be employed to set the one-sidednesses of those individual positions over against one another and to eliminate them. This will make it clear precisely wherein the particularity of the previous conceptions consists. Not until this ground has been cleared is it possible on the basis of one's own judgment to arrive at a more inclusive solution, which overcomes the one-sidednesses that have become apparent. The conception of utopia which we have used above seems in this sense to be the most inclusive. It strives to take account of the dynamic character of reality, inasmuch as it assumes not a

" reality as such " as its point of departure, but rather a concrete historically and socially determined reality which is in a constant process of change (cf. pp. 84 ff. and p. 111, footnote 1). It proposes further to arrive at a qualitatively, historically, and socially differentiated conception of utopia, and finally to keep distinct the " relatively " and " absolutely utopian ".

All this happens in the last analysis because it is our intention not to establish purely abstractly and theoretically some sort of arbitrary relationship between existence and utopia, but rather if possible to do justice to the concrete fullness of the historical and social transformation of utopia in a given period. Furthermore, we do this because we not only seek to view contemplatively and to describe morphologically this transformation of form in the conception of utopia but also because we wish to single out the living principle which links the development of utopia with the development of an existing order. In this sense, the relationship between utopia and the existing order turns out to be a " dialectical " one. By this is meant that every age allows to arise (in differently located social groups) those ideas and values in which are contained in condensed form the unrealized and the unfulfilled tendencies which represent the needs of each age. These intellectual elements then become the explosive material for bursting the limits of the existing order. The existing order gives birth to utopias which in turn break the bonds of the existing order, leaving it free to develop in the direction of the next order of existence. This " dialectical relationship " was already well stated by the Hegelian Droysen, though in a formal and intellectualistic fashion. His definitions may serve for the preliminary clarification of this dialectical aspect. He writes as follows[1] :

§ 77

" All movement in the historical world goes on in this way : Thought, which is the ideal counterpart of things as they really exist, develops itself as things ought to be. . . .

§ 78

" Thoughts constitute the criticism of that which is and yet is not as it should be. Inasmuch as they may bring conditions to their level, then broaden out and harden themselves into

---

[1] Droysen, T. G., *Outline of the Principles of History*, tr. by E. Benjamin Andrews, Boston, 1893, pp. 45–6.

accord with custom, conservatism, and obstinacy, new criticism is demanded, and thus on and on.

§ 79

" That out of the already given conditions, new thoughts arise and out of the thoughts new conditions—this is the work of men."

This formulation of dialectical progression, of the situation, and of the contradictions to be found in the realm of thought should be regarded as nothing more than a formal outline. The real problem lies in tracing the concrete interplay of the differentiated forms of social existence with the corresponding differentiations in utopias. As a result, the problems raised become more systematic and more inclusive in so far as they reflect the richness and variety of history. The most immediate problem of research is to bring the conceptual system and empirical reality into closer contact with one another.

The observation may be made here that in general the conceptual framework of progressive parties is more suitable for systematic study—inasmuch as their social position offers the greater possibility for systematic thought.[1] Historical concepts emphasizing the uniqueness of events, on the other hand, are more likely to be the product of the conservative elements in society. At least there can be no doubt as to the correctness of this imputation for the epoch in which the idea of historical uniqueness, as over against generalization, arose.

Accordingly we may expect that the historian will criticize our definition of utopia as too much of an arbitrary construction because, on the one hand, it has not confined itself to the type of works which got their name from the *Utopia* of Thomas More, and on the other because it includes much which is unrelated to this historical point of departure.

This objection rests upon the historians' assumption that (a) his sole task is the presentation of historical phenomena in all the concrete uniqueness in which they present themselves; and that (b) he therefore should work only with descriptive concepts, i.e. concepts which from a systematic standpoint are not so rigidly defined as to prevent them from doing justice to the fluid character of the phenomena. Therefore, events are to be grouped and classified not on the basis of a principle of

---

[1] For the causes, cf. my *Das Konservative Denken*, loc. cit., pp. 83 ff.

similarity, but rather as phenomena whose relationship is discoverable (through discernible marks) as parts of the unique historical situation. It is clear that whoever approaches the study of historical reality with such presuppositions obstructs, by means of his conceptual apparatus, his road to systematic investigation. If it be conceded that history is more than a matter of concreteness and individuality, and that it has some structural organization and even to a certain extent follows laws (a supposition which must be kept open as one of the possibilities), how could these factors be discovered with such " naïve " concepts, which refer only to historical uniqueness ? Such an historically " naïve " concept would be, for example, that of " utopia " in so far as in its technical historical use it comprised structures which in the concrete are similar to the *Utopia* of Thomas More, or which in a somewhat broader historical sense refer to " ideal commonwealths ". It is not our intention to deny the utility of such individually descriptive concepts as long as the objective is the comprehension of the individual elements in history. We do deny, however, that this is the only approach to historical phenomena. The historians' claim then that history in and for itself is just such a chain of unique phenomena does not stand as an argument against our statement. How could history be anything better when, with the very statement of the problem and the formulation of concepts, the possibility of arriving at any other answer is already closed ? When concepts which are not designed to reveal structures are applied to history, how can we hope to demonstrate historical structures by means of them ? If our questions do not anticipate a certain type of theoretical answer, how can we hope to receive it ? (This is a repetition on a higher level of the procedure we had an opportunity to observe earlier in the case of conservatives and anarchists : the possibility of a certain undesirable answer is already blocked through the manner in which the problem is stated and through the formulation of concepts to be applied. Cf. pp. 176–178.)

Since the question we address to history is in its very nature designed to solve the problem whether there are not ideas as yet unrealized in reality which transcend a given reality, these phenomena may be stated as a problem-complex in the form of a concept. It would be in order, therefore, to raise the question whether this concept can be linked to the meaning of the term " utopia ". The question permits a twofold answer ; in so far as we define the term, " utopia shall signify such and such . . . " no one can object to our procedure, because we admit that the definition is designed only for certain purposes (Max Weber saw this perfectly). When, however, in addition we link such a definition with the historically evolved connotation of the term, it is done with the purpose of showing that the elements which we have emphasized in our conception of utopia are already present in the utopias as they have appeared in history. On that account, we are of the opinion that our abstract concepts are not just arbitrary and wilful intellectual constructions, but have their roots in empirical reality. The concepts which we have created exist not merely for purposes of speculation but to assist in reconstructing structural forces which are present in reality although not always obvious. A constructive abstraction is not the same as speculation where we never get beyond the concept and reflection about it. Constructive abstraction is a prerequisite for empirical investigation, which, if it fulfils the anticipations implicit in the concept or, more simply, if it supplies evidence for the correctness of the construct, gives to the latter the dignity of a reconstruction.

In general, the antithesis of historical procedure and systematic construction must be used only with the utmost caution. In the preliminary stages of the development of an idea it may indeed aid somewhat in clarification. When in the course of the historical development of this antithesis Ranke's ideas came to the fore, a good many differences were provisionally cleared up by contrasting these two procedures. For example, Ranke himself was thereby able to clarify his differences with Hegel. If out of this contrast we make an ultimate antithesis and an absolute opposition which carries us beyond historical development and the immanent structure of the phenomena, but which is legitimate and useful only as the first step in the development of an idea, the result will be that, as happens so often, we shall be guilty of making an absolute out of what is merely a particular stage in the unfolding of an idea. Here too, absolutism blocks the way to the synthesis of the systematic and historical approaches, and obstructs the comprehension of the total situation.[1]

[1] Concerning the practical dangers of historical conceptualization cf. C. Schmitt's criticism of Meinecke: Carl Schmitt, " Zu Friedrich Meineckes *Idee der Staatsräson*," *Archiv für Sozialwissenschaft und Sozialpolitik* (1926), lvi, pp. 226 ff. It is to be regretted that the problematic issues arising out of the controversy between these two typical representatives of their respective points of view has not been further elaborated in the literature.

Because the concrete determination of what is utopian proceeds always from a certain stage of existence, it is possible that the utopias of to-day may become the realities of to-morrow : " Utopias are often only premature truths " (" *Les utopies ne sont souvent que des verités prématurées* " (Lamartine)). Whenever an idea is labelled utopian it is usually by a representative of an epoch that has already passed. On the other hand, the exposure of ideologies as illusory ideas, adapted to the present order, is the work generally of representatives of an order of existence which is still in process of emergence. It is always the dominant group which is in full accord with the existing order that determines what is to be regarded as utopian, while the ascendant group which is in conflict with things as they are is the one that determines what is regarded as ideological. Still another difficulty in defining precisely what, at a given period, is to be regarded as ideology, and what as utopia, results from the fact that the utopian and ideological elements do not occur separately in the historical process. The utopias of ascendant classes are often, to a large extent, permeated with ideological elements.

The utopia of the ascendent bourgeoisie was the idea of " freedom ". It was in part a real utopia, i.e. it contained elements oriented towards the realization of a new social order which were instrumental in disintegrating the previously existing order and which, after their realization, did in part become translated into reality. Freedom in the sense of bursting asunder the bonds of the static, guild, and caste order, in the sense of freedom of thought and opinion, in the sense of political freedom and freedom of the unhampered development of the personality became to a large extent, or at least to a greater extent than in the preceding status-bound, feudal society, a realizable possibility. To-day we know just wherein these utopias became realities and to what extent the idea of freedom of that time contained not merely utopian but also ideological elements.

Wherever the idea of freedom had to make concessions to the concomitant idea of equality, it was setting up goals which were in contradiction to the social order which it demanded and which was later realized. The separation of the ideological elements in the dominant bourgeois mentality from those capable of

As regards the problem of the relation between history and systematization, cf. for recent statements : Sombart, W., " Economic Theory and Economic History," *Economic History Review*, ii, No. 1, January, 1929 Jecht, H., *Wirtschaftsgeschichte und Wirtschaftstheorie* (Tübingen, 1928).

subsequent realization, i.e. the truly utopian elements, could only be made by a social stratum that came later upon the scene to challenge the existing order.

All the hazards that we have pointed out as being involved in a specific definition of what is ideological and what utopian in the mentality of a given time, do indeed make the formulation of the problem more difficult, but do not preclude its investigation. It is only as long as we find ourselves in the very midst of mutually conflicting ideas that it is extremely difficult to determine what is to be regarded as truly utopian (i.e. realizable in the future) in the outlook of a rising class, and what is to be regarded as merely the ideology of dominant as well as ascendant classes. But, if we look into the past, it seems possible to find a fairly adequate criterion of what is to be regarded as ideological and what as utopian. This criterion is their realization. Ideas which later turned out to have been only distorted representations of a past or potential social order were ideological, while those which were adequately realized in the succeeding social order were relative utopias. The actualized realities of the past put an end to the conflict of mere opinions about what in earlier situationally transcendent ideas was relatively utopian bursting asunder the bonds of the existing order, and what was an ideology which merely served to conceal reality. The extent to which ideas are realized constitutes a supplementary and retroactive standard for making distinctions between facts which as long as they are contemporary are buried under the partisan conflict of opinion.

2. Wish-Fulfilment and Utopian Mentality

Wishful thinking has always figured in human affairs. When the imagination finds no satisfaction in existing reality, it seeks refuge in wishfully constructed places and periods. Myths, fairy tales, other-worldly promises of religion, humanistic fantasies, travel romances, have been continually changing expressions of that which was lacking in actual life. They were more nearly complementary colours in the picture of the reality existing at the time than utopias working in opposition to the *status quo* and disintegrating it.

Outstanding research in cultural history [1] has shown that the

[1] Doren, A., *Wunschräume und Wunschzeiten* (Lectures, 1924–5, of the Bibliothek Warburg (Leipzig, Berlin, 1927), pp. 158 ff.). This work is cited for future reference as the best guide for the treatment of the problem

forms of human yearnings can be stated in terms of general principles, and that in certain historical periods wish-fulfilment takes place through projection into time while, in others, it proceeds through projection into space. In accord with this differentiation, it would be possible to call spatial wishes utopias, and temporal wishes chiliasms. This definition of concepts, according to the interests of cultural history, aims merely at descriptive principles. We cannot, however, accept the distinction between spatial and temporal wish-projection as a decisive criterion for differentiating types of ideologies and utopias. We regard as utopian all situationally transcendent ideas (not only wish-projections) which in any way have a transforming effect upon the existing historical-social order. With this as an initial step in our investigation, we are led on to a number of problems.

Since in this connection we are primarily interested in the development of modern life, our first task is to discover the point at which situationally transcendent ideas for the first time become active, i.e. become forces leading to the transformation of existing reality. It would be well here to ask which of the situationally transcendent elements in the dominant mentality at different times assumed this active function. For in human mentality it is not always the same forces, substances, or images which can take on a utopian function, i.e. the function of bursting the bonds of the existing order. We will see in what follows that the utopian element in our consciousness is subject to changes in content and form. The situation that exists at any given moment is constantly being shattered by different situationally transcendent factors.

This change in substance and form of the utopia does not take place in a realm which is independent of social life. It could be shown rather, especially in modern historical developments, that the successive forms of utopia, in their beginnings are intimately bound up with given historical stages of development, and in each of these with particular social strata. It happens very often

from the point of view of cultural history and the history of ideas. It also contains an excellent bibliography. In our work, we cite merely those items which are not contained in the bibliographical references of Doren's work. Doren's essay may be classified as a *motif* history (somewhat in the manner of iconography on the history of art). For this purpose his terminology (" spatial yearning " and " temporal yearning ") is especially suitable, but for our own purpose, i.e. the construction of a sociological history of the structure of modern consciousness, it is only of indirect value.

that the dominant utopia first arises as the wish-fantasy of a single
individual and does not until later become incorporated into the
political aims of a more inclusive group which at each successive
stage can be sociologically determined with more exactness.
In such cases it is customary to speak of a forerunner and of his
role as a pioneer and to attribute this individual's achievement,
sociologically, to the group to whom he transmitted the vision
and in whose behalf he thought through the ideas. This involves
the assumption that the *ex post facto* acceptance of the new
view by certain strata only lays bare the impulse and the social
roots of the outlook in which the forerunner already participated
unconsciously, and from which he drew the general tendency
of his otherwise indisputably individual accomplishment. The
belief that the significance of individual creative power is to be
denied is one of the most widespread misunderstandings of the
findings of sociology. On the contrary, from what should the
new be expected to originate if not from the novel and uniquely
personal mind of the individual who breaks beyond the bounds
of the existing order ? It is the task of sociology always to show,
however, that the first stirrings of what is new (even though
they often take on the form of opposition to the existing order)
are in fact oriented towards the existing order and that the existing
order itself is rooted in the alignment and tension of the forces
of social life. Furthermore, what is new in the achievement
of the personally unique " charismatic " individual can only
then be utilized for the collective life when, from the very beginning, it is in contact with some important current problem,
and when from the start its meanings are rooted genetically
in collective purposes. We must not, however, overestimate the
significance of the prominence of the individual in relation to
the collectivity as we have been accustomed to do ever since the
Renaissance. Since that time the contribution of the individual
mind stands out relatively when set over against the role which
it played in the Middle Ages or in Oriental cultures, but its
significance is not absolute. Even when a seemingly isolated
individual gives form to the utopia of his group, in the final
analysis this can rightly be attributed to the group to whose
collective impulse his achievement conformed.

After having clarified the relations between the achievements
of the individual and the group, we are in a position to speak
of a differentiation of utopias according to historical epochs
and social strata, and to view history from this standpoint.

In the sense of our definition, an effective utopia cannot in the long run be the work of an individual, since the individual cannot by himself tear asunder the historical-social situation. Only when the utopian conception of the individual seizes upon currents already present in society and gives expression to them, when in this form it flows back into the outlook of the whole group, and is translated into action by it, only then can the existing order be challenged by the striving for another order of existence. Indeed, it may be stated further that it is a very essential feature of modern history that in the gradual organization for collective action social classes become effective in transforming historical reality only when their aspirations are embodied in utopias appropriate to the changing situation.

It is only because there existed a close correlation between the different forms of the utopia and the social strata which were transforming the existing order that the changes in modern utopian ideas are a theme of sociological investigation. If we may speak of social and historical differentiations of utopian ideas, then we must ask ourselves the question whether the form and substance that they have at any given time is not to be understood through a concrete analysis of the historical-social position in which they arose. In other words, the key to the intelligibility of utopias is the structural situation of that social stratum which at any given time espouses them.

The peculiarities of the individual forms of successively emerging utopias become in fact most nearly intelligible not merely by regarding them as a unilinear filiation of one from the other, but also by taking account of the fact that they came into existence and maintained themselves as mutually antagonistic counter-utopias. The different forms of the active utopias have appeared in this historical succession in connection with certain definite social strata struggling for ascendancy. Despite frequent exceptions, this connection continued to exist, so that, as time goes on, it is possible to speak of a co-existence of the different forms of utopia which at first appeared in temporal succession. The fact that they exist in an intimate connection with sometimes latently, and sometimes openly, mutually antagonistic strata is reflected in the form they take. The change of fortunes of the classes to which they belong are constantly expressing themselves in the concrete variations in the form of the utopias. The fundamental fact that they must orient themselves to one another, through conflict even if only in the sense

of opposition, leaves a definite imprint upon them. Consequently
the sociologist can really understand these utopias only as parts
of a constantly shifting total constellation.[1]

If social and intellectual history were concerned exclusively
with the previously outlined fact that every socially bound
form of utopia is subject to change, we would be entitled to
speak merely of a problem concerning the socially bound transformation of the " utopia ", but not of the problem of a transformation in the " utopian mentality ". One may rightly speak
of a utopian mentality only when the configuration of the utopia
at any one time forms not only a vital part of the " content "
of the mentality involved, but when, at least, in its general
tendency, it permeates the whole range of that mentality. Only
when the utopian element in this sense tends to be completely
infused into every aspect of the dominating mentality of the
time, when the forms of experience, of action, and of outlook
(perspective) are organized in accord with this utopian element,
are we truthfully and realistically entitled to speak not merely
of different forms of utopia but, at the same time, of different
configurations and stages of utopian mentality. It is precisely
the task of proving that such a thorough-going interrelationship
does exist that constitutes the culmination of our inquiry.

It is the utopian element—i.e. the nature of the dominant
wish—which determines the sequence, order, and evaluation of
single experiences. This wish is the organizing principle which
even moulds the way in which we experience time. The form
in which events are ordered and the unconsciously emphatic
rhythm, which the individual in his spontaneous observation
of events imposes upon the flux of time, appears in the utopia
as an immediately perceptible picture, or at least a directly
intelligible set of meanings. The innermost structure of the
mentality of a group can never be as clearly grasped as when
we attempt to understand its conception of time in the light
of its hopes, yearnings, and purposes. On the basis of these
purposes and expectations, a given mentality orders not merely
future events, but also the past. Events which at first glance
present themselves as a mere chronological cumulation, from this
point of view take on the character of destiny. Bare facts set

---

[1] It is the merit of Alfred Weber to have made this constellational
analysis into an instrument of cultural sociology. We are attempting
to apply his formulation of the problem, though in a specific sense, in
the case treated above.

themselves in perspective, and emphasis in meaning are distributed and apportioned to individual happenings in accordance with the fundamental directions in which the personality strives. It is in nothing but this meaningful ordering of events, extending far beyond mere chronological orderings, that the structural principle of historical time is to be discovered. But it is necessary to go even farther: this ordering of meaning is, in fact, the most primary element in the comprehension and interpretation of events. Just as modern psychology shows that the whole (*Gestalt*) is prior to the parts and that our first understanding of the parts comes through the whole, so it is with historical understanding. Here, too, we have the sense of historical time as a meaningful totality which orders events " prior " to the parts, and through this totality we first truly understand the total course of events and our place in it. Just because of this central significance of the historical time-sense, we will emphasize particularly the connections which exist between each utopia and the corresponding historical time-perspective.

When we refer to certain forms and stages of the utopian mentality, we have in mind concrete, discoverable structures of mentality as they were to be found in living, individual human beings. We are not thinking here of some purely arbitrarily constructed unity (like Kant's " consciousness as such "), or a metaphysical entity which is to be posited beyond the concrete minds of individuals (as in Hegel's " spirit "). Rather we mean the concretely discoverable structures of mentality as they are demonstrable in individual men. Therefore we will be concerned here with concrete thinking, acting, and feeling and their inner connections in concrete types of men. The pure types and stages of the utopian mind are constructions only in so far as they are conceived of as *ideal-types*. No single individual represents a pure embodiment of any one of the historical-social types of mentality here presented.[1] Rather in each single, concrete individual there were operative certain elements of a certain type of mental structure often mixed with other types.

When we proceed then to analyse the ideal types of utopian mentalities in their historical-social differentiations, we do not intend them as epistemological or metaphysical constructions. They are simply methodological devices. No individual mind, as it actually existed, ever corresponded completely to the

[1] Cf. pp. 52 ff. and p. 182 of the present book.

types and their structural interconnections to be described. Each individual mind in its concreteness, however (despite all mixtures), tends to be organized in general along the structural lines of one of these historically changing types. These constructions, like Max Weber's ideal-types, serve simply for the mastery of past and present complexities. In our case they are intended in addition for the understanding not only of psychological facts, but also for the comprehension, in all their " purity ", of the structures which are historically unfolding and operating in them.

3. Changes in the Configuration of the Utopian Mentality : Its Stages in Modern Times

(a) The First Form of the Utopian Mentality : The Orgiastic Chiliasm of the Anabaptists

The decisive turning-point in modern history was, from the point of view of our problem, the moment in which " Chiliasm " joined forces with the active demands of the oppressed strata of society.[1] The very idea of the dawn of a millenial kingdom on earth always contained a revolutionizing tendency, and the church made every effort to paralyse this situationally transcendent idea with all the means at its command. These intermittently reviving doctrines reappeared again in Joachim of Flores among others, but in his case they were not as yet thought of as revolutionizing. In the Hussites, however, and then in Thomas Münzer [2] and the Anabaptists these ideas became transformed into the activistic movements of specific social strata. Longings

[1] To fix the beginning of a movement at a given point in the stream of historical events is always hazardous and signifies a neglect of the forerunners of the movement. But the successful reconstruction of what is most essential in historical development depends upon the historian's ability to give the proper emphasis to those turning-points which are decisive in the articulation of phenomena. The fact that modern socialism often dates its origins from the time of the Anabaptists is in part evidence that the movement led by Thomas Münzer is to be regarded as a step in the direction of modern revolutionary movements. It is obvious, of course, that we are not yet dealing here with class-conscious proletarians. Similarly, it must be readily granted that Münzer was a social revolutionary from religious motives. However, the sociologist must pay particular attention to this movement, because in it Chiliasm and the social revolution were structurally integrated.

[2] Of the literature concerning Münzer, we mention only K. Holl, " Luther und die Schwärmer " (Gesammelte Aufsätze zur Kirchengeschichte, Tübingen, 1927, pp. 420 ff.), where a wide range of citations bearing upon a single

which up to that time had been either unattached to a specific goal or concentrated upon other-worldly objectives suddenly took on a mundane complexion. They were now felt to be realizable—here and now—and infused social conduct with a singular zeal.

The " spiritualization of politics ", which may be said to have begun at this turn in history, more or less affected all the currents of the time. The source of spiritual tension, however, was the emergence of the utopian mentality which originated in the oppressed strata of society. It is at this point that politics in the modern sense of the term begins, if we here understand by politics a more or less conscious participation of all strata of society in the achievement of some mundane purpose, as contrasted with a fatalistic acceptance of events as they are, or of control from " above ".[1]

The lower classes in the post-medieval period only very gradually assumed this motor function in the total social process and only bit by bit did they arrive at an awareness of their own social and political significance. Even though this stage is, as already indicated, still very far removed from the stage of " proletarian self-consciousness ", it is nevertheless the starting point of the process gradually leading to it. Henceforth the oppressed classes in society tend in a more clearly discernible fashion to play a specific role in the dynamic development of the total social process. From this time on we get an increasing social differentiation of purposes and psychic attitudes.

This by no means implies that this most extreme form of the utopian mentality has been the only determining factor in history since that time. None the less its presence in the social realm has exerted an almost continual influence even upon antithetical mentalities. Even the opponents of this extreme

problem is admirably assembled. In the references that follow, we simply cite the passage in Holl without reprinting it in detail.

For a characterization of Chiliasm, cf. especially Bloch, E., *Thomas Münzer als Theologe der Revolution* (Munich, 1921). An inner affinity between Münzer and this author has made possible a very adequate exposition of the essence of the phenomenon of Chiliasm. This has in part already been correctly evaluated in Doren, op. cit.

[1] Politics might, of course, be defined in a number of ways. In this case again we should keep in mind a statement made earlier : the definition is always related to its purpose and to the point of view of the observer. Our purpose here is the tracing of the relationship between the formation of the collective consciousness and political history, and consequently our definition, which selects certain facts, must be related to this formulation of the problem.

form of utopian mentality oriented themselves, though un-wittingly and unconsciously, with reference to it. The utopian vision aroused a contrary vision. The Chiliastic optimism of the revolutionaries ultimately gave birth to the formation of the conservative attitude of resignation and to the realistic attitude in politics.

This situation was of great moment not only for politics but also for those spiritual strivings which had become fused with practical movements and which had abandoned their detached and aloof position. Orgiastic energies and ecstatic outbursts began to operate in a worldly setting, and tensions, previously transcending day to day life became explosive agents within it. The impossible gives birth to the possible,[1] and the absolute interferes with the world and conditions actual events. This fundamental and most radical form of the modern utopia was fashioned out of a singular material. It corresponded to the spiritual fermentation and physical excitement of the peasants, of a stratum living closest to the earth. It was at the same time robustly material and highly spiritual.

Nothing would be more misleading than to try to understand these events from the point of view of the " history of ideas ". " Ideas " did not drive these men to revolutionary deeds. Their actual outburst was conditioned by ecstatic-orgiastic energies. The reality-transcending elements in consciousness which here were aroused to an active utopian function were not " ideas ". To see everything that occurred during this period as the work of " ideas " is an unconscious distortion produced during the liberal-humanitarian stage of utopian mentality.[2] The history of ideas was the creation of an " idea-struck " age, which involuntarily reinterpreted the past in the light of its own central experiences. It was not " ideas " that impelled men during the Peasant Wars to revolutionary action. This eruption had its roots in much deeper-lying vital and elemental levels of the psyche.[3]

If we are to come closer to an understanding of the true substance of Chiliasm and if we are to make it accessible to scientific comprehension, it is first of all necessary to distinguish from Chiliasm itself the images, symbols, and forms in which

[1] Münzer himself spoke of the " courage and strength to realize the impossible ". For citations, cf. Holl, p. 429.

[2] To be discussed in the next section.

[3] Münzer spoke of the " abyss of the spirit " which could be seen only when forces of the soul are laid bare. Cf. Holl, p. 428, note 6.

the Chiliastic mind thought. For nowhere else is our experience as valid as here, that what is already formed, and the expression things assume, tend to become detached from their origins and to go their own way independently of the motives that prompted them. The essential feature of Chiliasm is its tendency always to dissociate itself from its own images and symbols. It is precisely because the driving force of this utopia does not lie in the form of its external expression that a view of the phenomenon based upon the mere history of ideas fails to do it justice. Such a view constantly threatens to miss the essential point. If we use the methods of the history of ideas, we tend to put in place of the history of the substance of Chiliasm the history of frames of reference which have already been emptied of content, i.e. the history of mere Chiliastic ideas as such.[1] Likewise, the investigation of the careers of Chiliastic revolutionaries is apt to be misleading, since it is of the nature of Chiliastic experience to ebb in the course of time and to undergo an unremitting transformation in the course of the persons' experience. Hence, to adhere closely to the theme of investigation itself, we must seek out a method of research which will give a living view of the material and which will present it as if we were experiencing it ourselves. We must constantly ask ourselves whether the Chiliastic attitude itself is actually present in the forms of thought and experience with which we are dealing in a given case.

The only true, perhaps the only direct, identifying characteristic of Chiliastic experience is absolute presentness. We always occupy some here and now on the spatial and temporal stage but, from the point of view of Chiliastic experience, the position that we occupy is only incidental. For the real Chiliast, the present becomes the breach through which what was previously inward bursts out suddenly, takes hold of the outer world and transforms it.

The mystic lives either in recollection of ecstasy, or in longing for it. His metaphors describe this ecstasy as a psychic situation which cannot be conceived of in spatial and temporal terms as

---

[1] In the conflict between Münzer and Luther there is evidence of the above-mentioned divergence between emphasis upon the substance of faith which can only be experienced and the " ideas " which symbolize it. According to Münzer, Luther is one who believes exclusively in the letter of the Scriptures. For Münzer, such faith is a " stolen, unexperienced, apish mimicry ". Citations in Holl, p. 427.

P

a union with the closed world of the beyond.[1] It is perhaps this same ecstatic substance which turns with the Chiliast into the immediate here and now, but not in order simply to delight in it, but in order to whip it up and to make it a part of himself. Thomas Münzer, the Chiliastic prophet, expressed himself as follows : " For that reason, all prophets should speak in this manner, ' Thus saith the Lord,' and not, ' Thus said the Lord,' as if it had occurred in the past rather than in the present." [2]

The experience of the mystic is purely spiritual, and if there are some traces of sensual experience in his language it is because he has to express an inexpressible spiritual contact and can only find his symbols in the sensual analogies of everyday life. With the Chiliast, however, sensual experience is present in all its robustness, and is as inseparable from the spirituality in him as he is from his immediate present. It is as if through this immediate present he had first come into the world and entered into his own body.

To quote Münzer himself :—

" I seek only that you accept the living word in which I live and breathe, so that it should not come back to me empty. Take it to your hearts, I beseech you in the name of the red blood of Christ. I take an account of you and I wish to give you an account of myself. Can I not do this, may I be the child of temporal and eternal death. A higher pledge I cannot give you." [3]

---

[1] Meister Eckehart : " Nothing so much hinders the soul from knowing God as time and space" (Meister Eckehart, *Schriften und Predigten*, ed. by Büttner (Jena, 1921, i, p. 137). " If the soul is to perceive God, it must stand above time and space ! " (Ibid., p. 138). " If the soul is in the act of taking a leap beyond itself, and entering into a denial of itself and its own activities, it is through grace. . . ." (i, 201). On the distinction between medieval mysticism and the religiosity of Münzer, cf. Holl's pertinent comment. " Whereas the mystics of the Middle Ages prepared for God by artificial means, by asceticism, and, so to speak, tried to force union with divinity, Münzer believed that it is ' God himself Who takes the scythe to cut the weeds from among men '." (Cf. Holl, p. 483.)

[2] Münzer expresses himself similarly in the following : " He should and must know that God is within him and that he should not think of Him as if he were a thousand miles away." (Holl, p. 430, note 3.)
Elsewhere Münzer showed his spiritual and religious radicalism in his distinction between the honey-sweet and the bitter Christ. He accused Luther of representing only the former. (Holl, pp. 426–7.) For interpretation, cf. Bloch, op. cit., pp. 251 ff.

[3] In the creative art of this epoch, as represented by Grünewald's painting, there is to be found, carried to a grandiose extreme, a parallel to this intimate fusion of the most robust sensualism with the highest spirituality. Because so little is known of his life, it is impossible to determine whether he himself had connections with the Anabaptists.

The Chiliast expects a union with the immediate present. Hence he is not preoccupied in his daily life with optimistic hopes for the future or romantic reminiscences. His attitude is characterized by a tense expectation. He is always on his toes awaiting the propitious moment and thus there is no inner articulation of time for him. He is not actually concerned with the millenium that is to come [1] ; what is important for him is that it happened here and now, and that it arose from mundane existence, as a sudden swing over into another kind of existence. The promise of the future which is to come is not for him a reason for postponement, but merely a point of orientation, something external to the ordinary course of events from where he is on the lookout ready to take the leap.

Because of the peculiarity of its structure, medieval, feudal society did not know revolution in the modern sense.[2] Since the earliest appearance of this form of political change, Chiliasm has always accompanied revolutionary outbursts and given

The reference to Grünewald's art, however, is intended to illustrate what we said above. (Cf. Heidrich, E., *Die altdeutche Malerei* (Jena, 1909), pp. 39–41, 269.)

Cf. also Heidrich's instructive work, *Dürer und die Reformation* (Leipzig, 1909), in which he shows clearly the demonstrable relationship between the ecstatic enthusiasts and their followers among the painters Hans Sebald, Barthel Beham, and Georg Pencz in Nürnberg, and Dürer's defence against them. Heidrich sees in Dürer's art the expression of Lutheran religiosity, and in Grünewald's the parallel to the ecstatic religious enthusiasts.

[1] Münzer : " . . . that we earthly creatures of flesh and blood should become Gods through Christ's becoming a man, and thereby become with him God's pupils, taught by Him and in His spirit and become divine and totally transformed into Him and that earthly life should turn into heaven." (Citation from Holl, p. 431, note 1.)

On the sociology of the inward-turning of experience, and in general on the theory of the relationship of forms of experience and forms of political-public activity, it should be noted that, in the degree that Karlstadt and the South German Baptists fell away from Münzer, they turned more and more from the Chiliastic experience of immediacy towards prophetic experience and an optimistic hope for the future (cf. Holl, p. 458).

[2] One of the features of modern revolution already pointed out by Stahl is that it is no ordinary uprising against a certain oppressor but a striving for an upheaval against the whole existing social order in a thoroughgoing and systematic way. If this systematic aim is made the starting-point in the analysis and its historical and intellectual antecedents are sought out one arrives in this case also at Chiliasm. As unsystematic as Chiliasm may seem to be in other respects, in one phase it had a tendency towards abstract systematic orientation. Thus, for example, Radványi has pointed out that Chiliasm did not attack individual persons, but only attacked and persecuted the evil principle active in individuals and institutions. (Cf. his unpublished dissertation, *Der Chiliasmus*, Heidelberg, 1923, p. 98.) Further citations in Holl, p. 454.

them their spirit. When this spirit ebbs and deserts these movements, there remains behind in the world a naked mass-frenzy and a despiritualized fury. Chiliasm sees the revolution as a value in itself, not as an unavoidable means to a rationally set end, but as the only creative principle of the immediate present, as the longed-for realization of its aspirations in this world. " The will to destroy is a creative will," said Bakunin,[1] because of the Satan within him, the Satan of whom he loved to speak as working through contagion. That he was not fundamentally interested in the realization of a rationally thought-out world is betrayed by his statement : " I do not believe in constitutions or in laws. The best constitution would leave me dissatisfied. We need something different. Storm and vitality and a new lawless and consequently free world."

Whenever the ecstatic spirit wearies of broadened perspectives and imagery, we get a reappearance of the concrete promise of a better world, although it is in no way meant to be taken quite literally. For this mentality, promises of a better world removed in time and space are like uncashable cheques—their only function is to fix that point in the " world beyond events " of which we have spoken, and from which he, who is expectantly awaiting the propitious moment, can be assured of detachment from that which is merely in the process of becoming. Not being at one with whatever events transpire in the " evil " here and now, he awaits only the critical juncture of events and that moment when the external concatenation of circumstances coincides with the ecstatic restlessness of his soul.

Consequently, in observing the structure and course of development of the Chiliastic mentality, it is quite unimportant (although for the history of the variations in *motif*, it may be significant) that in place of a temporal utopia we get a spatial one, and that in the Age of Reason and Enlightenment the closed system of rational deduction comes to permeate the utopian outlook. In a certain sense the rational, axiomatic point of departure, the closed system of deductive procedure, and the internally balanced equilibrium of motives comprised in the body of axioms are quite as capable of insuring that inner coherence and isolation from the world as are the utopian dreams.[2]

[1] Literature on Bakunin is cited below. We shall later show that the anarchism of the Bakunian variety comes closest in our opinion to continuing the Chiliastic outlook in the modern world.

[2] Cf. Freyer, H., " Das Problem der Utopie," *Deutsche Rundschau*, 1928, vol. 183, pp. 321–345. Also Girsberger's book to be cited in detail below.

Furthermore, the remoteness from space and time of what is merely rationally correct and valid, is, in a certain sense, more likely to lead to the outside realm beyond experience than could be hoped for through these utopian dreams which are laden with the corporeal content of the world as it is.

Nothing is more removed from actual events than the closed rational system. Under certain circumstances, nothing contains more irrational drive than a fully self-contained, intellectualistic world-view. Nevertheless, in every formal rational system there is the danger that the Chiliastic-ecstatic element will ebb away behind the intellectual façade. Not every rational utopia, therefore, is tantamount to Chiliastic faith, and not every rational utopia in this sense represents a detachment and alienation from the world. The abstract nature of the rational utopia contradicts the intense emotional drive of a sensually alert Chiliastic faith in the complete and immediate present. Thus the rational utopian mentality although often born of the Chiliastic mentality may inadvertently become its prime antagonist, just as the liberal-humanitarian utopia tended more and more to turn against Chiliasm.

(b) The Second Form of the Utopian Mentality: The Liberal-humanitarian Idea

The utopia of liberal humanitarianism, too, arose out of the conflict with the existing order. In its characteristic form, it also establishes a " correct " rational conception to be set off against evil reality. This counter-conception is not used, however, as a blue-print in accordance with which at any given point in time the world is to be reconstructed. Rather it serves merely as a " measuring rod " by means of which the course of concrete events may be theoretically evaluated. The utopia of the liberal-humanitarian mentality is the " idea ". This, however, is not the static platonic idea of the Greek tradition, which was a concrete archetype, a primal model of things ; but here the idea is rather conceived of as a formal goal projected into the infinite future whose function it is to act as a mere regulative device in mundane affairs.

Some further distinctions need, however, to be made. Where, as in France, for instance, the situation matured into a political attack the intellectualistic utopia took on a rational form with decisively sharp contours.[1] Where it was not possible to follow

[1] About the French concept of " idea ", we read in Grimm's *Deutsches Wörterbuch* : " . . . at an earlier period French usage of the seventeenth

in this path, as in Germany, the utopia was introverted and assumed a subjective tone. Here the road to progress was not sought in external deeds or in revolutions, but exclusively in the inner constitution of man and its transformations.

Chiliastic mentality severs all relationship with those phases of historical existence which are in daily process of becoming in our midst. It tends at every moment to turn into hostility towards the world, its culture, and all its works and earthly achievements, and to regard them as only premature gratifications of a more fundamental striving which can only be adequately satisfied in Kairos.[1] The fundamental attitude of the liberal is characterized by a positive acceptance of culture and the giving of an ethical tone to human affairs. He is most in his element in the role of critic rather than that of creative destroyer. He has not broken his contact with the present—the here and now. About every event there is an atmosphere of inspiring ideas and spiritual goals to be achieved.

For Chiliasm the spirit is a force which suffuses and expresses itself through us. For humanitarian liberalism it is that " other realm ",[2] which, when absorbed in our moral conscience, inspires us. Ideas, and not bare ecstasy, guided the activity of that epoch immediately before and after the French Revolution which gave itself over to the reconstruction of the world. This modern humanitarian idea radiated from the political realm into all spheres of cultural life culminating finally in the " idealistic " philosophy in an attempt to achieve the highest attainable stage of self-consciousness. The most fertile period in the history of modern philosophy coincides with the birth and expansion of this modern idea, and when it begins again to be limited by narrower bounds in the political sphere this particular trend in philosophy, appropriate to the liberal-humanitarian outlook, begins to disintegrate.

century gave the word the rarified meaning of a mental representation, a thought, or a concept of something " (Littré, 2, 5c.) It is in this sense that we find the word " idea " under decisively French influence among German writers of the first half of the eighteenth century; and for a time the word is even written with the French accent.

[1] [In Greek mythology Kairos is the God of Opportunity—the genius of the decisive moment. The Christianized notion of this is given thus in Paul Tillich's *The Religious Situation*, translated by H. R. Niebuhr, New York, 1932, p. 138–139 : " Kairos is fulfilled time, the moment of time which is invaded by eternity. But Kairos is not perfection or completion in time." Translators' note.]

[2] Cf. Freyer, loc. cit., p. 323.

The fate of idealistic philosophy was too closely bound up with the social position of its protagonists for us to neglect to point out in this connection, at least, the most important stage in this relationship. As regards its social function, modern philosophy arose to overthrow the clerical-theological view of the world. It was first of all adopted by the two parties which were at that time in ascendancy—the absolute monarchy and the bourgeoisie. Not until later did it become exclusively the weapon of the bourgeoisie where it came to represent, at one and the same time, culture and politics. The monarchy, when it became reactionary, took refuge in theocratic ideas. Even the proletariat emancipated itself from the intellectualistic framework of idealist philosophy which it had previously held in common with the bourgeoisie, now its conscious adversary.

Modern liberal thought, which carries on a dual struggle is of a peculiar texture, highly elevated, a creation of the imagination. This idealist mentality avoids both the visionary conception of reality involved in the Chiliastic appeal to God, and also the conservative and often narrow-minded domination over things and men involved in the earth- and time-bound notion of the world. Socially, this intellectualistic outlook had its basis in a middle stratum, in the bourgeoisie and in the intellectual class. This outlook, in accordance with the structural relationship of the groups representing it, pursued a dynamic middle course between the vitality, ecstasy, and vindictiveness of oppressed strata, and the immediate concreteness of a feudal ruling class whose aspirations were in complete congruence with the then existing reality.

Bourgeois liberalism was much too preoccupied with norms to concern itself with the actual situation as it really existed. Hence, it necessarily constructed for itself its own ideal world. Elevated and detached, and at the same time sublime, it lost all sense for material things, as well as every real relationship with nature. In this context of meaning, nature, for the most part, signified reasonableness, a state of things regulated by the eternal standards of right and wrong. Even the art of the generation then dominant reflected the notions of its philosophy—the eternal, the unconditioned, and a world without body and individualization.[1]

Here, as in most other periods of history, art, culture and philosophy are nothing but the expression of the central utopia

[1] Cf. Pinder, *Das Problem der Generation in der Kunstgeschichte Europas* (Berlin, 1926), pp. 67 ff., 69.

of the age as shaped by contemporary social and political forces. Just as lack of depth and colour characterize the art corresponding to this theory, so a similar lack is apparent in the content of this liberal-humanitarian idea. The absence of colour corresponds to the emptiness of content of all the ideals dominant at the height of this mode of thought : culture in the narrower sense, freedom, personality, are only frames for a content, which, one might say, has been purposely left undetermined. Already in Herder's *Letters on Humanity*, and therefore in the early stages of the ideal of " humanity ", there is no definite statement of wherein the ideal consists : at one time it is " reason and justice " which appear as the goal ; at another it is the " well being of man " that he regards as worth striving for.

This overemphasis on form in philosophy as well as in other fields corresponds to this middle position and to the lack of concreteness of all its ideas. The absence of depth in the plastic arts and the dominance of the purely linear correspond to the manner of experiencing historical time as unilinear progress and evolution. This conception of unilinear progress is essentially derived from two separate sources.

One source arose in western capitalist development. The bourgeois ideal of reason, set up as the goal, contrasted with the existing state of affairs, and it was necessary to bridge the gap between the imperfection of things as they occurred in a state of nature and the dictates of reason by means of the concept of progress. This reconciliation of norms with the existing state of things succeeded through the belief that reality moves continually towards an ever closer approximation to the rational. Though this idea of continuously closer approximation was at first vague and indeterminate, it is given a relatively concrete and classic form by the Girondist, Condorcet. Condorcet, as Cunow [1] has rightly analysed from a sociological viewpoint, incorporated the disillusioning experience of the middle strata after the fall of the Girondists into the concept of history held by these strata. The ultimate aim of a state of perfection was not renounced, but the revolution was considered only as a mere transitional stage. The idea of progress placed difficulties in its own path by discovering the necessary steps and transitional stages involved in the process of development which was still believed to be unilinear. Whereas formerly everything that was

[1] Cunow, H., *Die Marxsche Geschichts-, Gesellschafts- und Staatstheorie* (Berlin, 1920), i, p. 158.

provisional was, from the point of view of reason, dismissed as error or prejudice, in Condorcet we find at least a concession of relative validity to these tentative stages which precede a state of perfection. The " prejudices " prevailing in any given epoch were recognized as unavoidable. As " parts of the historical picture " of the period they were assimilated into the idea of progress, which, as time went on, became more differentiated into stages and periods.

Another source of the idea of progress is to be found in Germany. In Lessing's *Erziehung des Menschengeschlechts*, the emergent idea of evolution had, according to the views of von der Goltz and Gerlich,[1] a secularized pietistic character. If, in addition to this derivation, one considers that Pietism, transplanted from Holland to Germany, originally contained certain Baptist elements, then the religious idea of development may be understood as an ebbing away of the Chiliastic impulse—as a process in which abiding faith (*Harren*) becomes, in the German milieu a " waiting and anticipation ", and the Chiliastic time-sense merges imperceptibly into an evolutionary one.

From Arndt, Coccejus, Spener, Zinzendorf, the line leads to Bengel, Lessing's pietistic contemporary, who already spoke of God's historical stewardship and of continuous and uniform progress from the beginning to the end of the world. It was from him that Lessing is supposed to have taken over the idea of the infinite perfectability of the human species, which he then secularized and blended with the belief in reason, and then passed on in this form as a heritage to German idealism.

In whatever manner this conception of progress may have arisen, whether as a continuous transformation of the religious mentality or as a counter-movement on the part of rationalism, there is already contained in it, in contrast with the Chiliastic mentality, an increasing concern with the concrete " here and now " of the ongoing process.

The fulfilment of Chiliastic expectations may occur at any moment. Now with the liberal-humanitarian idea the utopian element receives a definite location in the historical process—

---

[1] von der Goltz, " Die theologische Bedeutung J. A. Bengels und seiner Schüler," *Jahrbücher für deutsche Theologie* (Gotha, 1861), vol. vi, pp. 460–506. Gerlich, Fr., *Der Kommunismus als Lehre vom tausendjährigen Reich* (München, 1920). This book, written with propagandistic intent, is in many aspects over-simplified and superficial, but many basic ideas, as that cited above, seem to be rightly comprehended. (Cf. the appendix.) Doren (op. cit.) has already made an adequate estimate of the value of this book.

it is the culminating point of historical evolution. In contrast
with the earlier conception of a utopia which was suddenly to
break upon the world completely from the " outside ", this
signifies, in the long run, a relative toning down of the notion
of sudden historical change.   Henceforth, even the utopian
view sees the world moving in the direction of a realization of
its aims, of a utopia.   From another angle as well, utopianism
becomes increasingly bound up with the process of becoming.
The idea, which could be completely realized only in some distant
time, in the course of the continuous development of the present
becomes a norm, which, applied to details, effects gradual improvement.   Whoever criticizes details becomes bound up by that
very criticism with the world as it is.   Participation in the most
immediate trends of present-day cultural development, the
intense faith in institutionalism and in the formative power of
politics and economics characterize the heirs to a tradition
who are not interested merely in sowing, but who want to reap
the harvest now.

  But the politics of this ascendant social stratum still did not
come to actual grips with the real problem of society, and in the
epochs of liberal antagonism towards the state it still did not
understand the historical significance of what the dominant
strata placed absolute value upon, namely the significance of
power and of naked violence.   However abstract this outlook,
which rests theoretically upon culture in the narrower sense and
philosophy, and practically upon economics and politics, may
appear to be when viewed from the standpoint of the conservative,
it is nevertheless, in so far as it is concerned with mundane historical events, very much more concrete than the Chiliastic
mentality with its detachment from history.   This greater
proximity to the historical is betrayed by the fact that the
historical time-sense, always a reliable symptom of the structure
of a mentality, is much more definite than in the Chiliastic
mentality.   The Chiliastic mentality has, as we saw, no sense
for the process of becoming ; it was sensitive only to the abrupt
moment, the present pregnant with meaning.   The type of
mentality which remains on the Chiliastic level neither knows
nor recognizes—even when its opponents have already absorbed
this point of view—either a road that leads to a goal or a process
of development—it knows only the tide and ebb of time.   Revolutionary anarchism, for instance, in which the Chiliastic mentality
is preserved in its purest and most genuine form, regards modern

times, since the decline of the Middle Ages, as a single revolution. " It is part of the fact and the concept of revolution that, like a convalescent fever, it comes between two spells of sickness. It would not exist at all if it were not preceded by fatigue and followed by exhaustion." [1]   Thus, even though this outlook learns much from its opponents and takes on at one time a conservative cast, and at another a socialist, it emerges even now at decisive moments.

The Chiliastic absolute experience of the " now ", which precludes any possibility of experiencing development does, however, serve the sole function of providing us with a qualitative differentiation of time.   There are, according to this view, times that are pregnant with meaning and times that are devoid of meaning.   In this fact lies an important approach to the historico-philosophical differentiation of historical events.   Its significance can be estimated only after it has been made clear that even an empirical consideration of history is impossible without an historico-philosophical differentiation of time (often latent and hence imperceptible in its effects).   And even though at first glance it may seem improbable, the above-mentioned first attempt at a qualitative arrangement of historical times does arise from Chiliastic aloofness and ecstatic experience.   The normative-liberal mentality also contains this qualitative differentiation of historical events, and in addition holds in contempt as an evil reality everything that has become a part of the past or is part of the present.   It defers the actual realization of these norms into the remote future and, at the same time, unlike the Chiliast who anticipates its realization at some ecstatic point beyond history, it sees it as arising out of the process of becoming in the here and now, out of the events of our everyday life.   From this has developed, we have seen, the typically linear conception of evolution and the relatively direct connection between a formerly transcendental and meaningful goal and present actual existence.

The liberal idea is adequately intelligible only as a counterpart to the ecstatic attitude of the Chiliast which often hides behind a rationalist façade and which historically and socially offers a continual, potential threat to liberalism.   It is a battle cry against that stratum of society whose power comes from its inherited position in the existing order, and which is able to master the here and now at first unconsciously and later through

[1] Landauer, op. cit., p. 91.

rational calculation.   Here we see how different utopias can
shape the whole structure of consciousness itself, and can reflect
the divergence between two historical worlds and the two corresponding, fundamentally different social strata whose outlooks
they embody.

Chiliasm had its period of existence in the world of the decaying
Middle Ages, a period of tremendous disintegration. Everything
was in conflict with everything else. It was the world of nobles,
patricians, townsmen, journeymen, vagabonds, and mercenaries,
all warring against each other. It was a world in upheaval and
unrest, in which the deepest impulses of the human spirit sought
external expression.   In this conflict, the ideologies did not
crystallize quite clearly, and it is not always easy to determine
definitely the social position to which each of them belongs.
As Engels clearly saw, it was the Peasant Revolt that first
reduced to simpler and less ambiguous terms the spiritual and
intellectual whirlpool of the Reformation.[1] It becomes more
apparent now that the Chiliastic experience is characteristic
of the lowest strata of society. Underlying it is a mental structure
peculiar to oppressed peasants, journeymen, an incipient *Lumpen-
proletariat*, fanatically emotional preachers, etc.[2]

[1] Engels, Fr., *Der deutsche Bauernkrieg*, ed. by Mehring (Berlin, 1920),
pp. 40 ff.
[2] Holl (op. cit., p. 435) claims to see an argument against a sociological
interpretation in the fact that Münzer's ideas, which, according to Max
Weber's general typology (*Wirtschaft und Gesellschaft : Grundriss der
Sozialökonomik*, Pt. III, V, I, pp. 267 ff., § 7), are to be correlated with the
lower classes, were also accepted by the " intellectuals " of the period
(e.g. Seb. Franck, Karlstadt, Schwenkenfeld, etc.).   If one is going to
simplify the problem of sociology to such a degree as he has done, it
is no wonder that one finally rejects its conclusions. Max Weber always
insisted that his general typology was created in order to characterize
ideal-typical tendencies, and not immediately perceivable unique constellations (ibid., p. 10).   The sociology which seeks to analyse historically
unique constellations must proceed in an especially cautious manner
when it is concerned with determining sociologically the position of the
intellectuals.   It is necessary at this point to consider the following
questions in the statement of the problem :—
    (a) The question of their sociological ambivalence (is this not already
a particular sociological trait, when one considers that it is not characteristic of all strata of society ?).
    (b) At what particular point in time are the representatives of the
intellectuals driven into the one camp or another ?
    (c) In what manner are the ideas that the intellectuals derive from
other camps modified in the course of their assimilation ?   (It is often
possible to trace shifts in social position through the " angle of refraction "
with which ideas are taken over.)
Thus Holl himself (pp. 435 ff., 459, 460) presents very interesting
documentary corroboration of the correctness of the sociology which

A long time intervened until the appearance of the next form
of utopia. Meanwhile the social world had undergone complete
transformation. " The knight became an official, the yeoman
an obedient citizen " (Freyer). Nor was the next form of utopia
the expression of the lowest stratum in the social order, rather it
was the middle stratum that was disciplining itself through còn-
scious self-cultivation and which regarded ethics and intellectual
culture as its principal self-justification (against the nobility),
and unwittingly shifted the bases of experience from an ecstatic
to an educational plane.

However abstract the liberal idea may appear to have been
from the point of view of the Chiliast or from the concrete
approach of the conservative, it nevertheless gave life to one of
the most important periods of modern history. Its abstractness,
which was only gradually uncovered by the criticism of the
right and left, was never felt by the original exponents of the
idea. Perhaps there was precisely in this indeterminateness
which left open such a variety of possibilities and which
stimulated the phantasy, that fresh and youthful quality, that
suggestive and stimulating atmosphere which even the aged
Hegel, despite his turn to conservatism, felt, when in the last
days of his life he recalled the penetrating impact of the great
ideas of the revolutionary period. In contrast with the sombre

he opposes. He himself shows that when the educated took over Münzer's
views they were really unable to elaborate them any further, and they
never contributed anything fundamentally new to the doctrine.   They
drew more upon books and upon the writings of the German mystics,
particularly the " *Theologia deutsch* ", but also upon Augustine, than upon
their own immediate, inner experience. They did not bring even the
slightest enrichment of language. They distorted the singularly mystical
on decisive points and made an innocuous amalgam of the teachings
of the medieval mystics and Münzer's doctrine of the cross.   (All these
are direct supports for the sociological theory referred to above concerning
the determinability of the intellectual " angle of refraction " which exists
when the ideas of one stratum are taken over by another.)

Holl further tells us how the intellectuals among others, through their
above-mentioned leaders, withdrew more and more as the movement
progressed and became more radical ; how among others, Franck, in
his *Chronika*, condemned the Peasant War even more sharply than Luther
himself ; how, following this alienation from Münzer, his *Weltanschauung*
underwent a radical transformation ; how after the alienation from
Münzer this " intellectual " *Weltanschauung* took on misanthropic traits ;
how it lost its " social features " ; and how, in place of the Chiliastic
intransigence, there emerged the more tolerant almost syncretistic idea
of the " invisible Church " (ibid., pp. 459 ff.).

Here, too, there is much that can be understood sociologically, as long
as one asks the appropriate questions, and utilizes the conceptual apparatus
arising from these.

depths of Chiliastic agitation, the central elements of the intellectualistic mentality were open to the clear light of day. The dominating mood of the Enlightenment, the hope that at last light would dawn on the world, has long survived to give these ideas even at this late stage their driving power.

However, in addition to this promise which stimulated phantasy and looked to a distant horizon, the deepest driving forces of the liberal ideas of the Enlightenment lay in the fact that it appealed to the free will and kept alive the feeling of being indeterminate and unconditioned. The distinctive character of the conservative mentality, however, consisted in the fact that it dulled the edge of this experience. And if one wishes to formulate the central achievement of conservatism in a single sentence, it could be said that in conscious contrast to the liberal outlook, it gave positive emphasis to the notion of the determinateness of our outlook and our behaviour.

(c) The Third Form of the Utopian Mentality: The Conservative Idea

Conservative mentality as such has no predisposition towards theorizing. This is in accord with the fact that human beings do not theorize about the actual situations in which they live as long as they are well adjusted to them. They tend, under such conditions of existence, to regard the environment as part of a natural world-order which, consequently, presents no problems. Conservative mentality as such has no utopia. Ideally it is in its very structure completely in harmony with the reality which, for the time being, it has mastered. It lacks all those reflections and illuminations of the historical process which come from a progressive impulse. The conservative type of knowledge originally is the sort of knowledge giving practical control. It consists of habitual and often also of reflective orientations towards those factors which are immanent in the situation. There are ideal elements surviving in the present as hangovers from the tension of former periods in which the world was not yet stabilized and which operate now only ideologically as faiths, religions, and myths which have been banished to a realm beyond history. At this stage, thought, as we have indicated, inclines to accept the total environment in the accidental concreteness in which it occurs, as if it were the proper order of the world, to be taken for granted and presenting no problem. Only the counter-attack of opposing classes and their tendency to break through the limits of the existing order causes the conservative mentality to question the basis of its own dominance, and necessarily brings about among the conservatives historical-philosophical reflections concerning themselves. Thus, there arises a counter-utopia which serves as a means of self-orientation and defence.

If the socially ascendant classes had not in reality raised these problems and if they had not given them utterance in their respective counter-ideologies, the tendency of conservatism to become conscious of itself would have remained latent and the conservative outlook would have continued on a level of unconscious behaviour. But the ideological attack of a socially ascendant group representing a new epoch does, in fact, bring about an awareness of the attitudes and ideas which assert themselves only in life and in action. Goaded on by opposing theories, conservative mentality discovers its *idea* only *ex post facto*.[1] It is no accident that whereas all progressive groups regard the idea as coming before the deed, for the conservative Hegel the idea of an historical reality becomes visible only subsequently, when the world has already assumed a fixed inner form : " Only one word more concerning the desire to teach the world what it ought to be. For such a purpose, philosophy, at least, always comes too late. Philosophy as the thought of the world does not appear until reality has completed its formative process and made itself ready. History thus corroborates the teachings of the conception that only in the maturity of reality does the ideal appear as the counterpart to the real, apprehends the real world in its substance, and shapes it into an intellectual kingdom. When philosophy paints its

[1] We must also consider the ideology of absolutism in this connection, although we cannot deal with it in detail. It, too, shows an outlook originally oriented towards the mastery of a life-situation, acquiring the tendency to reflect in a rather cold-blooded way on the technique of domination—in the manner of what is called Machiavellianism. Only later (mostly when compelled by its opponents) does the need arise for a more intellectual and elaborate justification for occupying a position of power. For the corroboration of this more general proposition, we draw on a sentence of Meinecke in which this process is observed :—
" Thus arose the ideal of the modern state which aspires not merely to be a political state (*Machtstaat*), but also a cultural state, and the bare restriction of the *raison d'état* to the mere problems of the immediate maintenance of power, which largely occupied the attention of the theoreticians of the seventeenth century, was overcome." This refers particularly to the age of Frederick the Great. Meinecke, Fr., *Die Idee der Staatsräson in der neueren Geschichte* (München, Berlin, 1925), p. 353.

grey in grey, one form of life has become old, and by means of grey it cannot be rejuvenated, but only known. The owl of Minerva takes its flight only when the shades of night are gathering." [1] In the conservative mentality, the " owl of Minerva " does indeed begin its flight only with the approaching twilight.

In its original form, conservative mentality was, as we have mentioned, not concerned with ideas. It was its liberal opponent who, so to speak, forced it into this arena of conflict. The peculiar characteristic of intellectual development seems to lie precisely in the fact that the most recent antagonist dictates the tempo and the form of the battle. Certainly there is little truth in the so-called progressive idea that only the new has the prospect for further existence, and that all else dies off gradually. Rather, the older, driven by the newer, must continuously transform itself and must accommodate itself to the level of the most recent opponent. Thus, at present, those who have been operating with earlier modes of thought, when confronted with sociological arguments must also have recourse to these same methods. In the same manner, at the beginning of the nineteenth century, the liberal-intellectualist mode of thought compelled the conservatives to interpret themselves by intellectualist means.

It is interesting to observe that the original conservative social classes, which earlier had acquired stability through closeness to the land (Möser, v.d. Marwitz) did not succeed in the theoretical interpretation of their own position, and that the discovery of the conservative idea became the work of a body of ideologists who attached themselves to the conservatives.

The accomplishment in this direction of the conservative romantics, and particularly Hegel, consisted in their intellectual analysis of the meaning of conservative existence. With this as a point of departure, they provided an intellectual interpretation of an attitude toward the world which was already implicit in actual conduct but which had not yet become explicit. Hence, in the case of the conservatives, what corresponds to the *idea* is in substance something quite different from the liberal idea. It was Hegel's great achievement to set up against the liberal idea a conservative counterpart, not in the sense of artificially concocting an attitude and a mode of behaviour, but rather by raising an already present mode of experience to an intellectual level and by emphasizing the distinctive

[1] The famous final paragraph in Hegel's preface to his *Philosophy of Right*. Translated by J. W. Dyde (London, 1896), p. xxx.

characteristics that mark it off from the liberal attitude toward the world.

The conservatives looked .upon the liberal idea which characterized the period of the Enlightenment as something vaporous and lacking in concreteness. And it was from this angle that they levelled their attack against it and depreciated it. Hegel saw in it nothing more than a mere " opinion "— a bare image—a pure possibility behind which one takes refuge, saves oneself, and escapes from the demands of the hour.

As opposed to this mere " opinion ", this bare subjective image, the conservatives conceived of the idea as rooted in and expressing itself concretely in the living reality of the here and now. Meaning and reality, norm and existence, are not separate here, because the utopian, the " concretized idea ", is in a vital sense present in this world. What in liberalism is merely a formal norm, in conservatism acquires concrete content in the prevailing laws of the state. In the objectifications of culture, in art and in science, spirituality unfolds itself, and the idea expresses itself in tangible fullness.

We have already observed that, in the liberal utopia, in the humanitarian idea as contrasted with Chiliastic ecstasy, there is a relative approximation to the " here and now ". In con- servatism, we find the process of approximation to the " here and now " completed. The utopia in this case is, from the very beginning, embedded in existing reality.

To this, obviously, there corresponds the fact that reality, the " here and now ", is no longer experienced as an " evil " reality but as the embodiment of the highest values and meanings.

Although it is true that the utopia, or the idea, has become completely congruous with concretely existing reality, i.e. has been assimilated into it, this mode of experience—at least at the highest point in the creative period of this current—never- theless does not lead to an elimination of tensions and to an inert and passive acceptance of the situation as it is. A certain amount of tension between idea and existence arises from the fact that not every element of this existence embodies meaning, and that it is always necessary to distinguish between what is essential and what is non-essential, and that the present continually confronts us with new tasks and problems which have not yet been mastered. In order to arrive at some norm for orientation, we should not depend on subjective impulses, but must call upon those forces and ideas which have become objectified in us and in our past, upon the spirit which, up to now, has operated through us to create these, our works. But this idea, this spirit, has not been rationally conjured up and has not been arbitrarily chosen as the best among a number of possibilities. It is either in us, as a "silently working force" (Savigny), subjectively perceived, or as an entelechy which has unfolded itself in the collective creations of the community, of the folk, the nation, or the state as an inner form which, for the most part, is perceivable morphologically. The morphological perspective, directed towards language, art, and the state, develops from that point on. At about the same time that the liberal idea set the existing order into motion and stimulated constructive speculation, Goethe turned from this activistic approach to contemplation—to morphology. He set out to use intuitive apperception as an instrument of science. The approach of the historical school is in some ways analogous to that of Goethe. They follow up the emanation of "ideas" through the observation of language, custom, and law, etc., not by abstract generalizations but rather by sympathetic intuition and morphological description.

In this case also, the idea which assumes a central position in political experience (i.e. the form of utopia corresponding to this social position) helped in shaping that segment of intellectual life which was bound up with politics. In all the varieties of these quests for the "inner form" the same conservative attitude of determinateness persists and, when projected outward, finds expression also in the emphasis on historical determinateness. According to this view and from the standpoint of this attitude towards the world man is by no means absolutely free. Not all things in general and each thing in particular are possible at every moment and in every historical community. The inner form of historical individuality existing at any given time, be it that of an individual personality or of a folk spirit, and the external conditions together with the past that lies behind it, determine the shape of things that are to be. It is for this reason that the historical configuration existing at any given time cannot be artificially constructed, but grows like a plant from its seed.[1]

---

[1] "The constitutions of states cannot be invented; the cleverest calculation in this matter is as futile as total ignorance. There is no substitute for the spirit of a people, and the strength and order arising therefrom, and it is not to be found even in the brightest minds or in

Even the conservative form of the utopia, the notion of an idea embedded and expressed in reality, is in the last analysis intelligible only in the light of its struggles with the other coexistent forms of utopia. Its immediate antagonist is the liberal idea which has been translated into rationalistic terms. Whereas in the latter, the normative, the " should " is accentuated in experience, in conservatism the emphasis shifts to existing reality, the " is ". The fact of the mere existence of a thing endows it with a higher value, be it, as in the case of Hegel, because of the higher rationality embodied in it, or, as in the case of Stahl, because of the mystifying and fascinating effects of its very irrationality. " There is something marvellous about experiencing something of which it may be said ' it is ! '— ' This is your father, this is your friend, and through them you have arrived at this position.' ' Why precisely this ? ' ' Why are you just the person you are ? ' This incomprehensibility consists in the fact that existence can never be fully subsumed in thought, and that existence is not a logical necessity but has its basis in a higher autonomous power." [1] Here the pregnant antagonism between the idea embodied and expressed in reality, on the one hand, and that which merely exists, on the other (derived from the halcyon days of conservatism), threatens to transform itself into a complete congruence, and conservative quietism tends to justify, by irrational means, everything that exists at all.

The time-sense of this mode of experience and thought is completely opposed to that of liberalism. Whereas for liberalism the future was everything and the past nothing, the conservative mode of experiencing time found the best corroboration of its sense of determinateness in discovering the significance of the past, in the discovery of time as the creator of value. Duration did not exist at all for the Chiliastic mentality,[2] and existed for liberalism only in so far as henceforth it gives birth to progress. But for conservatism everything that exists has a positive and nominal value merely because it has come into existence slowly

the greatest geniuses." (Müller, Adam, *Über König Friedrich II. und die Natur, Würde, und Bestimmung der preussischen Monarchie* (Berlin, 1810), p. 49.) This idea, derived from romanticism, becomes the leading theme of the whole conservative tradition.

[1] Stahl, Fr. J., *Die Philosophie des Rechts*, i[4], p. 272.

[2] Münzer says further, " The intellectuals and scholars do not know why the Holy Scriptures should be accepted or rejected, but only that they come down from the remote past . . . the Jews, the Turks, and all other peoples also have such apish, imitative ways of giving support to their beliefs." (Holl, p. 432, note 2.)

and gradually. Consequently not only is attention turned to the past and the attempt made to rescue it from oblivion, but the presentness and immediacy of the whole past becomes an actual experience. In this view, history can no longer be thought of as a mere unilinear extension of time, nor does it consist in merely joining on to the line which leads from the present to the future that which led from the past to the present. The conception of time here in question has an imaginary third dimension which it derives from the fact that the past is experienced as virtually present. "The life of the contemporary spirit is a cycle of stages, which on the one hand still have a synchronous coexistence, and only from another view appear as a sequence in time that has passed. The experiences which the spirit seems to have behind it, exist also in the depths of its present being." (Hegel.) [1]

The Chiliastic experience had its locus outside the realm of time, but on those occasions when it broke through into the temporal realm it hallowed the chance moment.   Liberal experience establishes a connection between existence and utopia in shifting the idea as meaningful goal into the future, and, through progress, allowing the promises of the utopia, at least in certain respects, gradually to be realized in our own midst. Conservative experience merges the spirit, which at one time came upon us from beyond and to which we gave expression, with what already is, allowing that to become objective, to expand in all dimensions, and thereby endowing every event with an immanent, intrinsic value.

---

[1] Hegel, *Vorlesungen über die Philosophie der Geschichte* (Leipzig, Reclam, 1907), cf. pp. 123–5. Further references may be found in my *Das konservative Denken*, p. 98 f., where I attempted for the first time to understand the forms of the "historical time-sense" in the light of the structure of the political consciousness existing at any given time. For further references, cf. the following :—

Stahl seeks to characterize the feeling for time and life of Schelling, Goethe and Savigny, in the following words : " In these writers it is as in every stage and nuance of life : it seems as if what is had always been so. But then we turn back and find that what is has developed. But it is not so obvious to us where and how the transition from one stage to another occurred. In the course of the same invisible growth, the situations and surrounding circumstances emerge and change. Just as in our own life-situations and careers, so here too the feeling of eternal and necessary existence and, at the same time, that of temporal emergence and change comes over us.

This endless growth, this living process of becoming, also dominates Schelling's outlook and his system represents an unabating struggle to express it. Savigny in his own domain is marked by the same characteristic." (*Die Philosophie des Rechts,* i[4], pp. 394 ff.

The conservative mode of experience, apart from its struggle with the liberal idea, had to wage its own particular war with the Chiliastic outlook, which it had always regarded as an inner enemy. The same Chiliastic experience, which at the time of the Anabaptists began to play an active part in the world, had another fate awaiting it, somewhat different from those already mentioned. We have already seen three alternative tendencies in Chiliastic experience. Either it remains unchanged and persists in its original eruptive form, often bound up with the most fundamentally divergent ideologies—as for instance in extremist anarchism—or it subsides and disappears or becomes " sublimated " into an idea. It follows another path, departing from those mentioned above, when it maintains its supertemporal, ecstatic tendency by turning inward, whereupon it no longer dares to venture forth into the world, and loses its contact with worldly happenings. Compelled by external circumstances, the Chiliastic-ecstatic mode of experience in Germany followed to a very large extent this path of inward-turning. The Pietistic under-currents which may be traced over long periods in Germanic countries, represents such an inward-turning of what was once Chiliastic ecstasy.

Even when it is turned inward, ecstatic experience represents a danger to the existing order, for it is constantly under temptation to express itself outwardly, and only prolonged discipline and repression transform it into quietism. Orthodoxy therefore waged constant war against Pietism, and it entered into an open union with it only when the revolutionary onslaught necessitated the summoning of all the available forces for the spiritualization of the ruling powers. Under external pressure and because of the sociologically intelligible structural situations, Chiliastic experience, through this very inward-turning, naturally undergoes a change in character. Here, as elsewhere, the structural interpenetration of socially " external " and of " internal " factors may be followed out in detail. Whereas originally Chiliastic experience manifested a robust and corporeal drive, when repressed it became rather sweetly innocuous and vaporous, it became watered down into mere enthusiasm, and the ecstatic element came to life once more, though in a gently soothing form, only in the Pietistic " experience of awakening ".

What is most important, however, for the connections we wish to point out, is that through the loss of contact with the world in actual process of becoming (this contact when seen from the point of view of the whole takes place in the political and not the private sphere), this attitude develops an inner uncertainty. In place of the pontifical tone of Chiliastic prophecy comes uncertain vacillation, Pietistic indecision in the face of action. The " historical school " in Germany, with its quietism and its lack of standards, can be adequately understood only when its continuity with Pietism has been taken into account. Everything which in an active person expresses itself spontaneously and is taken for granted is here detached from its context and made into a problem. The " decision " becomes an independent phase of action which is overladen with problems, and this conceptual separation of the act from the decision only increases uncertainty instead of eliminating it. The inner illumination furnished by Pietism offers no solution to most of the problems of everyday life, and if suddenly it becomes necessary to act in the historical process, one seeks to interpret the events of history as if they were indications of the will of God. At this point sets in the movement towards the religious interpretations of history [1] through which it was hoped to eliminate the inner indecision in political activity. But instead of finding the solution to the problems of right conduct, and instead of history furnishing divine guidance, this inner uncertainty was projected into the world.

It is important for the activist, conservative mode of experience to subdue this form of utopia also, and to harmonize the latent, vital energies present there with its own spirit. What needs to be controlled here is the concept of " inner freedom ", which constantly threatens to turn into anarchism (it had once before turned into a revolt against the church). Here also the conservative idea, embedded in reality, has a subduing influence on the utopia espoused by the inner enemies. According to the dominant theory of conservatism, " inner freedom," in its undefined, worldly objective, must subordinate itself to the moral code which has already been defined. Instead of " inner freedom ", we have " objective freedom ", to which the former must adjust itself. Metaphysically this may be interpreted as a pre-stabilized harmony between internally subjectified and externally objectified freedom. That this current of the movement, which is characterized by introspective Pietistic attitudes, conforms to the above

[1] Some of the important aspects of this tendency have been well worked out by my student Requadt, P., *Johannes v. Müller und der Frühhistorismus* (München, 1929).

interpretation is to be explained only by its fatal helplessness in the face of worldly problems. On that account it yields the reins to the dominance of the realistic conservative group either by surrendering entirely or by retiring to some obscure corner. Even to-day there are arch-conservative groups who wish to hear nothing of the power politics of the Bismarckian epoch, and who see in the inward-turning direction of that current which set itself in opposition to Bismarck the truly valuable elements of the tradition.[1]

(d) The Fourth Form of the Utopian Mentality : The Socialist-Communist Utopia

Even the socialist-communist mode of thought and experience which, as regards its origins, may be treated as a unity, is best understood in its utopian structure by observing it as it is attacked from three sides.

On the one hand, socialism had further to radicalize the liberal utopia, the idea, and, on the other, it had to render impotent or in a given case to overcome completely the inner opposition of anarchism in its most extreme form. Its conservative antagonist is considered only secondarily, just as in political life one generally proceeds more sharply against the closely related opponent than against a distant one, because the tendency is much greater to glide over into his view, and consequently especial watchfulness must be exercised against this inner temptation. Communism, for example, fights more energetically against Revisionism than against conservatism. This helps us to understand why socialist-communist theory is in a position to learn much from conservatism.

The utopian element in socialism, due to this many-sided situation and the late stage of its origin, presents a Janus face. It represents not merely a compromise but also a new creation based upon an inner synthesis of the various forms of utopia which have arisen hitherto and which have struggled against one another in society.

Socialism is at one with the liberal utopia in the sense that both believe that the realm of freedom and equality will come into

---

[1] Cf., for example, the last section of v. Martin's essay, " Weltanschauliche Motive im altkonservativen Denken," *Deutscher Staat und deutsche Parteien : in Festschrift, Fr. Meinecke zum 60. Geburtstag dargebracht* (München, Berlin, 1922).

existence only in the remote future.[1] But socialism characteristically places this future at a much more specifically determined point in time, namely the period of the breakdown of capitalist culture. This solidarity of socialism with the liberal idea in its orientation towards a goal located in the future is to be explained by their common opposition to conservatism's immediate and direct acceptance and affirmation of the existing order. The far-reaching indefiniteness and spirituality of the remote goal corresponds, also, to the socialist and liberal rejection of Chiliastic excitement and their common recognition that latent ecstatic energies must be sublimated through cultural ideals.

But in so far as the question is one of the penetration of the idea into the evolving process and the gradual development of the idea, the socialist mentality does not experience it in this spiritually sublimated form. We are faced here with the idea in the form of a novel substance, almost like a living organism which has definite conditions of existence, the knowledge of which may become the aim of scientific investigation. In this context, ideas are not dreams and desires, imaginary imperatives wafted down from some absolute sphere; they have rather a concrete life of their own and a definite function in the total process. They die away when they become outmoded, and they can be realized when the social process attains to a given structural situation. Without such relevance to reality, they become merely obfuscating " ideologies ".

When one turns to the liberal, one discovers from a perspective quite different from the one employed by the conservative the purely formal abstract character of his idea. The ",mere opinion ", the mere image of the idea which realizes itself only in one's subjective attitude, is recognized here too as inadequate and is subjected to attack from another angle than that of the conservative opposition. It is not sufficient to have a good intention in the abstract and to postulate in the far-off future

---

[1] This assertion does not apply to socialism until we come to the nineteenth century. The utopian socialism of the eighteenth century Enlightenment, in a period when the Physiocrats were interpreting history in the light of the idea of progress, had its utopia located in the past, corresponding to the petty bourgeois reactionary mentality of its bearers. Sociologically this flight into the past has its roots in part in the persistence of certain remnants of the old " common " land holding system, which to some extent kept alive the memory of " communist " institutions in the past. Concerning this relationship, many details are to be found in Girsberger, H., *Der utopische Sozialismus des 18. Jahrhunderts in Frankreich und seine philosophischen und materiellen Grundlagen: Zürcher Volkswirtschaftliche Forschungen*, Heft 1., cf. esp. pp. 94 ff.

a realized realm of freedom, the elements of which are not subject to control. It is necessary rather to become aware of the real conditions (in this case economic and social) under which such a wish-fulfilment can at all become operative. The road which leads from the present to this distant goal must also be investigated in order to identify those forces in the contemporary process whose immanent, dynamic character, under our direction, leads step by step towards the realized idea. While conservatism depreciated the liberal idea as a mere opinion, socialism, in its analysis of ideology, worked out a coherent, critical method which was, in effect, an attempt to annihilate the antagonists' utopia by showing that they had their roots in the existing situation.

Henceforth, a desperate struggle takes place aiming at the fundamental disintegration of the adversary's belief. Each of the forms of utopian mentality which we have treated thus far turns against the rest of each belief it is demanded that it correspond with reality, and in each case a differently constituted form of existence is presented to the adversary as " reality ". The economic and social structure of society becomes absolute reality for the socialist. It becomes the bearer of that cultural totality which the conservatives had already perceived as a unity. The conservative conception of folk spirit (*Volksgeist*) was the first significant attempt to understand the apparently isolated facts of intellectual and psychic life as emanations from a single centre of creative energy.

For the liberals as well as for the conservatives, this driving force was something spiritual. In the socialist mentality, on the contrary, there emerges, out of the age-old affinity of oppressed strata for a materialistic orientation, a glorification of the material aspects of existence, which were formerly experienced merely as negative and obstructive factors.

Even in the ontological evaluation of the factors which constitute the world which is always the most characteristic criterion of any structure of consciousness, a hierarchy of values, which is the reverse of that employed by other modes of thought, gradually achieves dominance. The " material " conditions which were previously regarded merely as evil obstacles in the path of the idea are here hypostatized into the motor factor in world affairs, in the form of an economic determinism which is reinterpreted in materialistic terms.

The utopia which achieves the closest relationship to the

historical-social situation of this world, manifests its approximation not only by locating its goal more and more within the
framework of history, but by elevating and spiritualizing the
social and economic structure which is immediately accessible.
Essentially what happens here is a peculiar assimilation of the
conservative sense of determinism into the progressive utopia
which strives to remake the world.   The conservative, due to
his consciousness of being determined, glorified the past despite
or even because of its determinative function, and at the same
time, once and for all, gave an adequate indication of the significance of the past for historical development. For the socialists,
however, it is the social structure which becomes the most
influential force in the historical moment, and its formative
powers (in a glorified form) are regarded as the determinant
factors of the whole development.

The novel phenomenon which we meet with here, the feeling of
determinateness, is quite compatible, however, with a utopia
located in the future. While conservative mentality naturally
connected the feeling of determinateness with the affirmation
of the present, socialism merges a progressive social force with
the checks which revolutionary action automatically imposes
upon itself when it perceives the determining forces in history.

These two factors, which at first are immediately bound up
with each other, diverge in the course of time to form two opposing
but mutually interacting factions within the socialist-communist
movement. Groups which have recently gained power and which,
by participating in and sharing responsibility for the existing
order, become wedded to things as they are, come to exert a
retarding influence through their espousal of orderly evolutionary
change. On the other hand, those strata which as yet have no
vested interest in things as they are, become the bearers of the
communist (and also the syndicalist) theory which emphasizes
the overwhelming importance of revolution.

Before the split, however, which corresponds to a later stage
in the process, this progressive mentality first of all had to
establish itself in the face of the opposition of other parties.
Two obstacles to be overcome were the sense of historical
indeterminateness involved in Chiliasm, which took a modern
form in radical anarchism, and this same blindness to the
determining forces of history which goes with the sense of
indeterminateness of the liberal " idea ".

In the history of modern Chiliastic experience, the conflict between Marx and Bakunin was decisive.[1] It was in the course of this conflict that Chiliastic utopianism came to an end.

The more a group preparing to assume power strives to become a party, the less it will tolerate a movement which, in a sectarian and eruptive fashion, aims, in some undetermined moment, to take the fortresses of history by storm. Here, too, the disappearance of a fundamental attitude—at least in the form of which we have spoken—is closely connected with the disintegration of the social and economic reality which constitutes its background (as Brupbacher has shown.[2]) Bakunin's advance guard, the anarchists of the Jura Federation, disintegrated when the domestic system of watch manufacture, in which they were engaged and which made possible their sectarian attitude, was supplanted by the factory system of production. In the place of the unorganized, oscillating experience of the ecstatic utopia, came the well-organized Marxian revolutionary movement. Here again we see that the manner in which a group conceived of time displays most clearly the type of utopia in consonance with which its consciousness is organized. Time is experienced here as a series of strategical points.

This disintegration of the anarchist ecstatic utopia was abrupt and brutal, but it was dictated with a fatal necessity by the historical process itself. An outlook of passionate depth disappeared from the foreground of the political scene and the sense of determinism came to hold sway over an enlarged sphere.

Liberal thought is related to anarchist thought in that it too had a sense of indeterminism even though (as we have seen), through the idea of progress, it achieved relative nearness to the concrete historical process. The liberal's sense of indeterminism was based on faith in an immediate relationship to an absolute sphere of ethical imperatives—to the *idea* itself. This sphere of ethical imperatives did not derive its validity from history; nevertheless for the liberal the idea could become a driving force in it. It is not the historical process which produces ideas, but it is only the discovery of the ideas, the spreading of them, and

---

[1] Concerning Bakunin, cf. the writings of Nettlau, Ricarda Huch and Fr. Brupbacher. The work of the latter, *Marx und Bakunin* (Berlin-Wilmersdorf, 1922), offers a concise exposition of many important problems. The collected works of Bakunin have been brought out in German by the publishing house " Der Syndikalist ". Cf. further Bakunin's confession to Czar Nicholas I, discovered in the secret files of the chief of the third section of the chancellery of the late Czar, trans. by K. Kersten, Berlin, 1926.

[2] Brupbacher, op. cit., pp. 60 ff., 204 ff.

" enlightenment " about them, which make of them historical forces. A veritable Copernican revolution occurred when man began to regard not merely himself, not merely man, but also the existence, the validity, and the influence of these ideas as conditioned factors, and the development of ideas as bound up with existence, as integral to the historico-social process. It was important for socialism, first of all, not to combat this absolutist mentality among its opponents, but rather to establish in its own camp the new attitude in opposition to the still dominant idealism. Quite early, therefore, there took place this turning away from the utopias of the "big bourgeoisie", the best analysis of which is still to be found in Engels.

St. Simon, Fourier, and Owen were still dreaming their utopias in the older intellectualist style, although they already bore the impress of socialistic ideas. Their situation on the margin of society expressed itself in discoveries which broadened social and economic perspectives; in their method, however, they retained the indeterminate outlook characteristic of the Enlightenment. " Socialism is for all of them the expression of absolute truth, reason, and justice, and need only be discovered in order to conquer the world through its own power." [1] Here, too, one idea had to be vanquished, and accordingly the sense of historical determinateness displaced the other competing form of utopia. Socialist mentality, in a far more fundamental sense than the liberal idea, represents a redefinition of utopia in terms of reality. It is only at the end of the process that the idea remains in its prophetic indeterminateness and indefiniteness, but the road which leads from things as they are to the realization of the idea is already clearly staked out historically and socially.

Here again there is a difference in the manner of experiencing historical time : whereas the liberal conceived of future time as a direct and straight line leading to a goal, there now arises a distinction between the near and the remote, a distinction, the beginnings of which were already to be found in Condorcet and which is of significance for thought as well as action. Conservatism had already differentiated the past in such a manner, but since its utopia was tending more and more towards a complete harmony with the stage of reality already reached at the time, the future remained completely undifferentiated for the conservative. Only through the union of a sense of determinate-

[1] Engels, Fr., *Die Entwicklung des Sozialismus von der Utopie zur Wissenschaft*, 4th edit., Berlin, 1894.

ness and a living vision of the future was it possible to create an historical time-sense of more than one dimension. But this more complex perspective of historical time, which conservatism had already created for the past, has here a completely different structure.

It is not alone through the virtual presentness of every past event that every present experience embodies a third dimension which points back to the past, but it is also because the future is being prepared in it. It is not only the past but the future as well which has virtual existence in the present. A weighing of each of the factors existing in the present, and an insight into the tendencies latent in these forces, can be obtained only if the present is understood in the light of its concrete fulfilment in the future.[1]

Whereas the liberal conception of the future was completely formal, here we are dealing with a process of gradual concretization. Although this completion of the present by the future is, to begin with, imposed by the will and by wishful images, none the less this striving towards a goal acts as a heuristically selective factor both in research and in action. According to this point of view, the future is always testing itself in the present. At the same time the " idea " which was at first only a vague prophecy is constantly being corrected and rendered more concrete as the present lives on into the future. The socialist " idea ", in its interaction with " actual " events, operates not as a purely formal and transcendent principle which regulates the event from the outside, but rather as a " tendency " within the matrix of this reality which continuously corrects itself with reference to this context. The concrete investigation of the interdependence of the entire range of events from economic to psychic and intellectual must bring together isolated observations into a functional unity against the background of a developing whole.

Thereby our view of history obtains an ever more concrete,

[1] A corroboration of the above analysis and an almost exact mathematical corroboration of our theory concerning the socially and politically differentiated mode of experiencing historical time is provided by the following excerpt from an article by the Communist, J. Révai : " The present really exists only by virtue of the fact that the past and the future exist, the present is the form of the unnecessary past and of the unreal future. Tactics are the future appearing as present." (" Das Problem der Taktik," in *Kommunismus : Zeitschrift der Kommunistischen Internationale*, 1920, ii, p. 1676. The virtual presentness of the future in the present is clearly expressed herein. It stands in complete contrast to the citation from Hegel on page 212.) It should also be compared with the other materials cited throughout the text concerning the social differentiation of the historical time-sense (pp. 202–03, 211–12, 219, 228).

differentiated, but at the same time more flexible framework. We examine every event with a view to discovering what it means and what its position is in the total developmental structure.

To be sure, the area of free choice becomes more restricted thereby ; more determinants are discovered, for not only is the past a determining factor, but the economic and social situation of the present also conditions the possible event. The driving purpose here no longer consists in activity on the basis of random impulses toward some arbitrarily chosen here and now, but rather in fixing attention upon a favourable point of attack in the structural whole within which we exist. It becomes the task of the political leader deliberately to reinforce those forces the dynamics of which seem to move in the direction desired by him, and to turn in his own direction or at least to render impotent those which seem to be to his disadvantage. Historical experience becomes thereby a truly strategic plan. Everything in history may now be experienced as an intellectually and volitionally controllable phenomenon.

In this case, too, the point of view formulated primarily in the political arena penetrates all cultural life : out of the investigation into the social determination of history arises sociology, and it in its turn gradually becomes a key science whose outlook permeates all the special historical sciences which have arrived at a similar stage of development. A confidence and assurance, qualified by the feeling of determinateness, gives rise at the same time to a creative scepticism and a disciplined *élan*. A special kind of " realism " permeates the realm of art. The idealism of the bourgeois philistine of the middle nineteenth century has vanished and, as long as a productive tension between the ideal and existence persists, transcendent values, which are henceforth conceived of as embodied in actual existence, will be sought in the near and the immediate.

4. Utopia in the Contemporary Situation

At the present moment the problem has assumed its own unique form. The historical process itself shows us a gradual descent and a closer approximation to real life of a utopia that at one time completely transcended history. As it comes closer to historical reality, its form undergoes functional as well as substantial changes. What was originally in absolute opposition to historical reality tends now, after the model of conservatism, to lose its character as opposition. Of course, none of the forms of these dynamic forces which emerge in an historical sequence ever disappears entirely, and at no time is any one of them indisputably dominant. The coexistence of these forces, their reciprocal opposition, as well as their constant mutual interpenetration, bring into being forms from which the richness of historical experience first emerges.

In order not to obscure what is decisive by an excess of details, we purposely stressed only the important tendencies in all this variety and overemphasized them by portraying them as ideal-types. Even though in the course of history nothing actually ever is lost of this multiplicity of things and events, it is possible to show with increasing clarity various degrees of dominance and alignment of the forces at work in society. Ideas, forms of thought, and psychic energies persist and are transformed in close conjunction with social forces. It is never by accident that they appear at given moments in the social process.

In this connection there becomes visible a peculiar structural determinant, which is at least worth indicating. The broader the class which achieves a certain mastery of the concrete conditions of existence, and the greater the chances for a victory through peaceful evolution, the more likely is this class to follow the road of conservatism. This signifies, however, that the various movements will have relinquished the utopian elements in their own modes of life.

This is demonstrated most sharply in the already mentioned fact that the relatively purest form of modern Chiliastic mentality, as embodied in radical anarchism, disappears almost entirely from the political scene, as a result of which an element of tension was eliminated from the remaining forms of the political utopia.

It is, of course, true that many of the elements constituting the Chiliastic attitude were transmuted into and took refuge in syndicalism and in Bolshevism, and were assimilated and incorporated into the activity of these movements. Thus the function devolves upon them, particularly in Bolshevism, of accelerating and catalyzing rather than deifying the revolutionary deed.

The general subsidence of utopian intensity occurs in still another important direction, namely that each utopia, as it is formed at a later stage of development, manifests a closer approximation to the historical-social process. In this sense, the liberal, the socialist, and the conservative ideas are merely different stages, and indeed counter-forms in the process which moves continually farther away from Chiliasm and approximates more closely to the events transpiring in this world.

All of these counter-forms of the Chiliastic utopia develop in close connection with the fate of those social strata which originally espouse them. They are, as we have seen, already moderated forms of the original Chiliastic ecstasy but in the course of further development they discard these last utopian vestiges and unwittingly approach more closely to a conservative attitude. It appears to be a generally valid law of the structure of intellectual development that when new groups gain entry into an already established situation they do not take over without further ado the ideologies which have already been elaborated for this situation, but rather they adapt the ideas which they bring with them through their traditions to the new situation. Thus liberalism and socialism, as they entered a situation more conducive to conservatism, did intermittently take over the ideas which conservatism offered them as a model, but on the whole preferred to adapt the original ideologies that they brought with them to the new situation. When these strata had come to occupy the social position previously held by the conservatives, they quite spontaneously developed a feeling for life and modes of thought which were structurally related to conservatism. The initial insight of the conservative into the structure of historical determinism, the emphasis, and, wherever possible, the overemphasis of the silently-working forces, the continuous absorption of the utopian element into everyday life appeared also in the thinking of these strata, sometimes in the form of a new and spontaneous creation, sometimes as a reinterpretation of older conservative patterns.

Thus we note that, conditioned by the social process, there develops a relative departure from the utopia at many points and in various forms. This process, which has already a dynamic quality of its own, is accelerated even further in its tempo and intensity by the fact that different coexistent forms of utopian mentality are destroying one another in reciprocal conflict. Such a reciprocal conflict of the various forms of the utopia does not necessarily lead to the annihilation of utopianism itself, for struggle in and by itself only heightens the utopian intensity. The modern form of reciprocal conflict is nevertheless peculiar in that the destruction of one's adversary does not take place on a utopian level, a fact which is most clearly perceptible in the way the socialists have gone about unmasking the ideologies of their antagonists.[1] We do not hold up to the adversary that he is worshipping false gods ; rather we destroy the intensity of his idea by showing that it is historically and socially determined.

Socialist thought, which hitherto has unmasked all its adversaries' utopias as ideologies, never raised the problem of determinateness about its own position. It never applied this method to itself and never checked its own desire to be absolute. It is nevertheless inevitable that here too the utopian element disappears with an increase in the feeling of determinateness. Thus we approach a situation in which the utopian element, through its many divergent forms, has completely (in politics, at least) annihilated itself. If one attempts to follow through tendencies which are already in existence, and to project them into the future, Gottfried Keller's prophecy—" The ultimate triumph of freedom will be barren " [2]—begins to assume, for us at least, an ominous meaning.

Symptoms of this " barrenness " are revealed in many contemporary phenomena, and can be clearly understood as radiations of the social and political situation into the more remote spheres of cultural life. Indeed, the more actively an ascendant party collaborates in a parliamentary coalition, and the more it gives up its original utopian impulses and with it its broad perspective, the more its power to transform society is likely to be absorbed by its interest in concrete and isolated details. Quite parallel to the change that may be observed in the political realm runs a change in the scientific outlook which conforms to political demands, i.e. what was once merely a formal scheme and abstract, total view, tends to dissolve into the investigation of specific and discrete problems. The utopian striving towards a goal and the closely related capacity for a broad perspective disintegrate in the parliamentary advisory council and in the trade-union movement into a mere body of directions for mastering a vast number of concrete details with a view to taking a political stand with reference to them. Likewise in the realm of research, what was formerly a correspondingly unified and systematized *Weltanschauung* becomes, in the attempt to deal

---

[1] The change in the meaning of the concept ideology which we attempted to present in Part II is merely a phase of this more general process (pp. 53 ff.).

[2] " Der Freiheit letzter Sieg wird trocken sein."

R

with individual problems, merely a guiding perspective and a heuristic principle. But since all the mutually conflicting forms of utopia pass through the same life-cycle, they become in the realm of science, as in the realm of parliamentary practice, less and less mutually conflicting articles of faith, and more and more competing parties, or possible hypotheses for research. Whereas in an age of liberal ideals philosophy best reflected the social and intellectual situation, to-day the internal condition of the social and intellectual situations is reflected most clearly in the diverse forms of sociology.

The sociological view of classes acceding to power undergoes transformation along particular lines. These sociological theories, like our contemporary everyday conception of the world, embody the conflicting " possible points of view " which are nothing but the gradual transformations of earlier utopias. What is peculiar to this situation is that in this competitive struggle for the correct social perspective, all these conflicting approaches and points of view do not by any means " discredit " themselves ; i.e. do not show themselves to be futile or incorrect. Rather it is shown with increasing clarity that it is possible to think productively from any point of view, although the degree of fruitfulness attainable varies from position to position. Each of these points of view reveals the interrelationships in the total complex of events from a different angle, and thus the suspicion grows that the historical process is something more inclusive than all the existing individual standpoints, and that our basis of thought, in its present state of atomization does not achieve a comprehensive view of events. The mass of facts and points of view is far greater than can be accommodated by the present state of our theoretical apparatus and systematizing capacity.

But this throws a new light upon the necessity of being continuously prepared for a synthesis in a world which is attaining one of the high points of its existence. What had previously grown up in random fashion from the particular intellectual needs of restricted social circles and classes suddenly becomes perceptible as a whole, and the profusion of events and ideas produces a rather blurred picture.

It is not out of weakness that a people of a mature stage in social and historical development submits to the different possibilities of viewing the world, and attempts to find for these a theoretical framework which will comprehend them all. This submission arises rather from the insight that every former intellectual certainty has rested upon partial points of view made absolute. It is characteristic of the present time that the limits of these partial points of view should have become obvious.

At this mature and advanced stage of development, the total perspective tends to disappear in proportion to the disappearance of the utopia. Only the extreme left and right groups in modern life believe that there is a unity in the developmental process. In the former we have the neo-Marxism of a Lukács, with his profoundly important work, and in the latter the universalism of a Spann. It would be superfluous at this time to demonstrate the differences in the sociological points of view of these two extremes by referring to the differences in their conceptions of totality. We are not interested in completeness in this connection, but rather in a provisional determination of the phenomena which are symptomatic of the present situation.

Unlike those mentioned above, who regard the category of totality as an ontological-metaphysical entity, Troeltsch used it as a working hypothesis in research. He employed it in a somewhat experimental fashion as an ordering principle for an approach to the mass of data and, resorting to different lines of attack on the materials, he sought to uncover the elements which at any one time make it a unity. Alfred Weber seeks to reconstruct the whole of a past historical epoch rather as a *Gestalt*—a configurational unity by means of what can be intuitively observed. His method stands in decided contrast to rationalist dogmatism which relies upon deduction. That Troeltsch and Alfred Weber, as democrats, stand between the two extremes of Lukács and Spann is reflected in their respective mental structures. Although they accept the conception of totality, the former avoids any metaphysical and ontological assumption when speaking of it, and the latter rejects the rationalistic attitude usually connected with it as used by radicals.

In contrast to those who are associated with Marxism or the conservative-historical tradition in their conception of totality, another element in the middle group attempts to disregard entirely the problem of totality, in order, on the basis of this renunciation, to be able to concentrate its attention more fully on the wealth of individual problems. Whenever the utopia disappears, history ceases to be a process leading to an ultimate end. The frame of reference according to which we evaluate facts vanishes and we are left with a series of events all equal as far as their inner significance is concerned. The concept of historical time which led to qualitatively different epochs disappears, and history becomes more and more like undifferentiated space. All those elements of thought which are rooted in utopias are now viewed from a sceptical relativist point of view. Instead of the conception of progress and dialectics we get the search for eternally valid generalizations and types, and reality becomes nothing but a particular combination of these general factors (cf. the general sociology of Max Weber).

The conceptual framework of social philosophy which stood behind the work of the last centuries seems to disappear with the faith in utopias as collective ends of human strivings. This sceptical attitude, in many ways fruitful, corresponds primarily to the social position of a bourgeoisie already in power, whose future has gradually become its present. The other strata of society manifest the same tendencies in the measure that they too approach a realization of their aims. Nevertheless, the concrete development of their present mode of thought is also to some extent sociologically determined by the historical situation in which they had their beginnings. If the dynamic conception of time is cancelled out of the Marxian sociological method, here too is obtained a generalizing theory of ideology which, since it is blind to historical differentiations, would relate ideas exclusively to the social positions of those who hold them irrespective of the society in which they occur or of the particular function they may there fulfil.

The outlines of a sociology which is indifferent to the historical time-element were already perceivable in America, where the dominant type of mentality became more completely and more quickly congruent with the reality of capitalistic society than was the case in German thought. In America, the sociology derived from the philosophy of history was discarded at a rather early date. Sociology, instead of being an adequate picture of the structure of the whole of society, split up into a series of discrete technical problems of social readjustment.

" Realism " means different things in different contexts. In Europe it meant that sociology had to focus its attention on the very severe tension between the classes, whereas in America, where there was more free play in the economic realm, it was not so much the class problem which was considered as the " real " centre of society but the problems of social technique and organization. Sociology for those forms of European thought which found themselves in opposition to the *status quo*, signified the solution of the problem of class relations—more generally, a scientific diagnosis of the present epoch ; to the American, on the contrary, it meant the solution of the immediate, technical problems of social life. This helps to explain why, in the European formulation of sociological problems, there is always asked the uneasy question about what the future has in store, and similarly it throws light on the closely related drive for a total perspective ; likewise it is possible to explain, on the basis of this difference, the type of thought involved in the American formulation of the problem, as represented by the following : How can I do this ? How can I solve this concrete individual problem ? And in all these questions we sense the optimistic undertone : I need not worry about the whole, the whole will take care of itself.

In Europe, however, the complete disappearance of all reality-transcending doctrines—utopian as well as ideological—took place not merely through the fact that all these notions were shown to be relative to the social-economic situation, but also by other means. The sphere of ultimate reality rested in the economic and social sphere for it was to this that Marxism, in the last analysis, related all ideas and values ; it was still historically and intellectually differentiated, i.e. it still contained some fragment of historical perspective (due largely to its Hegelian derivation). Historical materialism was materialist only in name ; the economic sphere was, in the last analysis, in spite of occasional denial of this fact, a structural interrelationship of mental attitudes. The existent economic system was precisely a " system ", i.e. something which arises in the sphere of the mind (the objective mind as Hegel understood it). The process which first started by undermining the validity of spiritual elements in history proceeded further to disturb that sphere of the mind, and reduced all happenings to functions of human drives which were completely detached from historical and spiritual elements. This, too, made possible a generalizing theory ; the reality-transcending elements, ideologies, utopias, etc.—were now no longer relative to social group-situations but to drives—to eternal forms in the structure of human impulses (Pareto, Freud, etc.). This generalizing theory of drives was already adumbrated in the English social philosophy and social psychology of the seventeenth and eighteenth centuries. Thus, for example, Hume, in his *Enquiry concerning Human Understanding*, says :

" It is universally acknowledged that there is a great uniformity among the actions of men, in all nations and ages, and that human nature remains still the same, in its principles and operations. The same motives always produce the same actions. The same events always follow from the same causes. Ambition, avarice, self-love, vanity, friendship, generosity, public spirit : these passions, mixed in various degrees, and distributed through society, have been from the beginning of the world, and still are, the source of all the actions and enterprises which have ever been observed among mankind." [1]

This process of the complete destruction of all spiritual elements, the utopian as well as the ideological, has its parallel in the most recent trends of modern life, and in their corresponding tendencies in the realm of art. Must we not regard the disappearance of humanitarianism from art, the emergence of a " matter of factness " (*Sachlichkeit*) in sexual life, art, and architecture, and the expression of the natural impulses in sports—must all these not be interpreted as symptomatic of the increasing regression of the ideological and utopian elements from the mentality of the strata which are coming to dominate the present situation ? Must not the gradual reduction of politics to economics towards which there is at least a discernible tendency, the conscious rejection of the past and of the notion of historical time, the conscious brushing aside of every " cultural ideal ", be interpreted as a disappearance of every form of utopianism from the political arena as well ?

Here a certain tendency to act on the world is pressing forward an attitude for which all ideas have been discredited and all utopias have been destroyed. This prosaic attitude which is now dawning is in large measure to be welcomed as the only instrument for the mastery of the present situation, as the transformation of utopianism into science, as the destruction of the deluding ideologies which are incongruent with the reality of our present situation. It would require either a callousness which our generation could probably no longer acquire or the unsuspecting naïveté of a generation newly born into the world to be able to live in absolute congruence with the realities of that world, utterly without any transcendent element, either in the form of a utopia or of an ideology. At our present stage

---

[1] Hume, *Enquiries concerning the Human Understanding and concerning the Principles of Morals*. Ed. by L. A. Selby-Bigge, 2nd ed. (Oxford, 1927), p. 83.

of self-consciousness this is perhaps the only form of actual existence that is possible in a world which is no longer in the making. It is possible that the best that our ethical principles have to offer is " genuineness " and " frankness " in place of the old ideals. " Genuineness " (*Echtheitskategorie*) and frankness seem to be nothing more than the projection of the general " matter-of-factness " or " realism " of our time into the realm of ethics. Perhaps a world that is no longer in the making can afford this. But have we reached the stage where we can dispense with strivings ? Would not this elimination of all tension mean the elimination also of political activity, scientific zeal—in fact of the very content of life itself ?

Thus, if we are not to rest content with this " matter-of-factness ", we must carry our quest farther and ask whether there are not, besides those social strata who by their satisfied attitude promote this decreased psychological tension, other forces active in the social realm ? If the question is put in this manner, however, the answer must be as follows :

The apparent absence of tension in the present-day world is being undermined from two sides. On the one side are those strata whose aspirations are not yet fulfilled, and who are striving towards communism and socialism. For these the unity of utopia, point of view, and action is taken for granted as long as they are outsiders in relation to the world as it now exists. Their presence in society implies the uninterrupted existence of at least one form of utopia, and thus, to a certain extent, will always cause the counter-utopias to rekindle and flare up again, at least whenever this extreme left wing goes into action. Whether this will actually happen depends largely on the structural form of the developmental process which confronts us at present. If, through peaceful evolution, we are able, at a later stage, to reach a somewhat superior form of industrialism, which will be sufficiently elastic and which will give the lower strata a degree of relative well-being, then they too will undergo the type of transformation which has already been evidenced by the classes in power. (From this point of view it makes no difference whether this superior form of social organization of industrialism, through the arrival at a position of power on the part of the lower strata, will eventuate in a capitalism which is sufficiently elastic to insure their relative well-being, or whether this capitalism will first be transformed into communism.) If this later stage in industrial development can be attained only through revolution, then the utopian and ideological elements in thought will flare up once more with fresh vigour on all sides. However this may be, it is in the social power of this wing of the opposition to the existing order that there is to be found one of the determinants upon which the fate of reality-transcending concepts depends.

But the future form of the utopian mentality and of intellectuality does not depend only on the vicissitudes of this extreme social stratum. In addition to this sociological factor, there is yet another which should be reckoned with in this connection, namely, a distinct social and intellectual middle stratum which, although it bears a definite relation to intellectual activity, has not been considered in our previous analysis. Hitherto all classes have included, in addition to those who actually represented their direct interests, a stratum more oriented towards what might be called the realm of the spirit. Sociologically, they could be called " intellectuals ", but for our present purpose we must be more precise. We are not referring here to those who bear the outward insignia of education, but to those few among them who, consciously or unconsciously, are interested in something else than success in the competitive scheme that displaces the present one. No matter how soberly one looks at it, one cannot deny that this small group has nearly always existed. Their position presented no problem as long as their intellectual and spiritual interests were congruous with those of the class that was struggling for social supremacy. They experienced and knew the world from the same utopian perspective as that of the group or social stratum with whose interest they identified themselves. This applies as well to Thomas Münzer as to the bourgeois fighters of the French Revolution, to Hegel as well as to Karl Marx.

Their situation always becomes questionable, however, when the group with which they identify themselves arrives at a position of power, and when, as a result of this attainment of power, the utopia is released from politics, and consequently the stratum which was identified with that group on the basis of this utopia is also set free.

The intellectuals will also be released from these social bonds as soon as the most oppressed stratum of society comes to share in the domination of the social order. Only the socially unattached intellectuals will be even more than now in increasing proportions recruited from all social strata rather than merely from the most privileged ones. This intellectual section of society, which is becoming more and more separated from the rest and thrown upon its own resources, is confronted at another angle by what we have just now characterized as a total situation tending towards the complete disappearance of social tension.   But since the intellectuals by no means find themselves in accord with the existing situation and so completely congruent with it that it no longer presents a problem to them, they aim also to reach out beyond that tensionless situation.

The four following alternatives are open to the intellectuals who have thus been cast up by the social process : the first group of intellectuals which is affiliated with the radical wing of the socialist-communist proletariat actually does not concern us here at all. For it, at least to that extent, there are no problems. The conflict between social and intellectual allegiance does not yet exist for it.

The second group, which was cast up by the social process at the same time that its utopia was discarded, becomes sceptical and proceeds, in the name of intellectual integrity, to destroy the ideological elements in science, in the manner described above (M. Weber, Pareto).

The third group takes refuge in the past and attempts to find there an epoch or society in which an extinct form of reality-transcendence dominated the world, and through this romantic reconstruction it seeks to spiritualize the present. The same function, from this point of view, is fulfilled by attempts to revive religious feeling, idealism, symbols, and myths.

The fourth group becomes shut off from the world and consciously renounces direct participation in the historical process. They become ecstatic like the Chiliasts, but with the difference that they no longer concern themselves with radical political movements. They take part in the great historical process of disillusionment, in which every concrete meaning of things as well as myths and beliefs are slowly cast aside. They therefore differ from the Romanticists, who aim essentially at conserving the old beliefs in a modern age. This a-historical ecstasy which had inspired both the mystic and the Chiliast, although in different ways, is now placed in all its nakedness in the very centre of experience. We find one symptom of this, for example, in modern expressionistic art, in which objects have lost their original meaning and seem simply to serve as a medium for the communication of the ecstatic. Similarly in the field of philosophy, many non-academic thinkers like Kierkegaard, in the quest for faith, discard all the concrete historical elements in religion, and are ultimately driven to a bare ecstatic " existence as such ". Such a removal of the Chiliastic element from the midst of culture and politics might preserve the purity of the ecstatic spirit but it would leave the world without meaning or life. This removal will, in the end, be fatal for Chiliastic ecstasy as well, since, as we have already seen, when it turns inward and gives up its conflict with the immediate concrete world, it tends to become gentle and innocuous, or else to lose itself in pure self-edification.

It is inevitable that after such an analysis we should ask ourselves what the future holds ; and the difficulty of this question lays bare the structure of historical understanding. To predict is the task of prophets, and every prophecy of necessity transforms history into a purely determinate system, depriving us thereby of the possibility of choice and decision. As a further result, the impulse to weigh and to reflect with reference to the constantly emerging sphere of new possibilities dies away.

The only form in which the future presents itself to us is that of possibility, while the imperative, the " should ", tells us which of these possibilities we should choose. As regards knowledge, the future—in so far as we are not concerned with the purely organized and rationalized part of it—presents itself as an impenetrable medium, an unyielding wall. And when our attempts to see through it are repulsed, we first become aware of the necessity of wilfully choosing our course and, in close connection with it, the need for an imperative (a utopia) to drive us onward. Only when we know what are the interests and imperatives involved are we in a position to inquire into the possibilities of the present situation, and thus to gain our first insight into history. Here, finally, we see why no interpretation of history can exist except in so far as it is guided by interest and purposeful striving. Of the two conflicting tendencies in the modern world—the utopian trends on the one hand, struggling against a complacent tendency to accept the present on the other hand—it is difficult to tell in advance which one will finally conquer, for the course of historical reality which will determine it still lies in the future. We could change the whole of society to-morrow if everybody could agree. The real obstacle is that every individual is bound into a system of established relationships which to a large extent hamper his will.[1] But these " established relationships " in the last analysis rest again upon uncontrolled decisions of individuals. The task, therefore, is to remove that source of difficulty by unveiling the hidden motives behind the individual's decisions, thus putting him in a position really to choose. Then, and only then, would his decisions *really* lie with him.

All that we have said so far in this book is meant to help the individual to disclose these hidden motives and to reveal the implications of his choice. For our own more restricted analytical purpose, however, which we may designate as a sociological history of modes of thought, it became clear that the most important changes in the intellectual structure of the epoch we have been dealing with are to be understood in the light of the transformations of the utopian element. It is possible, therefore, that in the future, in a world in which there is never

---

[1] Here, too, in such ultimately decisive questions as these, the most fundamental differences in possible modes of experiencing reality are revealed. The anarchist, Landauer, may again be quoted to represent one extreme :—

" What do you understand then by the hard objective facts of human history ? Certainly not the soil, houses, machines, railroad tracks, telegraph wires, and such like. If, however, you are referring thereby to tradition, custom, and complexes of relations, which are the objects of pious reverence, such as the state and similar organizations, conditions, and situations, then it is no longer possible to dismiss them by saying they are only appearances. The possibility and the necessity of the social process as it fluctuates from stability, to decay, and then to reconstruction is based on the fact that there is no organism that has grown up that stands above the individual, but rather a complex relationship of reason, love, and authority. Thus again and again there comes a time in the history of a social structure, which is a structure only as long as individuals nourish it with their vitality, when those living shy away from it as a strange ghost from the past, and create new groupings instead. Thus I have withdrawn my love, reason, obedience, and my will from that which I call the " state ". That I am able to do this depends on my will. That you are not able to do this does not alter the decisive fact that this particular inability is inseparably bound up with your own personality and not with the nature of the state." (From a letter of Gustav Landauer to Margarete Susmann, reprinted in *Landauer, G., sein Lebensgang in Briefen*, edited by Martin Buber (1929), vol. ii, p. 122.)

At the other extreme, cf. the following citation from Hegel :—

" Since the phases of the ethical system are the conception of freedom, they are the substance of universal essence of individuals. In relation to it, individuals are merely accidental. Whether the individual exists or not is a matter of indifference to the objective ethical order, which alone is steadfast. It is the power by which the life of individuals is ruled. It has been represented by nations as eternal justice, or as deities who are absolute, in contrast with whom the striving of individuals is an empty game, like the tossing of the sea." Hegel, *Philosophy of Right*, trans. by J. W. Dyde (London, 1896), p. 156, § 145, addition.

anything new, in which all is finished and each moment is a repetition of the past, there can exist a condition in which thought will be utterly devoid of all ideological and utopian elements. But the complete elimination of reality-transcending elements from our world would lead us to a " matter-of-factness " which ultimately would mean the decay of the human will. Herein lies the most essential difference between these two types of reality-transcendence : whereas the decline of ideology represents a crisis only for certain strata, and the objectivity which comes from the unmasking of ideologies always takes the form of self-clarification for society as a whole, the complete disappearance of the utopian element from human thought and action would mean that human nature and human development would take on a totally new character. The disappearance of utopia brings about a static state of affairs in which man himself becomes no more than a thing. We would be faced then with the greatest paradox imaginable, namely, that man, who has achieved the highest degree of rational mastery of existence, left without any ideals, becomes a mere creature of impulses. Thus, after a long tortuous, but heroic development, just at the highest stage of awareness, when history is ceasing to be blind fate, and is becoming more and more man's own creation, with the relinquishment of utopias, man would lose his will to shape history and therewith his ability to understand it.

V. THE SOCIOLOGY OF KNOWLEDGE

1. THE NATURE AND SCOPE OF THE SOCIOLOGY OF KNOWLEDGE

(a) Definition and Subdivisions of the Sociology of Knowledge

The sociology of knowledge is one of the youngest branches of sociology ; as theory it seeks to analyse the relationship between knowledge and existence ; as historical-sociological research it seeks to trace the forms which this relationship has taken in the intellectual development of mankind.

It arose in the effort to develop as its own proper field of search those multiple interconnections which had become apparent in the crisis of modern thought, and especially the social ties between theories and modes of thought. On the one hand, it aims at discovering workable criteria for determining the interrelations between thought and action. On the other hand, by thinking this problem out from beginning to end in a radical, unprejudiced manner, it hopes to develop a theory, appropriate to the contemporary situation, concerning the significance of the non-theoretical conditioning factors in knowledge.

Only in this way can we hope to overcome the vague, ill-considered, and sterile form of relativism with regard to scientific knowledge which is increasingly prevalent to-day. This discouraging condition will continue to exist as long as science does not adequately deal with the factors conditioning every product of thought which its most recent developments have made clearly visible. In view of this, the sociology of knowledge has set itself the task of solving the problem of the social conditioning of knowledge by boldly recognizing these relations and drawing them into the horizon of science itself and using them as checks on the conclusions of our research. In so far as the anticipations concerning the influence of the social background have remained vague, inexact, and exaggerated, the sociology of knowledge aims at reducing the conclusions derived to their most tenable truths and thereby to come closer to methodological mastery over the problems involved.

237

(b) *The Sociology of Knowledge and the Theory of Ideology*

The sociology of knowledge is closely related to, but increasingly distinguishable from, the theory of ideology, which has also emerged and developed in our own time. The study of ideologies has made it its task to unmask the more or less conscious deceptions and disguises of human interest groups, particularly those of political parties. The sociology of knowledge is concerned not so much with distortions due to a deliberate effort to deceive as with the varying ways in which objects present themselves to the subject according to the differences in social settings. Thus, mental structures are inevitably differently formed in different social and historical settings.

In accordance with this distinction we will leave to the theory of ideology only the first forms of the " incorrect " and the untrue, while one-sidedness of observation, which is not due to more or less conscious intent, will be separated from the theory of ideology and treated as the proper subject-matter of the sociology of knowledge. In the older theory of ideology, no distinction was made between these two types of false observation and statement. To-day, however, it is advisable to separate more sharply these two types, both of which were formerly described as ideologies. Hence we speak of a *particular* and of a *total* conception of ideology. Under the first we include all those utterances the " falsity " of which is due to an intentional or unintentional, conscious, semi-conscious, or unconscious, deluding of one's self or of others, taking place on a psychological level and structurally resembling lies.

We speak of this conception of ideology as *particular* because it always refers only to specific assertions which may be regarded as concealments, falsifications, or lies without attacking the integrity of the *total mental structure* of the asserting subject. The sociology of knowledge, on the other hand, takes as its problem precisely this mental structure *in its totality*, as it appears in different currents of thought and historical-social groups. The sociology of knowledge does not criticize thought on the level of the assertions themselves, which may involve deceptions and disguises, but examines them on the structural or noological level, which it views as not necessarily being the same for all men, but rather as allowing the same object to take on different forms and aspects in the course of social development. Since suspicion of falsification is not included in the total conception of ideology, the use of the term " ideology " in the sociology of knowledge has no moral or denunciatory intent. It points rather to a research interest which leads to the raising of the question when and where social structures come to express themselves in the structure of assertions, and in what sense the former concretely determine the latter. In the realm of the sociology of knowledge, we shall then, as far as possible, avoid the use of the term " ideology ", because of its moral connotation, and shall instead speak of the " perspective " of a thinker. By this term we mean the subject's whole mode of conceiving things as determined by his historical and social setting.

2. THE TWO DIVISIONS OF THE SOCIOLOGY OF KNOWLEDGE

A. THE THEORY OF THE SOCIAL DETERMINATION OF KNOWLEDGE

The sociology of knowledge is on the one hand a theory, and on the other hand an historical-sociological method of research. As theory it may take two forms. In the first place it is a purely empirical investigation through description and structural analysis of the ways in which social relationships, in fact, influence thought. This may pass, in the second place, into an epistemological inquiry concerned with the bearing of this interrelationship upon the problem of validity. It is important to notice that these two types of inquiry are not necessarily connected and one can accept the empirical results without drawing the epistemological conclusions.

The Purely Empirical Aspect of the Investigation of the Social Determination of Knowledge. In accord with this classification and disregarding the epistemological implications as far as possible, we will present the sociology of knowledge as a theory of the social or existential determination of actual thinking. It would be well to begin by explaining what is meant by the wider term " existential determination of knowledge " (" *Seinsverbundenheit* [1] *des Wissens* "). As a concrete fact, it may be best approached by means of an illustration. The existential determination of thought may be regarded as a demonstrated fact in those realms of thought in which we can show (*a*) that

---

[1] Here we do not mean by " determination " a mechanical cause-effect sequence : we leave the meaning of " determination " open, and only empirical investigation will show us how strict is the correlation between life-situation and thought-process, or what scope exists for variations in the correlation. [The German expression " *Seinsverbundenes Wissens* " conveys a meaning which leaves the exact nature of the determinism open.]

the process of knowing does not actually develop historically in accordance with immanent laws, that it does not follow only from the " nature of things " or from " pure logical possibilities ", and that it is not driven by an " inner dialectic ". On the contrary, the emergence and the crystallization of actual thought is influenced in many decisive points by extra-theoretical factors of the most diverse sort. These may be called, in contradistinction to purely theoretical factors, existential factors. This existential determination of thought will also have to be regarded as a fact (*b*) if the influence of these existential factors on the concrete content of knowledge is of more than mere peripheral importance, if they are relevant not only to the genesis of ideas, but penetrate into their forms and content and if, furthermore, they decisively determine the scope and the intensity of our experience and observation, i.e. that which we formerly referred to as the " perspective " of the subject.

Social Processes Influencing the Process of Knowledge. Considering now the first set of criteria for determining the existential connections of knowledge, i.e. the role actually played by extra-theoretical factors in the history of thought, we find that the more recent investigations undertaken in the spirit of the sociologically oriented history of thought supply an increasing amount of corroborative evidence. For even to-day the fact seems to be perfectly clear that the older method of intellectual history, which was oriented towards the *a priori* conception that changes in ideas were to be understood on the level of ideas (immanent intellectual history), blocked recognition of the penetration of the social process into the intellectual sphere. With the growing evidence of the flaws in this *a priori* assumption, an increasing number of concrete cases makes it evident that (*a*) every formulation of a problem is made possible only by a previous actual human experience which involves such a problem ; (*b*) in selection from the multiplicity of data there is involved an act of will on the part of the knower ; and (*c*) forces arising out of living experience are significant in the direction which the treatment of the problem follows.

In connection with these investigations, it will become more and more clear that the living forces and actual attitudes which underlie the theoretical ones are by no means merely of an individual nature, i.e. they do not have their origin in the first place in the individual's becoming aware of his interests in the course of his thinking. Rather, they arise out of the collective purposes of a group which underlie the thought of the individual, and in the prescribed outlook of which he merely participates. In this connection, it becomes more clear that a large part of thinking and knowing cannot be correctly understood, as long as its connection with existence or with the social implications of human life are not taken into account.

It would be impossible to list all the manifold social processes which, in the above sense, condition and shape our theories, and we shall, therefore, confine ourselves to a few examples (and even in these cases, we shall have to leave the detailed proof to the instances cited in the index and bibliography).

We may regard competition as such a representative case in which extra-theoretical processes affect the emergence and the direction of the development of knowledge. Competition[1] controls not merely economic activity through the mechanism of the market, not merely the course of political and social events, but furnishes also the motor impulse behind diverse interpretations of the world which, when their social background is uncovered, reveal themselves as the intellectual expressions of conflicting groups struggling for power.

As we see these social backgrounds emerge and become recognizable as the invisible forces underlying knowledge, we realize that thoughts and ideas are not the result of the isolated inspiration of great geniuses. Underlying even the profound insight of the genius are the collective historical experiences of a group which the individual takes for granted, but which should under no conditions be hypostatized as " group mind ". On closer inspection it is to be seen that there is not merely one complex of collective experience with one exclusive tendency, as the theory of the folk-spirit maintained. The world is known through many different orientations because there are many simultaneous and mutually contradictory trends of thought (by no means of equal value) struggling against one another with their different interpretations of " common " experience. The clue to this conflict, therefore, is not to be found in the " object in itself " (if it were, it would be impossible to understand why the object should appear in so many different refractions), but in the very different expectations, purposes, and impulses arising out of experience. If, then, for our explanation we are thrown back upon the play and counterplay of different impulses

---

[1] For concrete examples cf. the author's paper " Die Bedeutung der Konkurrenz im Gebiete des Geistigen," op. cit.

within the social sphere, a more exact analysis will show that the cause of this conflict between concrete impulses is not to be looked for in theory itself, but in these varied opposing impulses, which in turn are rooted in the whole matrix of collective interests. These seemingly " pure theoretical" cleavages may, in the light of a sociological analysis (which uncovers the hidden intermediate steps between the original impulses to observe and the purely theoretical conclusion), be reduced, for the most part, to more fundamental philosophical differences. But the latter, in turn, are invisibly guided by the antagonism and competition between concrete, conflicting groups.

To mention only one of the many other possible bases of collective existence, out of which different interpretations of the world and different forms of knowledge may arise, we may point to the role played by the relationship between differently situated generations. This factor influences in very many cases the principles of selection, organization, and polarization of theories and points of view prevailing in a given society at a given moment. (This is given more detailed attention in the author's essay entitled " Das Problem der Generationen ".[1]) From the knowledge derived from our studies on competition and generations, we have concluded that what, from the point of view of immanent intellectual history, appears to be the " inner dialectic " in the development of ideas, becomes, from the standpoint of the sociology of knowledge, the rhythmic movement in the history of ideas as affected by competition and the succession of generations.

In considering the relationship between forms of thought and forms of society, we shall recall Max Weber's [2] observation that the interest in systematization is in large part attributable to a scholastic background, that the interest in " systematic " thought is the correlate of juristic and scientific schools of thought, and that the origin of this organizing form of thought lies in the continuity of pedagogical institutions. We should also mention at this point Max Scheler's [3] significant attempt to establish the relationship between various forms of thought and

---

[1] *Kölner Vierteljahrshefte für Soziologie* (1928), vol. viii.

[2] Cf. Max Weber, *Wirtschaft und Gesellschaft*, op. cit., particularly the section on the sociology of law.

[3] Cf. especially his works, *Die Wissensformen und die Gesellschaft*, Leipzig, 1926, and *Die Formen des Wissens und der Bildung*, i, Bonn, 1925.

certain types of groups in which alone they can arise and be elaborated.

This must suffice to indicate what is meant by the correlation between types of knowledge and of ideas, on the one hand, and the social groups and processes of which they are characteristic.

The Essential Penetration of the Social Process into the "Perspective" of Thought. Are the existential factors in the social process merely of peripheral significance, are they to be regarded merely as conditioning the origin or factual development of ideas (i.e. are they of merely genetic relevance), or do they penetrate into the "perspective" of concrete particular assertions? This is the next question we shall try to answer. The historical and social genesis of an idea would only be irrelevant to its ultimate validity if the temporal and social conditions of its emergence had no effect on its content and form. If this were the case, any two periods in the history of human knowledge would only be distinguished from one another by the fact that in the earlier period certain things were still unknown and certain errors still existed which, through later knowledge were completely corrected. This simple relationship between an earlier incomplete and a later complete period of knowledge may to a large extent be appropriate for the exact sciences (although indeed to-day the notion of the stability of the categorical structure of the exact sciences is, compared with the logic of classical physics, considerably shaken). For the history of the cultural sciences, however, the earlier stages are not quite so simply superseded by the later stages, and it is not so easily demonstrable that early errors have subsequently been corrected. Every epoch has its fundamentally new approach and its characteristic point of view, and consequently sees the "same" object from a new perspective.

Hence the thesis that the historico-social process is of essential significance for most of the domains of knowledge receives support from the fact that we can see from most of the concrete assertions of human beings when and where they arose, when and where they were formulated. The history of art has fairly conclusively shown that art forms may be definitely dated according to their style, since each form is possible only under given historical conditions and reveals the characteristics of that epoch. What is true of art also holds *mutatis mutandis* good for knowledge. Just as in art we can date particular forms on the ground of their definite association with a particular period of history so in the case of knowledge we can detect with increasing exactness the perspective due to a particular historical setting. Further, by the use of pure analysis of thought-structure, we can determine when and where the world presented itself in such, and only in such a light to the subject that made the assertion, and the analysis may frequently be carried to the point where the more inclusive question may be answered, *why* the world presented itself in precisely such a manner.

Whereas the assertion (to cite the simplest case) that twice two equals four gives no clue as to when, where, and by whom it was formulated, it is always possible in the case of a work in the social sciences to say whether it was inspired by the " historical school ", or " positivism ", or " Marxism ", and from what stage in the development of each of these it dates. In assertions of this sort, we may speak of an " infiltration of the social position " of the investigator into the results of his study and of the " situational-relativity " (" *Situations-gebundenheit* "), or the relationship of these assertions to the underlying reality.

" Perspective " in this sense signifies the manner in which one views an object, what one perceives in it, and how one construes it in his thinking. Perspective, therefore, is something more than a merely formal determination of thinking. It refers also to qualitative elements in the structure of thought, elements which must necessarily be overlooked by a purely formal logic. It is precisely these factors which are responsible for the fact that two persons, even if they apply the same formal-logical rules, e.g. the law of contradiction or the formula of the syllogism, in an identical manner, may judge the same object very differently.

Of the traits by which the perspective of an assertion may be characterized, and of the criteria which aid us to attribute it to a given epoch or situation, we will adduce only a few examples : analysis of the meaning of the concepts being used ; the phenomenon of the counter-concept ; the absence of certain concepts ; the structure of the categorical apparatus ; dominant models of thought ; level of abstraction ; and the ontology that is presupposed. In what follows, we intend to show, by means of a few examples, the applicability of these identifying traits and criteria in the analysis of perspective. At the same time, it will be shown how far the social position of the observer affects his outlook.

We will begin with the fact that the same word, or the same concept in most cases, means very different things when used by differently situated persons.

When, in the early years of the nineteenth century, an old-style German conservative spoke of " freedom " he meant thereby the right of each estate to live according to its privileges (liberties). If he belonged to the romantic-conservative and Protestant movement he understood by it " inner freedom ", i.e. the right of each individual to live according to his own individual personality. Both of these groups thought in terms of the " *qualitative conception of freedom* " because they understood freedom to mean the right to maintain either their historical or their inner, individual distinctiveness.

When a liberal of the same period used the term " freedom ", he was thinking of freedom *from* precisely those privileges which to the old-style conservative appeared to be the very basis of all freedom. The liberal conception was, then, an " *equalitarian conception of freedom* ", in the case of which " being free " meant that all men have the same fundamental rights at their disposal. The liberal conception of freedom was that of a group which sought to overthrow the external, legal, non-equalitarian social order. The conservative idea of freedom, on the other hand, was that of a stratum which did not wish to see any changes in the external order of things, hoping that events would continue in their traditional uniqueness ; in order to support things as they were, they also had to divert the issues concerning freedom from the external political realm to the inner non-political realm. That the liberal saw only one, and the conservative only another side of the concept and of the problem was clearly and demonstrably connected with their respective positions in the social and political structure.[1] In brief, even in the formulation of concepts, the angle of vision is guided by the observer's interests. Thought, namely, is directed in accordance with what a particular social group expects. Thus, out of the possible data of experience, every concept combines within itself only that which, in the light of the investigators' interests, it is essential to grasp and to incorporate. Hence, for example, the conservative concept of *Volksgeist* was most probably formulated as a counter-concept in opposition to the progressive concept of " the spirit of the age " (*Zeitgeist*). The analysis of the concepts in a given conceptual

[1] Cf. the author's " Das konservative Denken," *Archiv für Sozialwissenschaft und Sozialpolitik*, vol. 57, pp. 90 ff.

scheme itself provides the most direct approach to the perspective of distinctively situated strata.

The absence of certain concepts indicates very often not only the absence of certain points of view, but also the absence of a definite drive to come to grips with certain life-problems. Thus, for example, the relatively late appearance in history of the concept " social " is evidence for the fact that the questions implied in the concept " social " had never been posited before, and likewise that a definite mode of experience signified by the concept " social " did not exist before.

But not only do the concepts in their concrete contents diverge from one another in accordance with differing social positions, but the basic categories of thought may likewise differ.

So, for example, early nineteenth century German conservatism (we draw most of our illustrations from this epoch because it has been studied more thoroughly from a sociological point of view than any other), and contemporary conservatism too, for that matter, tend to use morphological categories which do not break up the concrete totality of the data of experience, but seek rather to preserve it in all its uniqueness. As opposed to the morphological approach, the analytical approach character-istic of the parties of the left, broke down every concrete totality in order to arrive at smaller, more general, units which might then be recombined through the category of causality or· functional integration. Here it becomes our task not only to indicate the fact that people in different social positions think differently, but to make intelligible the causes for their different ordering of the material of experiences by different categories. The groups oriented to the left intend to make something new out of the world as it is given, and therefore they divert their glance from things as they are, they become abstract and atomize the given situation into its component elements in order to recombine them anew. Only that appears configuratively or morphologically which we are prepared to accept without further ado, and which, fundamentally, we do not wish to change. Still further, by means of the configurative conception, it is intended to stabilize precisely those elements which are still in flux, and at the same time to invoke sanction for what exists because it is as it is. All this makes it quite clear to what extent even abstract categories and principles of organization, which are seemingly far removed from the political struggle, have their origin in the meta-theoretical pragmatic nature of the human mind, and in the more profound depths of the psyche and of consciousness. Hence to speak here of conscious deception in the sense of creating ideologies is out of the question.

The next factor which may serve to characterize the perspective of thought is the so-called thought-model; i.e. the model that is implicitly in the mind of a person when he proceeds to reflect about an object.

It is well known, for instance, that once the typology of objects in the natural sciences was formulated, and the categories and methods of thought derived from these types became models, it was thenceforth hoped to solve all the problems in the other realms of existence, including the social, by that method. (This tendency is represented by the mechanistic-atomistic conception of social phenomena.)

It is significant to observe that when this happened, as in all similar cases, not all the strata of society oriented themselves primarily to this single model of thought. The landed nobility, the displaced classes, and the peasantry were not heard from during this historical period. The new character of cultural development and the ascendant forms of orientation towards the world belonged to a mode of life other than their own. The forms of the ascendant world-perspective, modelled on the principles of natural science, came upon these classes as if from the outside. As the interplay of social forces brought other groups, representing the above-mentioned classes and expressing their life-situation, into the forefront of history, the opposing models of thought, as, for instance, the " *organismic* " and the " *personalistic* " were played off against the " functional-mechanistic " type of thought. Thus Stahl, for instance, who stood at the apex of this development, was already able to establish connections between thought-models and political currents.[1]

Behind every definite question and answer is implicitly or explicitly to be found a model of how fruitful thinking can be carried on. If one were to trace in detail, in each individual case, the origin and the radius of diffusion of a certain thought-model, one would discover the peculiar affinity it has to the social position of given groups and their manner of interpreting the world. By these groups we mean not merely classes, as a dogmatic

---

[1] The history of theories of the state, especially as viewed by Oppenheimer, F., in his *System der Soziologie* (vol. ii, " Der Staat ") is a treasure of illustrative material.

type of Marxism would have it, but also generations, status groups, sects, occupational groups, schools, etc. Unless careful attention is paid to highly differentiated social groupings of this sort and to the corresponding differentiations in concepts, categories, and thought-models, i.e. unless the problem of the relation between super- and sub-structure is refined, it would be impossible to demonstrate that corresponding to the wealth of types of knowledge and perspectives which have appeared in the course of history there are similar differentiations in the substructure of society. Of course we do not intend to deny that of all the above-mentioned social groupings and units class stratification is the most significant, since in the final analysis all the other social groups arise from and are transformed as parts of the more basic conditions of production and domination. None the less the investigator who, in the face of the variety of types of thought, attempts to place them correctly can no longer be content with the undifferentiated class concept, but must reckon with the existing social units and factors that condition social position, aside from those of class.

Another characteristic of the perspective is to be found by investigating the level of abstraction, beyond which a given theory does not progress, or the degree to which it resists theoretical, systematic formulation.

It is never an accident when a certain theory, wholly or in part, fails to develop beyond a given stage of relative abstractness and offers resistance to further tendencies towards becoming more concrete, either by frowning upon this tendency towards concreteness or declaring it to be irrelevant. Here, too, the social position of the thinker is significant.

Precisely in the case of Marxism and the relation it bears to the findings of the sociology of knowledge can it be shown how an interrelationship can often be formulated only in that form of concreteness which is peculiar to that particular standpoint. It can be shown in the case of Marxism that an observer whose view is bound up with a given social position will by himself never succeed in singling out the more general and theoretical aspects which are implicit in the concrete observations that he makes. It might have been expected, for instance, that long ago Marxism would have formulated in a more theoretical way the fundamental findings of the sociology of knowledge concerning the relationship between human thought and the conditions of existence *in general*, especially since its discovery of the theory of ideology also implied at least the beginnings of the sociology of knowledge. That this implication could never be brought out and theoretically elaborated, and at best only came partially into view, was due, however, to the fact that, in the concrete instance, this relationship was perceived only in the thought of the opponent. It was probably due, furthermore, to a subconscious reluctance to think out the implications of a concretely formulated insight to a point where the theoretical formulations latent in it would be clear enough to have a disquieting effect on one's own position. Thus we see how the narrowed focus which a given position imposes and the driving impulses which govern its insights tend to obstruct the general and theoretical formulation of these views and to restrict the capacity for abstraction. There is a tendency to abide by the particular view that is immediately obtainable, and to prevent the question from being raised as to whether the fact that knowledge is bound up with existence is not inherent in the human thought-structure as such. In addition to this, the tendency in Marxism to shy away from a general, sociological formulation may frequently be traced to a similar limitation which a given point of view imposes on a method of thinking. For instance, one is not even allowed to raise the question whether " impersonalization " (*Verdinglichung*), as elaborated by Marx and Lukács, is a more or less general phenomenon of consciousness, or whether capitalistic impersonalization is merely one particular form of it. Whereas this overemphasis on concreteness and historicism arises out of a particular social location, the opposite tendency, namely the immediate flight into the highest realms of abstraction and formalization, may, as Marxism has rightly emphasized, lead to an obscuring of the concrete situation and its unique character. This could be demonstrated once more in the case of " formal sociology ".

We do not wish in any way to call into question the legitimacy of formal sociology as one possible type of sociology. When, however, in the face of the tendency to introduce further concreteness into the formulation of sociological problems, it sets itself up as the only sociology, it is unconsciously guided by motives similar to those which prevented its historical forerunner, the bourgeois-liberal mode of thought, from ever getting beyond an abstract and generalizing mode of observation in its theory. It shies away from dealing historically, concretely, and individually with the problems of society for fear that its own inner antagonisms, for instance the antagonisms of capitalism itself, might become visible. In this it resembles the crucial bourgeois discussion of the problem of freedom, in which the problem usually was and is posited only theoretically and abstractly. And even when it is so posited, the question of freedom is always one of political, rather than of social, rights, since, if the latter sphere were considered, the factors of property and class position in their relation to freedom and equality would inevitably come to light.

To summarize : the approach to a problem, the level on which the problem happens to be formulated, the stage of abstraction and the stage of concreteness that one hopes to attain, are all and in the same way bound up with social existence.

It would be appropriate finally to deal with the underlying substratum in all modes of thought, with their presupposed ontologies and their social differentiations. It is precisely because the ontological substratum is fundamentally significant for thinking and perceiving that we cannot deal adequately in limited space with the problems raised thereby, and we refer, therefore, to more elaborate treatments to be found elsewhere.[1] At this point, let it suffice to say that, however justified the desire of modern philosophy may be to work out a " basic ontology ", it is dangerous to approach these problems naïvely, without first taking into account the results suggested by the sociology of knowledge. For if we approached this problem naïvely, the almost inevitable result would be that, instead of obtaining a genuine basic ontology, we would become the victims of an arbitrary accidental ontology which the historical process happens to make available to us.

These reflections must suffice in this connection to clarify the notion that the conditions of existence affect not merely the historical genesis of ideas, but constitute an essential part of the products of thought and make themselves felt in their content and form. The examples we have just cited should serve to clarify the peculiar structure and the functions of the sociology of knowledge.

The Special Approach Characteristic of the Sociology of Knowledge. Two persons, carrying on a discussion in the same universe of discourse—corresponding to the same historical-social conditions—can and must do so quite differently from two persons

---

[1] Cf. the author's " Das konservative Denken " (loc. cit., pp. 489 ff., and especially p. 494), and pp. 78 ff., 87 ff., 174 ff. of this volume.

identified with different social positions.   These two types of discussion, i.e. between socially and intellectually homogeneous participants and between socially and intellectually heterogeneous participants, are to be clearly distinguished.   It is no accident that the distinction between these two types of discussion is explicitly recognized as a problem in an age like ours.   Max Scheler called our contemporary period the " epoch of equalization " (*Zeitalter des Ausgleichs*), which, if applied to our problems, means that ours is a world in which social groupings, which had hitherto lived more or less isolated from one another, each making itself and its own world of thought absolute, are now, in one form or another, merging into one another.   Not only Orient and Occident, not only the various nations of the west, but also the various social strata of these nations, which previously had been more or less self-contained, and, finally, the different occupational groups within these strata and the intellectual groups in this most highly differentiated world—all these are now thrown out of the self-sufficient, complacent state of taking themselves for granted, and are forced to maintain themselves and their ideas in the face of the onslaught of these heterogeneous groups.

But how do they carry on this struggle ?   As far as intellectual antagonisms are concerned, they usually do so with but few exceptions by " talking past one another " ;   i.e. although they are more or less aware that the person with whom they are discussing the matter represents another group, and that it is likely that his mental structure as a whole is often quite different when a concrete thing is being discussed, they speak as if their differences were confined to the specific question at issue around which their present disagreement crystallized.   They overlook the fact that their antagonist differs from them in his whole outlook, and not merely in his opinion about the point under discussion.

This indicates that there are also types of intellectual intercourse between heterogeneous persons.   In the first, the differences in the total mental structure remain obscurely in the background in so far as the contact between the participants is concerned.   Consciousness for both is crystallized about the concrete issue.   For each of the participants the " object " has a more or less different meaning because it grows out of the whole of their respective frames of reference, as a result of which the meaning of the object in the perspective of the other person remains, at least in part, obscure. Hence " talking past one another " is an inevitable phenomenon of the " age of equalization ".

On the other hand, the divergent participants may also be approached with the intention of using each theoretical point of contact as an occasion for removing misunderstandings by ascertaining the source of the differences. This will bring out the varying presuppositions which are implied in the two respective perspectives as consequences of the two different social situations. In such cases, the sociologist of knowledge does not face his antagonist in the usual manner, according to which the other's arguments are dealt with directly. He seeks rather to understand him by defining the total perspective and seeing it as a function of a certain social position.

The sociologist of knowledge has been accused, because of this procedure, of avoiding the real argument, of not concerning himself with the actual subject-matter under discussion, but, instead, of going behind the immediate subject of debate to the total basis of thought of the assertor in order to reveal it as merely one basis of thought among many and as no more than a partial perspective. Going behind the assertions of the opponents and disregarding the actual arguments is legitimate in certain cases, namely, wherever, because of the absence of a common basis of thought, there is no common problem. The sociology of knowledge seeks to overcome the " talking past one another " of the various antagonists by taking as its explicit theme of investigation the uncovering of the sources of the partial disagreements which would never come to the attention of the disputants because of their preoccupation with the subject-matter that is the immediate issue of the debate. It is superfluous to remark that the sociologist of knowledge is justified in tracing the arguments to the very basis of thought and the position of disputants only if and in so far as an actual disparity exists between the perspectives of the discussion resulting in a fundamental misunderstanding. As long as discussion proceeds from the same basis of thought, and within the same universe of discourse, it is unnecessary. Needlessly applied, it may become a means for side-stepping the discussion.

The Acquisition of Perspective as a Pre-condition for the Sociology of Knowledge. For the son of a peasant who has grown up within the narrow confines of his village and spends his whole life in the place of his birth, the mode of thinking and speaking characteristic of that village is something that he takes entirely for granted. But for the country lad who goes to the city and adapts himself gradually to city life, the rural mode of living and thinking ceases to be something to be taken for granted. He has won a certain detachment from it, and he distinguishes now, perhaps quite consciously, between " rural " and " urban " modes of thought and ideas. In this distinction lie the first beginnings of that approach which the sociology of knowledge seeks to develop in full detail. That which within a given group is accepted as absolute appears to the outsider conditioned by the group situation and recognized as partial (in this case, as " rural "). This type of knowledge presupposes a more detached perspective.

This detached perspective can be gained in the following ways : (*a*) a member of a group leaves his social position (by ascending to a higher class, emigration, etc.) ; (*b*) the basis of existence of a whole group shifts in relation to its traditional norms and institutions [1] ; (*c*) within the same society two or more socially determined modes of interpretation come into conflict and, in criticizing one another, render one another transparent and establish perspectives with reference to each other. As a result, a detached perspective, through which the outlines of the contrasting modes of thought are discovered, comes within the range of possibility for all the different positions, and later gets to be the recognized mode of thinking. We have already indicated that the social genesis of the sociology of knowledge rests primarily upon the last mentioned possibility.

Relationism. What has already been said should hardly leave any doubt as to what is meant when the procedure of the sociology of knowledge is designated as " relational ". When the urbanized peasant boy, who characterizes certain political, philosophical, or social opinions to be found among his relatives as " rustic ", he no longer discusses these opinions as a homogeneous participant, that is, by dealing directly with the specific content of what is said. Rather he relates them to a certain mode of interpreting the world which, in turn, is ultimately related to a certain social structure which constitutes its situation. This is an instance of the " relational " procedure. We shall deal later with the fact that when assertions are treated in this way it is not implied that they are false. The sociology of knowledge goes beyond what, in some such crude way as this,

[1] A good example is furnished by Karl Renner, in *Die Rechtsinstitute des Privatrechts* (J. C. B. Mohr, Tübingen, 1929).

people frequently do to-day, only in so far as it consciously and systematically subjects all intellectual phenomena without exception, to the question :   In connection with what social structure did they arise and are they valid ?   Relating individual ideas to the total structure of a given historico-social subject should not be confused with a philosophical relativism which denies the validity of any standards and of the existence of order in the world.   Just as the fact that every measurement in space hinges upon the nature of light does not mean that our measurements are arbitrary, but merely that they are only valid in relation to the nature of light, so in the same way not relativism in the sense of arbitrariness but *relationism* applies to our discussions.   Relationism does not signify that there are no criteria of rightness and wrongness in a dicussion.   It does insist, however, that it lies in the nature of certain assertions that they cannot be formulated absolutely, but only in terms of the perspective of a given situation.

Particularization.   Having described the relational process, as conceived by the sociology of knowledge, the question will inevitably be raised :   what can it tell us about the validity of an assertion that we would not know if we had not been able to relate it to the standpoint of the assertor ?   Have we said anything about the truth or falsity of a statement when we have shown that it is to be imputed to liberalism or to Marxism ?

Three answers may be made to this question :—

(*a*) It may be said that the absolute validity of an assertion is denied when its structural relationship to a given social situation has been shown.   In this sense there is indeed a current in the sociology of knowledge and in the theory of ideology which accepts the demonstration of this sort of relationship as a refutation of the opponents' assertion, and which would use this method as a device for annihilating the validity of all assertions.

(*b*) In opposition to this, there may be another answer, namely that the imputations that the sociology of knowledge establishes between a statement and its assertor tells us nothing concerning the truth-value of the assertion, since the manner in which a statement originates does not affect its validity. Whether an assertion is liberal or conservative in and of itself gives no indication of its correctness.

(*c*) There is a third possible way of judging the value of the assertions that the sociologist of knowledge makes, which represents our own point of view. It differs from the first view in that it shows that the mere factual demonstration and identification of the social position of the assertor as yet tells us nothing about the truth-value of his assertion. It implies only the suspicion that this assertion might represent merely a partial view. As over against the second alternative, it maintains that it would be incorrect to regard the sociology of knowledge as giving no more than a description of the actual conditions under which an assertion arises (factual-genesis). Every complete and thorough sociological analysis of knowledge delimits, in content as well as structure, the view to be analysed. In other words, it attempts not merely to establish the existence of the relationship, but at the same time to particularize its scope and the extent of its validity. The implications of this will be set forth in greater detail.

What the sociology of knowledge intends to do by its analysis was fairly clearly brought out in the example we cited of the peasant boy. The discovery and identification of his earlier mode of thought as " rural ", as contrasted with " urban ", already involves the insight that the different perspectives are not merely particular in that they presuppose different ranges of vision and different sectors of the total reality, but also in that the interests and the powers of perception of the different perspectives are conditioned by the social situations in which they arose and to which they are relevant.

Already upon this level the relational process tends to become a particularizing process, for one does not merely relate the assertion to a standpoint but, in doing so, restricts its claim to validity which at first was absolute to a narrower scope.

A fully developed sociology of knowledge follows the same approach which we have illustrated above in the case of the peasant boy, except that it follows a deliberate method. With the aid of a consistently elaborated analysis of the perspective, particularization acquires a guiding instrument and a set of criteria for treating problems of imputation. The range and degree of comprehension of each of these several points of view becomes measurable and delimitable through their categorical apparatus and the variety of meanings which each presents. The orientation towards certain meanings and values which inheres in a given social position (the outlook and attitude conditioned by the collective purposes of a group), and the concrete reasons for the different perspectives which the same situation presents to the different positions in it thus become even more determinable, intelligible, and subject to methodical study through the perfection of the sociology of knowledge.[1]

With the growing methodological refinements in the sociology of knowledge, the determination of the particularity of a perspective becomes a cultural and intellectual index of the position of the group in question. By particularizing, the sociology of knowledge goes a step farther than the original determination of the facts to which mere relationism limits itself. Every analytical step undertaken in the spirit of the sociology of knowledge arrives at a point where the sociology of knowledge becomes more than a sociological description of the facts which tell us how certain views have been derived from a certain *milieu*. Rather it reaches a point where it also becomes a critique by redefining the scope and the limits of the perspective implicit in given assertions. The analyses characteristic of the sociology of knowledge are, in this sense, by no means irrelevant for the determination of the truth of a statement ; but these analyses, on the other hand, do not by themselves fully reveal the truth because the mere delimitation of the perspectives is by no means a substitute for the immediate and direct discussion between the divergent points of view or for the direct examination of the facts. The function of the findings of the sociology of knowledge lies somewhere in a fashion hitherto not clearly understood, between irrelevance to the establishment of truth on the one hand, and entire adequacy for determining truth on the other. This can be shown by a careful analysis of the original intention of the single statements of sociology of knowledge and by the nature of its findings. An analysis based on the sociology of knowledge is a first preparatory step leading to direct discussion, in an age which is aware of the heterogeneity of its interests and the disunity of its basis of thought, and which seeks to attain this unity on a higher level.

B. THE EPISTEMOLOGICAL CONSEQUENCES OF THE SOCIOLOGY OF KNOWLEDGE

In the opening paragraph of this chapter we maintained that it was possible to present the sociology of knowledge as an

[1] For further details, cf. the treatment of the relationship of theory and practice, *supra*, Part III, where we have endeavoured to carry out such a sociological analysis of the perspective.

empirical theory of the actual relations of knowledge to the social situation without raising any epistemological problems. On this assumption, all epistemological problems have been avoided or put into the background. This reserve on our part is possible, and this artificial isolation of a purely abstracted set of problems is even desirable as long as our goal is merely the disinterested analysis of given concrete relationships, without distortion through theoretical preconceptions. But once the fundamental relationships between social situations and corresponding aspects are reliably established, one cannot but devote oneself to the frank disclosure of the valuations following from them. Anyone who has a sense for the interconnection of problems which inevitably arise out of the interpretation of empirical data, and who at the same time is not blinded by the intricacy of specialization in modern learning, which very often prevents a direct attack on problems, must have noticed that the facts presented under the section of " Particularization " are in their very nature hard to accept as mere facts. They transcend bare fact, and call for further epistemological reflection. On the one hand, we have the mere fact that when, through the sociology of knowledge, a relationship is pointed out between an assertion and a situation, there is contained in the very intent of this procedure the tendency to " particularize " its validity. Phenomenologically, one may take cognizance of this fact without disputing the claim to validity implied in it. But, on the other hand, the further fact that the position of the observer does influence the results of thought, and the fact (intentionally dealt with by us in great detail) that the partial validity of a given perspective is fairly exactly determinable, must sooner or later lead us to raise the question as to the significance of this problem for epistemology.

Our point is not, therefore, that the sociology of knowledge will, by its very nature, supplant epistemological and noological inquiry, but rather that it has made certain discoveries which have more than a mere factual relevance, and which cannot be adequately dealt with until some of the conceptions and prejudices of contemporary epistemology have been revised. In the fact, then, that we always attribute only partial validity to particular assertions, we find that new element which compels us to revise the fundamental presuppositions of present-day epistemology. We are dealing here with a case in which the pure determination of a fact (the fact of the partiality of a

T

perspective which is demonstrable in concrete assertions) may become relevant for determining the validity of a proposition and in which the nature of the genesis of an assertion may become relevant to its truth (*wo eine Genesis Sinngenesis zu sein vermag*). This, to say the least, furnishes an obstacle to the construction of a sphere of validity in which the criteria of truth are independent of origins.

Under the dominant presuppositions of present-day philosophy it will be impossible to utilize this new insight for epistemology, because modern theory of knowledge is based on the supposition that bare fact-finding has no relevance to validity. Under the sanctions of this article of faith, every enrichment of knowledge arising out of concrete research, which—seen from a wider point of view—dares to open up more fundamental considerations, is stigmatized with the phrase " sociologism ". Once it is decided and elevated into the realm of the *a priori* that nothing can come out of the world of empirical facts which has relevance for the validity of assertions, we become blind to the observation that this *a priori* itself originally was a premature hypostatization of a factual interrelationship which was derived from a particular type of assertion and was formulated over-hastily into an epistemological axiom. With the peace of mind that comes from the *a priori* premise that epistemology is independent of the " empirical " special sciences, the mind is once and for all closed to the insight which a broadened empiricism might bring. The result is that one fails to see that this theory of self-sufficiency, this gesture of self-preservation, serves no other purpose than that of a bulwark for a certain type of academic epistemology which, in its last stages, is attempting to preserve itself from the collapse which might result from a more developed empiricism. The holders of the older view overlook the fact that they are thereby perpetuating not epistemology as such and preserving it from revision at the hands of the individual sciences, but rather merely one specific kind of epistemology, the uniqueness of which consists only in the fact that it once was at war with an earlier stage of a more narrowly conceived empiricism. It then stabilized the conception of knowledge which was derived from merely one particular segment of reality and represented merely one of the many possible varieties of knowledge.

In order to discover where the sociology of knowledge may lead us, we must once more go into the problem of the alleged primacy of epistemology over the special sciences. Having opened the problem by a critical examination, we shall be in a position to formulate, at least sketchily, a positive presentation of the epistemology already implicit in the very problem of the sociology of knowledge. First we must adduce those arguments which undermine or at least call into question the absolute autonomy and primacy of epistemology as over against the special sciences.

Epistemology and the Special Sciences. There is a twofold relationship between epistemology and the special sciences. The former, according to its constructive claims, is fundamental to all the special sciences, since it supplies the basic justifications for the types of knowledge and the conceptions of truth and correctness which these others rely upon in their concrete methods of procedure, and affects their findings. This, however, does not alter the fact that every theory of knowledge is itself influenced by the form which science takes at the time and from which alone it can obtain its conception of the nature of knowledge. In principle, no doubt, it claims to be the basis of all science but in fact it is determined by the condition of science at any given time. The problem is thus made the more difficult by the fact that the very principles, in the light of which knowledge is to be criticized, are themselves found to be socially and historically conditioned. Hence their application appears to be limited to given historical periods and the particular types of knowledge then prevalent.

Once these interrelationships are clearly recognized, then the belief is no longer tenable that epistemology and noology, because of their justifiable claim to foundational functions, must develop autonomously and independently of the progress of the special sciences, and are not subject to basic modifications by these. Consequently we are forced to recognize that a wholesome development of epistemology and noology is possible only if we conceive of their relationship to the special sciences in the following sense :—

New forms of knowledge, in the last analysis, grow out of the conditions of collective life and do not depend for their emergence upon the prior demonstration by a theory of knowledge that they are possible ; they do not therefore need to be first legitimized by an epistemology. The relationship is actually quite the reverse : the development of theories of scientific knowledge takes place in the preoccupation with empirical data and the fortunes of the former vary with those of the latter. The revolutions in methodology and epistemology are always sequels and repercussions of the revolutions in the immediate empirical procedures for getting knowledge. Only through constant recourse to the procedure of the special empirical sciences can the epistemological foundations be made sufficiently flexible and extended so that they will not only sanction the claims of the older forms of knowledge (their original purpose) but will also support the newer forms. This peculiar situation is characteristic of all theoretical, philosophic disciplines. Its structure is most clearly perceivable in the philosophy of law which presumes to be the judge and critic of positive law, but which is actually, in most cases, no more than a *post facto* formulation and justification of the principles of positive law.

In saying this, no denial is made of the importance of epistemology or philosophy as such. The basic inquiries which they undertake are indispensable, and indeed, if one attacked epistemology and philosophy on theoretical grounds, one could not avoid dealing with theoretical principles oneself. Such a theoretical attack would, of course, precisely to the extent that it penetrates into fundamental issues, be in itself a philosophical concern. To every factual form of knowledge belongs a theoretical foundation. This basic function of theory, which is to be understood in a structural sense, must never be misapplied by using its character to give an *a priori* certainty to particular findings. If misused in this manner it would frustrate the progress of science and would lead to the displacement, by *a priori* certainties, of views deriving from empirical observations. The errors and the partiality in the theoretical bases of science must continually be revised in the light of the new developments in the immediate scientific activities themselves. The light that is thrown by new factual knowledge upon the theoretical foundation must not be allowed to be obscured by the obstacles to thought which theory may possible erect. Through the particularizing procedure of the sociology of knowledge, we discover that the older epistemology is a correlate of a particular mode of thought. This is one example of the possibility of extending our field of vision by allowing newly discovered empirical evidence to throw new light upon our theoretical foundations. We are thus implicitly called upon to find an epistemological foundation appropriate to these more varied modes of thought. Moreover we are required to find if possible a theoretical basis under which can be subsumed all the modes of thought which, in the course of history, we have succeeded in establishing. We can now examine how far it is true that the hitherto dominant epistemologies and noologies furnish only one particular foundation for a single type of knowledge.

3. THE DEMONSTRATION OF THE PARTIAL NATURE OF TRADITIONAL EPISTEMOLOGY

(a) *The Orientation Towards Natural Science as a Model of Thought.* The particularity of the theory of knowledge holding sway to-day is now clearly demonstrable by the fact that the natural sciences have been selected as the ideal to which all knowledge should aspire. It is only because natural science, especially in its quantifiable phases, is largely detachable from the historical-social perspective of the investigator that the ideal of true knowledge was so construed that all attempts to attain a type of knowledge aiming at the comprehension of quality are considered as methods of inferior value. For quality contains elements more or less intertwined with the *Weltanschauung* of the knowing subject. At a moment when historical-social forces place other types of knowledge in the centre of the arena it is necessary to revise the older premises which had been, if not exclusively, at least to a large extent formulated for the understanding and justification of the natural sciences. Just as Kant once laid the foundations for modern epistemology by asking about the already existent natural sciences, " How are they possible ? " so to-day we must ask the same question concerning the type of knowledge which seeks qualitative understanding and which tends, at least, to affect the whole subject. We must ask further how and in what sense can we arrive at truth by means of this type of thought.

(b) *The Relationship between Criteria of Truth and the Social-Historical Situation.* We are faced here with an even more deeply rooted connection between epistemology in its concrete historical varieties and the corresponding " existential situation ". The theory of knowledge takes over from the concrete conditions of knowledge of a period (and thereby of a society) not merely its ideal of what factual knowledge should be, but also the utopian conception of truth in general, as for instance in the form of a utopian construction of a sphere of " truth as such ".

The possible utopias and wish-images of an epoch as conceptions of the not-yet-real are oriented about what has already been realized in this epoch (and are not therefore chance, undetermined phantasies, or the results of inspiration). Similarly, the utopian pattern of correctness, the idea of truth, arises out of the concrete modes of obtaining knowledge prevailing at a given time. Thus the concept of truth has not remained constant through all time, but has been involved in the process of historical change. The exact physiognomy of the concept of truth at a given time is not a chance phenomenon. Rather is there a clue to the construction of the conception of truth of that time, in the representative modes of thought and their structure, from which a conception is built up as to the nature of truth in general. We see, therefore, not merely that the notion of knowledge in general is dependent upon the concretely prevailing form of knowledge and the modes of knowing expressed therein and accepted as ideal, but also that the concept of truth itself is dependent upon the already existing types of knowledge. Thus, on the basis of these intermediate stages, there exists a fundamental although not readily apparent nexus between epistemology, the dominant forms of knowing, and the general social-intellectual situation of a time. In this manner the sociology of knowledge at a given point, through its analysis by means of the particularizing method, also penetrates into the realm of epistomology where it resolves the possible conflict among the various epistemologies by conceiving of each as the theoretical substructure appropriate merely to a given form of knowledge. The final solution of the problem so presents itself that only after the juxtaposition of the different modes of knowledge and their respective epistemologies can a more fundamental and inclusive epistemology be constructed.

4. The Positive Role of the Sociology of Knowledge

Once we realize that although epistemology is the basis of all the empirical sciences, it can only derive its principles from the data supplied by them and once we realize, further, the extent to which epistemology has hitherto been profoundly influenced by the ideal of the exact sciences, then it is clearly our duty to inquire how the problem will be affected when other sciences are taken into consideration. This suggests the following arguments :—

Revision of the Thesis that the Genesis of a Proposition is under all Circumstances Irrelevant to its Truth. The abrupt and absolute dualism between " validity " and " existence "—between " meaning " and " existence "—between " essence " and " fact " is, as has often been pointed out, one of the axioms of the " idealistic " epistemology and noology prevailing to-day. It is regarded as impregnable and is the most immediate obstacle to the unbiased utilization of the findings of the sociology of knowledge.

Indeed, if the type of knowledge represented by the example $2 \times 2 = 4$ is subjected to examination, then the correctness of this thesis is fairly well demonstrated. It is true of this type of knowledge that its genesis does not enter into the results of thought. From this it is only a short step to construct a sphere of truth in itself in such a manner that it becomes completely independent of the knowing subject. Moreover, this theory of the separability of the truth-content of a statement from the conditions of its origin had great value in the struggle against psychologism, for only with the aid of this theory was it possible to separate the known from the act of knowing. The observation that the genesis of an idea must be kept separate from its meaning applies also in the domain of explanatory psychology. It is only because in this realm it could be demonstrated in certain cases that the psychological processes which produce meanings are irrelevant to their validity, that this statement was legitimately incorporated into the truths of noology and epistemology. Between, for instance, the laws of the mechanism of association and the judgment arrived at by this associative mechanism, there exists a gap, which makes it plausible that a genesis of that kind does not contribute anything to the evaluation of meaning. There are, however, types of genesis which are not void of meaning, the peculiarities of which have until now never been analysed. Thus, for example, the relationship between existential position and the corresponding point of view may be considered as a genetic one, but in a sense different from that used previously. In this case, too, the question of genesis is involved, since there can be no doubt that we are here dealing with the conditions of emergence and existence of an assertion. If we speak of the " position behind a point of view " we have in mind a complex of conditions of emergence and existence which determine the nature and development of an assertion. But we would be falsely characterizing the existential situation of the assertor if we failed to take into account its meaning for the validity of the assertion. A position in the social structure carries with it, as we have seen, the probability that he who occupies it will think in a certain way. It signifies existence oriented with reference to certain meanings (*Sinnausgerichtetes Sein*). Social position cannot be described in terms which are devoid of social meanings as, for example, by mere chronological designation. 1789 as a chronological date is wholly meaningless. As historical designation, however, this date refers to a set of meaningful social events which in themselves demarcate the range of a certain type of experiences, conflicts, attitudes, and thoughts. Historical-social position can only be adequately characterized by meaningful designations (as, for instance, by such designations as " liberal position ", " proletarian conditions of existence ", etc.). " Social existence " is thus an area of being, or a sphere of existence, of which orthodox ontology which recognizes only the absolute dualism between being devoid of meaning on the one hand and meaning on the other hand takes no account.[1] A genesis of this sort could be characterized by calling it a " meaningful genesis " (*Sinngenesis*) as contrasted with a " factual-genesis " (*Faktizitätsgenesis*). If a model of this sort had been kept in mind in stating the relationship between being and meaning, the duality of being and validity would not have been assumed as absolute in epistemology and noology. Instead, there would have been a series of gradations between these two poles, in which such intermediate cases as " being invested with meaning " and " being oriented to meaning " would have found a place and been incorporated into the fundamental conception.

The next task of epistemology, in our opinion, is to overcome its partial nature by incorporating into itself the multiplicity of relationships between existence and validity (*Sein und Geltung*) as discovered by the sociology of knowledge, and to give attention to the types of knowledge operating in a region of being which is full of meaning and which affects the truth-value of the assertions. Thereby epistemology is not supplanted by the sociology of knowledge but a new kind of epistomology is called for which will reckon with the facts brought to light by the sociology of knowledge.

Further Consequences of the Sociology of Knowledge for Epistemology. Having seen that most of the axioms of the prevailing

---

[1] Cf. the essay previously referred to, " Ideologische und soziologische Interpretation geistiger Gebilde," loc. cit.

noology and epistemology have been taken over from the quantifiable natural sciences and are, so to speak, mere extensions of the tendencies singularly characteristic of this form of knowledge, it becomes clear that the noological problem must be reformulated with reference to the counter-model of more or less existentially determined varieties of knowledge. We intend now in a few words to state the new formulation of the problem which is deemed necessary once we have recognized the partial character of the older noology.

The Discovery of the Activistic Element in Knowledge. That in the " idealistic " conception of knowledge knowing is regarded mostly as a purely " theoretical " act in the sense of pure perception, has its origins, in addition to the above-mentioned orientation toward mathematical models, in the fact that in the background of this epistemology there lies the philosophical ideal of the " contemplative life ". We cannot concern ourselves here with the history of this ideal or the manner in which the purely contemplative conception of knowledge first penetrated into epistemology. (This would require examination of the pre-history of scientific logic and of the development of the philosopher from the seer, from whom the former took over the ideal of the " mystic vision ".) It suffices for us to point out that this great esteem for the contemplatively perceived is not the outcome of the " pure " observation of the act of thinking and knowing, but springs from a hierarchy of values based on a certain philosophy of life. The idealistic philosophy, which represents this tradition, insisted that knowledge was pure only when it was purely theoretical. Idealistic philosophy was not upset by the discovery that the type of knowledge represented by pure theory was only a small segment of human knowledge, that in addition there can be knowledge where men, while thinking, are also acting, and finally, that in certain fields knowledge arises only when and in so far as it itself is action, i.e. when action is permeated by the intention of the mind, in the sense that the concepts and the total apparatus of thought are dominated by and reflect this activist orientation. Not purpose *in addition* to perception but purpose *in* perception itself reveals the qualitative richness of the world in certain fields. Also the phenomenologically demonstrable fact that in these fields the activist genesis penetrates into the structure of the perspective and is not separable from it could not deter the older noology and epistemology either from overlooking

this type of knowledge, which is integrated with action, or from
seeing in it only an " impure " form of knowledge. (It is interesting to note that the connotations of the designation " impure
knowledge " seems to point to a magical origin of the term.) The
problem henceforth consists not in rejecting this type of knowledge from the very beginning, but in considering the manner
in which the concept of knowing must be reformulated so that
knowledge can be had even where purposeful action is involved.
This reformulation of the noological problem is not intended to
open the gates to propaganda and value-judgments in the
sciences. On the contrary, when we speak of the fundamental
intent of the mind (*intentio animi*) which is inherent in every
form of knowledge and which affects the perspective, we refer
to the irreducible residue of the purposeful element in knowledge
which remains even when all conscious and explicit evaluations
and biases have been eliminated. It is self-evident that science
(in so far as it is free from evaluation) is not a propagandistic
device and does not exist for the purpose of communicating
evaluations, but rather for the determination of facts. What
the sociology of knowledge seeks to reveal is merely that,
after knowledge has been freed from the elements of propaganda
and evaluation, it still contains an activist element which, for
the most part, has not become explicit, and which cannot be
eliminated, but which, at best, can and should be raised into
the sphere of the controllable.

*The Essentially Perspectivistic Element in Certain Types of
Knowledge.* The second point of which we must take cognizance
is that in certain areas of historical-social knowledge it should
be regarded as right and inevitable that a given finding should
contain the traces of the position of the knower. The problem
lies not in trying to hide these perspectives or in apologizing
for them, but in inquiring into the question of how, granted these
perspectives, knowledge and objectivity are still possible. It is
not a source of error that in the visual picture of an object in
space we can, in the nature of the case, get only a perspectivistic
view. The problem is not how we might arrive at a non-
perspectivistic picture but how, by juxtaposing the various
points of view, each perspective may be recognized as such
and thereby a new level of objectivity attained. Thus
we come to the point where the false ideal of a detached,
impersonal point of view must be replaced by the ideal
of an essentially human point of view which is within the

limits of a human perspective, constantly striving to enlarge itself.

The Problem of the Sphere of Truth as Such. In examining the philosophy of life, which furnishes the background for the idealistic epistemology and noology, it became clear that the ideal of a realm of truth as such (which, so to speak, pre-exists independently of the historical-psychological act of thought, and in which every concrete act of knowing merely participates) is the last offshoot of the dualistic world-view which, alongside of our world of concrete immediate events, created a second world by adding another dimension of being.

The positing of a sphere of truth which is valid in itself (an offshoot of the doctrine of ideas) is intended to do the same for the act of knowing as the notion of the beyond or the transcendental did for dualistic metaphysics in the realm of ontology, namely to postulate a sphere of perfection which does not bear the scars of its origins and, measured by which, all events and processes are shown to be finite and incomplete. Furthermore, just as in this extreme spiritualistic metaphysics the quality of " being human " was conceived as " merely being human "—which had been stripped of everything vital, corporeal, historical, or social—so an attempt was made to set forth a conception of knowledge in which these human elements would be submerged.   It is necessary to raise the question time and again whether we can imagine the concept of knowing without taking account of the whole complex of traits by which man is characterized, and how, without these presuppositions we can even think of the concept of knowing, to say nothing of actually engaging in the act of knowing.

In the realm of ontology, in modern times, this dualistic view (which originated for the purpose of proving the inadequacy of " this " world) was, furthermore, gradually broken down in the course of empirical research.   In noology and epistemology, however, it is still a force. But since here the basic presuppositions in the field of the theory of science are not quite so transparent, it was believed that this ideal of a superhuman, supertemporal sphere of validity was not a possible construction arising out of one's world-view, but an essential datum and prerequisite for the interpretation of the phenomenon of " thinking ".   Our discussion here is intended to show that from the point of view of the phenomenology of thought, there is no necessity to regard knowledge as though it were an intrusion from the sphere of actual happenings into a sphere of " truth in itself ". Such a construction at best is of a heuristic value for such modes of thought as are represented by the example $2 \times 2 = 4$. Our reflections aim, on the contrary, to show that the problem of knowing becomes more intelligible if we hold strictly to the data presented by the real factual thinking that we carry on in this world (which is the only kind of thinking known to us, and which is independent of this ideal sphere) and if we accept the phenomenon of knowing as the act of a living being. In other words, the sociology of knowledge regards the cognitive act in connection with the models to which it aspires in its existential as well as its meaningful quality, not as insight into " eternal " truths, arising from a purely theoretical, contemplative urge, or as some sort of participation in these truths (as Scheler still thought), but as an instrument for dealing with life-situations at the disposal of a certain kind of vital being under certain conditions of life. All these three factors, the nature and structure of the process of dealing with life-situations, the subjects' own make-up (in his biological as well as historical-social aspects), and the peculiarity of the conditions of life, especially the place and position of the thinker—all these influence the results of thought. But they also condition the ideal of truth which this living being is able to construct from the products of thought.

The conception of knowledge as an intellectual act, which is only then complete when it no longer bears the traces of its human derivation, has, as we have already indicated, its greatest heuristic value in those realms where, as in the example $2 \times 2 = 4$, the above-mentioned characteristics can phenomenologically, with greater or less justification, be shown actually to exist. It is misleading, however, and tends to obscure fundamental phenomena in those broader realms of the knowable where, if the human historical element is overlooked, the results of thought are completely denatured.

Only the phenomenological evidence derived from the existing models of thought may be used as an argument for or against certain concepts involved in knowledge. Disguised motives, arising out of a certain outlook on the world, have no bearing on the matter. There is no reason for retaining in our noology the disdain for corporeal, sensual, temporal, dynamic, and social things characteristic of the type of human being presupposed in the " idealistic " philosophy. At the present moment there are confronting each other two types of knowledge which are of representative significance, and correspondingly there are two possibilities of noological and epistemological explanations of knowledge. For the moment it would be well to keep these two approaches separate and to make the differences between them stand out rather than to minimize them. Only in the process, of trial and error will it become clear which of these bases of interpretation is the more sound and whether we get farther if, as has been done hitherto, we take the situationally detached type of knowledge as our point of departure and treat the situationally conditioned as secondary and unimportant or contrariwise, whether we regard the situationally detached type of knowledge as a marginal and special case of the situationally conditioned.

If we were to inquire into the possible directions of epistemology if it followed the last-mentioned model of thought and recognized the inherent " situational determination " of certain types of knowledge and made it the basis for its further reflections, we should be confronted with two possible alternatives. The scientist, in this case has the task, first of all, of making explicit the possibilities of the further implications of his problem and to point out all the eventualities that are likely to come into his range of vision. He should content himself with asserting only what, in his present stage of penetration into the problem, he can honestly determine. The function of the thinker is not to pronounce judgment at any cost when a new problem first arises, but rather, in full awareness of the fact that research is still under way, to state only that which has become definitely perceivable. There are two alternatives that he may follow once he has arrived at this stage.

The Two Directions in Epistemology. One of the two directions taken by epistemology emphasizes the prevalence of situational determination, maintaining that in the course of the progress of social knowledge this element is ineradicable, and that, therefore, even one's own point of view may always be expected to be peculiar to one's position. This would require revision of the theoretical basis of knowledge by setting up the thesis of the inherently relational structure of human knowledge (just as the essentially perspectivistic nature of visually perceived objects is admitted without question).

This solution does not imply renunciation of the postulate of objectivity and the possibility of arriving at decisions in factual disputes ; nor does it involve an acceptance of illusionism according to which everything is an appearance and nothing can be decided. It does imply rather that this objectivity and this competence to arrive at decisions can be attained only through indirect means. It is not intended to assert that objects do not exist or that reliance upon observation is useless and futile but rather that the answers we get to the questions we put to the subject-matter are, in certain cases, in the nature of things, possible only within the limits of the observer's perspective. The result even here is not relativism in the sense of one assertion being as good as another. Relationism, as we use it, states that every assertion can only be relationally formulated. It becomes relativism only when it is linked with the older static ideal of eternal, unperspectivistic truths independent of the subjective experience of the observer, and when it is judged by this alien ideal of absolute truth.

In the case of situationally conditioned thought, objectivity comes to mean something quite new and different : (a) there is first of all the fact that in so far as different observers are immersed in the same system, they will, on the basis of the identity of their conceptual and categorical apparatus and through the common universe of discourse thereby created, arrive at similar results, and be in a position to eradicate as an error everything that deviates from this unanimity ; (b) and recently there is a recognition of the fact that when observers have different perspectives, " objectivity " is attainable only in a more roundabout fashion. In such a case, what has been correctly but differently perceived by the two perspectives must be understood in the light of the differences in structure of these varied modes of perception. An effort must be made to find a formula for translating the results of one into those of the other and to discover a common denominator for these varying perspectivistic insights. Once such a common denominator has been found, it is possible to separate the necessary differences of the two views from the arbitrarily conceived and mistaken elements, which here too should be considered as errors.

The controversy concerning visually perceived objects (which, in the nature of the case, can be viewed only in perspective) is not settled by setting up a non-perspectivist view (which is impossible). It is settled rather by understanding, in the light of one's own positionally determined vision, why the object appeared differently to one in a different position. Likewise, in our field also, objectivity is brought about by the translation of one perspective into the terms of another. It is natural that here we must ask which of the various points of view is the best. And for this too there is a criterion. As in the case of visual perspective, where certain positions have the advantage of revealing the decisive features of the object, so here pre-eminence is given to that perspective which gives evidence of the greatest comprehensiveness and the greatest fruitfulness in dealing with empirical materials.

The theory of knowledge can also pursue a second course by emphasizing the following facts : The impetus to research in the sociology of knowledge may be so guided that it will not absolutize the concept of " situational determination " ; rather, it may be directed in such a fashion that precisely by discovering the element of situational determination in the views at hand, a first step will be taken towards the solution of the problem of situational determination itself. As soon as I identify a view which sets itself up as absolute, as representing merely a given angle of vision, I neutralize its partial nature in a certain sense. Most of our earlier discussion of this problem moved quite spontaneously in the direction of the neutralization of situational determination by attempting to rise above it. The idea of the continuously broadening basis of knowledge, the idea of the continuous extension of the self and of the integration of various social vantage points into the process of knowledge—observations which are all based on empirical facts—and the idea of an all-embracing ontology which is to be sought for—all move in this direction. This tendency in intellectual and social history is closely connected with the processes of group contact and interpenetration. In its first stage, this tendency neutralizes the various conflicting points of view (i.e. deprives them of their absolute character) ; in its second stage, it creates out of this neutralization a more comprehensive and serviceable basis of vision. It is interesting to note that the construction of a broader base is bound up with a higher degree of abstractness and tends in an increasing degree to formalize the phenomena with which we are concerned. This formalizing tendency consists in relegating to a subordinate position the analysis of the concrete qualitative assertions which lead in a given direction, and substituting in place of the qualitative and configurative description of phenomena a purely functional view modelled after a purely mechanical pattern. This theory of increasing abstractness will be designated as the theory of the social genesis of abstraction. According to this sociological derivation of abstraction (which is clearly observable in the emergence of the sociological point of view itself), the trend towards a higher stage of abstraction is a correlate of the amalgamation of social groups. The corroboration of this contention is found in the fact that the capacity for abstraction among individuals and groups grows in the measure that they are parts of heterogeneous groups and organizations in more inclusive collective units, capable of absorbing local or otherwise particular groups. But this tendency towards abstraction on a higher level is still in accord with the theory of the situational determination of thought, for the reason that the subject that engages in this thinking is by no means an absolutely autonomous " mind in itself ", but is rather a subject which is ever more inclusive, and which neutralizes the earlier particular and concrete points of view.

All the categories justifiably formulated by formal sociology are products of this neutralizing and formalizing operation. The logical conclusion of this approach is that, in the end, it sees only a formal mechanism in operation. Thus, to cite an illustration from formal sociology, domination is a category which can only be abstracted from the concrete positions of the persons involved (i.e. the dominator and the dominated), because it contents itself with emphasizing the structural inter-relationship (the mechanism, so to speak) of the behaviour involved in the process of interaction. This it does by operating with concepts like sub- and super-ordination, force, obedience, subjectibility, etc. The qualitative content of domination in the concrete (which would immediately present " domination " in an historical setting) is not accessible through this formula, and could be adequately portrayed only if the dominated as well as the dominator were to tell what their experiences actually were in the situations in which they live. For not even the formal definitions that we discover float in thin air ; they arise rather out of the concrete problems of a situation. At this point the notion arises, which of course needs detailed verification, that the problem of perspectivism concerns primarily the qualitative aspect of a phenomenon. Because, however, the content of social-intellectual phenomena is primarily meaningful and because meaning is perceived in acts of understanding and interpretation, we may say that the problem of perspectivism in the sociology of knowledge refers, first of all, to what is understandable in social phenomena. But in this we are by no means denoting a narrowly circumscribed realm. The most elementary facts in the social sphere surpass in complexity the purely formal relations, and they can only be understood in referring to qualitative contents and meanings. In short, the problem of interpretation is a fundamental one.

Even where formalization has gone farthest and where we are concerned with mere relations, so to speak, there is still a minimum of evidence of the investigator's general direction of interest which could not be entirely eliminated. For example, when Max Weber, in classifying types of conduct, distinguished between " purposeful-rational " and " traditional " conduct, he was still expressing the situation of a generation in which one group had discovered and given evaluative emphasis to the rationalistic tendencies in capitalism, while another, demonstrably impelled by political motives, discovered the significance of tradition and emphasized it as over against the former. The interest in the problem of a typology of conduct itself arises out of this particular social situation. And when we find that precisely these types of conduct were singled out and formalized in precisely this direction, we must seek the source of this tendency towards abstraction in the concrete social situation of the epoch which was preoccupied with the phenomenon of conduct as seen from this angle. If another age had attempted a formal systematization of the types of conduct, it would no doubt have arrived at quite another typology. In another historical situation, different abstractions would have been found and singled out from the total complex of events. In our judgment the sociology of knowledge, by virtue of its premises, does not need to deny the existence or possibility of formalized and abstract thought. It need show only that, in this respect, too, thought is not independent of " existence ", for it is not a super-social, super-human subject which is expressing itself in " as such " categories in this typology. Rather the neutralizations of the qualitative differences in the varying points of view, arising in certain definite situations, result in a scheme of orientation which allows only certain formal and structural components of the phenomena to emerge into the foreground of experience and thought. In a rudimentary form this process is already observable in the rules of etiquette and social intercourse which arise spontaneously in the contact between different groups. There, too, the more fleeting the contacts the less concern

U

there is with the qualitative understanding of the mutual relationship, which is formalized to such an extent that it becomes a "formal sociological category" indicating, so to speak, only the specific role of the relationship. The other party is regarded merely as an "ambassador", "stranger", or "train conductor". In social intercourse we react to the other only with reference to these characteristics. In other words, the formalization in such cases is itself an expression of certain social situations, and the direction which formalization takes (whether we pick out, as we do in the case of the "ambassador", his function as a political representative or whether, as we do in the case of the "stranger", single out his ethnic traits) is dependent on the social situation, which enters, even though in a diluted form, into the categories that we use. In a similar vein, the observation may be made that in jurisprudence formalized law takes the place of informal justice, which arises out of concrete issues and represents a qualitative judgment derived from the situation and expressing the sense of right of a community, whenever an exchange economy reaches the point where its very existence depends on knowing in advance what the law will be. Henceforth, it is less important to do full justice to each case in its absolute uniqueness than to be able more and more correctly to classify and subsume each case under pre-established formalized categories.

As already indicated, we are not yet in a position to-day to decide the question as to which of the two above-mentioned alternatives the nature of the empirical data will force a scientific theory of knowledge to follow. In either case, however, we will have to reckon with situational determination as an inherent factor in knowledge, as well as with the theory of relationism and the theory of the changing basis of thought. In either case we must reject the notion that there is a "sphere of truth in itself" as a disruptive and unjustifiable hypothesis. It is instructive to note that the natural sciences seem to be, in many respects, in a closely analogous situation, especially if we use as our basis for comparison the interpretation of their present plight that has been so skilfully presented by W. Westphal. According to this view, once it was discovered that our conventional standards for measurement, such as clocks, etc., and the everyday language associated with them are possible and usable only for this everyday, common sense scheme of orientation, it began to be understood that in the quantum theory, for instance, where we are dealing with the measurement of electrons, it is impossible to speak of a result of measurement which can be formulated independently of the measuring instrument used. For in the latter case the measuring instrument is interpreted as an object which itself relevantly influences the position and velocity of the electrons to be measured. Thus the thesis arose that position and velocity measurements are expressible only in " indeterminate relations " (Heisenberg) which specify the degree of indeterminacy. Furthermore, the next step from this idea was the denial of the assertion, which was closely allied to the older method of thinking, that the electrons *in themselves* must in reality have well-defined paths, on the ground that such " as such " assertions belong to that type of completely contentless assertion which, to be sure, do communicate a sort of intuitively derived image, but which are completely devoid of content, since no consequences can be drawn from them. The same was held to apply to the assumption that bodies in motion must have an absolute velocity. But since according to Einstein's relativity this is, in principle, not determinable, this assumption in the light of modern theory belongs quite as much with these empty assertions as the thesis that in addition to our world there exists another world which is, in the nature of the case, inaccessible to our experience.

If we followed this trend of thought, which in its unformulated relationism is surprisingly similar to our own, then the setting-up of the logical postulate that a sphere of " truth in itself " exists and has validity seems as difficult to justify as all of the other empty existential dualisms just mentioned. Because, as long as we see only relational determinabilities in the whole realm of empirical knowledge, the formulation of an " as such " sphere has no consequences whatsoever for the process of knowing.

5. PROBLEMS OF TECHNIQUE IN HISTORICAL-SOCIOLOGICAL RESEARCH IN THE FIELD OF THE SOCIOLOGY OF KNOWLEDGE

The most important task of the sociology of knowledge at present is to demonstrate its capacity in actual research in the historical-sociological realm. In this realm it must work out criteria of exactness for establishing empirical truths and for assuring their control. It must emerge from the stage where it engages in casual intuitions and gross generalities (such as the crude dichotomy involved in the assertion that here we find

bourgeois thinking, there we find proletarian thinking, etc.)
though even this may involve sacrificing its slogan-like clear-
cutness. In this it can and must learn from the methods and
results of the exact procedure of the philological disciplines,
and from the methods used in the history of art with particular
reference to stylistic succession.

In the latter, the methods of " dating " and " placing "
different works of art are especially advanced, and from them,
mutatis mutandis, there is much to be learned. The basic task
of research in the sociology of knowledge in this connection is to
determine the various viewpoints which gradually arise in the
history of thought and are constantly in process of change.

These various positions are determined by the method of
imputation. This involves a clear conception of the perspective
of each product of thought and bringing of the perspective thus
established into relationship with the currents of thought of
which it is a part. These currents of thought, in turn, must
be traced back to the social forces determining them (this step
has not yet been taken by the history of art in its own domain).

There are two levels on which the task of imputation may
proceed. The first (*Sinngemässe Zurechnung*) deals with general
problems of interpretation. It reconstructs integral styles of
thought and perspectives, tracing single expressions and records
of thought which appear to be related back to a central
Weltanschauung, which they express. It makes explicit the whole
of the system which is implicit in the discrete segments of
a system of thought. In styles of thought which are not
avowedly a part of a closed system, it uncovers the underlying
unity of outlook. Even after this has been done, the problem
of imputation on this level is not yet completely solved. Even
if, for instance, we were successful in showing that in the first
half of the nineteenth century most intellectual activities and
products could, from the standpoint of their meanings, be subsumed under and imputed to the polarity of " liberal " and
" conservative " thought, the problem would still arise whether
this explicit reference to a central outlook which proceeds purely
on an intellectual level actually corresponds to the facts. It is
quite possible that the investigator will succeed in building
up out of fragments of expression the two antithetical, closed
systems of conservative thought on the one hand and liberal
thought on the other, although the liberals and conservatives of
the period might not, in actuality, have thought that way at all.

The second level of imputation (*Faktizitätszurechnung*) operates by assuming that the ideal types built up through the process above described are indispensable hypotheses for research, and then asking to what extent liberals and conservatives actually did think in these terms, and in what measure, in individual cases, these ideal-types were actually realized in their thinking. Every author of the time accessible to us must be examined from this point of view and the imputation in each case must be made on the basis of the blends and crossings of points of view which are to be found in his assertions.

The consistent carrying out of this task of imputation will finally produce the concrete picture of the course and direction of development which has actually taken place. It will reveal the actual history of these two styles of thought. This method offers the maximum reliability in the reconstruction of intellectual development, since it analyses into its elements what at first was merely a summary impression of the course of intellectual history, and by reducing this impression to explicit criteria makes possible a reconstruction of reality. Thereby it succeeds subsequently in singling out the anonymous, unarticulated forces which are operative in the history of thought. It does this, however, not merely in the bare form of surmises, nor in narrative terms (which is still the level of our political and cultural history), but rather in the form of the controllable determination of facts. Of course, it is precisely in the process of detailed investigation that much that previously appeared to be certain becomes problematic. Thus, for example, there may be a great deal of controversy, in view of the ambivalent character of mixed types, as to the style to which they should be imputed. The fruitfulness of the historical method in the study of artistic styles, however, is not refuted but rather re-enforced when questions arise as to whether the work of certain artists is imputable to the Renaissance or to Baroque.

When the structures and the tendencies of two styles of thought have been worked out, we are faced with the task of their sociological imputation. As sociologists we do not attempt to explain the forms and variations in conservative thought, for example, solely by reference to the conservative *Weltanschauung*. On the contrary, we seek to derive them firstly from the composition of the groups and strata which express themselves in that mode of thought. And, secondly, we seek to explain the impulse and the direction of development of conservative thought through the structural situation and the changes it undergoes within a larger, historically conditioned whole (such as Germany, for instance), and through the constantly varying problems raised by the changing structure.

By constantly taking account of all the various types of knowledge, ranging from earlier intuitive impressions to controlled observation, the sociology of knowledge seeks to obtain systematic comprehension of the relationship between social existence and thought. The whole life of an historical-social group presents itself as an interdependent configuration ; thought is only its expression and the interaction between these two aspects of life is the essential element in the configuration, the detailed interconnections of which must be traced if it is to be understood.

Foremost among those who are advancing the sociology of knowledge and the sociological history of ideas are those scholars who, in their specific researches, use a conscious method in dealing with concrete materials. The controversy concerning particular problems of imputation in the sociology of knowledge is evidence of the transition from impressionistic conjectures to a stage of actual empirical research.

6. BRIEF SURVEY OF THE HISTORY OF THE SOCIOLOGY OF KNOWLEDGE

The most essential causes which gave rise to the sociology of knowledge have already been treated in the preceding pages. Because it is a discipline which arose out of the exigencies of social development, it is clear that the intellectual steps and attitudes which led up to it were made slowly, under the most diverse conditions and at different times. Here we must confine ourselves exclusively to the most important names and stages in its history. The sociology of knowledge actually emerged with Marx, whose profoundly suggestive *aperçus* went to the heart of the matter. However, in his work, the sociology of knowledge is still indistinguishable from the unmasking of ideologies since for him social strata and classes were the bearers of ideologies. Furthermore, although the theory of ideology appeared within the framework of a given interpretation of history, it was not as yet consistently thought out. The other source of the modern theory of ideology and of the sociology of knowledge is to be found in the flashes of insight of Nietzsche who combined concrete observations in this field with a theory of drives and a theory of knowledge which remind one of pragmatism. He too made sociological imputations, using as his chief categories " aristocratic " and " democratic " cultures, to each of which he ascribed certain modes of thought.

From Nietzsche the lines of development lead to the Freudian and Paretian theories of original impulses and to the methods developed by them for viewing human thought as distortions and as products of instinctive mechanisms. A related current leading to the development of a theory of ideology is to be noted in positivism, which led from Ratzenhofer through Gumplowicz to Oppenheimer. Jerusalem, who stimulated more recent discussions, may also be counted among the positivists. However, he did not see the difficulties in the problem arising from historicism and from Dilthey's position on the cultural sciences.[1]

The method of the sociology of knowledge was worked out in a more refined manner on two main lines : the first was through Lukács, who goes back to Marx and who elaborates the fruitful Hegelian elements contained in the latter. In this manner he arrived at a very fertile, schematic, and dogmatic solution of the problem, but one which suffers from the one-sidedness and the hazards of a given philosophy of history. Lukács did not go beyond Marx in so far as he failed to distinguish between the problem of unmasking ideologies on the one hand and the sociology of knowledge on the other. It was to Scheler's credit that, in addition to many valuable observations, he attempted to integrate the sociology of knowledge into the structure of a philosophical world-view. The emphasis in Scheler's achievement, however, is to be sought more in the direction of a metaphysical advance. This accounts for the fact that he more or less ignored the internal conflicts inhering in this new intellectual orientation and the dynamic implications and new problems arising out of it. It is true that he desired to do full justice to the new perspective opened up by the sociology of knowledge, but only in so far as it could be reconciled with the ontology, metaphysics, and epistemology which he represented. The outcome was a grandiose systematic sketch, full of profound intuitions, but lacking in a clear practicable method of investigation suited to a sociologically oriented, cultural science.

If in this summary presentation of the sociology of knowledge

[1] The works representing this tendency, including investigations of the French sociologists concerning " primitive thought ", are not treated here.

we did not present it in all its variety but only in the form in which the author conceives of it and which is elaborated in the first four parts of this book, it is because we desired to present the problem in as unified a form as possible in order to facilitate discussion.

BIBLIOGRAPHY

(The numbers in parentheses after the title refer to other topics in the Bibliography to which the book or article cited is relevant.)

I. EPISTEMOLOGICAL ASPECTS OF THE SOCIAL SCIENCES

1. PRESUPPOSITIONS

ABEL, THEODORE. *Systematic Sociology in Germany.* A critical analysis of some attempts to establish sociology as an independent science. Columbia University Studies in History, Economics, and Public Law, No. 310. New York and London, 1929. (I, 2, 3, 4, 5, 7.)

DEWEY, JOHN. "The Need for a Recovery in Philosophy," in *Creative Intelligence,* pp. 3–69. New York, 1917.

—— *Essays in Experimental Logic.* Chicago, 1919. (I, 3, 7.)

GINSBERG, MORRIS. "Recent Tendencies in Sociology," in *Economica,* vol. 39, pp. 22–39. February, 1933. (I, 6, 7.)

—— *Studies in Sociology,* pp. 1–43. London, 1932. (I, 6.)

KNIGHT, FRANK H. "The Limitations of Scientific Method in Economics," in *The Trend of Economics,* pp. 229–267, ed. by R. G. Tugwell. New York. (I, 6, 7.)

LANDHEER, BARTH. "The Problem of Presupposition in Sociology," *American Journal of Sociology,* xxxvii. 1932. (I, 5 ; II, 3.)

LÖWE, A. *Economics and Sociology.* A plea for co-operation in the social sciences. London, 1936.

MACIVER, R. M. "Social Causation," *Publication of the American Sociological Society,* xxvi, 3, pp. 28–36. August, 1932.

SPRANGER, EDUARD. "Sinn der Voraussetzungslosigkeit in den Geisteswissenschaften," *Abhandlungen der preussischen Akademie der Wissenschaften : Philosophisch-historische Klasse.* Berlin, 1931. (I, 5.)

2. BIAS AND PERSPECTIVE

BURKE, KENNETH. *Permanence and Change.* New York, 1935.

CALVERTON, V. F. "Modern Anthropology and the Theory of Cultural Compulsives," intro. to *The Making of Man,* pp. 1–37. New York, 1931. Also printed as "The Compulsive Basis of Social Thought," in *American Journal of Sociology,* xxxvi, 5, pp. 689–720. 1931. And in *Psyche.* 1930. (I, 3.)

DEWEY, JOHN. *The Influence of Darwin on Philosophy.* New York, 1910. (I, 3, 7.)

HOBSON, JOHN A. *Free Thought in the Social Sciences.* New York and London, 1926.

LEISEGANG, HANS. *Denkformen.* Berlin and Leipzig, 1928.

LITT, THEODOR. *Erkenntnis und Leben.* Untersuchungen über Gliederung, Methoden u. Beruf der Wissenschaft. Leipzig, 1923. (I, 3, 4, 5, 7 ; III, 4.)

—— *Individuum und Gemeinschaft.* Grundlegung der Kulturphilosophie. Leipzig, 1924. (I, 3, 4, 5, 6, 7.)

OGBURN, W. F. " Bias, Psychoanalysis and the Subjective in Relation to Culture," *Publication of the American Sociological Society,* xvii, pp. 62–74. 1923.

SPENCER, HERBERT. *The Study of Sociology.* New York, 1882. (X, 1, 3, 5.)

VAIHINGER, HANS. *The Philosophy of "As If".* A system of the theoretical, practical, and religious fictions of mankind. Tr. by C. K. Ogden. New York and London, 1924. (I, 1, 3, 7 ; IV, 1.)

WOLFE, A. B. *Radicalism, Conservatism, and Scientific Method.* New York, 1923. (I, 3.)

3. OBJECTIVITY

BECKER CARL. " Detachment and the Writing of History," *Atlantic Monthly,* October, 1910.

COHEN, MORRIS. *Reason and Nature,* pp. 333–385. New York, 1931. Also published in *The Social Sciences and their Interrelations,* pp. 437–466 ; ed. by Ogburn, W. F., and Goldenweiser, A. A. Boston and New York, 1927. (I, 1, 2, 4, 5, 6, 7.)

COOLEY, CHAS. H. " The Roots of Social Knowledge," in *Sociological Theory and Social Research,* pp. 287–312. New York, 1930. And in *American Journal of Sociology,* xxxii, 1 (1926), pp. 59–79. (I, 1, 2.)

CULVER, D. C. *Methodology of Social Science Research A Bibliography.* Berkeley, 1936.

DEWEY, JOHN. *The Quest for Certainty.* London, 1929. (I, 7 ; III, 1.)

—— *Experience and Nature.* Chicago and London, 1925. (I, 4.)

DURKHEIM, ÉMILE. *Les Règles de la méthode sociologique.* Paris, 1927. 8th ed. (I, 1, 7.)

GROLMANN, A. v. " Das Wissen um das Verhältnismässige in der Paradoxie des Seins," in *Zeitschrift f. deutsche Philosophie.* Vol. ii, 1, p. 57 ff.

HOBSON, E. W. *The Domain of Natural Science.* Cambridge, 1926.

HOOK, SIDNEY. "A Pragmatic Critique of the Historico-Genetic Method," in *Essays in Honor of John Dewey,* pp. 156–174. New York, 1929. (I, 2.)

HUSSERL, E. *Ideas.* General introduction to Pure Phenomenology. Tr. by W. R. Boyce-Gibson. New York, 1931. (I, 2, 4.)

JAMES, WILLIAM. *Pragmatism.* New York, 1907. (I, i, 2 ; III, 1, 5.)

KLÜVER, H. " Contemporary German Psychology." Appendix to Murphy, Gardner. *Historical Introduction to Modern Psychology.* New York, 1929. (I, 1.)

MACIVER, R. M. " Is Sociology a Natural Science ? " *Publication of the American Sociological Society,* xxv, 2, pp. 25–35. May, 1931. (I, 1.)

MANNHEIM, KARL. *Strukturanalyse der Erkenntnistheorie.* Ergänzungsheft 57. Kant-Studien. Berlin, 1922. (I, 2 ; II, 3.)

MEAD, G. H. " Scientific Method and the Individual Thinker," in *Creative Intelligence,* pp. 176–227. New York, 1917. (I, 7).

PEIRCE, C. S. S. *Pragmatism and Pragmaticism.* Vol. v of *Collected Papers of C. S. Peirce,* ed. by C. Hartshorne and P. Weiss. (I, 4, 7.)

RICE, STUART A. (ed.). *Methods in Social Science.* Chicago, 1931. Cf. also review by Mannheim, K., in *Amer. Journal of Sociology,* xxxvii (September, 1932).

SCHELTING, ALEXANDER V. *Max Weber's Wissenschaftslehre.* Tübingen, 1933. (I, 1, 2, 4, 5, 6, 7 ; IV, 2.)

SEIDLER, ERNST. *Die sozialwissenschaftliche Erkenntnis.* Ein Beitrag zur Methodik der Gesellschaftslehre. Jena, 1930. (I, 1, 7.)

SIMMEL, GEORG. *Probleme der Geschichtsphilosophie.* Second completely revised edition. Leipzig, 1905. (I, 2, 4, 5, 6.)

SMALL, ALBION. *The Origins of Sociology.* Chicago, 1924. (I, 6.)

SPIEGELBERG, H. *Antirelativismus. Kritik des Relativismus und Skeptizismus der Werte und des Sollens.* Zürich, Leipzig, 1935.

UNGER, R. " Zur Entwicklung des Problemes der historischen Objektivität : Eine prinzipiengeschichtliche Skizze." *Deutsche Vierteljahrsschrift für Literatur- und Geistesgeschichte,* Jhg. I, Heft 1, S. 104.

WEBER, MAX. " Die Objektivität sozialwissenschaftlicher und sozialpolitischer Erkenntnis," in *Gesammelte Aufsätze zur Wissenschaftslehre.* pp. 146–214. Tübingen, 1922.

—— " Der Sinn der , Wertfreiheit ' der soziologischen und ökonomischen Wissenschaften," in *Gesammelte Aufsätze zur Wissenschaftslehre,* pp. 451–502. Tübingen, 1922. (I, 1, 2, 4, 5, 6, 7 ; III, 2.)

4. SYMBOLS, MEANING, COMMUNICATION, AND LANGUAGE

AHLMANN, E. " Das Normative Moment im Bedeutungsbegriff," *Ann. Acad. Scient.,* Feun. Ser. B., Tom. xviii, No. 2. Helsingfors, 1926.

BALDWIN, J. M. *The Individual and Society, or Psychology and Sociology.* Boston, 1911.

—— *Social and Ethical Interpretations in Mental Development.* A study in social psychology. New York and London, 1913.

BENJAMIN, W. " Probleme der Sprachsoziologie," *Zeitschrift für Sozialforschung,* iv, 2. 1935.

BENTHAM, J. *The Theory of Fictions,* ed. by C. K. Ogden. London and New York, 1932.

BINSWANGER. " Verstehen und Erklären in der Psychologie," in *Zeitschrift für die Gesamte Neurologie und Psychologie,* vol. 107. 1927.

BURROW, N. TR. "Social Images *versus* Reality," *Journal of Abnormal Psychology and Social Psychology,* vol. xix.

—— *The Social Basis of Consciousness.* London and New York, 1927.

COOLEY, CHAS. H. *Human Nature and the Social Order.* New York, 1902.
—— *Social Process.* New York, 1918.
—— *Social Organization.* New York, 1909. (III, 4.)

CASSIRER, E. *Die Begriffsform im mythischen Denken.* Stud. d. Bibliothek Warburg. Leipzig, 1922.
—— "Erkenntnistheorie nebst den Grenzfragen der Logik und Denkpsychologie," in *Jahrb. der Philos.*, vol. 3, 1927.
—— *Philosophie der symbolischen Formen.* 3 vols. Berlin, 1923-1931.

DE LAGUNA, GRACE. *Speech, its Function and Development.* New Haven and London, 1927.

DEWEY, JOHN. *Human Nature and Conduct.* New York, 1922. (III, 1.)

DURKHEIM, E. "Representations individuelles et rep:esentations collectives," in *Revue de Metaphysique et de Morale*, vi (1898), pp. 273–302. Republished in *Sociologie et Philosophie*, ch. i. Paris, 1925. (I, 1, 2.)

ESPER, E. A. "A Contribution to the Experimental Study of Analogy," in *Psych. Rev.*, 25, 1918.

GINSBURG, I. *National Symbolism* in Kosok, P., *Modern Germany*. A Study of Conflicting Loyalties. pp. 292 ff. Chicago, 1933.

GOMPERZ, H. Über Sinn u. Sinngebilde : Verstehen u. Erklären. Tübingen, 1929.

GOTTL-OTTLILIENFELD, F. v. *Wirtschaft als Leben.* Jena, 1925.

GREEN, G. H. *The Daydream. A Study of Development.* London, 1923.

HEAD, H. "Disorders of Symbolic Thinking and Expression," *Brit. Journ. of Psychol.*, 1920–1.

HOERNLÉ, R. F. A. "Image, Idea, and Meaning," *Mind.* N.S. 16, 1907.

HOFFMANN, E. *Die Sprache und die archaische Logik.* Heidelb. Abh. zur. Philos. u. ihrer Gesch. No. 3. Tübingen, 1935.

HOFFMANN, PAUL. "Das Verstehen von Sinn und seine Allgemeingültigkeit," *Jahrbuch für Charakterologie*, vol. vi.

JASPERS, KARL. *Allgemeine Psychopathologie*, 3rd ed. Berlin, 1923. (I, 1, 7.)

JORDAN, L. "Sprache und Gesellschaft," in *Hauptprobleme d. Soziologie.* Erinnerungsgabe für Max Weber, vol. 1. München, Leipzig, 1923.

JUNG, C. G. *Psychology of the Unconscious.* A Study of the Transformations and Symbolisms of the Libido. New York and London, 1916.

LAYENDECKER, H. *Zur Phänomenologie der Täuschungen.* Halle, 1913.

LEISEGANG, H. Denkformen. Berlin and Leipzig, 1928.

MAIER, H. Psychologie des emotionalen Denkens. Tübingen, 1908.

MALGAUD, W. *De l'Action à la pensée.* Bibliothèque de Philosophie Contemporaine. Paris, 1935.

MALINOWSKI, B. " The Language of Magic and Gardening," vol. ii of *Coral Gardens and their Magic*. London, 1935.

—— " Magic, Science, and Religion," in Needham, J., ed. *Science, Religion, and Reality*. 1925.

—— *Myth in Primitive Psychology*, Psyche Miniatures. 1926.

—— " The Problem of Meaning in Primitive Languages," in C. K. Ogden and J. Richards, *The Meaning of Meaning*. New York and London, 1923.

MARKEY, JOHN F. *The Symbolic Process*. New York and London, 1928.

MAROUZEAU, J. Langage affectif et langage intellectuel. *J. d. Psych.*, 20, 1923.

MAYER-GROSS, W., and LIPPS, H. " Das Problem der Primitiven Denkformen," *Philosophischer Anzeiger*, iv, I.   1930.

MEAD, G. H. " Social Consciousness and the Consciousness of Meaning," *Psychological Bulletin*, vii (1910), pp. 397–405.

—— " The Mechanism of Social Consciousness." *Journal of Philosophy* ix, 15 (1912), 401–6. (I, 1, 2, 3.)

—— " A Behavioristic Account of the Significant Symbol." *Journal of Philosophy*, xix, 6 (1922), 157–163.

—— " The Genesis of the Self and Social Control," *International Journal of Ethics*, vol. 35 (1925), pp. 251–277. Reprinted in *Philosophy of the Present*. Chicago and London, 1932. (I, 3.)

—— *Mind, Self, and Society*. Chicago, 1934. (I, 2, 3.)

NAUMANN, H. " Ueber das sprachliche Verhältnis von Ober- zur Unterschicht," in *Jahrb. für Philologie*, i, p. 55 ff., 1925.

OGDEN, C. K. " The Magic of Words," in *Psyche*, an annual of general and linguistic psychology, vol. xiv, 1934.

—— *Jeremy Bentham*, in Psyche Miniatures, No. 46. London, 1932.

—— and RICHARDS, I. A.   *The Meaning of Meaning*. A study of the influence of language upon thought and of the science of symbolism. New York and London, 1923.

REINACH. Cultes, mythes, religions. 3 vols. Paris (Leroux), 1905–8.

ROFFENSTEIN, G. *Das Problem des psychologischen Verstehens*. Stuttgart, 1926.

ROYCE, JOSIAH. *The World and the Individual*, 2nd series. *Nature, Man, and the Social Order*, pp. 153–204. New York, 1904.

SAPIR, EDWARD. " Communication," *Encyclopædia of the Social Sciences*, vol. 4.

SCHILDER, P. *Wahn und Erkenntnis*. Berlin, 1918.

SCHÜTZ, ALFRED. *Der sinnhafte Aufbau der sozialen Welt*. Vienna, 1932. (I, 1, 2, 3, 6, 7 ; III, 1.)

SOMBART, WERNER. " Das Verstehen." With discussion by Stoltenberg, Wach, Rothacker, Mannheim, Singer. *In Verhandlungen des 6ten deutschen Soziologentages*, pp. 208–226. Tübingen, 1929. (I, 1, 2, 3, 5.)

SPRANGER, EDUARD. " Zur Theorie des Verstehens : Zur Geistes-wissenschaftlichen Psychologie," *Festschrift für Johannes Volkelt.* Munich, 1918. (I, 1, 7.)

—— *Die Psychologie des Jugendalters.* Leipzig, 1931. (I, 1.)

STERN, G. " Meaning and Change of Meaning," *Göteborgs Högskolas Arsskrift,* xxxviii, 1932, 1. Göteborg, 1931.

STOK, WILHELM. *Geheimnis, Lüge und Missverständnis.* Beiträge zur Beziehungslehre, vol. 2. Munich and Leipzig, 1929. (II, 1.)

STORCH, ALFRED. *Das archaisch-primitive Erleben u. Denken der Schizophrenen.* Berlin, 1922.

VOSSLER, K. " Die Grenzen der Sprachsoziologie," in *Hauptprobleme der Soziologie.* Erinnerungs gabe für Max Weber. München, 1913.

WACH, JOACHIM. *Das Verstehen.* Grundzüge einer Geschichte der hermeneutischen Theorie im 19ten Jahrhundert. Vol. 1. "Die Grossen Systeme," 1926. Vol. 2. " Die theologische Hermeneutik von Schleiermacher bis Hoffmann," 1929. Vol. 3. " Das Verstehen in der Historik von Ranke bis zum Positivismus," 1933. Tübingen 1926–1933.

WEISGERBER, E. *Muttersprache und Geistesbildung.* Göttingen. 1929.

—— " Sprachwissenschaft und Philosophie zum Bedeutungs-problem" in *Blätter für deutsche Philosophie,* iv, 1930, p. 77 ff.

—— Art. " Sprache " in *Vierkandt's Handwörterbuch der Soziologie.*

WERNER, H. *Ursprünge der Metapher. Arbeiten zur Entwicklungs-psychologie,* iii. Leipzig, 1919.

WHITEHEAD, A. N. *Symbolism, its Meaning and Effects.* 1927.

YOUNG, K. " Language, Thought, and Social Reality," in *Social Attitudes,* ed. by Young, K. New York, 1931.

5.   EVALUATIVE AND NON-EVALUATIVE SOCIAL SCIENCE

DIEHL, KARL. " The Life Work of Max Weber," *Quarterly Journal of Economics,* xxxviii (1924), 87–107. (I, 1, 2, 3.)

LANDSHUT, S. *Kritik der Soziologie.* Freiheit und Gleichheit als Ursprungsproblem der Soziologie, ch. ii and iii. Munich and Leipzig, 1929. (I, 2, 6, 7 ; II, 3.)

LÖWITH, KARL. " Max Weber and Karl Marx," *Archiv für Sozial-wissenschaft und Sozialpolitik,* vol. 67, pp. 213 ff. (I, 2, 3, 4.)

SPANN, OTHMAR. *Gesellschaftslehre,* 3rd ed. revised. Leipzig, 1930.

—— *Tote und lebendige Wissenschaft.* Jena, 1921.

—— *Kategorienlehre.* Jena, 1924.

WEBER, MAX. " Wissenschaft als Beruf," *Gesammelte Aufsätze zur Wissenschaftslehre,* pp. 524–555. Tübingen, 1922. (III, 2.)

—— " Der Sinn der ' Wertfreiheit ' der soziologischen und ökonomi-schen Wissenschaften," *Gesammelte Aufsätze zur Wissenschafts-lehre,* pp. 451–502. Tübingen, 1927. (III, 2.)

—— " Die Objektivität sozialwissenschaftlicher und sozialpolitischer Erkenntnis," *Gesammelte Aufsätze zur Wissenschaftslehre,* pp. 146–214. Tübingen, 1922.

6. HISTORICISM

BELOW, GEORG V. *Über historische Periodisierung.* Berlin, 1925.

CROCE, BENEDETTO. *History, its Theory and Practice*, tr. by Douglas Ainslie. New York, 1923.

DILTHEY, WILHELM. *Einleitung in die Geisteswissenschaften.* Versuch einer Grundlegung für das Studium der Gesellschaft u. der Geschichte. *Gesammelte Schriften*, i. Leipzig and Berlin, 1922. (I, 1, 2, 3, 4, 5, 7.)
Der Aufbau der geschichtlichen Welt in den Geisteswissenschaften, Gesammelte Schriften, vii. Leipzig and Berlin, 1927. (I, 2, 3.)

DROYSEN, J. G. *Grundriss der Historik*, 1st ed., 1858 ; new ed. by E. Rothacker. Halle/S., 1935. English translation by ANDREWS, E. B., "Outline of the Principles of History." Boston, 1893.

FREYER, HANS. *Soziologie als Wirklichkeitswissenschaft.* Logische Grundlegung des Systems der Soziologie. Leipzig and Berlin, 1930. (I, 1, 2, 3, 7.)

HEUSSI, KARL. *Die Krisis des Historismus.* 1932.

MANNHEIM, KARL. "Historismus." *Archiv für Sozialwissenschaft und Sozialpolitik.* (I, 7.)

RANKE. Das politische Gespräch (1836), ed. by E. Rothaker, Halle a. d. Sale, 1925.

REQUADT, P. *Johannes, v. Müller und der Frühhistorismus.* München, 1929.

ROTHENBÜCHER, KARL. *Uber das Wesen des Geschichtlichen und die gesellschaftlichen Gebilde.* Tübingen, 1926.

SIMMEL, GEORG. "Das Problem der historischen Zeit," *Philosophische Vorträge der Kant Gesellschaft.* Berlin, 1916. (I, 1.)

TEGGART, FREDERICK J. *Theory of History.* New Haven, 1925.

TROELTSCH, ERNST. *Der Historismus und seine Probleme. Gesammelte Schriften*, vol. iii. Tübingen, 1923.

WIPPER, R. *The Crisis in Historical Science.* Kazan, 1921.

7. GENERALIZATIONS

ALEXEYEV, N. N. *The Social and Natural Sciences in the Mutual Relationship of their Methods.* Essays in the History and Methodology of the Social Sciences. Moscow, 1912. (I. 6.)

BRIDGMAN, P. W. *The Logic of Modern Physics.* New York, 1927. (I, 2, 3.)

DEWEY, JOHN. "Philosophy," in Gee, Wilson. *Research in the Social Sciences*, pp. 241–268. New York, 1929. (I, 1.)

DOBRETSBERGER, J. "Historische und soziale Gesetze," in *Handwörterbuch der Soziologie*, ed. by A. Vierkandt. Stuttgart, 1931.

EULENBERG, F. "Sind historische Gesetze möglich," in *Hauptprobleme der Soziologie.* Erinnerungsgabe für Max Weber, ed. by Melchior Pályi, vol. 1. Leipzig and Munich, 1923.
—— "Über Gesetzmässigkeit in der Geschichte (historische Gesetze)," *Archiv für Sozialwissenschaft und Sozialpolitik*, vol. 35, pp. 299 ff. (1912).
—— "Naturgesetze und soziale Gesetze," *Archiv für Sozialwissenschaft und Sozialpolitik*, vol. 31, 32 (1910).

HAR, KYUNG DURK. *Social Laws.* A study of the validity of sociological generalizations. Chapel Hill, N.C., 1930.

KLÜVER, H. " The Problem of Type in Cultural Science Psychology," *Journal of Philosophy*, vol. 22 (1923), pp. 225–234.

—— " Weber's Ideal Type in Psychology," *Journal of Philosophy*, vol. 23 (1926).

MISES, LUDWIG. *Grundprobleme der Nationalökonomie.* Unter-suchungen über Verfahren, Aufgaben, Inhalt der Wirtschafts- und Gesellschaftslehre. Jena, 1933. Esp. ch. ii, " Soziologie und Geschichte," reprinted from *Archiv für Sozialwissenschaft und Sozialpolitik*, vol. 61 (1929). (I, 6.)

PARK, R. E., and BURGESS, E. W. *Introduction to the Science of Sociology*, ch. i. Chicago, 1921. (I, 5, 6.)

PFISTER, BERNHARD. *Die Entwicklung zum Idealtypus.* Tübingen, 1928. (I, 3.)

RICKERT, HEINRICH. *Die Grenzen der naturwissenschaftlichen Begriffsbildung.* Eine logische Einleitung in die historischen Wissenschaften, 5th revised edition. Tübingen, 1929.

—— *Kulturwissenschaft und Naturwissenschaft*, 3rd revised edition. Tübingen, 1915. (I, 1, 2, 6.)

ROGIN, LEO. " Werner Sombart and the ' Natural Science ' Method in Economics," *Journal of Political Economy*, xli (1933), 222–236. (I, 1.)

ROTHACKER, ERICH. *Einleitung in die Geisteswissenschaften*, 2nd edition. Tübingen, 1930. (I, 1, 2, 3, 4, 5, 6.)

RUEFF, JACQUES. *From the Physical to the Social Sciences.* Baltimore and London, 1929. (I, 1, 3, 5.)

SCHELTING, ALEXANDER V. " Die logische Theorie der Kultur-wissenschaft von Max Weber, insbesondere sein Begriff des Ideal-typus," *Archiv für Sozialwissenschaft und Sozialpolitik*, 49. (I, 1, 3, 6.)

SIMMEL, GEORG. *Soziologie*, ch. i. Munich and Leipzig, 1908.

SNELL. " Zur naturwissenschaftlichen Begriffsbildung im Griech-ischen," in *Philos. Anzeiger*, iii, 1928, p. 234 ff. (I, 4).

SOMBART, WERNER. *Die drei Nationalökonomien.* Munich and Leipzig, 1930. (I, 1, 2, 3, 4, 5, 6.)

SPRANGER, EDUARD. *Types of Men*, tr. by Pigors. Halle (Saale), 1928.

WEBER, MAX. *Wirtschaft und Gesellschaft.* Part III of *Grundriss der Sozialökonomik*, ch. i. Tübingen, 1925. Also printed in part in *Gesammelte Aufsätze zur Wissenschaftslehre* as " Metho-dische Grundlagen der Soziologie," pp. 503–523.

—— " Über einige Kategorien der verstehenden Soziologie," in *Gesammelte Aufsätze zur Wissenschaftslehre*, pp. 403–480. (I, 1, 3, 4, 5, 6.)

WINDELBAND, WILHELM. *Geschichte und Naturwissenschaft.* Strass-bourg, 1894. Also reprinted in *Präludien*, vol. 2, 5th ed. Tübingen, 1915.

" A Symposium on the Observability of Social Phenomena with Respect to Statistical Analysis," *Sociologus*, 8, 4, and 9, 1.

II. SOCIAL MOVEMENTS AND INTELLECTUAL LIFE

1. IDEAS AND IDEOLOGIES

ADLER, GEORG. *Die Bedeutung der Illusionen für Politik und soziales Leben.* Jena, 1904. (I, 2 ; III, 1, 5.)

ADAMS, E. D. *The Power of Ideals in American History.* New Haven, 1913.

BEHRENDT, RICHARD. *Politischer Aktivismus.* Leipzig, 1932. (II, 2 ; III, 5.)

BERNSTEIN, E. " Idee und Interesse in der Geschichte," *Ethos,* i, 1 (1928).

COURNOT, R. A. *Traité de l'enchaînement des idées fondamentales dans les sciences et dans l'histoire.* Paris, 1861.

—— *Considérations sur la marche des idées.* Paris, 1872.

CZOBEL, E.-HAJDU, P. " Die Literatur über Marx, Engels und über Marxismus seit Beginn des Weltkrieges (mit ausnahme d. russ.). Mit Beilage : Die Lassalle Literatur derselben Epoche." *Marx-Engels Archiv,* i, 467–537. 1926.

DIETRICH, A. " Kritik der politischen Ideologien," *Archiv für Geschichte u. Politik* (1923).

DUPRAT, G. L. *Le Mensonge.* Paris, 1913.

ELLINGER, G. *Das Verhältnis der öffentlichen Meinung zu Wahrheit und Lüge im 10, 11, 12 Jh.* Berlin, 1884, (III, 5.)

GUÉRARD, A. *Reflections on the Napoleonic Legend.* London, 1924.

—— *The Life and Death of an Ideal. France in the Classical Age.* London, 1929.

GINZBURG, B. " Hypocrisy as a Pathological Symptom," *Intern. Journ. of Ethics,* xxii, p. 164.

GROETHUYSEN, BERNARD. *Les Origines de l'esprit bourgeois en France.* Paris, 1927.

HESSLEIN, H. *Ideale und Interessen,* tr. by E. Nascher. Berlin, 1911.

HONIGSHEIM, PAUL. " Zur Soziologie der mittelalterlichen Scholastik " (Die Soziologische Bedeutung des Nominalismus), *Hauptprobleme der Soziologie.* Erinnerungsgabe für Max Weber, ed. by M. Pályi. vol. ii. Munich and Leipzig, 1923. (II, 3, 4 ; III, 1.)

HUTH, H. *Soziale und individualistische Auffassung im 18. Jhdt. vornehmlich bei Adam Smith und Adam Ferguson.* Leipzig, 1907.

JANKELEVITCH. " Du rôle des idées dans l'évolution des sociétés," *Revue philosophique,* 66 (1908), pp. 256 ff.

JUNGMANN, EVA. *Spontaneität und Ideologie als Faktoren in der Gewerkschaftsbewegung* (Dissertation). Heidelberg, 1920.

KNIGHT, FRANK H. " Social Science and the Political Trend," *University of Toronto Quarterly,* iii, 4, 407–427 (July, 1934). (I, 4.)

KOLNAI, AUREL. " Versuch einer Klassifizierung einer allgemein-sozialen Machtidee," *Archiv für system. Philosophie u. Soziologie,* vol. 31, 1 and 2 (1928), pp. 125 ff. (II, 3.)

KRACAUER, S. " Die Gruppe als Ideenträger," in *Archiv. für Sozialwissenschaft u. Sozialpolitik,* 49, 3, p. 594.

LARSON, I. A. *Lying and its Detection. A Study of Deception and Reception Tests.* In collaboration with G. W. Haney and L. Keeler. The University of Chicago Press.

LIPMANN, O. and PLAUT, PAUL (ed.). *Die Lüge.* Leipzig, 1927.

LOEBELL, F. W. " Das reale und das ideale Element in der geschichtlichen Überlieferung," in *Hist. Zeitschr.*, 1859, p. 269.

MAN, HENRI DE. *The Psychology of Socialism*, tr. by E. and C. Paul. New York, 1928. (II, 2, 3, 4.)

MASSON-OURSEL, P. *Comparative Philosophy.* New York and London, 1926. (I, 1, 2.)

MILLIOUD, M. " La formation de l'idéal," *Revue philosophique*, 66 (1908), pp. 138 ff. (II, 2.)

OESTERREICH, T. K. *Vom Machtideal zum Kulturideal.* Charlottenburg, 1919.

PARETO, VILFREDO. *Traité de sociologie générale*, tr. by P. Boven. 2 vols. Lausanne and Paris, 1917, 1919. (I, 1, 2, 3, 5, 6, 7 ; II, 2, 3, 4 ; III, 1, 3 ; IV, 1.)

———The Mind and Society . . . edited by A. Livingston. London, 1935.

——— *Les systèmes socialistes.* 2 vols. Paris, 1902–3. (II, 2, 3, 4 ; III, 5.)

RIEZLER, K. *Erforderlichkeit des Unmöglichen.* Prolegomena zu einer Theorie der Politik und zu anderen Theorien. München, 1913.

——— " Idee und Interesse in der politischen Geschichte," in *Die Dioskuren.* 1927.

ROBERTY, E. DE. " La Nature sociale de l'idée," in *Revue Intern. de Sociol.* 1907.

——— *Sociologie de l'action. La Genèse sociale de la raison et les origines rationnelles de l'action.* Paris, 1908.

ROMIER, L. *L'explication de notre temps.* Paris, 1925. (II, 3.)

SALOMON, GOTTFRIED. " Geschichte als Ideologie," in *Wirtschaft und Gesellschaft.* Festschrift für Franz Oppenheimer. pp. 417 ff. Frankfurt a.M., 1924.

———*Die Mittelalter als Ideal der Romantik.* Munich, 1922. (II, 3.)

SOMBART, WERNER. *Der proletarische Sozialismus.* 2 vols. Jena, 1924. (II, 3 ; III, 3.)

SZENDE, PAUL. " Eine soziologische Theorie der Abstraktion," *Archiv für Sozialwissenschaft u. Sozialpolitik*, vol. 50, pp. 407 ff.

——— " Verhüllung und Enthüllung," *Archiv für die Geschichte des Sozialismus und der Arbeiterbewegung.* 1922. (II, 2, 3, 4.)

TAYLOR, H. O. *The Medieval Mind.* 2 vols. London, 1911.

TROELTSCH, ERNST. *Social Teachings of the Christian Churches.* Tr. by Olive Wyon. 2 vols. New York and London, 1931. (II, 2, 3 ; III, 1.)

ZILSEL, EDUARD. *Die Entstehung des Geniebegriffes.* Tübingen, 1926. (II, 4.)

2. UTOPIAN MENTALITY

BALDENSPERGER, W. *Das Selbstbewusstsein Jesu im Lichte der messianischen Hoffnungen seiner Zeit.* 1. Hälfte : *Die messianisch-apokalyptischen Hoffnungen des Judentums.* 3rd ed. Strassburg, 1903.

BIBLIOGRAPHY 291

BERNSTEIN, EDUARD. *Cromwell and Communism.* London, 1930. (II, 3.)

BLOCH, E. *Thomas Münzer als Theologe der Revolution.* München, 1921.

DELAISI, FRANÇOIS. *Political Myths and Economic Realities.* Eng. tr. New York, 1925. (II, 1; III, 3.)

DÖLLINGER, J. J. I. VON. " Der Weissagungsglaube und das Prophetentum in der christlichen Zeit," in *Kleinere Schriften.* Stuttgart, 1890.

DOREN, A. " Wunschträume und Wunschzeiten," in *Vorträge,* 1924-5, der Bibliothek Warburg. Leipzig, Berlin, 1927.

ENGELS, FR. *The Peasant War in Germany,* tr. by M. Olgin. New York, 1926. (II, 3.)

GIRSBERGER, H. *Der utopische Sozialismus des 18. Jahrhunderts in Frankreich und seine Philosophischen und materiellen Grundlagen.* Zuricher Volkswirtschaftl. Forschungen. Heft 1. (II, 1, 3.)

HERTZLER, J. O. *History of Utopian Thought.* London, 1923.

HOFFMANN, F. " Erscheinungen der Parteienideologie," *Kölner Vierteljahrshefte für Soziologie,* v, 1 and 2 (1925), 63 ff.

HOLL, K. " Luther und die Schwärmer," in *Gesammelte Aufsätze z. Kirchengeschichte.* Tübingen, 1927.

KAMPERS, F. " Kaiserprophetien und Kaisersagen im Mittelalter," in *Historische Abhandlungen,* ed. by Heigel and Grauert. München, 1895.

KAUTSKY, KARL. *Communism in Central Europe at the Time of the Reformation.* Eng. tr., J. L. and E. G. Mullikan. London, 1897. (II, 3.)

—— *Foundations of Christianity.* Eng. tr. New York and London, 1925.

LANDAUER, GUSTAV. *Die Revolution.* Vol. 13 of the series *Die Gesellschaft,* edited by Martin Buber. Frankfurt a.M., 1923.

LORENZ, EMIL. *Der politische Mythus.* Beiträge zur Mythologie der Kultur. Leipzig, Vienna, and Zurich, 1923.

MANNHEIM, KARL. " Utopia," *Encyclopædia of the Social Sciences,* vol. 15.

MUMFORD, LEWIS. *The Story of Utopias.* New York, 1922.

NIEBUHR, REINHOLD. *Reflections on the End of an Era.* New York, 1934. (II, 1, 3, 4; III, 1, 5.)

REINKE, L. *Die messianischen Weissagungen bei den grossen und kleinen Propheten des A. T.* 4 vols. Giessen, 1859-1862.

REITZENSTEIN, R. *Das iranische Erlösungsmysterium,* Bonn, 1921.

RENAN, E. *History of the People of Israel.* 5 vols. Boston, 1888.

—— *Histoire des origines du christianisme.* 7 vols. Paris, 1863-1883. (II 3; III, 1, 5.)

ROHR, J. " Die Prophetie im letzten Jahrhundert vor der Reformation als Geschichtsquelle und Geschichtsfaktor," *Hist. Jhb.,* 19.

ROSENKRANZ, A. " Prophetische Kaisererwartungen im ausgehenden Mittelalter," *Preuss. Jb.,* vol. 119, 508-524. 1905.

WADSTEIN, E. " Die eschatologische Ideengruppe Antichrist, Weltsabbat, Weltende und Weltgericht in den Hauptmomentum ihrer christlich mittelalterlichen Gesamtentwicklung," in *Zeitschr. f. wissensch. Theologie.* Vol. 38 (1895), p. 538 ff., vol. 39 (1896), p. 79 ff., p. 251 ff.

WALTER, L. G. *Thomas Münzer et les luttes sociales à l'époque de la réforme.* Paris (Picard), 1927.

WEBER, MAX. *Gesammelte Aufsätze zur Religionssoziologie,* i, 207–236, 237–275. Tübingen; 1920. (II, 1, 3, 4.)

——— *Wirtschaft und Gesellschaft.* Part III of *Grundriss der Sozialökonomik.* " Religionssoziologie," i, pt. ii, ch. iv, 227–356. Tübingen, 1925. (II, 1, 3, 4.)

3. SOCIAL STRATIFICATION AND WELTANSCHAUUNG.—SOCIOLOGY OF LITERATURE

ADLER, MAX. " Wissenschaft und soziale Struktur," *Verhandlungen des 4ten deutschen Soziologentages,* pp. 180–212. Tübingen, 1925. (IV, 2.)

BALDENSPERGER, F. *La littérature, Création, Succès, Durée.* Paris (E. Flammarion), 1913.

BARTLETT, F. C. " Temperament and Social Class," *Eugenics Rev.,* 20, 1. London.

BAUER, OTTO. " Das Weltbild des Kapitalismus," *Der lebendige Marxismus,* ed. by O. Jenssen. Jena, 1924. (II, 1.)

BEHN, S. Romantische und Klassische Logik. München, 1925. (i, 4.)

BERNHEIM, E. *Mittelalterliche Zeitanschauungen in ihrem Einfluss auf Politik und Geschichtschreibung.* Tübingen, 1918.

BORKENAU, FRANZ. *Der Übergang vom feudalen zum bürgerlichen Weltbild.* Schriften des Instituts für Sozialforschung, iv. Paris, 1934. (II, 1, 4 ; IV, 2.)

BRÜGGEMANN, F. " Der Kampf um die bürgerliche Welt- und Lebensanschauung in der deutschen Literatur des 18. Jahrhunderts," *Deutsche Vierteljahrsschrift für Literaturwissenschaft und Geistesgesch.* iii, Halle a. S. 1925.

BUDDEBERG, TH. " Zur Soziologie des europäischen Denkens," *Jahrbuch für Soziologie,* iii, p. 157 ff, ed. by G. Salomon. Karlsruhe, 1927.

BUKHARIN, N. I. " Theory and Practice from the Standpoint of Dialectical Materialism," in *Science at the Cross-Roads.* London, 1931. (I, 2, 5 ; IV, 2.)

CRAIN. " Weltansschauung und Technik," in *Technik und Wirtschaft,* vii, 1919.

DILTHEY, WILHELM. *Philosophie der Philosophie* : Abhandlungen zur Weltanschauungslehre, in *Gesammelte Schriften,* viii. Leipzig and Berlin. (II, 1, 2.)

FLICKENSCHILD, H. " Lebensform und Weltbild des altpreussischen Bauerntums zur Zeit des Vormärz," *Arch. f. Angewandte Soziologie.* Bd. v, Heft 2, S. 101 ff.

GIESE, F. *Bildungsideale im Maschinenzeitalter.* Halle a. d. S. 1931.

GOMPERZ, H. *Weltanschauungslehre.* 2 vols. Jena, 1908.

GUÉRARD, ALBERT. *Literature and Society.* Boston, 1935.

HELLPACH, W. *Nervenleben und Weltanschauung.* Ihre Wechsel-beziehungen im deutschen Leben von Heute. Wiesbaden, 1906.

HIELSCHER, HANS. " Das psychologische Verhältnis zwischen d. allg. Bildungsstufe eines Volkes u. d. in ihm sich gestaltenden Weltanschauungen," *Arch. f. ges. Psych.,* ix, 1. 1907.

JASPERS, KARL. *Man in the Modern Age.* Eng. tr. by E. and C. Paul. New York, 1934. (III, 5.)

—— *Psychologie der Weltanschauungen.* 2nd ed. Berlin, 1922. (I, 2.)

KAUTSKY, KARL. *Die materialistische Geschichtsauffassung.* 2 vols. Berlin, 1927. (I, 6 ; II, 2 ; IV, 1.)

KOHN-BRAMSTEDT, E. " Probleme der Literatursoziologie," *Neue Jahrbücher für Wissenschaft und Jugendbildung,* vii (1931), Heft 8.

KORSCH, KARL. " Marxismus und Philosophie," *Archiv für die Geschichte des Sozialismus und der Arbeiterbewegung,* xi (1925), 53–112. (I, 2, 5, 7 ; II, 1.)

LEDERER, E. " Aufgaben einer Kultursoziologie," in *Erinnerungs-gabe für Max Weber,* vol. 2. München, Leipzig, 1923.

LÖWENTHAL, L. " Zur gesellschaftlichen Lage der Literatur," *Zeitschrift für Sozialforschung,* F. 96 ff.

MANNHEIM, KARL. " Beiträge zur Theorie der Weltanschauungs-interpretation," in *Kunstgeschichtliche Einzeldarstellungen,* ii. Vienna, 1923. Also in *Jahrbuch für Kunstgeschichte,* i (xv, 1921–1922). (IV, 1.)

—— " Die Bedeutung der Konkurrenz im Gebiete des Geistigen," *Verhandlungen des 6ten deutschen Soziologentages in Zürich.* pp. 35–83. Tübingen, 1929. (I, 1, 4 ; IV, 1.)

—— " Das konservative Denken. Soziologische Beiträge zum Werden des politisch-historischen Denkens in Deutschland," *Archiv für Sozialwissenschaft und Sozialpolitik,* vol. 57, 1 and 2. (II, 1, 4 ; IV, 1.)

—— " Das Problem der Generationen," *Kölner Vierteljahrshefte für Soziologie,* vii, 2 and 3 (1927), 128 ff., 309 ff. (IV, 1.)

MARR, H. " Grosstadt als politische Lebensform in *Grosstadt und Volkstum.* Hamburg, 1917.

MARTIN, A. VON. " Weltanschauliche Motive im altkonser-vativen Denken," in *Deutschers Staat und deutsche Parteien. Festschrift, Fr. Meinecke zum 60ten Geburtstag.* München, Berlin, 1922. (II, 1 ; IV, 2.)

MAYO, ELTON. *The Human Aspects of an Industrial Civilization.* New York, 1933.

OPPENHEIMER, FRANZ. " Tendencies in Recent German Sociology," *Sociological Review,* xxiv (1932), 1–13 ; 125–137 ; 248–260.

ROFFENSTEIN, G. " Das Problem der Ideologie in der materiali-stischen Geschichtsauffassung und das moderne Parteiwesen," in *Partei und Klasse im Lebensprozesse der Gesellschaft,* ed. by R. Thurnwald. Leipzig, 1926. (II, 1.)

SCHÜCKING, LEVIN. *Die Soziologie der literarischen Geschmacks-bildung,* 2. Bd. 1931.

SZENDE, PAUL. " Das System der Wissenschaften und die Gesellschaftsordnung," in *Kölner Vierteljahrshefte für Sozialwissenschaft*, ii, 4 (1922), 5 ff. (I, 1, 2, 5.)

TAINE, H. *Introduction to the History of English Literature*. Paris (Hachette et Cie), 1863.

VAERTING, M. " Der Korpsgeist bei Herrschenden und Beherrschten," *Archiv für system. Philosophie u. Soziologie*, xxxi, 1 (1928), 142 ff.

WEBER, A. *Ideen zur Staats- und Kultursoziologie*. Karlsruhe, 1927.

WEBER, MAX. *Gesammelte Aufsätze zur Religionssoziologie*. 3 vols. Tübingen, 1920-1. (II, 4.)

WECHSLER, E. " Denkform und Weltanschauung in der Geschichte der deutschen Bildung," in *Zschr. f. Gesch. d. Erziehung u. d. Unterrichts* 20, 1930 " (I, 4.)

WITTICH, W. " Der soziale Gehalt von Goethes Roman ‚Wilhelm Meisters Lehrjahre ‘," in *Erinnerungsgabe für Max Weber*, vol. 2. München, Leipzig, 1923.

4. THE INTELLIGENTSIA AND ITS ROLE

BARBUSSE, HENRI. *Le couteaux entre les dents : aux intellectuels*. Paris, 1921.

BENDA, JULIEN. *The Great Betrayal*. Tr. into English by R. Aldington. New York and London, 1928.

BERTH, ED. *Les Méfaits des intellectuels*. Introd. by G. Sorel. Paris, 1914.

BOURNE, RANDOLPH S. *The War and the Intellectuels*. New York, 1917. Reprinted in his *Untimely Papers*. New York, 1919.

BRANDES, G. M. C. *Main Currents of European Literature in the 19th Century*. 6 vols. London, 1901-5. (II, 1, 2, 3.)

DAUDET, LEON. *The Stupid 19th Century*, tr. into English by L. Galantière. New York, 1928.

DÖBLIN, A. *Wissen und Verändern. Offene Briefe an einen jungen Menschen*. Berlin, 1931.

FLEXNER, ABRAHAM. *Universities : American, English, German*. New York, 1930.

FOGARASI, A. " Die Soziologie der Intelligenz und die Intelligenz der Soziologie," *Unter dem Banner des Marxismus*, iv, 3 (1930). (IV, 2.)

HEINRICH, H. " Die Intelligenz und ihre Stellung zur bürgerlichen Ideologie und zur Gedankenwelt des Sozialismus," *Archiv für die Geschichte der Philosophie*, 39, 1 and 2 (1929), 150 ff.

HELLPACH, W. " Die Arbeitsteilung im geistigen Leben," *Archiv für Sozialwissenschaft und Sozialpolitik*, 35, p. 665 ; 36, p. 79.

LANDSBERG, P. *Wesen und Bedeutung der platonischen Akademie*. Schriften zur Philosophie u. Soziologie, i. Bonn, 1923.

MAN, HENRI DE. *Die Intellektuellen und der Sozialismus*. Jena, 1926.

MASARYK, TH. G. *The Spirit of Russia*, tr. by E. and C. Paul. 2 vols. New York and London, 1929.

MICHELS, ROBERTO. " Intellectuals," *Encyclopædia of the Social Sciences*, vol. viii.
—— " Zur Soziologie der Bohême und ihre Zusammenhänge mit dem geistigen Proletariat," *Jahrbücher für Nationalökonomie und Statistik*, 3rd series, 81, 6 (1932).
—— *Political Parties*, tr. by E. and C. Paul. New York, 1915.
—— *Umschichtungen in den Herrschenden Klassen nach dem Kriege*. (Kap. III : Zur intellektuellen Oberschicht.) Stuttgart, 1934.
MIRSKY, (DIMITRI SVYATOPOLK), Prince. *The Intelligentsia of Great Britain*. London, 1935.
NAUMANN, FRIEDRICH. *Die Stellung der Gebildeten im politischen Leben*. Berlin, 1907.
NOMAD, MAX. *Rebels and Renegades*. New York, 1932.
RAUECKER, B. *Die Proletarisierung der geistigen Arbeiter*. Munich, 1920.
SPEIER, HANS. " Die Intellektuellen und ihr sozialer Beruf." *Neue Blätter für den Sozialismus*. 12/13. Potsdam, 1930.
—— " Zur Soziologie der bürgerlichen Intelligenz in Deutschland," *Die Gesellschaft*, pp. 58–72. 1929. (IV, 2.)
THIBAUDET, ALBERT. *La république des professeurs*. Paris, 1927.
VEBLEN, THORSTEIN. *The Higher Learning in America*. A memorandum on the conduct of universities by business men. New York, 1918.
WEBER, ALFRED. " Die Not der geistigen Arbeiter," *Schriften des Vereins für Sozialpolitik*. Leipzig, München, 1920.
WEBER, MAX. *Gesammelte Aufsätze zur Religionssoziologie*. 3 vols. Tübingen, 1920–1.
WITTFOGEL, KARL A. *Die Wissenschaft der bürgerlichen Gesellschaft* Berlin, 1922. (II, 1 ; IV, 2.)
ZEHRER, H. " Die Revolution der Intelligenz," *Die Tat*, vol. 21. 1929.

III. THE SOCIAL ROLE OF KNOWLEDGE

1. RATIONALITY AND DOGMA

BURY, J. B. *A History of Freedom of Thought*. New York, 1913.
DEWEY, JOHN. *How we Think*. Revised ed. Boston, 1933. (III, 2.)
JAMES, W. *The Will to Believe*. New York, 1897. (I, 2 ; II, 2.)
JORDAN. *The Development of Religious Toleration in England*, 1932.
MANNHEIM, KARL. *Rational and Irrational Elements in Contemporary Society*. Hobhouse Memorial Lecture. Oxford, 1934.
PARETO, V. *Traité de Sociologie générale*. Lausanne, Paris, 1917–18.
PARSONS, TALCOTT. " Capitalism in Recent German Literature : Sombart and Weber," *Journal of Political Economy*, xxxvii, and xxxviii (1928–9), 641–661 ; 31–51. (II, 1, 3.)
—— " Ultimate Values in Sociological Theory," *International Journal of Ethics*, xlv, 3 (April, 1935).
REIK, TH. " Dogma und Zwangsidee," *Imago*, xiii, 1927.
ROBERTSON, J. M. *Short History of Free Thought* (rev. ed., 2 vols.), 1936.

ROBINSON, J. H. *The Mind in the Making.* The relation of Intelligence to Social Reform. New York and London, 1921.

RUGGIERO, G. DE. *The History of European Liberalism,* tr. by R. G. Collingswood. London, 1927.

SANTAYANA, G. *Reason in Society : The Life of Reason,* ii, New York, 1905.

SIMMEL, GEORG. *Philosophie des Geldes.* Leipzig, 1900.

SUMNER, W. G. *Folkways.* Boston, 1906. (II, 1 ; III, 2.)

WALLAS, GRAHAM. *The Art of Thought.* New York, 1926.

—— *Social Judgment.* New York, 1935. (I, 2.)

WEBER, MAX. *Wirtschaft und Gesellschaft.* Tübingen, 1925.

—— *Gesammelte Aufsätze zur Religionssoziologie.* 3 vols. Tübingen, 1920–1.

—— *Gesammelte Aufsätze zur Wissenschaftslehre.* Tübingen, 1922.

2. EDUCATION AND INDOCTRINATION

APPENS, W. *Die pädagogischen Bewegungen des Jahres 1848.* Elberfeld, 1914.

BEARD, CH. A. *A Charter for the Social Sciences in the Schools.* Report of the Commission on Social Studies. New York, 1931. (III, 4, 5.)

—— *The Nature of the Social Sciences in Relation to Objectives of Instruction.* Report of Commission on Social Studies. New York, 1934.

Conclusions and Recommendations of the Commission. Report of the Commission on the Social Studies. American Historical Association. New York, 1934.

COUNTS, G. S. *The American Road to Culture.* New York, 1930.

—— *Dare the School Build a New Social Order ?* John Day Pamphlets, 11. New York, 1932.

—— *The Social Composition of Boards of Education.* A study in the social control of education. Chicago, 1927.

—— *Social Foundations of Education.* Report of the Commission on Social Studies. New York, 1934. (II, 3, 4, 5.)

—— *School and Society in Chicago.* New York, 1928. (III, 3, 4, 5.)

DOBBS, A. E. *Education and Social Movements, 1700–1850.* London, 1919.

GIESE, G. *Staat und Erziehung-Grundzüge einer politischen Pädagogik.* Hamburg, 1935.

HARPER, S. N. *Civic Training in Soviet Russia.* Chicago, 1929. (III, 3, 4.)

HOOK, SIDNEY. " The Importance of a Point of View," *Social Frontier,* i, 1 and 2 (October, November, 1934).

KARSEN, F. " Neue Literatur über Gesellschaft und Erzichung," in *Zeitschrift für Sozialforschung,* iii, 1, 1934.

KIRKPATRICK, W. (ed.) *The Educational Frontier.* New York, 1931.

KOSOK, P. *Modern Germany : a Study of Conflicting Loyalties.* Chicago, 1933. (III, 3, 4.)

LÜDDEKE, TH. *Die Tageszeitung als Mittel der Staatsführung.* Hamburg, 1933.

MERRIAM, C. E. *The Making of Citizens*. A comparative study of methods of civic training. Chicago, 1931. (III, 3, 4.)
—— *Civic Training in the United States*. Report of the Commission on Social Studies. New York, 1933. (III, 4.)
NOHL, H., and PALLAT. *Handbuch der Pädagogik*, vol. 2 : *Die soziologischen Grundlagen der Erziehung*. 1929.
PIERCE, B. L. *Citizens' Organizations and the Civic Training of Youth*. Report of the Commission on Social Studies. New York, 1933. (III, 3, 5.)
—— *Public Opinion and the Teaching of History*. New York, 1926. (III, 3, 5.)
—— *Civic Attitudes in American School Text-books*. Chicago, 1930.
RUSSELL, B. *Education and the Social Order*. London, 1932.
SCHNEIDER, H. W., and CLOUGH, S. B. *Making Fascists*. Chicago, 1929. (III, 3, 4.)
SCHMIDT, T.-HARTEFELD. *Das Erziehungsziel als Ausdruck des sozialen Lebens*. 1931.
SINCLAIR, U. *The Goslings*. A study of the American schools. Pasadena (Calif.), 1924. (III, 3.)
—— *The Goose-Step*. A study of American education. Pasadena (Calif.), 1923. (III, 3.)
Social Frontier. Published monthly. New York, 1934.

3. PROPAGANDA

LASSWELL, H. D. " Propaganda," *Encyclopædia of the Social Sciences*, vol. xii.
—— *Psychopathology and Politics*. Chicago, 1930.
—— " Strategy of Revolutionary and War Propaganda," in *Public Opinion and World Politics*. Ed. by Quincy Wright. Chicago, 1933. (II, 3, 4.)
—— *Propaganda Technique in the World War*. New York and London, 1927.
—— *Personal Insecurity and World Politics*. New York, 1935.
LASSWELL, H. D., D. CASEY, BRUCE LANNES SMITH. *Propaganda and Promotional Activity*. An annotated Bibliography. Minnesota, Minneapolis and London, 1935.
LUMLEY, F. E. *The Propaganda Menace*. New York and London, 1933.
RASSAK, J. *Psychologie de l'opinion et de la propaganda politique*. Paris, 1927. (III, 5.)
SCHULZE-PFAELZER, G. *Propaganda, Agitation, Reklame*. Berlin, 1923.
STERN-RUBARTH, EDGAR. *Die Propaganda als politisches Instrument*. Berlin, 1921.
YOUNG, K., and LAWRANCE, R. B. *Bibliography on Censorship and Propaganda, University of Oregon Publication*. Journalism Series i, No. 1, March, 1928.

4. DISSEMINATION AND POPULARIZATION OF KNOWLEDGE

DEWEY, JOHN. *The School in the New Social Order.* New York.
—— *Democracy and Education.* New York, 1916. (III, 2, 5.)
HANSOME, MARIUS. *World Worker's Education Movements.* Columbia University Studies in History, Economics, and Public Law, 338. New York and London, 1931.
HIGHAM, C. F. *Looking Forward : Mass Education through Publicity.* London, 1920. (III, 2, 5.)
KALLEN, H. *Education, the Machine and the Worker.* An essay on the psychology of education in industrial society. New York, 1925. (III, 2.)
LIPPMAN, WALTER. *Liberty and the News.* New York, 1927.
MÜNZER, GERHARD. *Öffentliche Meinung und Presse.* Sozialwissenschaftliche Abhandlungen VI. Karlsruhe, 1928. (III, 5.)
PAUL, EDEN, and CEDAR. *Proletcult (Proletarian Culture).* New York, 1921. (III, 2, 5.)
ROBINSON, J. H. *The Humanizing of Knowledge.* New York, 1923.
SALMON, LUCY. *The Newspaper and Authority.* New York, 1924.
WIESE, LEOPOLD V. (Ed.) *Soziologie des Volksbildungswesens.* Schriften des Forschungsinstituts für Sozialwissenschaften in Köln, i. Munich and Leipzig, 1921.

5. PUBLIC OPINION AND COLLECTIVE ACTION.

ANGELL, NORMAN. *The Public Mind.* London, 1926.
BAUER, WILHEM. " Public Opinion," *Encyclopædia of the Social Sciences*, vol. xii.
—— *Die öffentliche Meinung und ihre geschichtliche Grundlagen.* Tübingen, 1914.
CHILDS, H. L. *A Reference Guide to the Study of Public Opinion, etc.* Princeton University, School of Public and Internat. Affairs. Princeton, New Jersey, 1934.
DEWEY, JOHN. *The Public and its Problems.* New York, 1927.
DURKHEIM, E. *Elementary Forms of Religious Life,* tr. by J. W. Swain. London, New York, 1915[1]; 1926[2].
FLAD, RUTH. *Studien zur politischen Begriffsbildung in Deutschland während der preussischen Reform. Der Begriff der öffentlichen Meinung bei Stein, Arudt und Humboldt.* Berlin, 1929. (I, 4; II, 1, 3, 4.)
GEIGER, TH. *Die Masse und ihre Aktion.* Ein Beitrag zur Theorie der Revolutionen. Stuttgart, 1926.
LE BON, GUSTAVE. *The Crowd.* A study of the popular mind. London, 1926.
—— *The Psychology of Revolution,* tr. by Bernard Miall. New York, 1913.
LIPPMAN, WALTER. *The Phantom Public.* New York, 1925.
—— *Public Opinion.* New York, 1922.
ODEGARD, P. H. *The American Public Mind.* New York, 1930.

PARK, R. E. "Human Nature and Collective Behavior," *American Journal of Sociology*, xxxii (1926–7), 733.
—— *Masse und Publikum*. Bern, 1904.
ROFFENSTEIN, G. "Zur Psychologie der politischen Meinung," in *Zeitschr. für Völkerpsychologie und Soziologie*, 3. 1927.
TARDE, GABRIEL. *L'Opinion et la Foule*. Paris, 1901.
TÖNNIES, FERDINAND. *Kritik der öffentlichen Meinung*. Berlin, 1922.

IV. THE SOCIOLOGY OF KNOWLEDGE

1. FORERUNNERS

ALLIER, R. *The Mind of the Savage*. London, 1929.
BOGDANOV, A. *Entwicklungsformen der Gesellschaft und die Wissenschaft*. Berlin, 1924.
ENGELS, FR. *Ludwig Feuerbach*. Eng. tr. New York, 1935. Cf. Marx, Karl.
GUMPLOWICZ, L. *Grundriss der Soziologie*, in *Ausgewählte Werke*, ii, ed. by G. Salomon. Innsbruck, 1926.
HINTZE, O. "Über Max Schelers Wissensformen und die Gesellschaft," *Zeitschrift für die gesamte Staatswissenschaft*, vol. 81.
HOOK, SIDNEY. *Towards the Understanding of Karl Marx*. New York, 1933. (I, 2, 3, 5 ; II, 1, 2, 3.)
JERUSALEM, W. "Soziologie des Erkennens," *Die Zukunft*, 1909.
—— "Soziologie des Erkennens" (Bemerkungen zu Schelers Aufsatz), *Kölner Vierteljahrshefte für Sozialwissenschaften*, i, 3 (1921), 28 ff.
LEVY-BRÜHL, LUCIEN. *How Natives Think*, tr. by Lilian A. Claire. New York, 1926.
—— *The " Soul " of the Primitive*, tr. by Lilian A. Claire. New York, 1926.
—— *Primitive Mentality*, tr. by Lilian A. Claire. New York, 1923. (II, 1 ; III, 1.)
LUKÁCS, G. *Geschichte und Klassenbewusstsein*. Studien über marxistische Dialektik. Berlin, 1923 (I, 2, 6, 7 ; II, 1, 2, 3, 4 ; III, 1, 3, 5).
MARX, KARL. *Die deutsche Ideologie*. *Marx-Engels Gesamtausgabe*, pt. i, vol. v. Berlin, 1931.
——*Die heilige Familie*. *Marx-Engels Gesamtausgabe*, pt. i, vol. iii. Berlin, 1932.
—— *The Poverty of Philosophy*. Eng. tr. by H. Quelch. Chicago, 1910.
—— and ENGELS, FR. *The Communist Manifesto*, ed. by D. Ryazanov. New York, 1931.
NIETZSCHE, FR. *The Will to Power*. 2 vols. Tr. by A. M. Ludovici. London and Edinburgh, 1924.
—— *Geneology of Morals*, tr. by H. B. Samuel. London, 1923. (II, 1, 2, 3, 4.)
OPPENHEIMER, FRANZ. *System der Soziologie*, i, pt. 1 ; ii. Jena, 1922.

PARETO, VILFREDO. *Traité de Sociologie générale.* 2 vols. Lausanne and Paris, 1917–19.
—— The Mind and Society, edited by A. Livingston. London, 1935.
—— *Les systèmes socialistes.* 2 vols. Paris, 1902–3.
SCHELER, MAX. " Die positivistische Geschichtsphilosophie des Wissens und die Aufgaben einer Soziologie der Erkenntnis," *Kölner Vierteljahrshefte für Sozialwissenschaften,* i, 1 (1921), pp. 12 ff.
—— " Zu W. Jerusalem's Bemerkungen," *Kölner Vierteljahrshefte für Sozialwissenschaften,* i, 3 (1924), pp. 34 ff.
—— " Weltanschauungslehre, Soziologie und Weltanschauungssetzung," *Kölner Vierteljahrshefte für Sozialwissenschaften,* ii, 1 (1922), pp. 18 ff. (II, 3.)
—— *Schriften zur Soziologie und Weltanschauungslehre,* vols. i–iii. Leipzig, 1923 and 1924.
——(ed.) *Versuche einer Soziologie des Wissens.* Schriften des Forschungsinstituts für Sozialwissenschaften in Köln, vol. ii. Munich and Leipzig, 1924.
—— *Die Formen des Wissens und die Bildung.* Bonn, 1925. (III, 4.)
—— *Die Wissensformen und die Gesellschaft.* Leipzig, 1926. (II, 1, 2, 3, 4.)
—— " Universität und Hochschule." In same volume as above.
—— " Erkenntnis und Arbeit." In same volume as above. (I, 1.)
—— and ADLER, M. " Wissenschaft und soziale Struktur," in *Verhandlungen des IV. deutschen Soziologentages am 29.–30. Sept. 1924.* Tübingen, 1925.
SOREL, GEORGES. *La Ruine du monde antique.* 2nd ed. Paris, 1925. (II, 1, 2.)
—— " La Matérialisme historique," *Bulletin de la Société française de philosophie,* ii (1902). (I, 2, 3, 5.)
—— *Reflections on Violence,* tr. by T. E. Hulme. (II, 1, 2 ; III, 1, 5.)
—— *La Décomposition du marxisme.* Paris, 1908. (I 5 ; II. 1, 3 ; III, 1, 5.)
—— *Les Illusions du progrès.* Paris, 1911. (II, 1, 2, 3, 4.)
—— *De l'Utilité du pragmatisme.* Paris, 1921. (I, 3, 5, 7.)
—— *Matériaux d'une théorie du prolétariat.* Paris, 1921.
TAINE, H. A. *History of English Literature.* Eng. tr. by H. van Laun. New York, 1879.
—— *Philosophy of Art.* Eng. tr. by John Durand. 2nd ed. New York, 1873.
WEBER, MAX. *Wirtschaft und Gesellschaft,* in *Grundriss der Sozialökonomik,* iii, 2 vols. Tübingen, 1925.
—— *Gesammelte Aufsätze zur Religionssoziologie.* 3 vols. Tübingen, 1920–21.

2. PRESENT STATUS

ADLER, M. *Das Soziologische in Kants Erkenntniskritik.* Wien, 1924. (I, 1, 3, 5, 7.)
ANDREI, P. *Die soziologische Auffassung der Erkenntnis.* Leipzig, 1923.

ARENDT, H. " Philosophie und Soziologie. Anlässlich K. Mannheim : Ideologie und Utopie," *Die Gesellschaft*, vii, 2 (1930), pp. 163 ff.

ARON, R. " Sociologie du savoir," in *La Sociologie allemande contemporaine*, pp. 75–96. Paris (Alcan), 1935.

BRINKMANN, C. " Der Überbau und die Wissenschaften von Staat und Gesellschaft," *Schmollers Jahrbuch*, 54, 3 (1930).

CURTIUS, E. R. " Die Soziologie und ihre Grenzen," *Neue Schweizer Rundschau*, 10, pp. 727–36. 1929.

—— *Deutscher Geist in Gefahr*. Stuttgart, 1932.

DEMPF. ALOIS. " Wissenssoziologische Untersuchung des Übergangs vom Mittelalter zur Neuzeit," *Archiv für angewandte Soziologie*, iii, (1931), pp. 143 ff.

DOBRETSBERGER, J. " Zur Soziologie des ökonomischen Denkens," *Archiv für angewandte Soziologie*, iv, 75.

DUNKMANN, K. " Ideologie und Utopie," *Archiv für angewandte Soziologie*, ii, pp. 71 ff.

—— " Die soziologische Begründung der Wissenschaft," *Archiv für system. Phil. u. Soz.*, xxx, 1, 2 (1927), pp. 145 ff.

EHRENBERG, H. " Ideologische und soziologische Methode. Ein Wort zur Sozialisierung der Denkart," *Archiv für system. Phil. u. Soz.*, xxx, 1, 2 (1927), pp. 133 ff.

ELEUTHROPOULOS, A. " Sozialpsychologie und Wissenssoziologie," *Zeitschrift für Völkerpsychologie und Soziologie*, iii, 2 (1927), pp. 197 ff.

EPPSTEIN, PAUL. " Die Fragestellung nach der Wirklichkeit im historischen Materialismus," *Archiv für Sozialwissenschaft und Sozialpolitik*, 60 (1928), pp. 449 ff.

FREUND, M. " Karl Mannheim, Ideologie u. Utopie," *Deutsche Literaturzeitung*, 45 (1930).

FREYER, H. " Anmerkungen über das Problem der Ideologie und über Wissenssoziologie " in *Soziologie als Wirklichkeitswissenschaft*. Leipzig, Berlin, 1930.

GRUENEBERG, H. " Ende der Wissenschaft," *Die Tat*. (XXI, 8.)

GRÜNWALD, ERNST. *Das Problem einer Soziologie des Wissens*. Vienna and Leipzig, 1934. (IV, 1.)

GURIAN, W. Grenzen und Bedeutung der Soziologie. Ideologie und Utopie, *Germania*, 15 und 22 Juni, 1929.

HALBWACHS, MAURICE. *Les Cadres sociaux de la mémoire*. Paris, 1925. (I, 4 ; II, 3.)

HEINRICH, H. " Über den bürgerlichen und sozialistischen Begriff der Freiheit," *Der Kampf*, 21 (1928), pp. 288 ff.

HORKHEIMER, MAX. " Ein neuer Ideologiebegriff ? " *Archiv für die Geschichte des Sozialismus und der Arbeiterbewegung*, xv, (1930).

KANELLOPOULOS, PANOJOTIS. " Das Individuum als Grenze des Sozialen und der Erkenntnis. Soziologie contra Soziologismus," *Archiv für angewandte Soziologie*, iii, 79.

KRAFT, JULIUS. " Soziologie oder Soziologismus," *Zeitschrift für Völkerpsychologie und Soziologie*, v, 4 (1929).

Landsberg, P. L. *Wesen und Bedeutung der Platonischen Akademie.*
Schriften zur Philosophie und Soziologie. Bd. 1. ed. by
M. Scheler. Bonn, 1923. (II, 3, 4.)
—— " Zur Soziologie der Erkenntnistheorie," *Schmollers Jahrbuch,*
55, ii (1931).
Landshut, S. " Drei Konstitutive Forschungscharaktere und ein
Exkurs über Wissenssoziologie (Karl Mannheim) in his *Kritik
der Soziologie.* München, Leipzig, 1929.
Lewalter, E. " Wissenssoziologie und Marxismus. Eine Aus-
einandersetzung mit Karl Mannheims Ideologie und Utopie
von marxistischer Position aus." *Archiv für Sozialwissenschaft
und Sozialpolitik,* lxiv, 1 (1930).
Mannheim, Karl. " Das Problem einer Soziologie des Wissens,"
Archiv für Sozialwissenschaft und Sozialpolitik, vol. 54 (1925).
Tübingen. (IV, 1.)
—— " Ideologische und soziologische Interpretation der geistigen
Gebilde," *Jahrbuch für Soziologie,* ii, ed. by G. Salomon.
Karlsruhe, 1926.
—— *Mensch und Gesellschaft im Zeitalter des Umbaus.* Leiden, 1935.
(II, 1, 2, 3, 4 ; III, 1, 2, 3, 4, 5.)
—— *El Hombre y la Sociedad en la Epoca de Crisis.* tr. by F. Ayala.
Madrid. 1936.
—— " The Place of Sociology," in *Conference on the Social Sciences :
their Relations in Theory and Teaching.* London. 1936.
—— " German Sociology " (1918–1933), *Politica,* 1, 1934.
—— Zur Problematik der Soziologie in Deutschland. *Neue Schweizer
Rundschau,* 11. 1929.
Marck, Siegfried. " Marxistische Grundprobleme in der Soziologie
der Gegenwart," *Die Gesellschaft,* iv, 2 (1927), pp. 136 ff.
—— " Zur Problem der Seinsverbundenheit des Wissens," *Archiv
für Philosophie u. Soziologie,* pt. 2, pp. 238 ff. Festgabe für
Ludwig Stein. Berlin, 1929.
Marcuse, H. " Zur Wahrheitsproblematik der soziologischen
Methode Karl Mannheims Ideologie und Utopie," *Die Gesell-
schaft,* vi, 1929.
Martin, A. v. Soziologie als Resignation u. Mission. *Neue
Schweizer Rundschau,* 1930.
Menzel, H. " Ideologie und Utopie," *Zeitschr. f. Nationalökonomie,*
pp. 408–417, 1931.
Plessner, Helmuth. " Abwandlungen des Ideologiegedankens,"
Kölner Vierteljahrshefte für Soziologie, x, 2 (1931), pp. 163 ff.
(IV, 1.)
Renner, Karl. " Ist der Marxismus Ideologie oder Wissenschaft ? "
Der Kampf, xxi (1928), pp. 245 ff.
Rothacker, E. " Zur Lehre vom Menschen." Ein Sammelreferat
über Neuerscheinungen zur Kultursoziologie. *Deutsche Viertel-
jahrsschrift für Literaturwissenschaft und Geistesgeschichte,* xi, 1.
Salis, Jean-R. de. " Remarques sur le mouvement sociologique
en Allemagne," in *Revue de la synthèse historique,* vol. 1, Nos.
148–150, pp. 57–69 (1930).

SALOMON, G. " Über Politik als Wissenschaft," *Festschrift für Otto Köbner* (1930), pp. 52 ff.
—— " Historischer Materialismus und Ideologienlehre," Jahrbuch für Soziologie, ed. by G. Salomon, ii, pp. 386 ff. Karlsruhe, 1926.
SPEIER, HANS. " Soziologie oder Ideologie," *Die Gesellschaft*, vii, 4 (1930).
—— " Die Geschichtsphilosophie Lassalles." *Archiv für Sozialwissenschaft und Sozialpolitik*, vol. lxi, 1 and 2 (1929), pp. 103 ff.
SPRANGER, E. Ideologie und Wissenschaft. Rede gehalten in der Preuss. Akademie der Wissenschaften. cf. *Forschungen und Fortschritte*. Nachrichtenblatt der Deutschen Wissenschaft und Technik. Berlin, 1st April, 1930.
STERN, GUENTHER. " Über die sogenannte ‚Seinsverbundenheit' des Bewusstseins. Anlässlich Karl Mannheims Ideologie und Utopie," *Archiv für Sozialwissenschaft und Sozialpolitik*, vol. lxiv (1930), pp. 492 ff.
TILLICH, PAUL. " Ideologie und Utopie," *Die Gesellschaft*, vi, 10 (1929), pp. 348-355.
WITTFOGEL, K. A. " Wissen und Gesellschaft. Neuere deutsche Literatur zur Wissenssoziologie," *Unter dem Banner des Marxismus*, v, 1 (1931).
WOLFF, K. " *La Sociologia del Sapere, Ricerca di una Definizione*," Tesi di Laurea in Filosofia. Manoscritto, Biblioteca della Facoltà di Lettere e Filosofia della R. Università degli Studi di Firenze, 1935. (I, 1, 2, 3, 5, 6, 7 ; II, 1, 3 ; IV, 1, 2.)
ZIEGLER, H. O. Ideologienlehre. *Archiv für Sozialwissenschaft und Sozialpolitik*, 57, 1927, pp. 657 ff.

3. ATTEMPTS AT AN APPLICATION OR MODIFICATION OF THE METHOD AS PRESENTED IN THIS BOOK IN RECENT EMPIRICAL RESEARCH

BAKER R. J. *The Sociological Function of Intellectuals in Modern Society : A Study of some Social Movements in Post-War Germany* (Ph.D. Thesis, London School of Economics and Political Science, 1936). (Unpublished.) (I, 2, 4, 5 ; II, 1, 3, 4 ; III, 3, 4, 5 ; IV, 2.)
CARLÉ, W. *Weltanschauung und Presse* (Dissertation, Frankfurt a.M.) Leipzig, 1931. (I, 4 ; II, 1, 3, 4, 5 ; IV, 2.)
ELIAS, N. *Die höfische Gesellschaft. Untersuchungen zur Soziologie des Adels, des Königtums und des Hofes, vor allem in Frankreich des XVII ten Jahrhunderts*. (Unpublished.) (II, 1, 3, 4 ; IV, 1.)
ELIASBERG, W. " Die widersprechenden sachverständigen Gutachten. Was sollen die Richter, die öffentliche Meinung und die Sachverständigen tun, wenn die Gutachten sich widersprechen," in *Abhandlungen aus den Grenzgebieten der Psychologie und Medizin. Festschrift für A. Mohl*. Berlin, 1932.
FREUND, G. *La Photographie en France au dix-neuvième Siècle. Essai de sociologie et d'esthétique*. Paris, 1936. (II, 3, 4 ; IV, 2).

GERTH, H. "*Die sozialgeschichtliche Lage der bürgerlichen Intelligenz um die Wende des 18. Jahrhunderts.*" *Ein Beitrag zur Soziologie des deutschen Frühliberalismus.* (Dissertation, Frankfurt a.M.) (V.D.I-Verlag, G.m.b.H., Berlin, N.W. 7.) 1935. (II, 1, 3, 4 ; III, 1, 3, 5 ; IV, 2.)

HERRMANN, O. "*Die Anfänge Gustav Freytags.*" *Ein soziologischer Beitrag zur geschichte der deutschen bürgerlichen Intelligenz im 19. Jahrhundert.* (Dissertation.) Hamburg, 1934. (II, 1, 3, 4 ; IV, 2.)

KOHN-BRAMSTEDT, E. "*Class Distinctions as Reflected in the German Novel of the Nineteenth Century : Aristocracy, Middle Classes, Intellectuals, 1830–1900.*" *A study in sociology of literature.* (Ph.D. Thesis. London School of Economics and Political Science. 1936.) (Unpublished.) (II, 3, 4 ; IV, 2.)

LÜTKENS, CH. "Das Problem der Amerikanischen Intelligenz." (Unpublished). (II. 1, 3, 4 ; IV. 2.)

MANHEIM, E. *Die Träger der öffentlichen Meinung.* Studien zur Soziologie der Öffentlichkeit. Brünn, Prag, Leipzig, Wien, 1933. (II, 1, 3, 4 ; III, 4, 5 ; IV, 2.)

MARTIN, A. von. *Soziologie der Renaissance. Physiognomik und Rhythmik der bürgerlichen Kultur.* Stuttgart, 1932. (II, 1, 3, 4 ; III, 5 ; IV, 2).

—— "Der Humanismus als soziologisches Phänomen. Ein Beitrag zum Problem des Verhältnisses zwischen Besitzschicht und Bildungsschicht," in *Archiv. für Sozialwissenschaft und Sozialpolitik.* Vol. 65. Tübingen, 1931. (II, 1, 3, 4 ; IV, 2.)

—— Kultursoziologie des Mittelalters. Art. in Vierkandt's *Handwörterbuch der Soziologie.* Stuttgart, 1931. (II, 1, 3, 4 ; IV, 2.)

—— Kultursoziologie der Renaissance. Art. in Vierkandt's *Handwörterbuch der Soziologie.* Stuttgart, 1931. (II, 1, 3, 4 ; IV, 2.)

TRUHEL, K. *Sozialbeamte. Ein Beitrag zur Sozioanalyse der Bürokratie.* (Dissertation, Frankfurt a. Main.) Sagan (Benjamin Krause), 1934. (II, 1, 3, 4.)

WEIL, H. *Die Entstehung des deutschen Bildungsprinzips,* Schriften zur Philosophie und Soziologie. ed. by K. Mannheim. Bonn, 1930. (II, 1, 3, 4 ; III, 5 ; IV, 2.)

INDEX OF NAMES

Y

INDEX OF SUBJECTS

International Library of Psychology, Philosophy & Scientific Method

Editor: C K Ogden

(Demy 8vo)

Philosophy

Anton, John Peter, **Aristotle's Theory of Contrariety** *276 pp. 1957.*
Black, Max, **The Nature of Mathematics** *242 pp. 1933.*
Bluck, R.S., **Plato's Phaedo** *226 pp. 1955.*
Broad, C. D., **Five Types of Ethical Theory** *322 pp. 1930.*
  The Mind and Its Place in Nature *694 pp. 1925.*
Burtt, E. A., **The Metaphysical Foundations of Modern Physical Science**
  A Historical and Critical Essay *364 pp. 2nd (revised) edition 1932.*
Carnap, Rudolf, **The Logical Syntax of Language** *376 pp. 1937.*
Cornford, F. M., **Plato's Theory of Knowledge** *358 pp. 1935.*
  Plato's Cosmology, The Timaeus of Plato *402 pp. Frontispiece. 1937.*
  Plato and Parmenides *280 pp. 1939.*
Crawshay-Williams, Rupert, **Methods and Criteria of Reasoning**
  312 pp. 1957.
Hulme, T. E., **Speculations** *296 pp. 2nd edition 1936.*
Lazerowitz, Morris, **The Structure of Metaphysics** *262 pp. 1955.*
Mannheim, Karl, **Ideology and Utopia** *360 pp. 1954.*
Moore, G. E., **Philosophical Studies** *360 pp. 1922. See also* Ramsey, F.P.
Ogden, C. K. and Richards, I. A., **The Meaning of Meaning**
  With supplementary essays by B. Malinowski and F. G. Crookshank
    394 pp. 10th Edition 1949. (6th Impression 1967.)
Ramsey, Frank Plumpton, **The Foundations of Mathematics and other**
  Logical Essays *318 pp. 1931.*
Richards, I. A., **Principles of Literary Criticism** *312 pp. 2nd edition, 1926.*
  Mencius on the Mind. Experiments in Multiple Definition
    190 pp. 1932.
Smart, Ninian, **Reasons and Faiths** *230 pp. 1958.*
Vaihinger, H., **The Philosophy of As If**
  428 pp. 2nd edition 1935.
Wittgenstein, Ludwig, **Tractatus Logico-Philosophicus** *216 pp. 1922.*
Wright, Georg Henrik von, **Logical Studies** *214 pp. 1957.*
Zeller, Eduard, **Outlines of the History of Greek Philosopohy**
  248 pp. 13th (revised) edition 1931.

Psychology

Adler, Alfred, **The Practice and Theory of Individual Psychology**
  368 pp. 2nd (revised) edition 1929.
Eng, Helga, **The Psychology of Children's Drawings**
  240 pp. 8 colour plates. 139 figures. 2nd edition 1954.
Koffka, Kurt, **The Growth of the Mind** *456 pp. 16 figures. 2nd edition*
  (revised) 1928.